**MEN
WITHOUT
WOMEN**

MEN WITHOUT WOMEN

Masculinity and Revolution in

Russian Fiction, 1917–1929

Eliot Borenstein

DUKE UNIVERSITY PRESS

Durham and London 2000

© 2000 Duke University Press
All rights reserved

Designed by Rebecca M. Giménez
Typeset in Minion with Gill Sans
display by Tseng Information Systems, Inc.
Library of Congress Cataloging-
in-Publication Data appear on the
last printed page of this book.

FOR

Deborah Kandall Borenstein

(1929–1997)

«Память о матери питает
в нас сострадание, как океан,
безмерный океан питает реки,
рассекающие вселенную»

— из «Конармии»

CONTENTS

Acknowledgments ix

Note on Translations and Transliteration xiii

Introduction
Brothers and Comrades 1

Chapter One
The Ladykillers: Bolshevik Chivalry, Female Sacrifice, and the End of the Marriage Plot 43

Chapter Two
Isaak Babel: Dead Fathers and Sons 73

Chapter Three
The Family Men of Yuri Olesha 125

Chapter Four
The Object of *Envy*: Androgyny, Love Triangles, and the Uses of Women 162

Chapter Five
Puritans and Proletarians: Andrei Platonov's Asexual Revolution, 1919–1923 191

Chapter Six
Chevengur: Buried in the Family Plot 225

Conclusion
Fathers and Furies 264

Notes 277

Works Cited 327

Index 341

ACKNOWLEDGMENTS

It is only fitting that a book about comradeship should start by acknowledging all the advice, help, and support the author received in the many years it took to bring the project to fruition. Like so many first books, it began as a doctoral dissertation, and my first debt of gratitude goes to my professors and colleagues at the University of Wisconsin. My adviser, David Bethea, was always ready to discuss even the most unorthodox of approaches and was a strong and enthusiastic supporter from the very beginning. My coursework with Clare Cavanagh and Judith Kornblatt gave me the opportunity to develop many of the ideas that would result in this book; both Clare and Judith were also discerning and critical readers of numerous papers and drafts that eventually found their way into the final version. Rounding out my dissertation and exam committees were Gary Rosenshield and Tomislav Longinović, whose invaluable insights helped me along the way. I am grateful to all of them for encouraging me to take on a project that I thought too large for a doctoral dissertation. And I am particularly indebted to Arlene Forman at Oberlin College for her help with this topic long before it even vaguely resembled its present form.

While in Madison, I was supported financially by grants from the Mellon Foundation and the University of Wisconsin, and intellectually by my fellow graduate students and friends, many of whom read drafts and listened to hours of aimless ranting about masculinity and revolution: Amy Singleton Adams, Angela Brintlinger, Luke Ellenberg, Ann Gleason, Paul Klanderud, Dianne Sattinger, Maya Hoptman, Laurie Iudin-Nelson, Francis Poulin, and Jenifer Presto.

Much of the original work was completed in Moscow, where I benefited from fascinating conversations with Galina Yevgenievna Khutorskaya and from the patient support of Natasha Lipkina. I am grateful to my colleagues and friends Catherine Sevcenko at the U.S. Embassy's Cultural Section, Marina Abbot and Inga Pagava at the Moscow Fulbright Office, Bill James at the United States Information Agency, and Laurie Calhoun, Carol Hoyer, and Andy Riess at the Council for International Exchanges of Scholars, for their patience with me as I juggled my job and dissertation responsibilities. Their support (and their lenience!) was much appreciated. Marina Abbott, Dan Davidson, and Catherine Sevcenko all shuttled the manuscript back and forth across the Atlantic, as did a very kind, but unfortunately nameless, man I met while waiting on line at the American Embassy.

The transition from dissertation to book was facilitated by the generosity of New York University and the National Endowment for the Humanities, which gave me the opportunity to study utopianism in greater depth at a summer seminar run by Gary Saul Morson and Michael Williams at Northwestern University. The Tri-City Jewish Center in Rock Island, Illinois, provided me a place to write during two nomadic weeks in the summer of 1996.

At the University of Virginia, David Herman and Karen Ryan were good colleagues and friends who contributed useful comments and suggestions to various drafts and presentations. Laura Botta, Mark McCuen, Cale Parrish, and Michelle Viise, graduate students in a seminar called "Sex or Communism in 1920s Fiction," were a captive audience for many of the ideas elaborated in this book. I am also grateful for the encouragement of Charlotte Douglas, Stephen Rudy, and Valentina Zaitseva at the New York University Russian and Slavic Studies Department, as well as for the unfailing good humor of Genya Altman. My graduate students Rachel Borst, Maryl Hallett, and Vanessa Marling all contributed to a fruitful dialogue on gender and sexuality in Russian literature, both in class and in their master's theses.

I received a great deal of useful feedback from Caryl Emerson, Sona Hoisington, Harriet Murav, Gary Rosenshield, and Margaret Ziolkowski when I presented some of this material at the 1994 AAASS. The Harriman Institute's works-in-progress *kruzhok* also provided me a forum for what would become chapter 1, and I am grateful to Fred Corney, Cathy Nepomnyashchy, Ludmilla Trigos, and Mark von Hagen for their comments.

Adele Barker, Beth Holmgren, Eric Naiman, and Thomas Seifrid all read versions of this manuscript, providing much-needed encouragement and saving me from numerous embarrassing errors and oversights (those that remain are, of course, my own). Valerie Millholland, my editor at Duke University Press, has been a strong ally and a delightful correspondent. Miriam Angress diligently shepherded the manuscript through production.

I owe a particular debt of gratitude to Helena Goscilo and Mark Lipovetsky for their consistent enthusiasm and staunch friendship, and most of all to Frances Bernstein, in whom I have had the good fortune to find not only a scholar who shares my somewhat disreputable academic interests, but a partner who shares my life as well.

Finally, I would like to acknowledge my gratitude to my family: my brothers, Nathaniel and Seth Borenstein, my father, Stanley Borenstein, and my mother, Deborah Borenstein, who I wish had had the chance to see this book in print.

NOTE ON TRANSLATIONS AND TRANSLITERATION

The Library of Congress transliteration system is used in this book whenever unfamiliar Russian words are introduced. For the sake of easier reading, however, when Russian authors are named in the body of the text, I have chosen the most familiar English spelling ("Dostoevsky" rather than "Dostoevskii"); last names containing a Russian "ë" are rendered with the letters "yo" rather than "e" ("Fyodorov" rather than "Federov"). The "Works Cited" section and internal citations use the Library of Congress system for ease of bibliographic reference; thus, the name of the author of "Twenty-six Men and A Girl" is given in the text as "Gorky" but listed in the citations as "Gor'kii." Fictional characters' names are rendered in a more "reader-friendly" fashion so that non-Russian speakers can better pronounce the names ("Volodya" rather than "Volodia").

All translations are my own unless otherwise noted.

> ... look
> everything's become masculine
> —Aleksei Kruchenykh, *Victory over the Sun* (1913)

> [C]ommunist society is essentially a society of men ... Humanity is courage (man), and not the embodiment of sex (woman). He who desires the truth cannot desire a woman.—Andrei Platonov, "The Future October" (1920)

Introduction

BROTHERS AND COMRADES

> The ideal of perfect manliness [мужественности] is prepared by the style and the practical demands of our era. Everything has become heavier and more enormous, and therefore man must also be harder, for man must be harder than everything on earth and must be to the earth as a diamond to glass. — Osip Mandelstam, "On the Nature of the Word" (1922)

> Lelya Goncharova: Woman must now think like a man. The Revolution. Male scores are being settled. — Yuri Olesha, *A List of Assets* (1931)

To many readers familiar with Russian literature, the title of this study, *Men without Women*, will probably appear an unsuitable import from a vastly different literary tradition.[1] Hemingway's collection by the same name is only one of his many works that center on exclusively male experience; his masculine focus was hardly at odds with American literary history, which, thanks to the topos of the Western frontier, consists of numerous novels and stories devoted to the lives of men in the absence of women.[2] Such is not the case with Russian literature: despite the familiar figures of the superfluous man and the underground man, women loom large over the Russian literary tradition. From Pushkin's Tatyana to Chekhov's three Prokhorov sisters, Russian literature of the nineteenth century is populated by unforgettable female characters. Placed on the imposing pedestal of what Barbara Heldt terms "terrible perfection," many of these strong heroines put their male counterparts to shame.[3] Whether or not one accepts Heldt's contention that such "underdescribed" female characters are "literarily the least interesting" (Heldt 13), it is impossible to imagine the classics of Russian literature without them.[4]

In the fiction and poetry that follows the revolution, continuity with any tradition cannot be taken for granted. This is not to say that the literature of the 1920s, the period to which this book is devoted, represents a complete break with the past; it would be naive to accept the declarations of novelty on the part of futurists and militant proletarians at face value. Anyone who takes issue with the thesis that this literature focuses almost exclusively on the masculine has a wealth of ammunition at her or his disposal, such as the eponymous heroine of Aleksandra Kollontai's "Vasilisa Mulygina," whose path to independence reflects the uneasy alliance between Bolshevism and women's liberation, and Dasha from Fedor Gladkov's *Cement* (*Tsement*, 1925), who places her party work higher than the welfare of her sickly child. Even Andrei Platonov, whose *Chevengur* is one of the central works analyzed in this study, published a story in 1927 that features the efforts of a female schoolteacher to transform the lives of her nomadic pupils in the desert ("The Teacher of the Sands" ("Peschanaia uchitel'nitsa"). Nor does the most ascetic of the masculine-centered socialist realist novels, Nikolai Ostrovsky's *How the Steel Was Tempered* (*Kak zakalialas' stal'*, 1932–34), lack female characters: Pavel Korchagin has both a wife and mother.[5]

My aim is not, however, to argue that there are no women in the Russian literature of the 1920s; even if this were the case, one would hardly need an entire book to prove the point. Female characters can be found in almost any literary work of the period, including the novels, stories, and poems I intend to examine. In the particular strain of Russian literature treated here, women are either barely present or more important for their physical absence. In Yuri Olesha's short novel *Envy* (*Zavist'*, 1927), the main "heroine," Valya, is an ethereal, underdescribed entity whose significance and role is determined by the men around her, hence the repeated associations between Valya and empty vessels, such as vases and incubators. Like the male characters who ostensibly vie for her, Valya has her doubles in the novel, but with the exception of the repulsive widow Anechka, they are not even human: Ophelia, Ivan's imaginary "universal machine" and substitute "daughter," as well as Volodya's own abstract ideal of the machine (a feminine noun in Russian). Andrei Platonov's *Chevengur* takes the phenomenon of the female abstraction to its extreme; not only does Platonov also play with the contrast between women and machines, but he presents a feminine ideal even more ethereal than Olesha's Ophelia. The quixotic Kopyonkin's chosen Dulcinea is the German revolutionary Rosa Luxemburg, dead and decaying in a faraway grave. Even Sonya, who comes close to being romantically involved with Sasha Dvanov, becomes little more than an abstraction to the novel's central character, while the man who does actually sleep with her views her as the embodiment of Russia and a consolation for the loss of his mother. The abstract women of both Olesha and Platonov are reinterpretations of the cult of the Eternal Feminine, a conscious parody of a shopworn motif. Each author seems to follow the Symbolist poet Alexander Blok down his well-known path from worship to disillusionment, from the idealized "Beautiful Lady" of his early verse to her counterpart, the worldly and hostile "Stranger" of the poem by the same name.

Of the three authors central to this study, it is Babel who, perhaps paradoxically, features the most women in his major work. Despite the fact that *Red Cavalry* (*Konarmiia*) has a military setting, women find their way into the better part of the stories of which the cycle is composed. Even here, however, absent women and feminine abstractions mix with the earthy camp followers and hostile crones: the mother to whom Vasily Kurdyukov addresses his letter, the women featured in Lyutov's dream, Lyutov's ex-wife, even the revolution and the Sabbath themselves. Where physical women do appear, they are often perceived by Babel's illiterate soldiers as just as much the enemy as the "bourgeois" women who threaten the integrity of Platonov's Chevengur: black marketeers, contemptuous secretaries, treacherous hags, and conniving nurses.

Nonetheless, the women in these works are secondary to the male relationships their authors describe, either facilitating or hindering the ties between men. Despite the prominent rhetoric of women's emancipation, the postrevolutionary literature of the 1920s constructs (and ultimately dismantles) the myth of a new, masculinized society. Domesticity and traditional femininity have no place in a world of factories and battlefields, which at least partly explains why women in these novels are under the ever-present threat of transformation into bodiless abstractions. With the notable exception of Platonov, few writers of the time state this principle explicitly, and yet the values associated with the new world are the hallmarks of a traditionally masculine ethos: production rather than reproduction, participation in the historic process rather than domestic ahistoricity, heavy industry, construction, and, of course, "the struggle."[6]

The frequent translation of the phrase *novyi chelovek* (literally, "new person") as "new man" is no accident, for the new man must be manly in the extreme.[7] "Revolutionary vanguardism," as one historian has noted, "had always been a male prerogative. The image of the revolutionary proletarian had strongly marked male characteristics in Bolshevik mythology" (Fitzpatrick, *Cultural Front* 237).[8] From 1919 on, Soviet iconography featured muscular workers and farmers who were praised as bold, resolute, and committed to the idea of revolutionary society (Bonnell 23–33; Waters 228, 232). The Soviet fixation on manliness is reflected in all the authors discussed here, often expressed as the fascination with the male body and envy of more "masculine" men.

The masculinization of society is, however, merely the form taken by a perhaps more fundamental shift. Many writers, regardless of their relation to the party line, felt that the revolution marked a complete rupture with the past, a cataclysm that transformed society down to its most basic units. War and revolution had already played havoc with the Russian family, leaving millions of orphans, widows, and divided spouses. Bolshevik social policy, the result of decades of revolutionary ideological debates, appeared to put the final nail in the family's coffin. The more radical social critics demanded the end of the traditional family, advocating the state and society as more suitable alternatives. Despite the wealth of utopian writings on the coming golden age, no one could be certain what form would be taken by the new social structures that would replace the family unit.

The literature of the period points to one possible feature of this new society: its masculinity.[9] With the family and femininity in disgrace, the building of the new world was implicitly a task for men and for those women who were willing to adopt traditionally male roles. So where did this leave those intellectuals whose attitude toward the revolution never quite corresponded with party doctrine? Much has already been written about the quandary of the 1920s intellectual who cannot find a place in the new world, but I submit that this dilemma must be seen in the light of the decline of the family and the cult of masculinity.[10] Igal Halfin argues that a particular strain of Nietzschean Marxism in 1920s Russia implicitly identified the proletariat as male and the intelligentsia as female; the encounter between the two classes was depicted not as the

Platonic union of two complementary principles, but rather as the brutal rape of the effete intelligentsia by a rugged and powerful proletariat (Halfin 90–92).[11] If the intellectual heroes of Babel and Olesha feel alienated from the "new men," they experience this problem as their own lack of "manliness." Neither Kavalerov nor Lyutov can compare to the rugged men whom they admire and resent, which results in feelings of inferiority and envy.

Olesha's and Babel's protagonists suffer from their inadequacy on both an individual and collective level. To some extent, this can be seen as a response to the writers' own tenuous status in the contemporary literary milieu. The first decade of Soviet power was a time of intense literary production, a brief period of relative artistic freedom bracketed by the abolition of tsarist censorship in 1917 and the institution of tight controls by the end of the 1920s. But although state interference in literature was limited, the most extreme of the many communist artistic movements that arose in the 1920s called openly for "proletarian control" over the arts and for banning works by non-party authors. Olesha and Babel were identified with a loose conglomeration of writers who, though not a movement, were referred to by the somewhat disparaging name of "fellow travelers" (*popoutchiki*), writers who accepted Soviet power but could not bring themselves to produce work from a thoroughly "communist" perspective. Their status throughout the 1920s was tenuous at best, and their literary protagonists often expressed a sense of dislocation and alienation with which the authors themselves were probably all too familiar. It would be a mistake, however, to reduce the dilemma of Olesha's and Babel's protagonists to the vagaries of literary politics, since close readings of their works show that the problem is also one of sexual and group identity. Not only are Babel's and Olesha's heroes physically inferior to the model revolutionaries who surround them, but they are also unable to join in the network of male relationships, the comradeships and pseudo-filial ties, that are formed by the revolutionary men. It is these male relationships that replace the family in much of the literature of the 1920s: Babel juxtaposes the traditional family with the comradeship of rugged warriors, while Olesha's protagonist cannot find a place for himself in an all-male family formed along ideological, rather than genealogical, lines. Platonov's characters would seem more fortunate than either Olesha's or Babel's, since they are full-fledged members of these male communities or all-male families, and yet their attempts to build an exclusively masculine revolutionary world are doomed to failure. To understand this phenomenon, however, it is first necessary to discuss the historical context.

TWO SEXUAL REVOLUTIONS

If the reader of Russian fiction of the 1920s is likely to have conflicting impressions of the relations between the sexes as depicted in literature, such confusion is understandable. In terms of both literature and life in the period preceding the First Five-Year Plan, Soviet Russia experienced not one sexual revolution, but two. Paradoxically, these two upheavals, which occupied places at opposite ends of the sociopolitical spectrum, developed simultaneously. The existing social, political, and family structures, already undermined by the cataclysm of World War I, were thought to be a thing of the past after the 1917 October Revolution brought into power a party whose social program was more radical than anything ever attempted in western Europe to date. In the heady days of early postrevolutionary society, many young communists saw the Bolshevik liberation of social policy, which included removing restrictions on abortion and divorce, as a tacit invitation to promiscuity.[12] The beginning of these reforms coincided with the Russian Civil War (1917–21), when the Bolsheviks' struggle to consolidate power throughout the former Russian empire led to draconian policies such as grain requisitioning and compulsory labor that came to be known as "War Communism." The coincidence of radical family legislation with the social shock of a continued state of war (lasting three years longer than in the rest of Europe) would have a profound effect on social mores. In 1921, the Soviet government, recognizing the devastation of the country and sheer exhaustion of the population, instituted the New Economic Policy (NEP), a retreat from the uncompromising stance adopted under War Communism. Limited forms of private enterprise were now legal; the money economy, which had virtually collapsed, was restored; and grain requisitioning ended. But reform of family law continued, and the population now had the opportunity to redefine familial and sexual relationships in conditions of peace rather than perpetual war.

If one's reading of the polemical fiction of the time is limited to Panteleimon Romanov's "Without Cherry Blossom" ("Bez cheremukhi," 1926), Gumilevsky's 1927 "Dog Street" ("Sobachii pereulok"), or Kollontai's too-often misunderstood story of changing sexual mores, "Love of Three Generations" ("Liubov' trekh pokalenii," 1923), one is left with the unshakable impression that the 1920s were a time of unlimited sexual license bordering on sexual anarchy.[13] The most notorious formulation of this new freedom was the infamous "glass of water" theory, mistakenly attributed to Kollontai: engaging in sexual relations is no more significant than sharing a glass of water.[14] The scant statistical evidence available suggests that the decade's reputation for libertinism, the result of Malashkin's and Gumilevsky's vaguely erotic Komsomol potboilers (and the inevitable media crusade against them), may well be undeserved.[15] It is in part this impression that the youth of the 1920s were a collection of hedonists concerned only with animal pleasure, as well as the enormous social cost of changing mores (the rise in the number of single mothers and abandoned children), that contributed to what Richard Stites calls the "Sexual Thermidor" of the 1930s (Stites, *Women's Liberation* 376).[16] By this time, the reaction had set in. Family laws were again tightened, and motherhood and responsibility became official ideals.[17] Soviet society had begun to rehabilitate family values and structures that had been disparagingly termed "bourgeois" only a few years before.[18]

The reactionary social policy of high Stalinism was not, however, simply the suppression of individual freedom on the part of a tyrant consolidating his power. Not only did the uncontrolled social upheaval of the 1920s earn Stalin's repressive measures significant popular support, but, as Stites convincingly argues, "[t]he Thermidorian mood was born with the Revolution" (Stites, *Women's Liberation* 376). Thus we come to the second sexual revolution, one whose development parallels the spread of "free love," but ultimately outlives its rival, albeit in a drastically altered form.[19] The decade following 1917 saw the rapid evolution of a social philosophy with deep roots in Russian radicalism and intellectual history: revolutionary asceticism.[20] One can by no means claim that such asceticism became the norm for Soviet life in the periods of Stalinism or stagnation; both eras placed far too great an emphasis on the family and domesticity for such an assertion to be valid.[21] Nonetheless, restraint came to triumph over license, at least in terms of official doctrine. In order to comprehend the literature and society that developed in the years of Soviet power, it is essential to understand both extremes of early Soviet sexual culture.

The uneasy coexistence of two vastly divergent attitudes toward sexuality and the family can be traced back to a novel that was attacked for its supposed endorsement of Sandian free love, yet was actually the primary model for revolutionary asceticism: Nikolai Chernyshevsky's much-maligned *What Is to Be Done?* (*Chto delat'?*, 1863) This novel, despite its dubious artistic merits, had a profound effect on the next two generations of radical-leaning young readers.[22] Conservatives saw in Chernyshevsky's work a frontal assault on what their twentieth-century counterparts now call family values; the unorthodox marriages of the heroine, Vera Pavlovna, were denounced as a particularly unsavory example of libertinism, although the civilized manner in which the heroes attempt to sort out their love triangle resembles nothing so much as a gentlemen's agreement. Nonetheless, Chernyshevsky's tale of young radicals who form and dissolve sexual ties within the framework of their revolutionary philosophy became the prototype for similar arrangements in the decades to come.[23]

Chernyshevsky's novel, however, cannot be dismissed as an artistically clumsy treatise on the virtues of serial monogamy. His "stories about the new people," as the novel is subtitled, provide a second model for the transformation of personal life: Rakhmetov.[24] If Vera Pavlovna, Kirsanov, and Lopukhov show how one can rationally "manage" sexuality and human relationships as part of a revolutionary life, the example of Rakhmetov establishes a pattern of radicalism that does without sex altogether. Even before his conversion to the cause of revolution, the young Rakhmetov is driven toward self-transformation and perfectionism, taking menial jobs in order to develop his muscles; once he has found his cause, he even sleeps on a bed of nails to test his strength and resolve. The story of his life is more hagiography than biography; miracle after miracle is recounted for the reader's edification.[25] Two factors stand out, however, in making him a model for generations of revolutionary ascetics to come. First, he lives according to a "completed system" (Chernyshevsky 257); Rakhmetov replaces a conventional, "natural" existence with a life based on a theory. Such attempts to transfigure everyday life according to a prepackaged plan would be a perennial feature of revolutionary writings, including those of Andrei Platonov.

The second factor can be seen as subordinate to the first, for it is part of the system that Rakhmetov has devised. This component, however, is an essential aspect of the literature to be discussed in the study: Rakhmetov categorically renounces sexuality for the sake of his goals. The narrator's explanation of Rakhmetov's choice merits special attention, for it presents a line of reasoning that would take on a life of its own in the 1920s:

> He said to himself: "I don't drink a drop of wine. I do not touch women." But his nature was passionate. "Why? Such extremes are unnecessary." "It's necessary. We demand complete enjoyment of life for people, and our lives should attest to the fact that we demand this not for the satisfaction of our own personal passions, not for ourselves personally, but for man in general, that we are speaking only from principle, not from predilection, from conviction, and not from personal necessity." (259)

Though Chernyshevsky's revolutionary knows that women are to be equal partners in the creation of the new society, on the individual level he nonetheless treats them as a bourgeois temptation that, like wine, must be avoided. Like a monk, Rakhmetov must suppress his "natural" passions (which the narrator tells us are quite strong in his case) for the sake of something more abstract. The one love affair of his adult life is a case study in monomaniacal renunciation: having seriously injured himself saving a young woman from being killed by her runaway horse, Rakhmetov falls in love as she nurses him back to health. Upon recovering, he declares his intent to cut off all ties with her, since "you see that such people as I have no right to link anyone's fate with theirs" (267). His beloved, who has in the meantime been converted to his way of thinking, agrees with him immediately. They part, never to see one another again.

On the surface, Rakhmetov's reasoning for renouncing sex seems almost a matter of public relations; the revolutionary must avoid even the appearance of impropriety. But Rakhmetov's declaration contains an implicit opposition between ties based on personal sympathy and the bonds that link the individual to all of humanity. His assertion that the individual must deny his own desires for the sake of the common good, when combined with his forswearing of women, amounts to a rejection of the family in favor of the masses. Despite their unconventional living arrangements, Vera Pavlovna and her husbands build the future within the context of the family, albeit in a more ideologically correct form. Rakhmetov has no time for such distractions, for he has dedicated every iota of his strength and every moment of his concentration to the cause. Virtuous as the novel's main characters may be, they are no match for Rakhmetov.[26] Vera Pavlovna herself recognizes Rakhmetov's superiority, noting that for people like him, "the common cause" completely replaces "personal life" (330). The narrator implicitly contrasts Rakhmetov with his other heroes when he states that "the mass of good and honest people is large, but such people [as Rakhmetov] are few."[27] It is the latter, however, who are the true hope for the future, "the engine of engines, the salt of the salt of the earth" (270–71).

Both Rakhmetov's asceticism and Vera Pavlovna's newfound freedom hinge upon novel approaches to the family.[28] The prospect of the family's abolition or transformation was part and parcel of the "woman question," which occupied the public consciousness to varying degrees in the second half of the nineteenth century. Whereas feminists fought for equality within the existing social system, the socialist champions of women's rights, who slowly began to eclipse their "bourgeois" counterparts, linked the emancipation of women with the destruction of the traditional family unit.[29] Radical socialists and communists, following Bebel, Marx, and Engels, saw woman's role in the family as a metaphor for all capitalist oppression. Thus the men who joined women in their struggle for freedom resembled the children of the upper classes who turned their back on their "bourgeois" roots: in each case, politicized youths of the later nineteenth century voluntarily surrendered the privilege to which they were born. Decades later, Lenin himself would emphasize "the necessity of altering male attitudes" and "rooting out the 'old master right of the man'" (Lapidus 42). Such renunciation further contributed to the rise of revolutionary asceticism: if equality of the sexes and the transformation of the family are described for women in terms of liberation, the men who, at least on paper, chose to give up their dominant role expressed their choice in the language of self-denial. For the revolutionary man, the rejection of the family could serve a dual role: at the same time that he forsook domestic tyranny, he showed his "toughness" and utter dedication to the cause. Pyotr Tkachev expressed his version of "Rakhmetovism" in his 1869 *Catechism of a Revolutionary:* "All the tender and disarming feelings of family relations, friendship, love, and gratitude, and even honor, must be stifled within [the revolutionary] by a cold and single-minded passion for the revolutionary cause" (Heller 15). Moved by either solidarity with the oppressed or the need for revolutionary discipline, young radicals on the eve of the Russian Revolution spurned the family in favor of the abstract masses and the cold, efficient revolutionary "cell."

By the turn of the century, radical calls for the rejection of the family had assumed a more or less standard form, running across the spectrum from arguments for the transformation of domestic life to declarations that the family unit must be utterly destroyed. Though Kollontai's defense of "winged eros" gained more attention, the majority of socialists took a line resembling that of Krupskaya: relationships between the sexes would be based on equality, and under socialism, "a man sees in a woman, and vice versa, above all not a creature of the opposite sex, but a person" (Stites, *Women's Liberation* 261). In his 1903 blueprint for the future society, the Marxist Andrei Isaev would take such views even further: sex would play only a small role in the life of men and women in the future, since their time and energy would be occupied by public activity (Stites, *Women's Liberation* 262).

It is Isaev who first described the vision of the familyless future that would haunt the artistic imagination of the 1920s; where other Marxists left the details for later, Isaev's *What Can Women Expect from Socialism?* painted a picture of a communist society that resembles an anthill more than any received notion of domestic life. The individual kitchen would be superseded by the cafeteria, where all the residents of the apartment-building-*cum*-commune would eat together (Stites, *Women's Liberation,* 266). Isaev's anti-kitchen rhetoric would be adopted by Kollontai and the workers of the postrevolutionary Zhenotdel ("Women's Section"); the "separation of the kitchen from marriage" would be proclaimed by Kollontai to be even more significant than the separation of church and state (Lapidus 85; Stites, *Women's Liberation* 355). Bolshevik family policy rested on four primary precepts: "free union, women's emancipation through wage labor, the socialization of housework, and the withering away of the family." Convinced that the rationality of their ideas would inevitably lead to their success, "the Bolsheviks attached little importance to the powerful emotional bonds between parents and their children" (Goldman, *Women* 11). Though crusaders such as Kollontai advocated public child care on a strictly voluntary basis (Stites, *Women's Liberation* 354–55), their reassurances did little to calm those women who felt their entire way of life was going to be altered against their will.[30] At the 1918 All-Russian Women's Congress, Inessa Armand's speech on the joys of nurseries and communal kitchens prompted some women to shout, "We won't give up our children." Three years later, Kollontai herself would admit that the majority of women were alienated from the new regime by their fears that it would destroy the family and take away their children (Stites, *Women's Liberation* 329–30).

Though Bolshevik rhetoric made the destruction of the family seem to be an imminent threat during the years immediately following the revolution, Soviet family policy implicitly accepted the impossibility of the family's immediate abolition (Heller 168). Like the "withering away of the State," the destruction of the family became a distant goal that would be pushed further and further into the radiant future.[31] By 1930, the entry on "Family Law" in the *Small Soviet Encyclopedia* (*Malaia Sovetskaia Entsiklopediia*) still contained the assertion that the family was destined for extinction in the near future (Heller 168), yet radical social policy was oriented in a different direction. In his 1924 tract *The Revolution and Youth* (*Revoliutsiia i molodezh*), Aron Borisovich Zalkind set the agenda in more manageable terms: "A destitute proletarian state does not yet have the resources, either educational or economic, to replace the family completely, and therefore it must be revolutionized. The part to be played in this matter by the younger generation is tremendous" (Zalkind, as quoted in Heller 168). By conceding that the total destruction of the family is not immediately possible, Zalkind comes close to admitting defeat, yet the alternative he proposes — the reconstruction of the family along ideological lines — is no less a threat to the traditional family.

Zalkind is most famous for his theory of "revolutionary sublimation": young people waste their time and energy on sex and love, squandering a scarce resource that would be better used for class-oriented activity (Stites, *Women's Liberation* 381). Zalkind's approach reflected a popular notion of "sexual economy" that resonates in many works of Russian literature of that period, most notable those of Andrei Platonov (see chapters 5 and 6): human beings have a limited reservoir of energy, and sexuality saps more than its fair share of an individual's strength.[32] Though this idea is not unique to the Soviet experience, in postrevolutionary Russia such antisexual notions were firmly tied to ideology.[33] The potentially destabilizing and debilitating force of sexuality must be harnessed according to the imperatives of the new society: "Sexual selection should be built along the lines of class, revolutionary-proletarian expediency" (Zalkind, as quoted in Popovskii 73).

It is in Zalkind's work that the twin strands of revolutionary asceticism and hostility to the family come together. The interests of class and politics must dictate not only the young person's choice of a mate, but also one's attitude towards one's parents. In his famous "twelve commandments" for sexual and familial behavior, Zalkind offers a chilling alternative to the biblical injunction "Honor thy father and thy mother": "The proletariat recommends that you should honor only a father who adopted a revolutionary-proletarian standpoint and who brings his children up in a spirit of devotion to the struggle of the proletariat" (Zalkind, as quoted in Heller 173). Thus ties of blood become secondary to the interests of ideology; loyalty to one's class is placed higher than filial piety. In its most benign form, this philosophy meant only greater calls for "proletarianizing" the family; at its worst, it lent support to the Pavlik Morozovs of the subsequent decade, children who reported on their parents to the NKVD (Narodnii komissariat vnutrennikh del, or People's Commissariat of Internal Affairs). In either case, the politicization of the family called for by Zalkind and his ilk did meet with limited success in transforming the family from domestic refuge to instrument of social control. The boundaries between the domestic and social spheres were forcibly blurred if not erased. Though Soviet social policy had some consequences, such as the softening of male domestic tyranny, that are now generally accepted to be improvements, the result was nonetheless a radical assault on the family as an institution. In areas that would seem to the contemporary Western observer both positive (the emancipation of women from their husbands' domination) and negative (the intrusion of the state in family life), a man's home ceased to be his castle, becoming instead the "basic cell of society" (Heller 168).

THE FAMILY AS METAPHOR

Given the strident rhetoric to which such extreme opponents of the traditional family were prone, it would be easy to assume that the attack on family bonds and conventional sexual relations is a distinctly Russian (or Soviet) phenomenon. While Soviet Russia has the dubious distinction of being the first country to be transformed on the basis of a totalizing theory, the Soviet assault on the family nonetheless fits into the context of the general upheavals of twentieth-century society. As the most famous literary works of the contemporary literature illustrate, modernism was characterized by a sense of dislocation and discontinuity in both the social and domestic spheres. Citing *Ulysses, Death in Venice,* and *The Waste Land* as examples, Edward Said finds that in the European literature of around 1900, "the failure of the generative impulse—the failure of the capacity to produce or generate children—is portrayed in such a way as to stand for a general condition afflicting society and culture together, to say nothing of individual men and women" (Said 16). The preponderance of "[c]hildless couples, orphaned children, aborted childbirths, and unregenerately celibate men and women" in the period of high modernism is evidence to Said that "few things are as problematic . . . as what we might have supposed to be the mere natural continuity between one generation and the next" (Said 16–17). This collapse of family ties, or, to use Said's term, "filiation," results in "pressure to produce new and different ways of conceiving relationships" based on social bonds rather than biology. Said calls these social bonds, which are the result of choice or affinity rather than genealogy, affiliation (Said 17). Where filial relationships were rooted in "natural bonds," the new affiliative ties become "transpersonal," based on such concepts as "guild consciousness, consensus, collegiality, professional respect, class, and the hegemony of a dominant culture" (Said 19).

Said sees in the dynamic of filiation and affiliation a three-part pattern that vaguely resembles the Hegelian thesis, antithesis, and synthesis. Filiation, which precedes affiliation and provides a model for it, collapses. Biological ties are superseded by affiliative structures. According to Said, affiliation is "a kind of contemporary order that, whether it is a party, an institution, a culture, a set of beliefs, or even a world-vision, provides men and women with a new form of relationship . . . which is also a new system." The third part of the pattern provides a limited recapitulation of filiation within affiliation: ultimately, the new order will be used "to reinstate vestiges of the kind of authority associated in the past with filiative order" (Said 19). The family may be superseded, but the new structures that arise in its place often take on the characteristics of the family it supplanted. Thus, in one of its forms, affiliation becomes a pseudo-family, more or less faithfully reproducing the family hierarchy even as it denies the importance of blood ties.

Though Said confines himself to a discussion of western European literature, his analysis provides a valuable conceptual framework for reading Russian literature of the 1920s. If the authors treated by Said were keenly aware of the insufficiency of the family and the need for alternatives, the phenomena they described were not part of any governmental or political program. Soviet writers of the 1920s, however, composed their novels and stories during a time when the decline of the family was a part of public policy, and the revolutionary government was making a concerted effort to create an ideologically suitable replacement for filial ties. If the rhetoric surrounding the family in Soviet Russia is examined in Said's terms, the debates of the 1920s show themselves to be a classic example of the struggle between affiliation and filiation. Whether the goal was to destroy the family or merely to transform it, the radical advocates of the proletarian family and revolutionary sublimation found filial ties to be an unsatisfactory basis for human relationships.

In exploring the larger implications of his model, Said asserts that his three-part pattern "can be considered an instance of the passage from nature to culture" in which the "filiative scheme belongs to the realms of nature and of 'life,' whereas affiliation belongs exclusively to culture and society" (Said 19–20). Once again, Said's ideas are, if anything, even more applicable to the early Soviet context than the western European. When the nature-culture dichotomy is conflated with the filiation-affiliation dialectic, the attack on the family reveals itself to be a part of a larger Soviet phenomenon: the struggle against nature. As one enthusiast wrote in *Komsomol Life* (*Komsomol'skii byt*) in 1927, "Not to subject oneself to nature but to subject nature to oneself—this is the worthy slogan of socialism. Nature is obsolete and in addition poorly organized. Nature is in very definite need of fundamental corrections" (Nina Vel't, as quoted in Lapidus 85).[34] The official Soviet policies of the 1920s are a modern ecologist's nightmare: nature is merely a hostile force to be transformed by the miracle of Soviet science. In his aptly titled article "Repairing the Earth" ("Remont zemli," 1920), Andrei Platonov writes that the earth is a machine and, like any other mechanism, needs humans to repair and alter it. The primary economic task of the Soviet regime was the transformation of a backward, agrarian society into an industrial giant, which in turn demanded that industry take priority over all else.

The veneration of scientific and industrial progress could not help but have an impact on Bolshevik social policy. If we reexamine the rhetoric surrounding women's emancipation and the abolition of the family in revolutionary Russia, it becomes clear that such social transformation was merely the handmaiden of industrial policy. The attacks on the kitchen, the calls to "free" women from domestic labor, the experiments in communal child rearing—all had as their goal the removal of woman from the domestic sphere into the realm of industry and "productive" work. The be-all and end-all of Soviet policy was production (*proizvodstvo*), which was considered a far more useful outlet than reproduction (*vosproizvodstvo*). Emancipated from domestic chores, women were expected to replace (or at least supplement) their second-class reproductive labor with more valuable efforts in the productive sphere.

It is now a commonplace of post-Soviet society to claim that women were "masculinized" by Soviet social policy, forced to sacrifice their "femininity" on the altar of the workers' state.[35] Such assertions can be easily refuted on the grounds that they are contradictory: on the one hand, such critics accept cultural conceptions of gender as biological fact, but on the other, they claim that "natural" sex differences were nonetheless distorted by social circumstances. All the same, the charge of "masculinization" has some validity, even if one takes issue with the conceptions of gender that it implies. Whether or not gender roles are biologically determined, Soviet social policy played havoc with the traditional notions of gender that were at the heart of Russian culture. One does not have to accept that factory labor is an inherently masculine occupation to admit that the shift of female labor from the domestic to the productive sphere amounted to a rejection of the traditional feminine role in favor of something generally accepted to be masculine. When the cult of (masculine) productive labor is combined with the degradation of (feminine) domestic and reproductive pursuits, one sees that postrevolutionary Soviet society was characterized by a reverence for traditionally masculine values at the expense of conventional femininity.[36] Domesticity, femininity, nature, and the family were objects of scorn for the Bolsheviks, while the social sphere, science, productive labor, and, implicitly, masculinity were established as ideals.[37]

If we return to the problem of the family, examining it in terms of both Said's writings and the masculinization of Soviet society, the outlines of the relationships between the family and the social sphere in a postrevolutionary context begin to take shape, at least in the literature of the time. The attack on the conventional family is a de facto assault on received notions of femininity; if the individual members of the shattered family unit are forced to abandon their places in the family hierarchy, it is women who undergo the greatest transformation. The men in a traditional family were always part of more than just domestic relationships: fathers and sons, no matter what family conflicts might arise between them, always had one foot in the social realm. Indeed, as the standard English rendering of Turgenev's title *Fathers and Children* (*Ottsy i deti*) as *Fathers and Sons* demonstrates, generational conflict between men was more often a metaphor for a struggle within the social sphere, rather than a "merely" domestic drama. Women, however, were firmly grounded in hearth and home; with some notable exceptions, their stories began and ended in the context of the family. In literature as well as life, women now found themselves part of a decidedly different plot.

Whether the family was destroyed or transformed, the result was the triumph of affiliation over filial ties, and, by extension, of masculinity and the social over femininity and the domestic. One again recalls Dasha from *Cement*, who places her work above the welfare of her child, ultimately making the regrettable but necessary sacrifice of her family life for the sake of the revolution. If female characters such as Dasha attract the reader's attention, it is because her shift between one role and another is so pronounced.[38] Many Soviet novels of the postrevolutionary period, however, examine the decline of filiation and the rise of new, socially oriented ties in a context where women are all but absent. Taking the collapse of the family as a given, these works explore the relationships that arise in its place. Though Soviet literature of the 1920s is so broad and varied that one can cite examples for nearly any point of view, it is nonetheless possible to identify a particular strain in the fiction of the period, a strain in which the masculinization of the new Soviet society is underscored by the family's replacement with all-male structures. These "men without women" group together because of ideology rather than filial ties. As Said's three-part schema suggests, these men ultimately form pseudo-families with ideology as their basis; with the passage of time, their relationships begin to resemble the family structure that has been rejected or destroyed, with one important exception: these "families" have no place for women.[39] The revolutionary society is an alliance of either fathers and sons or brothers and comrades, in which mothers and daughters play at best a marginal role.

Even given the traditional linkage of men to the social sphere, many readers would find themselves at a loss to describe a society based only on male relationships, especially if these ties take on a familial character. All-female utopian societies are a staple of feminist fiction; works ranging from Charlotte Perkins Gilman's *Herland* (1915) to Marge Piercy's *Woman on the Edge of Time* (1976) are central to the canon of feminist writing, but few authors have posited all-male societies that are neither monasteries nor military barracks.[40] Moreover, all-female worlds are, as a rule, strictly utopian; that is, the world described is presumed to be better than our own. Their male counterparts are almost invariably dystopian; the Russian myth of the self-sufficient community of Cossacks may well be the only exception (see below).[41] Yet a variety of cultural theorists argue that the greater part of all human associations are founded on the ties between men and thus have a specifically masculine character. Even the family, which for centuries was considered to be woman's "natural" realm, can be viewed as a male organization in which women fulfill a function marked out for them by men. The manner in which men exchange, distribute, or share women is at the heart of a post-Freudian anthropological theory that was put forth by Lévi-Strauss (1969) and reinterpreted by Rubin (1975) and Irigaray (1985).[42] Culture, according to Lévi-Strauss, originates with the incest taboo, whose function is to delineate the women to which an individual man has "access." By clearly prescribing the limits of sexual conduct, kinship rules provide "the only means of maintaining the group as a group, of avoiding the indefinite fission and segmentation which the practice of consanguineous marriages would bring about" (Lévi-Strauss 479). Viewed in these terms, marriage becomes an institution not between a man and a woman, but an exchange "between two groups of men, and the woman figures only as one of the objects of the exchange, not as one of the partners between whom the exchange takes place" (115). Irigaray sees this reduction of women to mere exchange value as the source of what she calls "hom(m)o-sexuality," the reigning patriarchal structure in which women exist only to facilitate relationships among men (Irigaray 171–75). Such a reinterpretation of patriarchal society still allows for the restriction of women to the domestic sphere, but its emphasis on the family as an institution structured by male relationships shows that the shift from filiation to the all-male pseudo-families of postrevolutionary Russian literature might not be as radical a transformation as it first appears. If one accepts Irigaray's approach, such new Soviet "families" differ from their traditional predecessors only to the extent that they dispense with the need for the female intermediary.

Despite their revisionist approaches, both Irigaray and Lévi-Strauss are indebted to Freud for their analysis of human social structures. It is Freud who, in *Totem and Taboo,* extrapolates his theory of the Oedipus complex to postulate the father-son conflict as the basis of the most fundamental human social structures. Freud notes that the "most primitive kind of organization that we actually come across ... consists of bands of males" united around an animal totem (Freud, *Totem* 141). Freud sees the "access to women" as the fundamental question determining the character of male interaction; unlike Irigaray and Lévi-Strauss, however, he sees this issue as a question of rivalry. In order to understand the roots of the totemic society, Freud is forced to hypothesize an even more hierarchical predecessor, the "patriarchal horde." As the name suggests, this horde was dominated by the "violent primeval father," who denied his sons access to the objects of their sexual desire. Eventually, the sons banded together to kill their father, taking power (and the women) into their own hands. After the father's death, the sons, who loved their father as well as feared and hated him, began to feel remorse; ironically, "the dead father became stronger than the living one had been" (Freud, *Totem* 143). Along with their guilt, these sons faced another problem: "Though the brothers had banded together in order to overcome their father, they were all one another's rivals in regard to the women" (Freud, *Totem* 144). Thus, in order to keep their new, fatherless grouping from falling apart under fratricidal pressures, the brothers reinstituted the very taboo on incest that sparked their murderous act. This taboo was reinforced by a renewed cult of the dead father, who was symbolically replaced by the animal totem. Essentially Freud creates a legend of prehistory in which all of (male) humanity acts out the crisis and resolution of the oedipal conflict; by showing how the brothers voluntarily reinstitute the paternal prohibition, Freud gives his reader a sociological parable of the creation of the individual superego, which is itself the internalization of the father's restrictive role.

Though *Totem and Taboo* is often viewed strictly in terms of a father-son rivalry that can end only in blood, Freud's myth does not leave the balance of power between father and son unchanged. Freud's projection of his oedipal theory onto prehistory postulates that the basic structure of human society is a compromise between fraternal impulses and paternal authority, rather than the unconditional triumph of one over the other. Totemic society is based on "deferred obedience" to the dead father rather than immediate compliance with the wishes of the living male parent. Even after an abstract version of paternal authority is restored, "the social fraternal feelings, which were the basis of the whole transformation, [continue] to exercise a profound influence on the development of society." These feelings take the form of the "sanctification of the blood tie"; added to the renewed prohibition on both symbolic and actual parricide is a new one on fratricide (Freud, *Totem* 146). Thus arises the fraternal clan, in which a society of brothers now extends the protection of taboo horizontally as well as vertically. The previous, purely oedipal prohibitions restricted the son's behavior in regard to his father and mother; now, his interactions with the male and female members of his own generation are similarly confined, but with these limits come guarantees of personal safety and social stability.

The eventual outcome is the rise of the patriarchal family structure that would be central to Freudian theory. Such a family is based on paternal authority, in both the literalized form of the biological father and the establishment of father-based religions, themselves merely an elaboration of the earlier totemic cult. But the modern family, in Freud's view, is a compromise between the claims of patriarchy and fraternity, in which the father is restored to a more limited version of the authority once enjoyed by the unrestricted patriarch of the primal horde. Though paternal authority is recognized, the "social achievements of the fraternal clan [have] not been abandoned" (Freud, *Totem* 149). Elsewhere Freud is inclined to portray the patriarchal family as an institution based on the father's absolute primacy, but *Totem and Taboo* paints a noticeably different picture of the family unit. If the family of *The Interpretation of Dreams* and *Three Essays on Sexuality* presents the father as despot, *Totem and Taboo* portrays a compromise between father and son that is reminiscent of constitutional monarchy.

Totem and Taboo thus describes both types of male relationships that are crucial to the present study: the father-son connection and the bond between men of the same generation. *Totem and Taboo* reminds us that revolt against the father is only one possible form that the relationships between the generations can take. Though Freud's central myth is the murder of the father, the subsequent rise of the father cult shows that patricidal rebellion and filial piety are not mutually exclusive. Freud's attempt at a psychoanalytic prehistory thus yields two important conclusions for this book: first, that the father-and-son relationship, despite its inherent rivalry, can run the gamut from open hostility to submission and adoration, and second, that the fraternal bond cannot be viewed separately from the father-son relationship.

At their most extreme, "fraternal" relations would appear to be directly opposed to the bond between father and son. John Remy calls both types of social order "andocracy," recognizing that treating "patriarchy" and "male domination" as synonyms is too facile an identification. In his framework, patriarchy is only one of the many forms andocracy can take. As the word implies, patriarchy is built on the supremacy of the father, but by extension, it presupposes the existence of the family. Rooted in the family, patriarchy sets aside a place for women, however subordinate that place may be. Remy contrasts patriarchy with the structure he calls "fratriarchy," which, unconcerned with the values or the needs of the family, "is based simply on the interest of the association of men itself." Fratriarchy groups together young, unmarried men, without the dominance of an older man or ties to any woman. The patriarchal family, though controlled by the father, is a "matrifocal" institution, centered around the home, which is maintained by the mother. Fratriarchal clubs, such as the modern American fraternity, allow young men to act as if they are fatherless and motherless, a group of "brothers" who answer to no paternal authority.

Remy's argument that men seek out such "brotherly" contact has much in common with the work of Lionel Tiger, whose *Men in Groups* (1969) places him on the opposite side of the political spectrum from the profeminist Remy. At the end of his book-length study of the "male bond," Tiger concludes that "men 'need' some haunts and/or occasions which exclude women" (208). Though he does not devote as much attention as Remy to the opposition of fraternity to family, he nonetheless finds that the family can be a threat to the all-male group: "It is conceivable that . . . men dominated by their wives and families may lose a certain constructive maleness of consequence to many of their activities" (210–11). The basic propositions of Tiger's study read like a fratriarchal manifesto:

> (1) . . . when they can, males choose their workmates in processes analogous to sexual selection; (2) . . . the bond established generates considerable emotion; (3) . . . males derive important satisfactions from male bonds and male interactions which they cannot derive from male-female bonds and interactions; . . . (4) . . . the sexual division of labor is a *consequence* of males' wishes to preserve their unisexual bonds. (Tiger 100; emphasis in the original)

As the wording of the above quote suggests, Tiger sees a biological imperative behind what Remy considers a purely cultural or social structure.[43] One need not accept Tiger's sociobiological premise, however, to recognize that Tiger provides a detailed description of the processes that create Remy's fratriarchy. Where Remy focuses on fratriarchy's rejection of the father, Tiger pays attention to the male group's exclusion of women. Tiger recognizes the emotional strength and appeal of male relationships, seeing in them an alternative to male-female interactions whose dynamics nonetheless have much in common with sexual relationships. His comparison of male bonding and sexual selection will have particular ramifications for the erotic side of the relationships discussed in this book, especially those described in Babel's *Red Cavalry*.

THE GENEALOGY OF COMRADESHIP

Soviet literary attempts to build male communities cannot be explained only in terms of Tiger's and Remy's sociological theories.[44] At the heart of the Bolshevik myth is a concept that shares much with Remy's fratriarchy and Tiger's male bonding but that nonetheless diverges from both at crucial points: comradeship (tovarishchestvo). The word "comrade" (tovarishch) of course predates the revolution, but it came into vogue among various radical movements in the previous century, eventually becoming a standard form of address in Soviet society.[45] Both in English and in Russian, comradeship is easy to mistake for a milder form of friendship, and yet, in the Soviet context, comradeship is to friendship what affiliation is to filiation. If friendship is, like love, an emotional bond that transcends rational categories, comradeship is a form of human interaction based on common experience or ideology. Ozhegov defines a tovarishch as a "person who is close to someone based on their common views, activity, living conditions, etc." (*Chelovek, blizkii kom-n po obshchnosti vzglaidov, deiatel'nosti, uslovii zhizni i t. p.*). Comradeship becomes one of the standard tropes of revolutionary literature, one that fits in with the general privileging of rational, affiliative bonds based on dedication to the "common cause" rather than sentimental or familial feelings.[46]

Comradeship is the expression of revolutionary male solidarity par excellence; though women can be, and often are, comrades in the literature of the 1920s, the experience of comradeship is based on traditionally masculine values.[47] In his study *The Warriors: Reflections on Men in Battle*, J. Glenn Gray differentiates between "friends" and "comrades" in a way that, though free of communist connotations, helps explain the phenomenon of comradeship in Soviet fiction. Gray defines friendship as a fundamentally individual phenomenon: "Only those men or women can be friends ... who possess an intellectual and emotional affinity for each other" (Gray 89). Comradeship lies on the other end of the spectrum, for its personal demands on the individual are minimal: "The essential difference between comradeship and friendship consists ... in a heightened awareness of the self in friendship and in the suppression of self-awareness in comradeship." Comradeship seeks to "break down the walls of self," where friendship "strives to keep them intact. The one relationship is ecstatic, the other is wholly individual" (Gray 90). One can be mistaken for the other, but they are qualitatively different. Comrades may "love one another like brothers" and may be deceived by their shared experience into believing that they are actually true friends; but when the danger is past, comrades "gradually become strangers" (Gray 89).[48]

Though Gray leaves this avenue unexplored, his contrast between friendship and comradeship is enlightening in terms of the Soviet experience. Friendship is an individual phenomenon that requires no intermediaries, goals, or groups, but comradeship is implicitly collective. "Comradeship," writes Gray, "is fortunately within reach of the vast majority. Suffering and danger cannot create friendship, but they make all the difference in comradeship" (89). If one succeeds in convincing a group of people that they share common goals and common obstacles, comradeship will be the result. That the term "comrade" became the normative form of address during the Russian Revolution and the ensuing civil war should come as no surprise.

In order to understand the importance of comradeship in Russia, however, one must try to look beyond the Soviet stamp with which the Russian word "comrade" is indelibly marked. Like so many social institutions, comradeship can be regarded as the "secularization" of an old family metaphor: brotherhood. Like many cultures, the Slavic world had a tradition of "blood brotherhood" (*pobratimstvo*) that predates the arrival of Christianity.[49] This rite, which involved the actual exchange of blood between two men, was a means of recognizing strong male friendship by recategorizing the relationship as biological: like children of the same parents, *pobratimy* shared the same blood. Like heterosexual marriage, *pobratimstvo* served to bridge the gap between filiation and affiliation: an elective affinity (whether friendship, love, or the result of marriage brokering) would now be recognized as part of the biological family unit. Once Christianity became the dominant religion, *pobratimstvo* became a problem for Orthodox clerics; some argued that *pobratimstvo* was a pagan holdover, to be punished by a year of fasting, while others felt that it was superfluous, since Christ made brothers of all mankind. Most troubling to the clergy was the problem of marriage: would a man's marriage to his blood brother's sister constitute incest?

Although *pobratimstvo* ceased to be an issue in modern Russia, the metaphor of brotherhood remained potent.[50] In part this is due to the Christian notion of universal brotherhood, which, when adapted to Slavophile national myths in the nineteenth century, fed into the idea of Russian *sobornost'* (communality, collective life): the Russian people as an organic, self-regulating organism. *Sobornost'* is, however, too abstract a concept to be responsible for the evolution of collectivism from *pobratimstvo* to comradeship; rather, mythologizers of the Russian collective spirit could look to a phenomenon that was unique to the Russian empire, one that, in Gogol's hands, could even become the allegorical embodiment of Orthodox *sobornost'*: the Cossack.[51] Though in reality these freewheeling warriors who lived on the margins of the Russian empire married and reproduced, the "basic premise of mythic Cossackdom" is that "women do not make Cossacks. Cossacks are male" (Kornblatt 61). A number of literary texts "suggest that entrance into the Cossack community resembles tonsure"; just as a monk "vows celibacy and marries the Church, the Cossack also departs from ordinary life with its established heterosexual, maternal, and marital bonds" (Kornblatt 62–63). The Russian (literary) Cossack encampment is based on an affiliative bond that fits nearly all the criteria of Remy's "fratriarchy"; only the focus on paternal authority in Gogol's "Taras Bulba" (1835 and 1842) suggests a place for some form of the biological family. Moreover, as Gogol's story of a Cossack son's betrayal of his father and community shows, being born to a Cossack father is not enough: whether born among Cossacks or brought into the fold later in life, a man becomes a Cossack by choice (Kornblatt 66). Nor is homoeroticism absent from the Cossack world; Kornblatt suggests that true Cossack sexuality is expressed in their "male comradeship, their bonding itself," which is assumed to be "grander, . . . holier, and more mythic than that of ordinary mortals (66). Finally, Gogol's Cossacks provide an explicit endorsement of antifamily, "comradely" relations that predates Soviet power by eight decades. Before battle, Bulba addresses his fellow Cossacks: "Nothing is holier than the love of comrades. The father loves his child, the mother loves her child, the child loves its father and mother; but that is not the same, brothers; the wild beast too loves its offspring, but only man can be akin in soul, though not in blood" (Gogol 2: 99). Bulba's denigration of reproduction and the family as part of man's "animal" nature, if couched in terms of revolutionary consciousness rather than Russian Orthodox solidarity, could well have issued from the lips of a Chevengurian or one of Olesha's "new men."[52]

As the example of Gogol demonstrates, the advocacy of an extrabiological alternative to the traditional family was not the sole provenance of political radicals. Though the nature of the Soviet attack on the family was dictated by left-wing ideology, the form of the projected new social relationships is largely indebted to Russian religious tradition. "In the nineteenth century," observes Olga Matich, "the ideals of love and religion took the semiotic form of their polar opposites — militant asceticism and atheism — but paradigmatically they performed the same function"; the focus on community (*obshchestvennost'*) remained unchanged and was common to all Russian utopian thinkers, radical as well as religious" ("Zinaida Gippius" 239). At the same time that radical utopians plotted the destruction of traditional family, a counterutopia based specifically on family ties was developed by Nikolai Fyodorov [Fedorov].

Fyodorov's "scientific exegesis of Christianity" (Lukashevich 15) might at first glance seem utterly alien to the avowedly rationalist plans of the Soviet Union's early leaders, yet echoes of his *Philosophy of the Common Cause* (*Filosofiia obshchego dela*), published posthumously in 1906) can be heard in the literature (and even the policies) of the early Bolshevik regime.[53] Fyodorov's thousand-page treatise is far too ornate to dwell upon at length, but certain aspects of Fyodorov's project are crucial in the evolution of comradeship. Like many Soviet ideologues of the 1920s, Fyodorov viewed nature as fundamentally hostile to humankind, a force to be regulated, if not conquered. Far and away the worst aspect of the natural order is that man is doomed to die like any other animal, and that he consoles himself for the loss of prior generations through sex and reproduction. For Fyodorov, sex and childbearing are intrinsically connected to the idea of progress, which he defines as the "consciousness of the superiority of, first of all, an entire generation (the living) over its predecessors (the dead), and, second, of the younger over the older" (Fedorov 76–77). Fyodorov proposes instead channeling all human energy, sexual as well as scientific, toward the physical resurrection of every human being who ever walked the earth. Men and women must live according to the ideals of "positive chastity," sublimating erotic desire in the name of the "common cause."[54]

The source of all our present troubles is, according to Fyodorov, humanity's "unrelatedness" (*nerodstvennost'*), its "unbrotherly" (*nebratskoe*) order: "By an unbrotherly state we mean all the juridical-economic relations, estates, and international dissension" (Fedorov 63). All humanity is one enormous family, descended from common ancestors who deserve to be revered, rather than consigned to oblivion; true reverence is found in the process of resurrecting "that demands a universal joining together, not only of external, but of internal, true brotherhood, a brotherhood based on fathers, on the fatherland, and not citizenship" (Fedorov 281). Fyodorov is not speaking metaphorically: to him, the brotherhood of man is an indisputable fact, from which follow indisputable consequences. Thus he makes no secret of his hostility to socialism, which he terms a "deceit" (*obman*) based on the substitution of brotherhood by "the comradeship of people who are alien to each other and connected only by external interests" (Fedorov 91).[55]

Yet no matter how vehemently Fyodorov argued that his brotherhood was not metaphorical, no matter how harshly he attacked socialist notions of "fraternity," the irony of Fyodorov's work is that, structurally, his Christian conception of brotherhood resembled the very idea of comradeship that he despised. It requires a leap of faith to look upon all men as literally brothers; one reflexively recognizes a difference between immediate biological kin and fellow Christians a continent away. Socialist theorists who followed Fyodorov were able to appropriate his plans for regulating weather, interstellar colonization, the conquest of nature, and, most important, the resurrection of the dead, leaving behind the philosopher's religiosity and hatred of progress.[56] So too was the doctrine of brotherhood easily assimilated into the rhetoric of secular comradeship. Here one recalls a debate over terminology in *Chevengur*, whose author without a doubt made a close study of Fyodorov's work: one of the leaders of the communist collective greets the new arrivals as "brothers," which another leader condemns as a "bald-faced lie ... We are not brothers, we are comrades" (Platonov 281).[57] Unlike Fyodorov, Platonov's Chevengurians deny a common paternity, rendering "brotherhood" an impossibility. Nonetheless, the appeal to a common cause and a common fate has recognizably Fyodorovian roots.

The secularization of brotherhood as comradeship did not happen overnight; the term "brother" continued to resonate as a powerful metaphor throughout the early Soviet period. Yet the reinterpretation of Fyodorov's universal brotherhood can be traced largely to the efforts of one communist theorist: Aleksandr Bogdanov. Bogdanov, whose early phenomenological Marxist "empiriomonism" provoked Lenin's book-length rebuttal *Materialism and Empiriocriticism* (1909), is best known for the invention of "tektology" (*tektologiia*), a "science of organization," and for being the ideological fount of the movement known as Proletarian Culture (*proletarskaia kul'tura*) commonly called the Proletcult (*Proletkul't*). Founded in 1917, the Proletcult was an attempt to create a class-based, collective art. Proletcult poetry typically has a cosmist bent, with planet-sized muscular laborers rejoicing to the mellifluous sound of the factory whistle.[58] Bogdanov would often find himself in disagreement with the more radical pronouncements of the poets he inspired, such as the threats to "burn Raphael, destroy museums, and stomp on the flowers of art" (*sozhzhem Rafaelia, / Razrushim muzei, rastopchem iskusstva tvsety*) in Vladimir Kirillov's 1917 poem "We" ("My") (Papernyi 228; Bogdanov 449). Yet despite his differences with the Proletcult's artistic program, it was Bogdanov who gave the Proletcult's emphasis on collectivism and comradeship.[59]

Though Bogdanov's conception of history rests on a faith in the very "progress" that Fyodorov abhors, variation on the latter's "common cause" are easily recognizable in the Marxist philosopher's work (the struggle for immortality, the goal of resurrection, and the emphasis on a communitarian social structure).[60] The earliest version of Bogdanov's project echoes Fyodorov in its very title: "The Gathering of Man" ("Sobiranie cheloveka," 1904).[61] Here Bogdanov proposes a four-stage model of historical development, which he would revise throughout his career. Reinterpreting Marx's analysis of history in terms of psychology, he bases his different stages of society on the types of labor that characterize them. Bogdanov postulates an initial "primitive" (*pervobytnoe*) human society, in which there is no personality and all knowledge and experience is collective (31–32). Eventually the "sum of collective experience grows to such an extent, that the individual can master it only towards the end of his life," and thus the institution of the "elder" (*starshii*) arises. The result is the second, "authoritarian" stage, in which the only individual personality is that of the leader. Bogdanov sees the authoritarian model as the source of all hierarchical systems, especially that of spirit (*dukh*) and body (*telo*). The mind-body distinction arises when a leader emerges as the "spirit" that guides his society's collective "body." This model leads both to monotheism (one God rules over the entire universe) and to the patriarchal family (32–34). When the sum of experience grows even further, society fragments into "specialists" who are experts in only a narrow field of endeavor. This third stage, "specialization," is characterized by individualism and egoism. No longer is society one amorphous mass with a single leader; rather, authoritarianism spreads itself out among smaller groups, each with its own "specialist" as leader. The power of the family increases (35–38). Finally, a new type of person appears, the factory worker, whose work by its very nature forces him to be both an organizer (*organizator*) and a performer (*ispolnitel'*) of his tasks. He both performs the work demanded of him and guides a machine to help with his labor (40). Thus authoritarian fragmentation is transcended. All workers have their own narrow specialty, and yet they all perform the same type of work. Eventually the commonality of their experience leads them to class consciousness, and their interactions are not authoritarian or hierarchical, but "comradely" (*tovarishcheskie*) (44). In a socialist world, man will be "collected," and workers will lose their sense of an individual "I" in favor of an all-encompassing "we" that will someday triumph over nature and achieve collective immortality (Williams 391).

Bogdanov's comradeship purports to be a "scientific" phenomenon, yet it shares an almost mystical reverence for the collective with Fyodorov's universal brotherhood. As Vladislav Todorov writes, "Comradeship [in Bogdanov] does not arise from religious love, but from the technological togetherness of bodies in the process of labor.... The human corporeality must become the immediate substance of comradeship" (48). For Bogdanov, that substance was the very same fluid that united the *pobratimy* of the medieval Slavic world: blood. Toward the end of his life, Bogdanov founded the Moscow Institute for Blood Transfusion, whose work he saw as being more than just medical: "For Bogdanov, blood is the very substance which should be exchanged between comrades and thus comradeship will flow directly into the bodies of the proletarians" (Todorov 49). In one of the many ironies of the 1920s, Bogdanov's fascination with blood would lead to his death from an experimental transfusion he performed upon himself.

The high value placed on comradeship and the collective in the early Soviet years is evident in leftist or communist literature, a phenomenon for which the utopianism of Bogdanov and Proletcult is only partly responsible. Robert Maguire has isolated a particular "brotherhood" theme characteristic of civil war literature.[62] During the civil war, utopian idealism becomes hopelessly intermeshed with a military ethos, thus reinforcing the masculine character of early Bolshevik ideology—the very term "War Communism" suggests a masculine society. Of course, such a focus on men's group identity is to be expected in war literature of any country and would indeed resurface in stories of World War II.[63] By the time of the NEP era, though, unadulterated affection for "barracks communism" (*kazarmennyi kommunizm*) had acquired a taint of the old fashioned; the evolving attitude toward this particular brand of collectivism is perhaps best seen in Pilnyak's "Mahogany" ("Krasnoe derevo," 1929): here the motley assemblage of ideologically pure holy fools, whose squalid living conditions are brightened only by their nostalgia for the days of War Communism, is treated by the rest of the town as a laughingstock. Comradeship also tarred by the brush of Communist Youth League maximalism; commentators and youth organizers appear to have recognized the distinction between friendship and comradeship long before it was formulated by Gray. Some even argued against any small groups of close friends, since such bonds of affection might weaken the solidarity of the collective. Thus some student communards in the 1920s insisted on swimming and attending the theater en masse, lest they be tempted by the lure of "bourgeois friendship" (Stites, *Revolutionary Dreams* 115). The arguments against friendship are reminiscent of the debates on sexual morality that were raging at the same time: both romantic love and personal (non-comradely) friendship were perceived as the enemies of comradeship.

What is perhaps most remarkable, however, is that the concern with comradeship is by no means restricted to proto-socialist realist writers, nor is it always the target of satire. Central among the themes of fellow-traveler literature is the predicament of the overeducated, wavering intellectual who wants the emotional and social benefits of comradeship but finds they are denied him. Though one of the best-known explorations of this motif is Babel's *Red Cavalry*, another example of civil war literature, the outsider's longing for fellowship is also at the heart of Kavalerov's "envy" in Olesha's 1927 short novel of the same name. Kavalerov's anger and shame revolve around his inability to find a place in a world that, however much he might disdain it, holds a distinct attraction for him. In contrast to Kavalerov, Volodya Makarov, the man who is most comfortable in the new world, is the quintessential team player, both on the soccer field and off: "Comradeship was the strongest feeling within him" (Olesha 81). For reasons that, without a doubt, cannot be explained only in terms of ideology, the idea of comradeship would cut across political and social lines.[64]

COMRADESHIP AND THE SPECTER OF FASCISM

If the appeal of male comradeship transcended allegiance to this or that communist faction, it is not only because the ideal of comradely relations has a long history in Russia, but because both comradeship and a "cult of masculinity" were an integral part of early-twentieth-century modernist discourse. George Mosse's groundbreaking *Nationalism and Sexuality* (1985) argues that an idealized "manliness" is at the heart of what he terms "the most powerful ideology of modern times," nationalism (Mosse 1). According to Mosse, the nineteenth century was marked by a "renewed emphasis on masculinity" that was "reinforced by the wars against Napoleon." The fraternity movement in Germany extolled the virtues of virility, while a general cult of manliness and manly beauty was encouraged by the Greek revival in the romantic era. Moreover, this manly ideal was deeply rooted in both medieval chivalry and the "popular culture surrounding modern wars" (Mosse 13).[65] Of particular relevance to modernism is Mosse's assertion that by the early twentieth century, "[m]asculinity was expected to stand both for unchanging values in a changing age and for the dynamic but orderly process of change itself, guided by an appropriate purpose" (Mosse 31). If the modernist era was a time of change and rupture, masculinity could paradoxically embody both a resistance to unwanted change and the appeal to a supposedly "timeless" manly ethos. Idealized masculinity signified change in that it was a rejection of the androgyny and sexual "perversions" of fin-de-siècle decadence.[66]

Mosse's identification of the cult of masculinity with the ideology of nationalism is reinforced by his emphasis on male friendship and comradeship. He traces the German preoccupation with comradeship in both the Weimar and the Nazi eras to the eighteenth-century German cult of friendship: "Friendship among men was thought superior to heterosexual love because it was based upon reason rather than the senses" (Mosse 68). The nineteenth century saw the development of the modern conception of homosexuality as an attribute of one's character rather than a set of particular sexual acts; as a result, the heightened intimacy of male sentimental friendship would ultimately acquire the taint of homoeroticism.[67] Even in the eighteenth century, Mosse argues, the ideal of friendship "attempted to strip itself of sexuality" through the creation of *Freundschaftbünde*: "The cult of friendship in Germany was articulated through groups rather than individuals" (Mosse 69).[68] Here we should recall Gray's distinction between friendship and comradeship: friendship is an intense and personal tie between individuals, while comradeship is the product of shared experiences and a common cause rather than any emotional or spiritual affinity. It should come as no surprise, then, that the turn toward "group friendship" should give rise to the rhetoric of comradeship.

Comradeship and the cult of "manliness" would truly come to the fore throughout Europe only with the outbreak of World War I. "A variety of motivations were at work as the generation of 1914 rushed to the colors at the outbreak of the war," writes Mosse, "but the quest for masculinity cut across them all . . . Withdrawing from a corrupt world, they would create a new and virile universe" in which "robust health was to replace the sickness of [the] weak, effeminate, and over-refined society" of fin-de-siècle Europe (Mosse 115–16). The poetry, fiction, and memoirs of such diverse writers as Rupert Brooke and T. E. Lawrence on one side of the trenches and Walter Flex and Rudolf Herzog on the other would praise both male beauty and the camaraderie inspired by wartime experiences.[69] Nor were the unifying effects of battle lost on Russian writers who either participated in or observed the Great War. Vladimir Mayakovsky, whose postrevolutionary poetry would extol the virtues of the collective, describes the feeling of solidarity found on the battlefield in 1914: "When the regiment launches an attack, you can't make out which voice belongs to Ivan in the general 'hurrah'; so, too, in the mass of flying deaths you can't make out which is mine and which is someone else's. Death spreads itself out among the whole crowd, the whole unit. After all, our common body remains, at war everyone breathes as one, and therefore there is immortality" (Maiakovskii 1: 332).

Yet despite the contemporary rhetoric of the Great War as a unique, transformative experience, the "war to end all wars," the comradeship it engendered conformed with Gray's assessment of such military bonds: it all but vanished when the conflict was over. Veterans' nostalgia for the wars of their youth is common enough, but the experience of World War I shows that such nostalgia can become a force to be reckoned when war has left the country unstable. In Germany, the "rough and ready manners in use among wartime comrades," writes Mosse, ". . . came to symbolize true masculinity in comparison to the weaklings who misruled the nation":

> The warfare on the Western front created a new feeling of community among those who lived in the trenches. Here that community

of affinity for which so many had longed in an ever more restrictive society seemed to come alive. This was a community of men, a *Männerbund* that symbolized strength and devotion, within which men could test and prove their manliness. Here was a dynamic which continued into the postwar world when the need for community seemed greater than before. Thus immediately after the war, one leader of the German war veterans talked about the creation of an invisible church within which men could find each other through love and faith, with former front-line soldiers as priests and the German forest as the altar. Though exaggerated, this was not an isolated expression as the war experience was transmuted into an abiding nostalgia for comradeship. (Mosse 154)

Such war nostalgia was common among those communists in Russia who felt betrayed by the New Economic Policy; some men who joined the party during the civil war came to identify the policies of War Communism with an idealized postwar order.[70] But where NEP Russia rejected the values of War Communism, fascism embraced military structures and disciplines; in Mosse's view, fascism "based itself on the continuity of the war into peacetime and presented itself as a community of men" (154). This was a particularly attractive alternative in Germany, where, as Klaus Theweleit writes, the "Great War touched the masculinity of several . . . male generations in its most sensitive area: in the conviction that German men were born to be warriors and victors" (Theweleit 2: 357). Theweleit's two-volume study of the Freikorps, the bands of mercenaries who crushed labor revolts and participated in German military actions on the country's postwar borders, not only establishes a direct link between this right-wing movement and Nazism, but also shows the powerful role that sexual anxieties and homosocial bonds played in both this protofascist movement and subsequent Nazi ideology. The first volume is devoted to the fascist revulsion for women and femininity, while the second contains an impressive array of visual and textual evidence arguing for the primacy of the cult of masculinity and comradeship in fascist discourse. In her study of masculinity in fascist Italy, Barbara Spackman notes that it is a "commonplace" to say that "an obsession with virility is one of the distinctive traits of fascist discourse" (3). Are the same forces at work behind this fascist "obsession" and the cult of male comradeship in postrevolutionary Russia?

On the surface, the similarities are difficult to deny. The ubiquitous rugged male worker in the Soviet iconography of the 1920s and 1930s does appear to be the counterpart of the firm and muscular bodies of Nazi propaganda. The virtues of the comradely bond are extolled by communists and fascists alike, while the public sphere takes priority over the family in both early Soviet ideology and the rhetoric of fascism.[71] Yet such similarities threaten to overshadow the substantial differences between the communist and fascist obsessions with masculinity and comradeship. Nazism and Italian fascism owed few debts to feminism; though female labor would prove useful to the war effort, neither regime felt the need even to pay lip service to the notion of female equality. The Soviet government, for all its inconsistencies in its attempts to resolve the "woman question," was publicly committed to the transformation of women into workers. As we have already noted, Bolshevism was heir to a long tradition of radicalism that presupposed equality between the sexes; even if the reality of Soviet life would fall far short of utopian expectations, blatantly antifemale rhetoric was incompatible with the policy and official ideals of the regime. The cult of masculinity that lies just beneath the surface of fascism is obscured and diluted by the early Soviet commitment to women's liberation. One might regard the explicit fascist obsession with masculinity as a kind of mirror to the Soviet unconscious: what Soviet discourse represses, fascism flaunts.

Here one must recall that communism and fascism did not develop in complete isolation from one another. As Theweleit convincingly argues, Bolshevism played the role of the menacing "Other" in the right-wing discourse of both Weimar and Nazi Germany (1: 68–69, 229–35). In the Soviet Union, it was only in the 1930s that fascism would occupy pride of place among the enemies of the revolution. By this time, Soviet culture could project its own anxieties about gender and sexuality onto a fascist other, and those who failed to understand the shift in the cultural code would have to pay the price. Thus in 1936, the attempt by Yuri Olesha and Abram Room to create a film about fictional Komsomol athletes would severely damage both men's careers. The film, *A Strict Youth* (*Strogii iunosha*), lavished what would be considered an inordinate amount of cinematic attention to the striking physiques of its two central male heroes. As Jerry Heil points out, the depiction of seminude practitioners of physical culture was a commonplace of visual propaganda in the 1930s, but by 1936, "it was realized that the athletic, usually blond(e) 'Aryan' type had become an essential image of the *Hitlerjungend* in fascist Germany . . . The parallel was more than embarrassing to the Soviet propaganda state . . . , and the imagery of Soviet youth marching into the glorious future began to be changed" (69). Ironically, the film was banned not because it was "anti-Soviet" but because it was, if anything, too faithful a representation of the very elements of Soviet iconography that were no longer acceptable.

THEORY AND PRACTICE

How, then, does one situate Soviet masculine utopianism in history? Fratriarchy, male bonding, the "exchange" of women, "hom(m)osexuality" and male comradeship are all different points on what Eve Kosofsky Sedgwick calls the continuum of "homosociality"—the "structure of men's relations with other men" (Sedgwick 2). Yet for Freud, Lévi-Strauss, Remy, Tiger, and Sedgwick, these institutions of masculine relationships are either ahistorical or transhistorical. The first four all appeal to a vague and distant prehistory: Freud bases his analysis on a myth of group parricide and repentance, Lévi-Strauss briefly postulates a society without the clan structures he describes, Remy's terminology is filled with references to Native American culture, and Tiger sees the roots of male bonding in hunter-gatherer societies. Gray's writings come out of the historical moment of World War II, yet imply that both war and comradeship are universal. Sedgwick examines homosociality as part and parcel of western culture, which keeps its men constantly on the verge of "homosexual panic": the fear that seemingly innocent homosocial relations will prove to have a latent homosexual component (89).[72]

All of these formulations are relevant to the present study, and each will enhance our understanding of the material at various points. Said, Remy, and Sedgwick provide a useful vocabulary for discussing the ties among men—filiation, fratriarchy, and homosociality, respectively—while Gray's distinction between comradeship and friendship is crucial for our understanding of the texts at hand. Freud, Lévi-Strauss, Sedgwick, and Girard offer useful models for approaching the role played by women in male relationships, and despite the fact that each of these theorists might pretend to universal applicability, I invoke their ideas to help explain discrete examples from texts rather than accepting their theories in their entirety. My approach is consciously eclectic in that I find something of value in all of these critics' work without being convinced that any of them can provide a complete and satisfactory explanation of male social structures in postrevolutionary Russian literature, if for no other reason than that the phenomenon cannot be examined outside of its historical context. Certainly, male relationships were an integral part of Russian literature before the revolution, as has been demonstrated by Joe Andrew in his study of female characters in the formative years of Russia's literary tradition.[73] Yet the decline of the family in the years following the revolution changed the character of masculine interactions, elevating them to a central role in postrevolutionary society.

Though the official antifamily (and implicitly masculine) ideology of the first decade of Soviet power was all pervasive, male relationships could not solidify into a monolithic institution in such a period of flux. The "new world" was a chimera; Soviet citizens of the 1920s were expected to devote their energy to building the new society, but the arrival of communism could not be expected in the near future. The collapse of old social structures was nonetheless a fact, making the discussions of the proper form of communist society all the more urgent. Most of these blueprints, like Isaev's communalist vision, never made the leap from paper to practice.

Thus, to a large extent, the masculinization of society, the replacement of filial bonds with affiliative male ties, was a process enacted in the realm of the imaginary. Whether or not society was itself transformed, the agenda for social discourse had been profoundly altered. It is natural that such a change would be felt most acutely in the literature of the period, for the grand social experiments to be realized in the future can be shown in fiction as a fait accompli. Literature allowed individual writers to confront the future in the present, forcing them to define their attitude toward a society that was only in the process of formation. Certainly, the history of utopian literature bears out the appeal of fiction as the forum for the elaboration of both the conscious aspirations expressed by a given ideological system and the unconscious anxieties that these ideologies attempt to repress.

If, as I argue above, masculinity is integral to postrevolutionary attempts to imagine the new Soviet man and the world in which he was to live, then it is only reasonable to expect the literature of the period to display a particular concern for the portrayal and examination of masculinity and the male character, especially in those texts that address ideological questions directly. Yet the rhetoric of "manliness" remains only partially recognized in traditional criticism of Soviet literature: certainly, the "positive hero" of the nascent socialist realist novel displays most of the traditional male virtues. He is resolute, brave, and strong, often in body and in will. Most likely he is from good working-class stock, a model physical specimen; but if, like the hero of Ostrovsky's *How the Steel Was Tempered*, he is beset by disease or injury, he endures his hardship "like a man," dedicating himself to the cause with every iota of his dwindling strength. Without a doubt, this hero is the polar opposite of the wavering superfluous man, the intellectual besieged by self-doubt. When we read Soviet socialist realism and its precursors, we understand implicitly that such texts provide not only a blueprint for humanity, but a specific model of masculinity. In the first fifteen years of Soviet power, this model was only in the process of formation, and the more prominent sources upon which official Soviet literature would draw yield a predictable set of masculine tropes and clichés that would find their way into the socialist realist canon after 1934.

Yet the point I hope to make about masculinity in the literature of the twenties is both larger and smaller than merely analyzing the roots of "official" masculinity in the works of dedicated communist ideologues: larger in that I wish to demonstrate the pervasiveness of the topos of masculinity throughout early Soviet literature, to show that the concern with masculinity transcended the boundaries of party affiliation; smaller in that, despite masculinity's importance, I have no intention of surveying all of the fiction and poetry of the 1920s in order to prove that every major literary figure foregrounded the changing role of men. Rather, my goal is to show the prominence of the "man question" by isolating a specific strain in Soviet literature, by examining those texts that address revolutionary masculinity in a particularly productive fashion. One cannot make grand generalizations about all of the literature of the time, because the conception of the new world, as well as the reaction to it, varied from author to author. Still, a number of writers, most notably Olesha, Babel, and Platonov, but also Mayakovsky, Gorky, and the proletarian poets, created individual visions of the new society in particularly masculine terms.[74] Gorky, Mayakovsky, and Platonov present an insider's view on the rise of the male collective, while Olesha and Babel describe the dilemma of individual men who struggle for acceptance into the masculine groups that both fascinate and intimidate them. For all of these authors, the death of the traditional family is a given and thus serves as the backdrop for the presentation of the new affiliative social structures. It is my contention that Olesha, Babel, and Platonov, more than any of their contemporaries, simultaneously create and interrogate revolutionary notions of masculinity. These authors were selected not because they shared a common political cause or point of view. On the contrary, the fact that their relations to the party are so varied only serves to advance my argument: the implicit emphasis on masculinity was so ubiquitous in the discourse of 1920s Russia that it was at least unconsciously recognized by writers who might well have found themselves on opposite sides of the hottest literary and political issues of their day.

Though Olesha, Babel, and Platonov all, at various times, show male groups that succeed in creating some form of community, the main focus is on their failure. Babel's Cossacks are an example of a successful male community, yet the cycle focuses more on Lyutov's futile attempts to gain their long-term acceptance. Lyutov does, in the end, find a form of brotherhood, but only with a dying man and a distant correspondent. Olesha's Kavalerov fails to become part of the Babichev-Makarov all-male "family"; he realizes the hopelessness of his situation when the German soccer player with whom he identifies is outclassed by Volodya during a soccer match. At a (male) athletic event, Kavalerov shows that he cannot even play the game, let alone win. Platonov does not dwell on the plight of the alienated individual, focusing instead on the men who try to build a community. *Chevengur*, however, chronicles the downfall of a commune that, by shunning women and labor, shows itself to be doomed from the very beginning. By the end of the novel, nearly every major character to whom the reader has been introduced lies dead, and the city is deserted. Written by a man who had been an outspoken proponent of male comradeship over the family, *Chevengur* is the swan song of the very idealism that made such visions possible.

To an extent, the persistence with which the authors describe failed comradeship is a reflection of their own frustrated attempts to find their place in communist society, both as writers and as individuals. Throughout the course of this book, I will invoke relevant information about the authors' biographies on those particular occasions when the parallels or contrasts between life and literature are too obvious to ignore: Babel's transformation of his own experiences in the Red Cavalry into notes purportedly authored by a man whose name happens to be Babel's own former pseudonym (Kirill Lyutov); the persistence of triangular relationships in Olesha's life as well as in his work; and, finally, Platonov's abandonment of extreme revolutionary romanticism and disenchantment with Soviet communism. On the whole, however, the texts examined in the present study are treated both as literary documents and as important responses to (and participators in) the contemporary utopian discourse on masculinity and the family. In the case of each of the three primary works discussed here, male comradeship is both admired and critiqued. Kavalerov and his motley allies lose at the end of *Envy*, and yet Olesha's "losers" are more lively and sympathetic than his "winners." And if the soccer game that serves as the novel's climax is, as many critics suggest, a metaphor for the central ideological struggle, then the outcome is not as clear as it would seem. Though everything in the match points to the triumph of Volodya's team, Kavalerov leaves the stadium before the reader can learn who won. Lyutov, in *Red Cavalry*, openly admires the Cossacks for their unfettered passion and physical grace, yet his failure to gain acceptance by them can be blamed at least in part on a fundamental unwillingness to obey the Cossack code. Platonov is even freer with his implied criticism of the male collective, showing the Chevengurians to be unrestrained theorists who, left to their own devices, slowly bring all activity in the town to a halt.

If male comradeship is inadequate, at least two of these three works suggest that the family they propose to replace cannot be so easily discounted. Olesha's short novel ends with a series of unwilling affirmations of biological ties, while *Chevengur*'s Dvanov leaves the ruined commune to go to his long-dead father. In these works, the return of the family and the critique of male affiliation can be seen as a recognition that nature cannot be completely replaced with culture. Like the Soviet experiment itself, the phenomenon of "men without women" is hard pressed to sustain itself when the theory is tested in (novelistic) reality.

Chapter One

THE LADYKILLERS

Bolshevik Chivalry, Female Sacrifice,
and the End of the Marriage Plot

Then the Cossacks entered the room. They laughed, and grabbed Sashka by the arm and threw her onto a mountain of materials and books. Sashka's body, blooming and stinking, like the meat of a freshly slaughtered cow, exposed itself, her raised skirts uncovered the legs of the squadron's lady, wrought-iron, firm legs, and Kurdyukov, a moronic lad, mounted Sashka and shook as though in the saddle, pretending to be carried away by passion. She threw him off and ran to the door. And only then, passing by the altar, did we proceed into the church. — Isaac Babel, "At Saint Valentine's" (1920/1924)

Among the tramps there was one girl, her eyes currant-colored and timid, as if someone had waved his arm over them, her hair flowed like a downpour onto her shoulders. She was silent throughout the trip, was silent when the tramps fought and she didn't look at Ivan; she silently followed them. "You've seen the tsaritsa," said the guide to Ivan. 'We brought her from the Caspian itself and watch over her like a bride. She's our only property." — Andrei Platonov, "A Story about Many Interesting Things" (1923)

Despite a common interest in wide-reaching social change, communism and feminism proved to be strange bedfellows; it was hardly a match made in heaven, and by the time Stalin's new family code was introduced in 1936, communism would abandon feminism, citing irreconcilable differences. Nor were the literary manifestations of this alliance free from conflict; though the equal status of women was an official component of the new postrevolutionary order, literary texts of the period are often indicative more of the anxiety over female equality rather than equality itself. While Dasha's development as a *bol'shevichka* (Bolshevik woman) in *Cement* may be compelling, her primary function is to highlight the lack of political consciousness of her otherwise heroic husband Gleb. Olga Zotova, the heroine of Aleksei Tolstoi's "Viper" ("Gadiuka" 1928) becomes a Red soldier, slaughters her White enemies, and more than earns her reptilian nickname. While she still travels with her fellow soldiers, Zotova tries her best to fit in unobtrusively, dressing and behaving like a man, but her presence among the men defies the conventions of both gender and genre: a woman in fiction usually signals the romance and marriage plots, while a woman in a bivouac is most likely a nurse or a camp follower. Inevitably, the plots of love and war become one, and the Viper finds herself pursuing the affections of her commander Emelyanov, who restrains himself admirably: "I'd make you my wife, Olya, but I can't now, you understand" (A. N. Tolstoi 4: 207). Zotova fights alongside the men for over a year, a virgin all the while.

Contrary to claims by many post-Soviet postfeminists in Russia, the *bol'shevichka* (or at least her fictional sister) was never so thoroughly "masculinized" by communism's "unnatural" assertions of total sexual equality that she could simply lose herself in the crowd and become "one of the boys." Zotova's feminine beauty, barely hidden by her soldier's garb, initially puts her comrades out of sorts: "the young cavalrymen fidgeted and the older ones were moody when Zotova . . . walked through the smoke-filled barracks" (A. N. Tolstoi 4: 93). Nor can Zotova overcome her modesty: she rejects all suggestions that she bathe with her fellow soldiers. Even the ideologues of Platonov's *Chevengur*, who so desperately want to see women revolutionaries as simply comrades, clearly consider such an attitude an act of iron will. Emelyanov in "The Viper" appears to have the necessary fortitude; rather than follow up on his obvious attraction to Zotova, it is his idea to cut her hair and dress her like a man. And yet his efforts to make "no distinction between her and the men" (*nichem ne vydelial sredi boitsov*) entail a constant struggle; sometimes Zotova is convinced he is gazing at her with an "unbrotherly feeling" (*nebratskim chuvstvom*), and after he sees her bathing at the well, he begins to keep his distance (A. N. Tolstoi 4: 199, 197).

Attempts to achieve equality between the sexes through a kind of "gender leveling" easily became grist for the Soviet satiric mill: when Professor Filipp Filippovich Preobrazhensky of Mikhail Bulgakov's *Heart of a Dog* (*Sobach'e serdtse*, 1925) is faced with a delegation from the local housing committee, his attention is immediately drawn to one of the "comrades," who, though dressed exactly like his fellow proletarians, is shorter than the rest and looks younger:

> "First of all, we are not gentlemen [*gospoda*]," . . . said the youngest of the four, who looked like a peach.
>
> "First of all," interrupted Filipp Filippovich, "are you a man or a woman?"
>
> The four again fell silent and opened their mouths. This time the first of them recovered himself . . .
>
> "What's the difference, comrade?" he asked haughtily.
>
> "I'm a woman," admitted the peachy boy in the leather jacket, and he blushed a deep red. Then one of them—the blond one in the fur hat—for some reason blushed thickly.
>
> "In that case you can keep your cap on, while I must ask you, sir, to remove your hat," said Filipp Filippovich imposingly. (Bulgakov 2: 135)

From this point on, the fourth comrade is referred to as "the boy who turned out to be a woman," "one woman dressed as a man," and the "boy-woman" (*iunosha-zhenshchina*) (2: 137, 206). When she refers to herself as the "director" (*zaveduiushchii*), he interrupts her: "Di-rec-tress" (*Za-ve-duiushchaiia*) (2: 139).

The rather disparate examples of Bulgakov and Aleksei Tolstoi show two important features of male-female relations in the fiction of the 1920s: first, attempts to deny gender differences inevitably fail; second, the female characters are outnumbered.[1] The fictional male collective in the earlier Soviet period was most often confronted by a single woman rather than by a group; thus, the woman's obvious difference from her male counterparts would be exacerbated by her minority or token status. Oddly enough, her position prefigures the perennial lament of the (usually female) Soviet salesclerk to the impatient mobs of frustrated shoppers: "There are lots of you and only one of me" (*Vas mnogo, ia odna*).

THE LADY VANISHES

If comradeship in Soviet fiction is characteristic of the male experience, where does this leave women? The problem immediately suggests an algebraic simile that is perhaps appropriate to the pretensions of "scientific" communism; it is as though the men have finally solved a particularly difficult mathematical problem, only to discover that they have left something out of the equation: the inevitable remainder is women. This masculine group would prefer to be completely sufficient unto itself, with no need of feminine support or interaction. However, the unavoidable encounter between the male collective and female outsiders (or would-be female members) leaves the group bereft of a viable model for incorporating the feminine. The traditional solution to this problem is exogamous marriage, which resolves the competing demands of the biological family (ties of blood) and social, extrabiological bonds by "wedding" the two into a unit that will, in turn, extend the family line into another generation.[2] Though marriage might seem to be a personal contract between one man and one woman, we recall Lévi-Strauss's theory that marriage has always served to facilitate the cohesion of the male group: it is through the exchange of women that potentially hostile entities establish peaceful ties. In fiction, marriage also served a distinct narrative function, acting as the signal that the novel's plot can now be considered finished; the author who employs the marriage plot resembles nothing more than an impatient matchmaker who cannot rest until all parties are safely married. Yet early Soviet literature underwent a generic conflict that mirrored the larger ideological struggle: work after work flirts with the marriage plot, only to reject it outright. Volodya Makarov's wedding plans in Olesha's *Envy* are anything but romantic; yes, he writes his benefactor, he and Valya will get married—three or four years from now (see chapter 4). In Ilya Ehrenburg's *Life and Downfall of Nikolai Kurbov* (1922), the romance between a *chekist* (secret policeman) and a counterrevolutionary idealist is doomed from the start, and not only because the lovers are on opposite sides of the political barrier. For the *chekist* Kurbov, marriage itself is an unthinkable compromise with his revolutionary ideals: "To get married and peacefully coexist?" Their love is consummated not in a wedding, but in Kurbov's suicide: "And with that he brought together two lovers, the gun barrel and his temple" (Erenburg 383–84).

If the marriage plot failed individual characters, it was so utterly alien to the collectivist works of hard-core proletarians as to be beyond all generic possibility. Though the socialist collective was often represented in the first few years of the Soviet state as one giant male worker, this communist "Frankenstein's monster" was never to demand of his creator a collective female bride. By the same token, though the collective was also portrayed as an aggregation of men rather than their symbolic conglomeration, group wedding ceremonies with corresponding female collectives would have to wait for the advent of Reverend Sun Myung Moon. After an examination of the bond that unites Soviet men into a single desiring subject, we shall explore the model adopted and distorted for its "courtship" of the female outsider and discover that no matter how diverse the relationships analyzed might be, the structure of the encounter is the same. The male collective must find a way to make the woman serve to cement, rather than rupture, the male bond: either the woman is exalted as a quasi-holy object of collective male desire, or she is an obstacle whose elimination serves to bind the collective together ever more tightly.

THE LADY IS A TRAMP

With the balance of power slanted in favor of the men, the woman's status will be largely contingent on the respect accorded her by the male collective; she can be either placed on a pedestal or derided for her unmanliness, but it is highly unlikely that she will simply be accepted as one among equals: difference will out.[3] When the men see her womanhood as a mark of distinction, the result might be called "Bolshevik chivalry"; the coarse, brutish men are uplifted by the presence of a divine feminine creature for whom they are willing to lay down their lives. Such is the case in Platonov's 1923 "A Story about Many Interesting Things" ("Rasskaz o mnogikh interesnykh veshchakh"), whose hero, Ivan Kopchikov, encounters a band of twenty Bolshevik beggars and one woman, whom they call the Caspian Bride (*Kaspiiskaia nevesta*). Far from being a source of rivalry or competition, the Caspian Bride unites the men together more firmly, a fact that Ivan quickly comes to understand: "Through her we listen to the world," Ivan said to himself. "Through her it's possible to become brothers [*pobratat'sia*] with everything, to be one with the sun and the stars, and there won't be any need for work, or spite, or struggle. Everywhere will be brotherhood, visible and invisible . . . There will be a brotherhood of stars, of beasts, of grasses and man" (Platonov, *Starik* 65).[4] A similar dynamic is at work in *Chevengur*, in which the quixotic Kopyonkin wants to unite the men of his regiment around the icon (or perhaps pin-up) of Rosa Luxemburg, a revolutionary idol who combines all the qualities that Platonov's men find desirable in a woman: she is ethereal, distant, and dead. While this is not quite what the Vera Pavlovnas of prerevolutionary radical fiction dreamed of, it is far more benign than the alternative: humiliation, gang rape, or ritual murder.

The two different reactions (Bolshevik chivalry vs. female sacrifice) seem reminiscent of that classic paradigm, the division of women into madonnas and whores. This is perhaps to be expected: if, as Gray suggests, the male comrades submerge their egos (and perhaps libidos) into that of the collective, there is no reason to assume that this attitude toward women should be substantially different from that of the individual men who form the group. In this case, it is phylogeny that recapitulates ontogeny. It would then also follow, however, that the male collective is no less prone to disenchantment than the individual idealist when the beloved fails to live up to impossible expectations. Thus it all too often happens that the Bolshevik madonna suddenly falls to the level of her despised earthly double; and if she does not share Rosa Luxemburg's fortune in being dead before the story begins, she may well be on her way to joining her.

While the opposition of madonna to whore is hardly exclusive to the Russian context, the juxtaposition (and even conflation) of the two was a commonplace of Russian literature before the Soviet period. The Russian literary tradition is quite tolerant of the fallen woman, but only of the woman who has *already* fallen, who is introduced to us not simply as a woman, but as a dilemma. When the male protagonist(s) encounter her, the narrative usually plays itself out within the paradigm of redemption and salvation.[5] That is, the male hero attempts to perform a kind of moral alchemy, transforming the base metal of the prostitute into the precious gold of the madonna. Mary Magdalene, the redeemed New Testament prostitute who shares the name of the Mother of God, held a fascination for both Dostoevsky and Tolstoi.[6] While the Mary Magdalene subtext is prominent in *The Idiot*, it leads to the virtual conflation of the madonna and whore in *Crime and Punishment*'s Sonya. Tolstoi's Katyusha Maslova also follows the Mary Magdalene pattern in *Resurrection*, but here her salvation is merely instrumental to the transformation of her long-ago seducer, Nekhlyudov. The impulse to "save" such women can be attributed to a variety of motives, from a combination of vanity and a misguided sense of social duty (Likhonin in Kuprin's *The Pit*) to a selfish need to dominate (*Notes from Underground*). Indeed, one might argue that the attempts at redemption work precisely in that they sublimate the initial sexual arousal provoked by the prostitute into a moral one: it is her plight, and not her body, that is considered provocative. Tolstoi's Maslova understands this better than anyone and early on resolves that "she would not give herself to him, would not allow her to use him spiritually as he had used her bodily" (L. N. Tolstoi 10: 259). For the attempt at salvation to be made, the male protagonist must first transform the prostitute in his own mind from a sex object to a moral object (or, in the eyes of Kuprin's doctor, lawyer, and journalist who visit a brothel under the pretext of "professional" interest, a "scientific" one). Structurally, however, the roles played by these women are identical: as sounding boards for fantasy and desire, they destroy the male subjects either sexually (by giving them syphilis) or morally (by causing financial ruin and nervous breakdowns).

The link between the prerevolutionary literary prostitute and the postrevolutionary male collective is not, however, limited to the hero's capacity to be disappointed in women. The connection is also structural, in that the encounter with the prostitute serves as one of the primary models for interaction between one woman and a group of men. It is customary to treat the theme of the prostitute in terms of her relationship with one particular man,[7] yet the actual meeting between the prostitute and the individual male protagonist usually takes place in anything but an intimate context. Here, in fact, we have the closest thing to the "collective group marriage" briefly entertained by Platonov's Chevengurians; time after time, the prostitute's client arrives at the brothel in the company of at least two of his male friends.[8] Even the misanthropic underground man first encounters the prostitute Liza only because his wounded pride prompts him to follow his old schoolmates on their expedition to a Petersburg brothel. The underground man has no money and had no apparent desire for female companionship on that night. Rather, he goes to the brothel for the same reason he invites himself to Zverkov's farewell dinner: to prove that he belongs in their company. "Either they'll fall to their knees, hugging my legs, begging for my friendship, or . . . or I'll give Zverkov a slap in the face!" (Dostoevskii 4: 512). Only after he discovers that he has arrived too late, that his schoolmates have already paired off with prostitutes and gone their separate ways, does the underground man notice Liza; sex with her becomes a consolation prize for his inability to become part of the male group.

Unlike the underground man, the hero of Chekhov's "A Nervous Breakdown" ("Pripadok") has no intention of visiting such a place but is dragged to one brothel after another by his friends, who insist that he accompany them. But the fullest realization of the collective expedition to the brothel belongs to Kuprin's *The Pit* (*Iama*, 1908–1915), whose encyclopedic catalog of nearly every literary "fallen woman" cliché has led some critics to call it the final word on the prostitute in Russian literature.[9] Likhonin, one prostitute's would-be savior, and Kolya, another prostitute's near-victim, arrive at Anna Markovna's two-ruble house as part of larger groups (as in "A Nervous Breakdown," the group visit is represented by the men involved as virtually obligatory). When the classicist Yarchenko objects to his comrades' plans, Ramzes, a lawyer, poses the question in terms of "professional" interest. Yarchenko eventually relents, but not because Ramzes' "sophistry" has convinced him: "No, it's just that I'd hate to break up our group" (*Net, prosto mne zhalko razbivat' kompaniiu*) (Kuprin 53).[10] Later, when Boris Sobashnikov leaves the brothel after an argument with Platonov, his fellow student Petrovsky cannot allow Sobashnikov's departure to be merely an individual matter:

> "The rest of you do as you like, gentlemen, that's a matter of your own personal views, but I am leaving with Boris on principle. Maybe he isn't right, and so on; we can pass a vote of censure on

him within our intimate group, but if one of our comrades has been insulted, I cannot remain here. I'm leaving."

"Good lord!" And here Likhonin scratched his temple with nervous annoyance. ". . . Just think, such corporate pride! Collective walk-outs from editorial boards, from political meetings, from brothels. We're not officers who have to cover up the stupidity of every one of our comrades." (77)

In focusing on the evident absurdity in Petrovsky's chivalric behavior, Likhonin nonetheless overstates his case. Their entire visit to Anna Markovna's brothel has, in fact, had a distinctly collective character. Indeed, while Likhonin's own desire to save the prostitute Lyubka is initially individual, the enterprise soon becomes a group endeavor, a veritable orgy of liberal interventionism: all of Likhonin's friends join in the effort to educate poor Lyubka. Though these efforts are ultimately in vain, the final "reformation" of the novel's prostitutes is also a collective enterprise: 100 angry soldiers stage an impromptu raid on the red-light district, destroying the brothels and ultimately prompting a governor's decree closing all houses of prostitution in the city. Ironically, the marauding soldiers succeed where the earnest liberals fail, and on a much larger scale: the fallen women are removed from the brothel once and for all.[11]

The soldiers' raid on the brothel is probably not the strongest impression that most contemporary readers would have taken away from *The Pit*. Thanks to the vagaries of parts publication and Kuprin's own work habits, most of the scandal that surrounded the novel was sparked before the author even got around to completing the book. This ending is only tenuously connected with what passes for the plot of this meandering novel; one has the sense that Kuprin, angered by the prior appearance of a novella that purported to be the end of *The Pit*, resorted to an extreme, dramatic measure in order to be done with both the book and the prostitutes who populated it. Yet the motif of group male violence against "unworthy" women would reappear in the most unlikely of places: the poetry of Aleksandr Blok.

SQUARING THE LOVE TRIANGLE

Blok's approach to the Symbolist topos of the Eternal Feminine, while explicitly chivalric, relies heavily on the tension between madonna and whore. As early as his 1901 collection of verses about the "beautiful lady" (*Stikhi o prekrasnoi dame*), Blok expresses the fear that his feminine ideal could reveal herself to be something altogether different: "I'm afraid: you will change your guise" (*No strashno mne: izmenish' oblik ty*); "What you will become—I do not know" (*No vo chto obratish'sia—ne vedaiu*). As Samuel Cioran notes in his study of Symbolist Sophiology, neither Blok nor Bely was "totally unaware of the possibility of the deceptive mask of Antichrist or 'anti-Sophia' which could be lurking behind the vision of heavenly beauty" (Cioran 110). When Blok's "beautiful lady" appears in her demonic hypostasis, her fall is both metaphysical and all too familiar; the prostitutes of "The Stranger" and "Humiliation" combine the cosmic imagery of Blok's hymns to the beautiful lady with the high heels and earthy manner of the prostitute. In his prerevolutionary verse, Blok's poetic persona is powerless before this frightening, yet attractive, creature; the heroes of Blok's postrevolutionary "The Twelve" ("Dvenadtsat'," 1918) would not be so passive.

"The Twelve," which represented a drastic poetic departure for Blok, was also a transitional work for the Russian literary tradition. Here, the old, familiar plot of the love triangle is juxtaposed with a newer, more distinctly Soviet genre: the adventures of the revolutionary male collective. Each plot makes its competing demands on the poems and on the characters: the triangular rivalry and jealousy of Petrukha-Katka-Vanka acts as a centrifugal force, destroying solidarity by driving the two former comrades apart. The story of the collective is decidedly centripetal: for the collective to function, it must cohere. In terms of narrative, the resolution of the love triangle is, for the twelve, a digression, an obstruction in their path. When they are introduced in the second verse, they are shown in motion: "The wind is playing, the snow is dancing / The twelve are marching" (*Guliaet veter, porkhaet sneg / Idut dvenadtsat' chelovek*) (349). The love triangle occupies the next several stanzas (with the exception of verse 3, whose action takes place in the past and future, but not the present), and when it is finally resolved by Katka's death, the progress of the twelve can continue: "And the twelve march once again") (*I opiat' idut dvenadtsat'*) (353).

Blok's juxtaposition of the triangle and the collective is crucial to our understanding of the relationship between the male collective and the female intruder in early Soviet literature. The result is a marked shift in the representation of triangular desire: whereas the classic Russian literary love triangle, as in Dostoevsky's *Eternal Husband,* conforms to a Girardian model of mediated desire (in which the woman serves as a justification for the more important relationship between the two male rivals), the replacement of one (or both) of the men with an entire group leads to a structure that is better understood with the help of Freud's concept of the "tendentious" or aggressive joke.[12] According to Freud, "a tendentious joke calls for three people: in addition to the one who makes the joke, there must be a second who is taken as the object of the hostile or sexual aggressiveness, and a third in whom the joke's aim of producing pleasure is fulfilled" (Freud, *Jokes* 118). Initially, the presence of the third person (the other man) might have been perceived by the first man as an obstacle to his "conquest" of the woman: now that he has an audience, it will be impossible for the first man to gain sexual fulfillment from the woman. Therefore, he must find a substitute for this basic satisfaction. Freud writes: "When the first person finds his libidinal impulse inhibited . . . , he develops a hostile trend against the second person [the woman] and calls on the originally interfering third person as his ally. Through the first person's smutty speech the woman is exposed before the third, who, as listener, has now been bribed by the effortless satisfaction of his own libido" (*Jokes* 119). For the purposes of the present study, it is of particular import that the joke triangle engenders humiliation in the woman while both facilitating and depending upon an alliance between the men. In her study of Freud's joke theory and postmodernism, Jerry Aline Flieger compares the comic triangle with Georges Bataille's definition of the erotic act: for Bataille, sex is a "witnessed sacrificial rite" that, like Freud's tendentious joke, involves three parties: "a 'priest' who officiates, a victim, and a spectator who experiences a vicarious sense of self-obliteration when witnessing the sacrificial drama between priest and victim." The similarity between Bataille and Freud is more than simply structural, for Freud himself calls the joke a substitute gratification of either a murderous or sexual impulse. Flieger surmises that the joke "might qualify as an instance of what Bataille calls 'ordered transgression',... a socially sanctioned erotic act (like sex in marriage or killing in war)" (Flieger 67–68). The juxtaposition with Bataille is helpful because it demonstrates how much Freud's comic triangle resembles the ritual sacrifice of the woman in question.

Triangular rivalry (at the women's expense) plays an important role in fictional male relationships after the revolution; Shklovsky's and Room's 1927 film *Bed and Sofa,* Platonov's *Chevengur,* and just about any work by Yuri Olesha show that the love triangle could not be dismissed as merely a bourgeois relic (see chapter 5). But after the revolution, the love triangle often becomes the ideologically impaired protagonist's substitute for the true comradeship of the male collective (this is especially true of Olesha). This does not mean that Freud's joke theory can be of no help to us here; on the contrary, I submit that this theory does much to elucidate the dynamic of female sacrifice at the hands of the male collective. The classic joking triangle enables the male bond to take the place of rivalry, whether potential or actual; in the case of the male collective, rivalry is not an issue, for the collective itself plays the role of both men in the paradigm. In Freud's model, the perpetrator of the joke receives immediate libidinal satisfaction, while the audience is both entertained by the humor and annoyed by being manipulated; in order to regain a sense of control and to receive further pleasure, the third man soon finds himself repeating or reenacting the joke, this time in the first position. For the male collective, the first position is sufficient in and of itself: the individual men that compose the group become the audience for each other. In any case, both Freud and Bataille create triangular models in which shame ensures that the third party is not absolutely essential; the butt of Freud's joke can feel shame even if no one sees or hears her, while both partners in Bataille's erotic sacrifice are always reminded of the "symbolic third party—the absent voyeur who assures that the sexual enjoyment is a guilty pleasure" (Flieger 67).

When the triangle is reduced to the male collective and the individual woman, all hostility is focused on the woman rather than on another man. Indeed, male solidarity is already a given, whereas in the joke triangle it is a result. Still, such encounters resemble both Bataille's sacrifice and Freud's joke in that the bond between men is strengthened when the story is completed.[13] Not only are the sacrificial elements emphasized by the presence of corpses or battered women at the story's end, but the joking dynamic is also just beneath the surface. The female enemy of the collective is usually portrayed as a deceiver, while the men achieve victory by uncovering her unworthiness and taking revenge: the joke is now on her.

In Blok's "The Twelve" we see the beginning of this new pattern, although here the conflict between the traditional triangular rivalry and the new collective hero has yet to be resolved; one could say, in fact, that this very conflict is the subject of the poem. Here Katka is not deliberately executed or humiliated by the group, for her death is accidental; Petrukha wanted to kill Vanka, the man who stole Katka from him. Yet it is precisely her death that ends the distracting love plot far more efficiently than would the defeat of any rival. Once Katka is dead, Petrukha has apparently lost all desire for revenge upon Vanka, who has disappeared from the text once and for all. More important is the fact that it is Katka, and not Vanka, who exerts a disruptive force on the collective. Vanka's defection from their ranks appears to have coincided with his successful wooing of Katka. Yet it is her effect on Petrukha that is most damaging. Even after Katka's death, Petrukha is still separate from his comrades: "Only the poor murderer / Looked stricken" (*Lish' u bednogo ubiitsy / Ne vidat' sovsem litsa*) (353). His admission of his love for Katka is met with his comrades' disdain: "So you want to bare your soul? / Enough! . . . / Get a hold of yourself!" (— *Verno, dushu naiznanku / Vzdumal vyvernut'? Izvol'!. . . / —Nad soboi derzhi kontrol'!*) (354). A true warrior has no time for love; indeed, excessive concern for a woman is in itself emasculating:[14] "What are you, Petka, a woman [*baba*]?" (*Chto ty, Pet'ka, baba chto l'*) (354).[15] Here we see the murder of a woman as a kind of rite of passage (as it is in Babel); as Irene Masing-Delic has asserted, by killing Katka, "Petrukha to some extent succeeds in killing the *baba* within himself. . . . the anarchic killer Petrukha becomes a disciplined member of a warrior collective of Red Guardsmen who presumably are undergoing, or already have undergone, similar psychological transformations" (207-9).[16] Almost immediately after being scolded by his comrades, Petrukha recovers from his sorrow: "He raises his head up again, / He's happy once more" (*On golovku vskidiváet. / On opiat' poveselel*) (354). The twelve soldiers are characterized by their unrelenting movement forward, and Petrukha's distance from his comrades had been shown by his inability to stay in step: "Faster and faster / Goes his step" (*Vse bystree i bystree / Utoraplivaet shag*) (353). Now Petrukha can resume the rhythms of the collective: "And Petrukha slows down / His hurried steps" (*I Petrukha zamedliaet / Toroplivye shagi*) (354).

A similar situation arises in Venyamin Kaverin's *The End of the Gang* (*Konets khazy*, 1924), although with an outcome that is less favorable for the male group. Though Kaverin's tale of the decline and fall of a Jewish criminal gang in Leningrad might seem too apolitical to have anything in common with Blok's poem of the revolution, the opposition of male solidarity to involvement with women is common to both. Where the plot of "The Twelve" ends in the affirmation of the male collective, however, Kaverin's story ends in the gang's defeat. Of course, the mores of 1924 Russia would demand that the gang be caught and punished, but their failure, like that of Platonov's Chevengurians, can be seen as the result of unresolved "female trouble." As in "The Twelve," a love triangle interferes with the proper functioning of the male group; in this case, it is the gang's kidnapping of the stenographer Ekaterina Ivanovna, whom one of their number had "stolen" from Sergei Vesalago while the latter was in prison. Sergei escapes from prison and kills his rival, but meanwhile, Baraban, the gang's leader, has taken a fancy to Ekaterina Ivanovna. It is Sergei's attempts to free Ekaterina Ivanovna, along with the leader's distracting infatuation, that lead to the gang's downfall. One of the gangsters puts it quite succinctly: "since Baraban kidnapped that girl, things have been going worse and worse" (Kaverin 286). Before the gang is destroyed, Ekaterina Ivanovna is murdered, having been mistaken for Sushka, the prostitute who supposedly "sold out" the gang. Once again we have the conflation of the madonna (the innocent stenographer) and the whore (Sushka), and yet this sacrifice is unsuccessful: the attempt to dispose of the woman occurs too late, and the death of Sergei's beloved leads him to tell his story to the militia.[17]

In a milder form, we see this dynamic in another of the revolutionary hero's predecessors, one who was perhaps the first expression of the collective hero in Russian fiction: the narrator of Gorky's 1899 short story "Twenty-six Men and a Girl" ("Dvadtsat' shest' i odna"). Indeed, Gorky's story is probably the purest example of the male collective in all of Russian literature: the first-person narrator never once utters the word "I." Though written well before the revolution, Gorky's story without a doubt has an anticapitalist theme: the men are "comrades," and the story of their work is the account of their exploitation by their cruel, unseen boss. The men make pretzels in a bakery under terrible conditions. The only joy in their miserable existence is the regular appearance of Tanya, who works upstairs. They feed Tanya pretzels, she smiles and chats with them, and that is the extent of their interactions. But when a handsome soldier comes to work in their building, one of the men grows tired of the newcomer's constant bragging about his successes with women and challenges him to seduce Tanya. Up to this point the men practically worship her. She is their "holy of holies" (*sviatynia*), and the twenty-six men treat her as if she had descended to them from the heavens rather than merely down the staircase that is the only view from their window (Gor'kii 4: 285). But if their underground confinement in the hot and dark bakery resembles an urban inferno, Tanya proves to be an unsatisfactory Beatrice. After the soldier seduces Tanya, the men surround her in the alleyway and shout abuse at her, stopping short of actually beating her. She leaves, cursing them, and they never see each other again.

"Twenty-six Men and a Girl" is a transitional work that reflects the neoromanticism of the Silver Age (through the idealization of Tanya) and the social concerns of prerevolutionary *engagé* fiction (the oppressed proletarian cannot hope for his love to be requited), while rendering literal the class consciousness and male group identity that would be so characteristic of the literature after 1917. A number of important features of the postrevolutionary male collective are already present in Gorky's story: not only is the woman who was once exalted now reviled, but her fate is, at several times in the story, completely in the hands of the male group. Certainly, she has disappointed them, and yet she would not have been in a position to do so had not the men challenged the handsome soldier to "conquer" her. After she fails this test, they confront her with the disapproval that would, after the revolution, prove fatal to its object.

GENTLEMEN'S AGREEMENT

In the canon of the postrevolutionary male collective, a special place must be reserved for Isaak Babel's *Red Cavalry*. The narrator of most of the stories that compose the cycle, Kirill Lyutov, is never at home in any of the close-knit groups that he encounters, and thus his perspective is always that of the outsider. Indeed, "My First Goose" can be seen as a prime example of Freud's joke triangle and Bataille's erotic sacrifice, with Lyutov and the Cossacks in roles one and three.[18] At other times, Lyutov watches impassively as his fellow soldiers engage in a sexualized violence that is beyond him; in "At Saint Valentine's" ("U sviatogo Valenta"), the Cossacks grab the nurse Sashka and pretend to rape her (see epigraph). As in "My First Goose," actual sex (and actual violence) has been replaced by a ritual reenactment, only this time, Lyutov, whose detached narration of the episode mostly likely connotes the same combination of fascination and revulsion with which he usually views the Cossacks' violence, does not join in. The scene of the "crime" is particularly important: Sashka is in a small room attached to the church's altar. The altar, the scene of both religious sacrifice and holy matrimony, underscores the function of this act: it "weds" the participants through Sashka, who is offered up as a sacrifice to the group.[19]

But Babel's *Red Cavalry* is more than just the tale of an outsider trying desperately to break in. On several occasions, Lyutov steps aside as primary narrator, reproducing the words of one of his less-educated comrades. Among these secondary narrators is Nikita Balmashev, whose consciousness is firmly grounded in the collective; his ungrammatical speech and uncompromising stance could not be more distant from the stylistic clarity and ideological vacillation of Lyutov (and, indirectly, Babel). Though Balmashev moves freely between the first-person singular and the first-person plural, the portrayal of group identity in "Salt" resembles nothing so much as the collective narrator of Gorky's "Twenty-six Men and a Girl."[20] The comrades of "Salt" are the unwashed heroes of "Twenty-six" after they have been through World War I, the revolution, and, in conjunction with their participation in the civil war, an only partly comprehended indoctrination into Marxist-Leninist philosophy. In each story, the members of the male collective rush to express their concern for the woman. In "Twenty-six Men and a Girl," each man takes turns giving her pretzels, while all of them continually advise her regarding her health and dress. In "Salt," every one of the men helps seat the woman, telling her to be good to her child and raise it well. The workers of Gorky's story speak coarsely about women who "don't deserve" to be talked about in any other way but never dare say anything crude about Tanya, whom they consider too pure for that sort of talk (Gor'kii 7: 283). Because they believe her to be a mother, Babel's soldiers are moved to spare the woman the fate of the two girls they rape during the night. In each story, the woman's fate is decided by the male collective; it is the workers who inspire the soldier to seduce Tanya, using the woman they worship as part of their rivalry with the dashing newcomer they envy. "Salt" is built on two collective decisions: first to let the woman on the train, then to kill her. Each story ends with the woman's betrayal and the men's reprisal.

The second sentence of "Salt" states the message of Balmashev and his comrades in no uncertain terms: "I want to write to you about women without political consciousness, who are dangerous to us" (*Ia khochu opisat' vam za nesoznatel'nykh zhenshchin, kotorye nam vrednye*) (2: 72). And, indeed, the story Balmashev tells is one of a continual power struggle between the men of his platoon and the women they encounter. When the women at the train station beg to be let on board, the soldiers, "having pity," let some on and turn others away. The selection process, however, has little to do with charity, since the two young girls pay dearly during the night for their ride. Even when the "model woman" (*predstavitel'naia zhenshchina*), supposedly a mother traveling with her child on the way to see her long-lost husband, asks to accompany them, the platoon responds that "after us she won't want her husband" (*oposle nas ona i muzha ne zakhochet*).

It falls to Balmashev to remind the Cossacks of the reverence that one should accord a mother. His reproach of the men for forgetting that they were once babes in their mothers' arms all but states the oedipal taboo baldly: "Remember your life, platoon, and how you yourselves were once your mother's children, and then it turns out that it's not right to talk like that" (2: 73). Though all the men take turns speaking to her and helping her on board, their words to the woman appear on paper as if the men spoke together in one voice: "Sit down, woman, . . . , caress your child, like mothers should, no one . . . will touch you, and you'll arrive at your husband's, untouched, as you wish, and we're counting on your conscience that you will raise a new generation to replace us, because the old gets older, and there's not much youth around" (2: 74). The Cossacks understand that the mother is doing her civic duty in raising the "new generation," and thus, in Balmashev's words, "elevate her as a laboring mother in the republic" (2: 74). They respect her for her reproductive and nurturing function, for which the revolution has yet to find an adequate replacement.

Like so many other signs of fertility in *Red Cavalry*, however, the woman's child is revealed to be nothing more than a cruel hoax. When the woman asks forgiveness for her deception, Balmashev once again offers her up to the collective judgment of the platoon. His accusations are revealing, for the woman stands charged with responsibility for events in which she had no part. He tells her that she must ask forgiveness not only of the Cossacks, but also of the two girls who have "suffered at our hands this night." She is also guilty before the soldiers' wives, who "are drained of their womanly strength without their husbands," and even those very husbands, who "out of harsh necessity rape the women who pass through their lives." In Balmashev's formulation, the men themselves are responsible for none of this; they do not choose to rape, but must rape. They use the women for sexual purposes, because sex and reproduction are the only two womanly functions they recognize. Left "untouched," the woman is guilty of tricking them not to use her for one function because she is supposedly preoccupied with the other. Essentially, the Cossacks have been the victim of a hoax, a cruel joke played on them by the "model woman."

Carried away by his own rhetoric, Balmashev proclaims her guilt before the highest feminine symbol, Russia, which prompts the woman to betray her true ideological affiliations. When Balmashev throws this "counterrevolutionary" ("worse than a White General") out of the train, he wants to jump out and kill her with his bare hands.[21] Once again, the Cossacks display their particular brand of "pity" (*sozhalenie*) and tell him as a group to shoot her. Now the tables have been turned: the "joke" is on the woman. As in Freud's classic joke paradigm, this particular "joke" becomes an affirmation of group solidarity: the decision to kill her reaffirms the closeness of the Cossack collective. Balmashev, who has both written the narrative and killed the woman on behalf of the group, ends his story with the declaration: "For all the fighters of the second platoon—Nikita Balmashev, soldier of the revolution" (2: 76). This same line also underscores the "contagious" quality of the joke: it must be retold, and the story that Balmashev has written for *The Red Cavalryman* transmits the joke from this Cossack platoon to the wider male collective of the Red Army.

The era of War Communism would prove particularly conducive to the development of a literature that explores both the appeal and the horrors of comradeship and collective male violence. In the Soviet imaginary, the Russian civil war was both the forger and the destroyer of bonds among men, simultaneously fratriarchal (encouraging a sense of community among otherwise unrelated male warriors) and fratricidal (like all civil wars, the years of fighting following the Russian Revolution constituted the struggle of "brother against brother," both literally and figuratively).[22] The futurist Velimir Khlebnikov managed to embody both these extremes in his 1921 poem about revolutionary violence, "Night Search" ("Nochnoi obysk"). Though the poem's composition is, as in Blok's "The Twelve," fragmentary and confusing, with a multitude of voices vying for narrative control, it tells a story that is deceptively simple: a group of Red soldiers force their way into an apartment in search of retreating Whites. They are met by an old woman, who tries to convince them to leave by giving them her pearls. But the soldiers find her son Vladimir, a young White soldier, and shoot him in the forehead after stripping him of his clothes. They subsequently discover Vladimir's young wife, whose hair has gone gray from the shock. They leave her alone, their violent urges apparently satisfied by "revolutionary" vandalism (they smash a piano and throw it out the window). Soon the sailors demand food and drink from their "hostesses," and one of their number engages in a protracted dialogue with an icon of Christ. Meanwhile, the old woman locks them in the room and starts a fire, presumably burning them to death.

On the surface, the poem is hardly flattering to the forces of revolution, who are portrayed as merciless, crude, and unnecessarily violent. The poem's date, 7–11 November 1921, only strengthens its apparent counterrevolutionary force: if Khlebnikov's dating is accurate, "Night Search" was composed on the fourth anniversary of the October Revolution. But Francis Poulin has persuasively argued that the poem's date refers not to the revolution and its anniversaries, but to the first and second Kronstadt rebellions. The sailors' uprising at the Kronstadt naval base on 28 February 1917 was a crucial event in the formation of Soviet revolutionary mythology, leading to the base's transfer to the authority of the Petrograd Workers' and Soldiers' Soviet. Exactly four years later, a second revolt took place, this one lasting nineteen days. This time, the sailors rose up against the Bolshevik regime, leading to thousands of casualties on both sides. Poulin argues that Khlebnikov, who was convinced that he had discovered the mathematical laws that determine historical events, linked the poem to both revolts by giving it the epigraph $3^6 + 3^6$, a formula that yields the exact time span between the two revolts.[23] Khlebnikov's poem, then, reflects the "strange reversal of fate" by which some of the very soldiers who executed tsarist loyalists in 1917 would in turn be killed by the Red Army 1,458 days later. Moreover, the connection to the Kronstadt revolts helps explain the chilling transformation of the poem's revolutionary sailors: by the end of "Night Search," the carousing Red sailors are sitting around the White table, behaving in the very manner of their despised enemies (Poulin 511–17).

Like the other works discussed in this chapter, "Night Search" depicts a group of male revolutionary comrades whose collectivity is emphasized at the expense of individual characterization. As in "The Twelve," the narrator at times seems to be either a nameless member of the group or an aggregate voice of the entire collective. Liberally spiced with exclamation points, the poem contains an unusually high number of imperative sentences that do not point back to any particular speaker, but are often addressed to the collective itself: "Take your rifle! / Kick, brothers!" (Khlebnikov 317). Two metaphors are used to convey the strength of the group's bonds, one supplied by the men themselves, the other by the old woman (but quickly adopted by the men): "brothers" and "sea." "Brothers" and "sea" are symmetrically related forms of address in the poem, linked together by the manner in which they are introduced. The first command issued by the group to itself uses a Russian term for "brothers," while the first command issued by the old woman to the collective calls them "sea": "Stop, sea!" (*Stoi, more!*) (Khlebnikov 317). Her use of the term "sea" conflates several associations: first, "sea" is an appropriate metonymic nickname for a gang of sailors. Second, the word for sea, *more,* can be used as a metaphor to describe a collection of things that is too large to handle (much like Hamlet's "sea of troubles"); this is clearly how the sailors themselves understand her use of the term, as a plea that there are too many of them for her to accommodate (once again we recall the famous lament of the Soviet cashier): *Ty nas—more—ne moroch'* (roughly, "Don't give us that 'sea' stuff") (Khlebnikov 317). Finally, the appellation "sea" functions much like the pervasive meteorological imagery of "The Twelve": the revolutionary sailors are a force of nature, the flooding sea to Blok's relentless blizzard.

For our purposes, however, it is the insistence on brotherhood that is particularly significant. In the third line of the poem, the nameless speaker calls the group *bratva,* a singular noun for "brothers." The closest approximations of *bratva* in English would be "brotherhood" or "fraternity," except that neither of these words has the same "folksy" ring to it, nor can either be used as a form of address. *Bratva* is invoked repeatedly throughout the poem and creates a number of important effects. The word reinforces the sense of the male group as a single, irreducible entity, since it allows for the entire collective to be addressed with singular rather than plural imperatives ("Naletai, bratva!"; "*Sadis', bratva!*") (Khlebnikov 318, 326). In addition, *bratva* resonates with a range of Russian "brotherly" metaphors and associations usually linked to war, particularly that of the "brotherly grave" (*bratskaia mogila*): when one of the drunken sailors tries to convince the others not to leave the table so soon, he cries, "Brothers! / Where will we see each other again? / In the brotherly grave?" (*Bratva! / My gde uvidimsia? / V mogile bratskoi?*) (Khlebnikov 329). Finally, the constant invocation of brotherhood as metaphor creates a stark contrast with the nonmetaphorical family that the *bratva* has just destroyed: by killing Vladimir, the sailors have deprived the three-person household of the one member who binds the others together—in a sense, the two women are no longer related, or rather, they are connected by the body and the blood that still lie on the floor (the father, as is often the case in the literature of the period, is missing).[24] The encounter between the metaphorical family and the biological family ends in mutual destruction: as revenge for the murder of her son, the old woman engineers the death of the entire *bratva*.

What "Night Search" seems to lack in order to make it a true "ladykillers" text is direct instances of male group violence against women. Contrary to generic expectation, neither mother nor wife is threatened with rape, perhaps because, despite the poem's explicit criticism of the soldiers, Khlebnikov may have been reluctant to portray Red soldiers as sexual marauders. Yet when the soldiers prepare the young woman for execution, the standard lexicon of the firing squad takes on decidedly sexual overtones:

> Pretty girl in white,
> Up against the wall! [*K stenke!*]
> —This one? That one?
> Which one?
> I'm ready! (Khlebnikov 321)

Vladimir's widow, however, is spared, for much the same reasons that Balmashev uses to convince his comrades not to rape the woman in "Salt": "We also have sisters" (Khlebnikov 321). Indeed, not a single woman dies in "Night Search," but all of the men do. Khlebnikov, I would argue, is drawing attention to the fratricidal symmetry of the two Kronstadt rebellions noted by Poulin: the men are both aggressor and victim. One might say that "Night Search" represents the pinnacle of the Soviet male group's exclusion of women: if Blok, Gorky, and Babel have the collective begin to take over both positions occupied by the male rivals in Freud's joke triangle, Khlebnikov has the men adopt the role of victim as well. In the apotheosis of male comradeship, even the "female" victims are men.

The key to the replacement of the female victim lies in the eroticization of execution. If the threatened shooting of Vladimir's widow is sexualized, the men prove to be all talk and no action: rather than consummating the "relationship," the sailors content themselves with the equivalent of flirtation. Such is not the case, however, when the object of aggression (and desire) is a man. For one thing, the violent "courtship" is not one-sided; Vladimir is found only after he fires his weapon at the sailors. When he is captured, he, too, is told to move toward the wall, although in somewhat less erotic terms than would be used toward his wife ("Stan', iunosha, u stenki"). As soon as they catch him, the sailors call attention to his pleasing appearance: "Little blond hairs, / Little golden whiskers" (*Volosiki ruskiki. / Zolotye usiki*) (Khlebnikov 318). Perhaps in order to put up a brave front, Vladimir adopts a playful tone with the sailors, asking their pardon for his poor aim. The erotics of execution are reinforced by his request for a quick death; the question of just where the soldiers will shoot him becomes, in the standard Russian parlance, a question of where they will "give it" to him:

> Do you give it in the forehead,
> Comrades-*bratva*,
> Guests from the sea?
> They say you're generous. (Khlebnikov 319)

The sailors are happy to do him this "favor" after they confer among themselves: "Shall we give it to the White gentlemen / in the forehead?" (*Daem v lob, chto li / Belomu gospodinu?*") But before they shoot, the men want to make sure that no valuable clothing is lost. In a scene repeated time and again throughout the literature of the civil war, the soldiers demand that their victim strip before dying.[25] First they tell him to take off his shirts, since "you can go to your grave naked. / There are no girls in the grave." Then they tell him, "Off with your pants / And off with everything!" (*Shtany doloi / I vse doloi!*) (Khlebnikov 319). As we shall see in the next chapter, Babel's civil war stories present face-to-face violence as the height of male intimacy; Khlebnikov's "Night Search" takes a similar line.

Male martyrdom has a particular and obvious New Testament subtext that female sacrifice lacks: the man who goes willingly to his death often does so in imitation of Christ.[26] Hence the bizarre hallucinatory encounter between one of the *bratva* and a distinctly androgynous icon of the savior. In the world of "Night Search," there is nothing more erotic than a male victim. The sailor notes that the icon has such dark blue eyes that "you want to fall in love / Like with a Girl. / And God's face is that of girls, / But only with a beard" (Khlebnikov 327). The face of Christ is also a reminder of the sailor's beautiful, dead victim, looking down disapprovingly upon these "murderous saints." Here Christ represents the sailor's guilty conscience, but it is a conscience that never ceases to think in terms of a penetration that is both violent and erotic. He asks the icon, "Are you going to give it to me in the forehead? / Give it to me in the forehead, girlish god, / After all you, too, have seven rounds" (*Daesh' v lob, chto li? / Daesh' mne v lob, bog devichii. / Ved' te zhe sem'zariadov u tebia*). Christ's eyes "fly right into [the sailor's] soul" (*letiat mne priamo v dushu*), and now the sailor wants the role reversal to be complete: Christ is now to be the executioner, and the sailor will be the victim: "But I want him to kill me / Here and now, on the tablecloth" (*No ia khochu, chto on ubil menia / Seichas i zdes'nad skatert'iu*) (Khlebnikov 327). By now, Christ has been almost entirely transformed into a woman, although one that perhaps only this particular sailor could love: "You are a girl, but with a beard / You walk through the field and pick flowers . . . Girl! Do you want / Me to give you perfume? / And you can set the / Day for our date" (Khlebnikov 328–29).[27] Though none of the victims in "Night Search" is a biological woman, the feminization of the victimized men (Vladimir, Christ, and, by implication, the sailors) nonetheless reinforces the dynamic we have established in this chapter: the position of victim is always a feminine one.

Finally, the events of the poem appear to validate Balmashev's position in "Salt" and "Betrayal": women in "Night Search" are dangerous and cannot be trusted.[28] Not only does the *bratva* die at the hands of a woman, but the "betrayal" by Vladimir's mother takes place precisely at the moment that the sailor who seems most like the group's leader is distracted by his imaginary romance with the icon of Christ-*cum*-bearded-lady. The sailors had forgotten about the old woman; once Vladimir is killed, they treat her as just another old woman obliged to play hostess.[29] But her hospitality has been provided under duress; she has no choice but to let the *bratva* have the run of the larder. The men are obliged to invite themselves to dinner, appropriating the polite words that, under normal conditions, would have been issued by the hostess: "Have a seat, *bratva*, have a drink!" For her part, the old woman stands as "straight as a pine tree" (Khlebnikov 326). In the end, the woman turns the tables on the men; where they broke down doors to force their way in, she locks the door from the outside, preventing them from forcing their way out.

Only then does the old woman finally utter words appropriate to her role as "hostess": when the panicked sailors ask their leader what they should do, shoot themselves or suffocate, the old woman replies, "As you like!" (*Kak khotite!*) (Khlebnikov 330). In a poem in which the men have taken on all the roles of Freud's joke triangle, it is only appropriate that the final joke be on them.

Like all jokes, the story of the comrades who bond together over the dead body of their female victim would eventually grow old and tired, no longer providing the pleasure it afforded when it was new. As early as 1918, Bogdanov appealed to his proletarian followers for moderation; in his 1918 "Critique of Proletarian Art" ("Kritika proletarskogo iskusstva"), Bogdanov writes:

> Our cruel, harsh time — the era of worldwide militarism in action — often suggests to artists cruel and harsh symbols. For example, let's say, a working man of letters [*rabochii-belletrist*], in order to sharply and sternly express the idea of the rejection of everything personal in the name of the great collectivist cause, symbolizes [this idea] in the hero's murder of a beloved woman who sympathized with him. [Our] criticism must say that such a symbol is unallowable: it contradicts the very idea of collectivism; for the collective, woman is not just a source of personal happiness, but a real or possible member of the very same collective. (Bogdanov 449)

Bogdanov's critique is remarkable on a number of accounts. First, the very choice of such an example suggests that violence against women was a familiar trope in revolutionary writing as early as 1918. Very likely Bogdanov had a particular poet in mind, since the next example in the very same paragraph, though also unnamed, is Vladimir Kirillov's poem "We," a call to arms against the last remains of a moribund world culture. Moreover, Bogdanov's critique conflates two seemingly unrelated issues, covering the proletarians' attitude toward both the art of the past and the women of the present in the same brief lines. Finally, Bogdanov's appeal to proletarian writers tacitly admits that the "collective" to which he addresses himself is not only predominantly male, but sees itself as male by definition.[30]

Bogdanov attributes the violence and misogyny of proletarian art to the martial spirit of his times, suggesting that collectivism has assumed a military (and hence masculine) cast. One might then expect the topos of collective male violence against individual women to be restricted to the literature of War Communism, in which case it would have had no place in the more pragmatic era of the NEP. Such was not the case; as Eric Naiman has shown, the "comradely" sharing of a single woman would move from the barracks of the Red Army to the dormitories of the Komsomol.[31] By this point, however, the act has taken on entirely different overtones: whereas before it had been the sign of male solidarity, now it was a weapon in the arsenal of sensationalist muckrakers who purported to "expose" the sexual decadence of NEP society even as they reveled in the details.[32] By 1926, it became next to impossible to represent such an act in anything but an unequivocally negative light: the rape of a young woman by a group of drunken young men in Leningrad's Chubarov Alley provoked outrage in the press and on the factory floor, especially when it was discovered that at least five of the rapists were Komsomol members. The group was numbered in the original news reports as a folkloric forty, but by the time of the trial, the number of defendants was reduced to a Gorkian twenty-six (Naiman, "Case of Chubarov Alley" 3, 22). If life was to imitate art, then art was going to have to set more edifying examples.

In the wake of this "Chubarovism" (*chubarovishchina*), a concerted media campaign was mounted in order to convert the Komsomol into a center of collective responsibility rather than of collective debauchery (Naiman, "Case of Chubarov Alley" 24–25). The literary encounter between the male group and the individual female could no longer escape the taint of Chubarovism, which at least partially explains the motif's decline. Platonov's Chevengurians never think to use a woman this way. The closest they come is Kopyonkin's desire to unite all his men around the image of Rosa Luxemburg: her beloved corpse is beyond any harm, and her death at the hands of the enemies of communism absolves the revolutionary collective of any possible guilt. The novel's pervasive necrophilia can be considered a compromise: one has the results of collective male violence without having to take any responsibility for the destructive impulse.[33]

SEVEN BRIDES OR SEVEN BROTHERS

It is Platonov's *Chevengur* that bring the logic of revolutionary male utopianism to its logical extremes (see chapter 6). After satisfying themselves that, through repeated exercises of expropriation and mass murder, they have finally built socialism in one village, the men of Platonov's utopian ghost town have the leisure to grow restless. Where, they ask, are the women? Chepurny, the leader of the Chevengurians, had earlier considered himself the mouthpiece for the vox populi, but he is at a loss to confront the masses' demands now that the revolutionary appeal for "peace, land, and bread" has been superseded by "peace, land, and brides." Chepurny's initial reluctance prompts him to accede to the request only partially; he tells one of the proponents of this pragmatic "New Erotic Policy" that "in woman you don't respect a comrade, but the surrounding element . . . If a woman is a comrade, go ahead and bring her, but if it's the other way around, then drive her out into the steppe!" (Platonov 261).[34] Thus women are acceptable only if they are not perceived as women; in fact, Chepurny's convoluted "Platonovese" reveals at least part of the threat posed by femininity. "If it's the other way around" is apparently intended to mean that if the woman is not a comrade, she should be driven out, but the ambiguity of the sentence allows another interpretation: drive out not only the woman (*baba*) who is not a comrade, but the comrade who turns out to be a woman. Indeed, the threat of homosexuality, always just barely beneath the surface of Platonov's all-male utopia, increases in direct proportion to the longing for women, since both are signs of the persistence of erotic desire.[35] Hence the peculiar sequence of events that frames this episode: first Zheev kisses Prokofy's "dry lips," then he makes his case for the inclusion of women: "Prosha, . . . , don't forget to find us some women too, at least some beggar women. We need them, brother, for tenderness, or else, see for yourself: I just kissed you" (261).

However, the unusual group dynamics of Chevengurian society cannot be reduced to homosexuality per se; the force that binds men together includes more than mere eroticism. It is what Sedgwick terms "homosociality"—"the structure of men's relations with other men" (2).[36] Homoeroticism threatens to undermine the distinctly antierotic culture of Chevengur, and yet the solution—bringing women to the town—is just as dangerous. When the desire for women spreads to the newly sated "miscellaneous" (*prochie*) who have been brought to repopulate the town, their longing for women is presented as a direct consequence of their growing indifference to the joys of male comradeship.[37] The miscellaneous have become "useless" for one another now that they are no longer freezing or starving, and they want the right to a family. Finally, Chepurny is obliged to give the command: he calls for women who are "just [feminine] enough to be different from men—no attractiveness, just deliver the raw element!" (*zhenshchin, no ele-ele, lish' by v nikh raznitsa ot muzhika byla,—bez uvlekatel'nosti, odnu syruiu stikhiiu dostav'!*) (327). In any case, things do not go according to plan; when the "brides" are finally delivered to the town, Dvanov declares that "[w]ives aren't like them. . . . They're like mothers" (379). Though the men do engage in a rather inventive ritual in which each one kisses all of the newly arrived women, even the quixotic Chevengurians reject any cross between "free love" and the *kolkhoz*, designating the newly arrived women their "sisters and mothers." The danger of mass marriage has been narrowly avoided.

For their part, the women have no concept of the social structures to which they have been introduced and indeed are portrayed as incapable of partaking of them within the framework prescribed by the town's leaders: "Not one woman believed in the fatherhood or brotherhood of the Chevengurians" (380). The Chevengurian rejection of marriage in favor of sororial adoption is unique and, within the context of Platonov's parodic masculine utopia, appropriately extreme: the encounter with women must be purged of all desire. And in fact, this rejection is short-lived, for the arrival of the women does spell the downfall of the male community feared by Dvanov's brother Prokofy ("when they get to Chevengur, women will set up lots of households instead of one Chevengur, where a single orphan family lives" [322–23]): many of the men do break off into their own family units with the women. In the joyless, antierotic world of Platonov's fiction, no desire can remain unpunished, and it is not long after the arrival of dozens of half-starved women that the town is overrun by mysterious, "machinelike" invaders. The utopian dream is dead, having succumbed to a terminal case of female trouble.

Before the coming of the "wives," however, Chevengur already had one female resident: an acquisitive schemer who bears the ungainly (and, to the Russian ear, vaguely obscene) name of Klavdyusha Klobzd. Dedicated only to pleasure and personal gain, Klavdyusha embodies everything that is hateful about the old order: she is scheming and acquisitive, always looking for a chance for personal gain. Kopyonkin repeatedly complains that Klavdyusha understands nothing of their comradeship, but her liaison with Prokofy guarantees her a place in the town. As in *The Twelve,* there is a love triangle: both Prokofy and Chepurny are infatuated with Klavdyusha, but only Prokofy consummates the relationship. In *Chevengur,* however, the potential violence of both the love triangle and the ladykillers plot has been defused: Chepurny refuses to believe that Klavdyusha will "reproduce" (*razmnozhat'sia*) with Prokofy, thus suspending the possibility of true rivalry. Instead, he sees Klavdyusha as the collective property of the town: "he respected her too much for her comradely comforting of the lonely communists in Chevengur" (247). After the women arrive in Chevengur, however, communal property becomes quickly privatized, and Prokofy asks Chepurny to give him Klavdyusha (376), after which she and Prokofy are repeatedly referred to as "spouses" (*suprug, supruga*). Ironically, the novel appears to prove the more strident Chevengurian correct: it is Klavdyusha who suspiciously resembles a Judas figure, because until the arrival of the miscellaneous, the city has eleven male inhabitants, with Klavdyusha as the twelfth.[38] Before the town is overrun by enemies, she manages to take a large amount of formerly communal possessions to her aunt's for safekeeping.

Written in 1929, *Chevengur* is a farewell both to the revolutionary decade and to the ideology of male collectivism that played such an important role in early Soviet discourse. Why is the encounter between the male group and the individual woman such a prominent motif throughout the 1920s, and why does it all but disappear by the decade's end?[39] Certainly, the Chubarov Alley incident goes a long way to explain the motif's suppression, but the problem of the male collective's relationship to women goes far beyond one isolated incident, no matter how sensational that incident may be. One cannot help but notice the irony that the isolated woman is faced with groups of marauding men during the very same decade when Russian women were organizing themselves as never before;

indeed, the life span of the fictional male collective corresponds almost exactly to that of the very real institution of the Zhenotdel, the communist party's "women's section," established in 1919 and dismantled in 1930. One might suppose that these texts are the Soviet male psyche's hostile response to a perceived female threat. Yet such an interpretation turns a male phenomenon, whose roots include men's experience during the civil war, into nothing more than a reaction to advances in women's emancipation; this reading transforms the male collective hero into a supporting character in a fundamentally feminist drama. But as the next five chapters will demonstrate, male comradeship is one of the primary myths of early Soviet culture, a myth that, though connected to the changing status of women, does not depend on women for its power.

Chapter Two

ISAAK BABEL

Dead Fathers and Sons

> You cannot carry around on your back the corpse of your father.
> You leave him with the other dead. —Guillaume Apollinaire,
> *The Cubist Painters* (1913)

Among the many "dramas of beset manhood" that would capture the attention of the new Soviet reader, Isaak Babel's *Red Cavalry* surely deserves pride of place. Though work after work in the 1920s would focus on the predominantly male domains of the factory and battlefield, few make masculinity itself such a dominant and apparent theme, and fewer still reflect masculine concerns in form as well as content. In 1927 Yuri Olesha's *Envy* would capture both the anxiety and the admiration felt by the ineffectual *intelligent* when gazing upon the man of the future, while any number of civil war tales extolled the manly virtues of the Soviet warrior. Yet Babel's cycle of stories foregrounds a number of issues that, taken together, make masculinity a key problem: the strength of the rugged soldier, the trials of the effete intellectual, the structure of the male collective, and the collective's encounter with the female interloper. The glue holding these disparate themes together appears to be ethnicity: Lyutov, the book's protagonist and primary narrator, is a Russian-speaking Jew traveling with a Cossack regiment. To the Russian consciousness, there could hardly be more antithetical male types than the Cossack and the Jew: one is the primal, violent man, the other is the weak, effeminate victim. Indeed, were it not for Babel's own well-documented experience among Budyonny's Cossack troops during the Russian Civil War, the cycle's premise might strike the reader as suspiciously reminiscent of a Jewish joke.

The conflict between Cossack and Jew is apparent even to the most casual reader and has been the subject of a number of thought-provoking studies on Babel's work. The role of masculinity has also been far from ignored.[1] Though I by no means intend to disregard the conflict between

Cossack and Jew, neither do I wish to allow this admittedly fundamental issue to lead us to lose sight of equally important features of Babel's work that have significant ramifications for the question of masculinity and revolution. On the thematic level, masculinity in *Red Cavalry* is constituted within three possible social and emotional bonds. First, Lyutov's difficult relationship with the Jewish tradition raises the issue of generational conflict, the inevitable struggle between fathers and sons. The protagonists of the cycle oscillate between two different kinds of human relationships: the vertical connection between father and son ("The Letter," "Sashka Christ") and the lateral bond of brotherhood, whether literal or metaphorical ("My First Goose"). The third bond that helps constitute masculinity is not, as might be expected, that of a man and a woman, for heterosexual interactions in Babel's work undermine the hero's sense of his masculinity as often as they support it; in the world of *Red Cavalry*, it is easier to find mutual understanding between different species than between different sexes. Here I am obliged to trot out yet another old warhorse of Babel criticism: the Cossack and his trusty steed. Examined separately, none of these problems constitutes new ground in Babel studies.[2] I am comforted, however, by the thought that one of Babel's own stories teaches us that "beating a dead horse" can be more productive than one might think. In "The Remount Officer," the former circus athlete Dyakov proves to a disgruntled peasant that the broken-down nag allotted to him by the cavalry has life in it yet: through a combination of his personal magnetism and a judicious use of the lash, Dyakov forces the horse to stand up tall. Perhaps a similar resuscitation can be performed on Babel's text. Horses, fathers, and brothers or comrades form the symbolic system of masculinity in Babel's work: they are the building blocks of revolutionary manhood. These figures take part in a complex system of often mystifying exchanges, a "triangular trade" of fathers to brothers to horses. The result is a masculine language whose aesthetic appeal to the narrator is, if anything, augmented by Lyutov's lack of fluency.

After an examination of masculinity as theme, however, this chapter ends with the proposition that *Red Cavalry* is "generically masculine." This does not entail an appeal to old-fashioned essentialism, nor does it constitute an attempt to define an *écriture masculine* as either antidote or men's auxiliary to French feminism. Babel continually added to his collection of war stories, and there is evidence that he intended to include at least one more story in *Red Cavalry* before he was arrested. Perversely, Babel included his new stories not in the middle of the cycle, where they might have been less obtrusive, but right at the end: the addition of "Argamak" to conclude the cycle seems to require a radically different interpretation of *Red Cavalry* than one in which "The Rebbe's Son" is the final chapter.³ Yet I submit that the story's multiple endings highlight the cycle's repeated subversion of continuity and closure. I will argue that the genre of *Red Cavalry* (the short-story cycle) is uniquely suited to embody the dilemma of Kirill Lyutov, the man whose inability to find permanent acceptance among other men reveals the fundamental problem of masculine identity: the need to prove oneself a man ad infinitum.

LIFE WITHOUT FATHER

In its first six editions, Isaak Babel's cycle of stories *Red Cavalry* starts with a dead father and ends with a dead son.⁴ The bodies of the young Jewish woman's father and the rebbe's son Ilya lie at either side of the intervening stories like bookends, shoring up the narrative that unfolds between them. They are hardly the only corpses to be found in the cycle: the text is littered with the bodies of the dead and dying victims of both Cossack and Polish slaughter. Physically and structurally, however, these two bodies are uniquely positioned. Chronologically, the death of the woman's father precedes the stories themselves, yet "Crossing the Zbrucz" ("Perekhod cherez Zbruch") hinges on the revelation that Lyutov has spent the night lying next to a dead man; "The Rebbe's Son" ("Syn rabbi") shows Lyutov voluntarily bending over a man whose death ends both the story and the cycle. In each case, the ordinarily squeamish Lyutov, who in one story maintains his distance as he refuses to end the suffering of a wounded soldier, finds himself close enough to touch a dead or dying man.

These two deaths raise the problem of kinship in *Red Cavalry*, of filiation and affiliation, of fathers and sons. Both dead men are Jews, and the narrator's closeness to each, unwanted in the first case but voluntarily sought in the second, highlights Lyutov's inability either to extricate himself from or to fully join any given group. That it is a dead father and son who frame the text calls into question the possibility of continuity between generations; the fact that each is Jewish scarcely bodes well for the group into which Lyutov was born. Motherhood holds out some hope in the first story, for even as the Jewish woman laments the death of her father, her body is nurturing the potential life of a new generation. In the last story, mothers are revealed to be only an "episode" in the drama of revolution, and when Ilya dies, an entire dynasty dies with him. As in the works of Olesha and Platonov, the hope for continuity and group identity held out by "The Rebbe's Son" lies not with the traditional family, but with a freely chosen association that both mimics and distorts filial bonds. These are the ties between men: Lyutov receives the last breath of his "brother," yet he and Ilya share no mother save the revolution, a noun that is feminine in Russian. With varying degrees of success, the men of *Red Cavalry* seek to forge "brotherly" or "comradely" ties from which women are at best a distraction, at worst a distinct threat.

These attempts presuppose that purely filial bonds are no longer valid; the few tales involving biological parents and children all end in death for at least one of the family's members.[5] Biological fathers and sons are openly at war in only one story, "A Letter," and even this tale yields a far from satisfactory resolution to the conflict: by the story's final page, son has killed father, father has killed son, and neither generation can claim victory. Mutual slaughter does not constitute a triumph, and the family unit itself, deprived of three of its members, becomes a casualty of war.

The social order of *Red Cavalry* initially appears paradoxical: Babel describes the downfall of the traditional family in favor of a new, thoroughly masculine structure that runs counter to patriarchal tradition.[6] The decline of patriarchy, however, results in anything but a feminist paradise. Instead, *Red Cavalry* describes the increasing dominance of the "brothers" or "comrades" at the expense of the "fathers" and "mothers." The Cossack regiments of *Red Cavalry* are perhaps the purest example of what John Remy calls "fratriarchy" to be described in postrevolutionary Russian literature. Not only are women excluded from the Cossack community, but new members must endure a period of ritual initiation in order to prove their manhood and their worthiness. Even the "Cossack myth," a term as appropriate to Babel's revolutionary soldiers as to Gogol's classic marauders, cannot explain the thoroughly fratriarchal nature of this military community. Though men often became Cossacks by choice rather than by birth, the Cossack myth was by no means hostile to patrimony or heredity.[7] On the contrary, Gogol's *Taras Bulba,* perhaps the most famous fictional realizations of the Cossack myth, is firmly rooted in a patriarchal order. In Gogol's work, both fathers and sons are obliged to be good Cossacks, and the rebellion of the son constitutes the betrayal of the entire community.[8]

The Cossack regiments of *Red Cavalry,* while maintaining the strong ties characteristic of their Cossack ancestors, have been released from the need to respect paternal authority. The war has taken such a toll on their ranks that even some of their commanders are barely in their twenties. More significant is their political affiliation: whether or not they understand the subtler points of Leninist doctrine, these men have allied themselves with the forces of revolution. Such a political stance is inherently antitraditional and obliges some of its adherents to fight their fathers to the death. Of all the works treated in this study, *Red Cavalry* most strictly conforms to the received notion of revolution as a struggle of the sons against the fathers.

It is this rejection of paternal authority that makes Lyutov's continued alienation from the Cossacks all the more painful, for it suggests that Lyutov and the Cossacks should have some common ground. Like his fellow soldiers, Lyutov has broken with family and tradition, but unlike them, he spends most of the cycle unsuccessfully searching for a community to replace these relationships. In rejecting the world of his fathers, Lyutov comes halfway to the new world being created around him, but he finds he can go no further. Lyutov is trapped in a constant liminal state, which is reinforced by the repeated rituals and initiations he must undergo in order to join the Cossacks. Only in the end is he able to form a community of sorts, one that nonetheless preserves his physical isolation: "The Rebbe's Son" affirms Lyutov's kinship with a dead man and with the intended reader of his letter.

The son's retreat from the father is reflected even in the arrangement of the stories. The first three stories of the cycle all concern fathers, and in each one the father is either already dead, absent, or fated to die by the tale's end. Two other fathers play important roles in the first half of

Red Cavalry, each one serving as an obstacle for his son's dreams.⁹ Rabbi Bratslavsky from "The Rebbe" is the father as jailer, keeping his prodigal son from leaving the world of tradition. Tarakanych, the stepfather of the eponymous protagonist "Sashka Christ," also stands in the way of his stepson's dream.¹⁰ Ultimately, each father is unsuccessful: Ilya Bratslavsky runs away to join the Red Army, and Sashka wins his freedom through blackmail. The sons' stories are not fully told in the few pages that introduce them to the reader: both Sashka and Ilya appear later in the book, unlike their fathers. The second half of the cycle belongs exclusively to the sons, or more accurately, to the brothers.¹¹ By the end of the cycle, the father ceases to be an issue. Like the characters themselves, *Red Cavalry* eventually leaves the fathers behind.

The first story of the collection, "Crossing the Zbrucz," establishes patterns involving Judaism, the family, masculinity, and femininity that are repeated and developed throughout the cycle. Like so much of Babel's work, "Crossing the Zbrucz" is built on contrasts: the portrayal of the blood-soaked Cossacks fording a river as the sun rolls across the sky "like a severed head" is followed by the narrator's contemptuous description of the squalid hovel in which he has been billeted. His hosts include a pregnant woman (the only character in the story besides Lyutov who speaks), two redheaded Jews, and a third man who Lyutov assumes is asleep. The Jews are seen only indoors, and the single activity we see them engaged in is cleaning; the Cossacks are outdoors, struggling against nature and casually committing murder. At this point the reader is not necessarily aware that Lyutov himself is Jewish (Kornblatt 113),¹² and Lyutov's depiction of the two men who "jump silently like apes or Japanese men in a circus" serves only to increase the distance between Lyutov and his hosts.¹³ He is repulsed by the mess and filth he sees there, and he observes the Jews and their surroundings with the distant condescension of an explorer during his first encounter with "the natives." He refers to the men as "Jews" rather than men, as if he himself were not also a Jew. His only words to his Jewish hostess are a command and a reproach.

When he sleeps that night, his dreams he is still outside, watching as Savitsky shoots another soldier in the eyes. That night, while lying in the ruins of domesticity, surrounded by pathetic, servile men, Lyutov dreams of Cossacks, horses, and slaughter: "I dream of [Savitsky]. He's chasing after the brigade commander on his heavy stallion and shoots two bullets into his eyes. The bullets pierce the brigade commander's skull, and both his eyes fall onto the ground" (2: 7). At this point the violence of his dream erupts into the waking world: the pregnant woman rouses him because he is kicking her father in his sleep. Only then does Lyutov discover that the old man is dead, his throat cut and his face split in two. Now Lyutov's harsh treatment of his hosts pales in comparison with the violence of the Poles (though the connection remains): the Poles murdered him brutally, whereas Lyutov only kicks him unwittingly. Yet the Jewish woman addresses him the same way she would a Pole: *pan*. For his part, Lyutov kicks the father as he dreams of a different, equally merciless killing. Now that Lyutov understands the true nature of his hosts' circumstances, however, these Jews are not so easy to dismiss. Lyutov's earlier condescension is completely absent in the last two paragraphs. Instead, he listens to the Jewish woman tell of her father's courage and dignity and notes that she suddenly speaks with "a horrible strength." In his small way, Lyutov had been complicit in the victimization of this family, seeing them as only apes or circus performers. But at the story's end, Lyutov's voice is eclipsed by that of the Jewish woman as she praises and laments her father.

In "Crossing the Zbrucz" we see the beginnings of a motif that describes male and female roles in *Red Cavalry:* men willfully commit acts of violence while women stand by as passive witnesses. This opposition begins in the story's second paragraph, when the Cossacks push their way through yielding, feminine nature. When one man sinks in the river, he "loudly defames the Mother of God" (*zvonko porochit bogoroditsu*). The fields they cross are filled with "virginal" (*devstvennaia*) buckwheat that "rises like the wall of a distant convent" (*vstaet . . . kak stena dal'nego monastyria*) (2: 6).[14] The feminine moon simply lies on the water as the men cross the river. Later in the story the moon is a silent witness to the night, holding its "carefree" (*bespechnuiu*) head in its arms (2: 7).

Only later in the cycle does the reader discover that Lyutov is not at home among the Cossacks and their rough ways. In *Red Cavalry*, Lyutov not only "feels other than any group he confronts" (Kornblatt 110); he consistently manages to act according to a different ethos than that of the people he encounters, whoever they may be. Lyutov defines himself only in opposition. Thus the Lyutov who is accused of being a *molokan* (a member of a pacifist vegetarian sect) for riding into battle with no ammunition repeatedly behaves like a marauder when he enters a private home or encounters a helpless old woman. He threatens one peasant woman with a gun ("The Song" ["Pesnia"]), sets fire to the house of another ("Zamość" ["Zamost'e"]), and insults a third as he brutally kills her goose and orders her to serve it ("My First Goose"). This is not to say that, by Cossack standards, Lyutov is acting inappropriately; on the contrary, his treatment of the woman in "My First Goose" earns him the approval, indeed, the "affection" (*laska*) of his new comrades. Rather, Lyutov shows his best Cossack behavior when dealing with non-Cossacks, specifically women. Only on the battlefield or at the army camp does Lyutov appear to be the reluctant conscience of his division; the women mentioned above would probably see little difference between him and his fellows. The simplest way for Lyutov to redefine himself in Cossack terms is a tried and true method: he treats women with contempt.

In the story's final paragraph, the problem of the passive witness is posed with new urgency. Throughout the stories, Lyutov fondly describes how he sleeps next to various comrades whom he admires; such intimacy is part of his reward for killing the goose and treating the old woman as a servant. Here a different kind of intimacy has been thrust upon him: unknowingly, he has spent part of the night lying next to a victim. Now he becomes a witness not only to the effects of the Poles' torture of the old man, but also to the description of his death: "he begged them: kill me out in the backyard, so my daughter won't see me die. But they did as they saw fit, and he died in this room, thinking of me" (2: 7). He listens to the woman's story without saying a word.

Lyutov, a Jew who has turned his back on his origins to join a group whose ethics are totally alien to everything he knows, is confronted at the story's end with a dead Jewish father. The pregnant woman despairs of ever filling the gap left by her father's death, but her words refer to Lyutov rather than herself: "I want to know where on earth you will find a father like my father" (2: 7).[15] The story ends with a challenge to Lyutov: go and find a father as good as mine.[16]

From the *Odyssey* onwards, great stories have often begun with the search for one's father. Robert Con Davis sees a link between the development of such narratives and the absence of the father: it is the lack of a father that forces the hero to strike out on his own, but it also limits his access to wisdom. He can depend only on his own efforts rather than received knowledge (Davis 5–8). Lyutov, too, can be viewed as fatherless, but he is enjoined to find not his own father, but a father who is as good as the one who died thinking only of his daughter. The heroes of Olesha and Platonov also do not seek actual fathers, preferring instead father figures. Lyutov's search is less straightforward: he does continually search for new ties in the absence of any familial bonds, but he does not have a particular need for fathers. In a later story, the shopkeeper Gedali can be seen as a surrogate father to Lyutov, but he is more important for the wider community of Hasidim to which he can provide access. Lyutov seeks brothers rather than fathers, and if Gedali is a father to Lyutov, it is only in his capacity to provide him with new "siblings." In essence, "Crossing the Zbrucz" ends with a question: "What does one do in the absence of a father?"[17] If we interpret the question more broadly in terms of the lack of the entire family structure and all its attendant traditions, this is the question that the subsequent stories try to answer.

Lyutov does not respond to the Jewish woman's rhetorical question at the end of "Crossing the Zbrucz," but "The Church in Novograd" ("Kostel v Novograde"), which immediately follows the first story, provides a parodic answer. Like "Crossing the Zbrucz," "The Church in Novograd" takes place in the wake of an absent "father." This one, however, has merely disappeared: "The Pater fled" (*Pater bezhal*) (2: 8). Just as the death of the old Jewish father is accompanied by the destruction of the family home and way of life, the priest's abandonment of the church undermines its hierarchy and authority.

Echoes of the previous story abound in "The Church in Novograd." The second story makes explicit what was unspoken in the first: when he enters the church, he is an intruder, a "violent newcomer." In each story, his hostess addresses him as *pan*, the Polish equivalent of "sir." More complex, however, is the two stories' conflicting presentations of fertility. In the first story, the Jewish woman speaks with "horrible force" of her indignation and loss, while her pregnancy is the only implicit ray of hope in the entire story. "The Church in Novograd" contains only sterility and a parody of fertility. In keeping with the traditions of Catholicism, the church had been populated only by celibate priests, monks, and old maids. The priest's assistant, Romuald, is called a "eunuch" (*skopets*) (2: 8). The icons of the Virgin Mary, rather than being exalted, are said to be "degraded" by the jewels that surround them. The last line of "The Church in Novograd" is a sharp counterpoint to the dignity of the previous story's pregnant Jewish woman: Lyutov tells himself he must get away from "these winking madonnas who have been deceived by soldiers" (2: 10). In this place of holy celibacy, sexuality appears where it is supposed to be absent: the priest hangs the bras of his lovers on the nails of his savior, while the latter's wounds are said to be "oozing semen" (2: 9).

The "father"-centered Catholic hierarchy can itself be seen as a parody of the patriarchal family, and here it has broken down completely. War and revolution have destroyed both the Jewish family and the Catholic church's family, and yet the nature and form of their destruction is markedly different. The first story gives no indication that the family itself was ready to collapse; indeed, reverence and love for the father remain in "Crossing the Zbrucz." In "The Church in Novograd," the priest's authority is first undermined by his abandonment of the church, then totally destroyed by the discovery of the wealth (and articles of women's clothing) that he had been hiding on church grounds.

It is fitting that the army commander has taken up residence in the priest's house: he is filling the power vacuum he himself has helped to bring about. Even the commander, however, contributes to the overall sense of paternal authority's collapse in the second story: "The Church in Novograd" begins with Lyutov's attempts to find the commander at the priest's house. The commander, like the priest, is absent, though he does appear at the story's end. Lyutov is obliged to seek him out in the church but even there does not find him.[18] The Jewish woman in the previous story had asked him where he could find a father like hers, and Lyutov spends the next story looking for one male authority figure who is supposed to be in a place abandoned by still another "father." The priest, meanwhile, has yet to be apprehended. Lyutov leaves the church in disgust, and the Jewish woman's question still awaits a satisfactory answer.

In "Crossing the Zbrucz," the father is dead; in "The Church in Novograd," he is missing; the third story in the cycle, "A Letter," presents the father as Chronos, devouring his children. From the vaguely oedipal realm of weak or absent fathers, we now find ourselves cast into the world of *Totem and Taboo,* in which family conflict turns to full-fledged murder.[19] Such a tale is beyond the emotional range of Kirill Lyutov; in "A Letter," Babel resorts to *skaz,* a device he uses repeatedly to describe senseless violence on the part of Lyutov's uneducated comrades, presenting the events in the words of a participant or bystander.[20] The narrator of "A Letter" is Vasily Kurdyukov, a boy who has survived to write his letter only because he was too young to be a combatant in the bloodshed he describes.

Vasily's narration continually strikes a dissonant note. No matter how brutal the events he describes, his style remains oddly formal, never giving any sense of his own feelings on the matter: "In the second part of this letter I hasten to describe how Papa killed my brother Fyodor Timofeich Kurdyukov one year ago" (2:12). The closest he comes to condemnation is when he describes his father's disguise, writing to his mother, "[Y]ou know father and how stubborn he is," a statement so banal and domestic that it could even be said with some grudging admiration. The strange formality of Vasily's letter, as well as the dispassionate manner in which he writes, is seen most clearly in the way he refers to his relatives. He addresses his mother using the formal *vy,* going so far as to call her "Dear Mother Evdokya Fyodorovna Kurdryukova." Throughout the letter, his father is referred to consistently as *papasha* ("daddy"), and is called by first name and patronymic only when he is being interrogated by the son who plans to put him to death. When discussing either his father or his two elder brothers, Vasily uses third-person plural verb forms, in the manner of a nineteenth-century servant addressing someone of higher rank (Brodal 29). Vasily's formality has a dual effect: besides producing estrangement, his style also constantly reinforces the reader's awareness of the hereditary connection between fathers and sons. When the sons are referred to by their full names, their patronymics are always evident; Fyodor (also referred to as "Fedya"), Son of Timofei, is killed by Timofei, son of Rodion, and avenged by Semyon, son of Timofei.

Though Vasily begins his letter with his greetings to a long list of relatives, Vasily displays concern only about "my Styopa," who turns out to be a horse rather than a human being (2: 13). At the end of his letter, Vasily once again urges his mother to take care of Styopa, adding that if she does so, "God will not abandon [her]" (2: 14). Here Vasily shows how much he has in common with the people who are, de facto, his new family. The Cossacks of the Red Army prize their horses above all else; in a later story, one notes that a horse is "a friend," while the other replies that a horse is "a father" (2: 84). Vasily, who has nothing but praise for the work of his division (2: 11), shares their bond with horses as well as their remorseless attitude toward violence and murder.

For Vasily's brothers themselves, the fraternal bond takes precedence over loyalty to the father. The elder Kurdyukov is the first to draw blood and also clearly sees himself as the victim of his sons' betrayal. In a scene reminiscent of *Taras Bulba,* Kurdyukov curses his son Fedya for siding with the Reds. In his abuse of his sons, Kurdyukov accuses them of taking after their mother rather than their father. Indeed, when Kurdyukov turns his anger on Vasily, it is because he has caught his son trying to send a letter to his mother. In a telling passage, Kurdyukov blames the collapse of his authority on his wife at the same time that he asserts the preeminence of the father: "you're your mother's children, you take after her, the slut, I knocked your mother up and I'll keep knocking her up . . . I'll destroy my seed in the name of justice, and so on" (2: 20). Kurdyukov tries to reestablish his authority by putting all the other family members back in their places. At the same time that he berates his sons for being "mama's boys," he denigrates the woman's role in reproduction. Earlier he calls Fedya a "son of a bitch" (*sukin syn*), and now he refers to his own wife as a "slut" (*potaskukha*). If his sons have risen against him, they cannot be his sons. Therefore, they take after their mother. Yet even as he curses his sons for taking after their mother, he calls them "my seed" and reserves the right to destroy them. All his abuse contains reminders that he is still their father. The boys may be their mother's sons, but it is the father who has "knocked her up" and will continue to do so. To the very end, Kurdyukov uses his son's mother as their weak point, attacking them by attacking her. The last words Vasily ever hears from his father are Kurdyukov's curses against his children's mother, the Holy Virgin, and his son Semyon. It is appropriate that, of all three of the Kurdyukov sons, it is Semyon who kills his father. As one infelicitous transliteration of the young man's name suggests, "Semyon" phonetically resembles *semia*, the Russian word for "seed" or "semen"; first Kurdyukov exercises his perceived prerogative to destroy his seed, but then his seed murders him in revenge.

The old Jewish man's family has been devastated by outside forces, the church has fallen victim to a combination of war and internal corruption, but the family of "A Letter" is destroyed by an internecine conflict that mirrors the war ravaging their country. In "A Letter," the patriarchal family collapses into a metaphor for the Russian Civil War.[21] From the father's point of view, it is his rebellious sons who are to blame for the blood between them, but the story itself is still driven by the father's struggle to maintain his primacy. Kurdyukov's strategy is to take no prisoners: in order to save the family, it is necessary to destroy it. The fathers in *Red Cavalry* never cease to be the engine that drives the family, even if they often drive it to total ruin. Kurdyukov is only the most extreme example of a father who, by insisting on his patriarchal rights, contributes to the downfall of the very institution he represents.

In their variations on the theme of father-son conflict, the first three stories of *Red Cavalry* gradually shift their focus from the vertical connections between generations to the horizontal bonds of comradeship that both the army and the regime offer as an alternative. In "Crossing the Zbrucz," Lyutov, the would-be revolutionary Russian soldier, is forcibly reminded of the dead weight of paternal tradition and of the emotional poverty left by the father's passing; though he dreams of Cossacks in battle, he is left alone to confront the ruins of the Jewish family that has been forced to quarter him. In "The Church in Novograd," the father figure may be alive, but in his absence there is chaos and confusion; again, Lyutov is primarily alone, but the plot of the story is predicated on his search for his commanding officer. Only in "The Letter" does the metaphor of intergenerational conflict become realized, and it is in this story that we see the beginnings of an affiliative alternative. The revolt of the sons against the father is, at first, still an intrafamily affair, but Vasily's older brother gives him entrée into a larger group of *bratsy* who share no blood relation. He even participates in the mock rape of the nurse Sashka in "At Saint Valentine's"; not only is collective aggression against individual women one of the classic tropes of revolutionary comradeship (see chapter 1), but it is just such a symbolic rape as Lyutov would perform in "My First Goose" (see the next section).

Once "A Letter" introduces the pattern of substituting "brotherly" comradeship for paternal authority, the father's role becomes markedly less dramatic: now the father is an obstacle on the way to comradely relations. Such is the case in "Sashka Christ," in which the hero casually dismisses the threat of open generational warfare by sacrificing all ties of blood in order to gain entry to a comradely world. From the very beginning, Sashka's family appears to be on the verge of extinction; like "The Church in Novograd," "Sashka Christ" constantly highlights sterility and decay rather than fertility. The story begins at the end of autumn, when the harvest is presumably over. Tarakanych, Sashka's stepfather, brings him to Grozny for the winter, since the farm will not need him then. The beggar woman who sells herself to Sashka and his step-father is old and gray; as Tarakanych lies with her, she laughs at the absurdity of their coupling: "Rain on an old lady ... Some crop I'll give you!" (*Dozhdik na starukhu... dvesti pudov s desiatiny dam*) (2: 51). Sashka and Tarakanych return to the farm in the spring to find that Tarakanych's children have died only a week before.

The sterility of the story's setting casts doubt on the continuity of the family. Tarakanych's children are dead, leaving him with a stepson whom Tarakanych considers more his wife's than his own. The very name Tarakanych ("son of a cockroach") is morphologically a patronymic, suggesting a perversion of paternity rather than the real thing.[22] Like so many other stories in the *Red Cavalry* cycle, "Sashka Christ" presupposes an absent father. If Sashka has a patronymic, it is never revealed to the reader. Instead, the young man is called only by his diminutive and nickname: "Sashka Christ." The narrator informs us that Sashka received this name for his "meekness" (*krotost'*), but it also ironically comments on his family status. Like Jesus, Sashka is raised by a carpenter who is not his natural father. His mother is no virgin, but she is free from venereal disease and is thus "pure" (*chistaia*).

Under the surface of Tarakanych's relationship with his stepson is the same hostility and potential for violence that lead the Kurdyukov family to bloodshed in "A Letter." Kurdyukov, and later Nikitinsky (in "The Life of Pavlichenko"), talk of "messing up" or "knocking up" the narrators' mothers as a verbal weapon, but Tarakanych is about to commit the very deed the other two men merely allude to. Both Kurdyukov and Tarakanych find that their "sons" take more after their mothers than themselves, but each one claims the right to destroy any "son" who is guilty of rebellion. In "A Letter," the father murders one of his sons but only talks of sex with the mother, while in "Sashka Christ" the reverse holds true: Tarakanych talks of violence, but actually does sleep with Sashka's mother. In the ethical system of *Red Cavalry*, however, the conflict in "Sashka Christ" is less consequential than that of "A Letter." Kurdyukov kills Fedya for betraying his father, but Sashka knows that Tarakanych won't kill him "over a woman" (*Ty ne stanesh' menia rubit' za babu*) (2: 53).

Sashka has learned a lesson from the very man who stands in the path of his goals. The beggar woman had asked Tarakanych to "pay attention to her position" (2: 50), which Tarakanych interprets as an invitation to sex. After the two men sleep with her, Tarakanych pays her for her time and sends her on her way. Tarakanych uses the beggar woman for his own convenience and allows Sashka to do the same. When Sashka realizes that his mother is about to catch syphilis from his stepfather, he first appeals to Tarakanych's higher feelings, telling Tarakanych to leave her alone because she is "clean" (*chistaia*) while they are "spoiled" (*porcheny*). But Sashka's other motive soon becomes clear: he will keep silent about his stepfather's illness if Tarakanych will let him become a shepherd. Sashka is willing to exchange his own mother for his freedom. Tarakanych is enraged by Sashka's blackmail, but he is facing the results of his own handiwork. Earlier Tarakanych had only claimed a tenuous connection to Sashka, saying that Sashka was "sort of" his boy, but actually his wife's (*Vrode moego ... zhenin*) (2: 51). Now Sashka proves Tarakanych wrong. In resisting his stepfather and sacrificing the well-being of his mother, he resembles none other than Tarakanych. Each is willing to use women as he sees fit, and each subordinates the health of Sashka's mother for the sake of his own desires.[23]

In *Red Cavalry*, all roads lead back to male society. Hence even the "meek" Sashka, who wants to be a saint, leaves women and the family behind for the world of men. He realizes his goal of becoming a shepherd (literally, joining the "society of shepherds" [*k obshchestvu v pastukhi*]), where he earns the affection of men and women alike. Then he is drafted and eventually finds himself in the service of Budyonny and "three brothers" (2: 54). He has been freed from his family and become part of a male community. Like Lyutov in "My First Goose," Sashka has paid the price of initiation: he has sacrificed a woman. Indeed, he and Lyutov develop a sort of friendship, and the end of the story leaves them both with the reward of male intimacy seen repeatedly in *Red Cavalry*: he and Lyutov sleep side by side, a horse tied at their feet.

Sashka's story is peculiarly doubled by "The Life of Pavlichenko, Matvei Rodionovich." Though Sashka does leave behind his family for the company of men, he does not undergo a transformation as drastic as Matvei's. Sashka's goal was to become a shepherd, whereas Matvei was already living a similarly rustic life at the beginning of the story that bears his name. The lives of both Sashka and Pavlichenko are changed by either losing or surrendering a beloved woman: each sacrifices the woman in his life. The central conflict of "The Life of Pavlichenko, Matvei Rodionych" revolves around Nikitinsky, a landowner who takes liberties with Nastya, the wife of the eponymous narrator. Had Pavlichenko never been involved with a woman, there would be no story. Each time Nikitinsky is confronted by Matvei, he responds by using women as a weapon. When Pavlichenko returns for revenge after the revolution, the landowner tries to placate his former servant by appealing to Pavlichenko's old love for Nastya. Pavlichenko agrees to see Nastya, but his resolve remains firm. He stomps the landlord to death over the course of an hour as Nastya watches. Now insane, Nastya has exchanged her role as disputed object and weapon in the struggle between men for the other standard function of woman characters in *Red Cavalry*: she becomes the witness of brutal male violence.

Nastya's new role merely reflects the central transformation of the story's main character. Pavlichenko starts life as a simple shepherd, living a pastoral life strongly connected to women and femininity. As a shepherd, he is "surrounded by cows on all sides, soaked to the bone in milk, smelling like a slit udder" (2: 55). Milk is one of the most basic feminine symbols, one that is often associated in *Red Cavalry* with conduct unbecoming a true, masculine Cossack. The milk imagery shows that Pavlichenko is "wasting away" as a herdsman instead of a warrior, that "he has not yet entered true adult Cossackdom" (Kornblatt 204). At work he is surrounded by cows, and after his marriage he spends all his time naked with his wife. In his relationship with Nastya, Matvei takes a passive role from the very beginning. He comes to talk to her only when she calls him and follows her lead when she runs. She asks him why he "lowers his head," to which he metaphorically all but admits to being a failure as a man: "my head is not a rifle, it has no musket and no sights, and my heart.... probably stinks of milk" (2: 56). Nastya laughs at him with a voice "like a drum," and soon they are married.

Pavlichenko comes into conflict with Nikitinsky over Nastya, but soon the animosity between the two men takes precedence over any concern for women. Nastya is only one of the commodities at issue; Nikitinsky has stolen Pavlichenko's wife, but Pavlichenko owes money for a broken yoke. When Pavlichenko returns, he demands revenge for his beating by Nikitinsky rather than for the loss of his wife. For Pavlichenko, reunion with his lost wife is not only impossible, but not even an issue: where before he found happiness in Nastya's arms, now he is reborn as a warrior and discovers where true contentment can be found. As he tramples Nikitinsky, Pavlichenko "learns all there is to know about life" (2: 59).

Battles with men have replaced contact with women. Now he finds his greatest pleasure when he allows himself to trample his foes rather than merely shoot them. Shooting, he tells us, is simply a method of doing away with a man; with bullets "you don't get to the soul, to where it is found in a man and to the way it shows itself" (2: 59). True intimacy with one's enemy can only be achieved by beating him to death. Matvei's story is the tale of his rebirth as a "man's man," a Cossack whose life finds purpose in the company of other men. Matvei's transformation makes sense only in the context of *Red Cavalry*'s masculine ethic. He has lost a wife but gained an enemy, which is more than fair compensation in the Cossack world. As Lyutov learns to his great regret, one needs to be able to make enemies in order to have comrades. In violence, Pavlichenko has learned true communion with other men, reaching their very souls.

He has also discovered the virtue of comradeship. By the time the story is told, he has become a "red general" who has found his place in the collective. The story's opening line is a call to his "countrymen, comrades, my dear brothers" (*Zemliaki, tovarishchi, rodnye moi brat'ia!*), a refrain repeated two pages later. From the point of view of the male collective, one could say that Nikitinsky has done Pavlichenko a favor: by taking his wife, Nikitinsky has forcibly removed him from the feminine world, and by beating him, he has taught Pavlichenko the joys of battle and hatred. Before attacking Matvei, Nikitinsky is twice said to "strut" (*petushit'sia*), a verb whose root is the word for "rooster." The term is appropriate, for Nikitinsky engages his shepherd in a primal struggle for dominance among males. Pavlichenko learns his lesson well; when he finally takes his revenge on his former master, Matvei's actions describe a violent sort of intimacy: "And then I grabbed him by his body, by his throat, by his hair" (2: 59). No longer passive, Pavlichenko has joined the world of men.

Though Sashka Christ, the Kurdyukov brothers, and Matvei Pavlichenko are vivid, unforgettable characters, their roles in *Red Cavalry* are episodic. They hold center stage for their brief, parodic hagiographies, only occasionally making cameo appearances in the other stories, and develop within the limits of a few short pages, whereupon their story is essentially told. In the reader's mind, the two men's lives contain only one turning point that irrevocably alters their fate, after which they are no longer subject to any fundamental changes.[24] In terms of narrative structure, Kirill Lyutov represents the other extreme: his presence can be felt in almost every story, but the reader is never privy to his biography. At times Lyutov seems to be more of a voice than a full-fledged character, a narrative function rather than a narrative participant. This is partly due to the passivity that he tries to overcome throughout the cycle; indeed, the crux of many of the stories is Lyutov's inability to take part in the action that superficially describes the plot. Babel develops Sashka, Pavlichenko, and the Kurdyukovs in compelling but compact stories that are the narrative equivalent to the bombs and battles of the war in Poland: they make a dramatic appearance, briefly absorb all attention, and disappear after having left a distinct and unforgettable impression. As for Lyutov, no truly military metaphors can appropriately describe his role in the cycle. If the minor characters are explosive weapons, Lyutov is the narrative equivalent to the cold war: he provides all the tension of war without ever picking up a gun. Thus his conflicts are always left partially unresolved, and all his victories are ephemeral. Lyutov does, indeed, repeatedly fight the same battle for acceptance by the Cossacks (Kornblatt 117).

> I was alone among these men [*liudei*] whose friendship I could not gain. — "Argamak"

COMRADES AND ENEMIES: A LOVE STORY

At first it would seem that Lyutov wins the battle for acceptance the very first time it is explicitly joined: the story "My First Goose" appears to recount Lyutov's unconditional initiation into Cossack society. As is often noted in the critical literature, "My First Goose" resembles a classic rite of passage into manhood: Lyutov is removed from his accustomed surroundings, initially finding himself in a liminal state between his comfortable old world and acceptance in the new, and is welcomed into the community only after performing a distasteful task.[25] In the case of "My First Goose," however, the term "initiation" can be misleading, for it implies an irreversible process: upon initiation into a group, one is presumably accepted for life, and any further testing is necessary only to achieve new status. Lyutov, however, is challenged to prove his worthiness again and again and often found lacking. This is partly attributable to the difference between him and the episodic characters that populate the cycle: the biographies of Matvei Pavlichenko and Sashka Christ are compressed into a few specific high points, before and after which their lives are presumably stable and uneventful. Lyutov, however, is the center of narrative attention for a longer period of time, and thus the section of his life described in *Red Cavalry* more closely resembles nonliterary daily life. Not everything that happens to Lyutov is eventful, and not all the dramatic moments change him as drastically as any individual story would lead the reader to believe. Thus, as an isolated story, "My First Goose" depicts Lyutov's successful integration into a violent male community, but as an episode in the *Red Cavalry* cycle, the story describes a limited victory that fails to have any permanent effect on Lyutov's status.

It is the nature of rituals that they are steeped in symbolism and substitution: the bread and the wine of the Catholic Mass serve as the body and blood of Christ. The Cossacks demand a human sacrifice from Lyutov, and Lyutov substitutes an animal for the suggested, if hypothetical, victim. The quartermaster warns Lyutov that a man in glasses will have a hard road with the Cossacks, but suggests that the sexual conquest of a "pure" woman will win favor with his new fellows. When Lyutov meets with abuse at the hands of the Cossacks, however, he turns to an easier target: intimidating an old woman, he savagely breaks the neck of her goose and orders her to cook it for him. At this point the Cossacks, who sit around their fire "like high priests" (*kak zhretsy*), welcome him into the fold and invite him to join in their communal meal: "This guy's all right" (*Paren' nam podkhodiashchii*) (2: 34). They even call him "brother" (*bratishka*), implying that he is truly one of them.

But Lyutov, perhaps unwittingly, has fooled them through ritual substitution. Lyutov's slaughter of the goose implies a capability for murder that he does not have; Lyutov cannot fulfill the promise implied by his actions. In his close reading of the story, Andrew sees the goose as a substitute for a wide range of people and concepts: Savitsky, "pure" women, Lyutov's own innocence, passive victims (Andrew 75–76). None of these sacrifices, however, descends from the realm of symbolism to the reality of the bivouac or battlefield. Lyutov has not succeeded in killing his own conscience. The story's last sentence belies the narrator's apparent success: far from being indifferent to the fate of the goose, Lyutov's heart, "turned scarlet by murder, creaked and bled" (2: 34).[26] Lyutov's acceptance *by* the Cossacks is as tenuous as his acceptance *of* the Cossacks; despite his rhapsodies over the Cossacks' masculine splendor, he can no more wholeheartedly approve of them than he can wholeheartedly join them. Even in the stories in which Lyutov is apparently successful in gaining their acceptance, he engages in a charade of Cossack behavior rather than the real thing. If his initiations never "take," it is because he never allows them to happen according to Cossack rules. Lyutov pays every price demanded by the Cossacks for entry into their community in a counterfeit currency.[27] Lyutov's perspective will never be that of a Cossack, nor can he do what his own actions imply: no matter how often Lyutov threatens old women with violence in *Red Cavalry*, he never commits rape or murder. The warrior brotherhood demands human sacrifice, for which no amount of metaphor or symbolism will substitute.

As a rite of passage, "My First Goose" signals a short-term success followed by a long-term failure. There is, however, another model for the events of the story. "My First Goose" takes place in a strongly eroticized context, which is usually alluded to but not discussed by the critics. Andrew refers to the story's "obvious sexual implications" as well as the "strong sexual overtones" of Lyutov's attitude toward Savitsky (Andrew 74, 75). Trilling rescues "My First Goose" from its homosexual implications by reducing the eroticism of Savitsky's description to "admiration and envy" which "[keep] the description from seeming sexually perverse." He adds: "It is remarkably not perverse; it is as 'healthy' as a boy's love of his hero of the moment" (Trilling 35). Ironically, critics of "My First Goose" repeat the very mechanism employed by the story's narrator: when faced with homoeroticism, they redirect it to more acceptable, if not more conventional, objects.

No doubt envy is inextricably linked to the attraction Babel's Cossacks hold for his narrator. In this respect Lyutov resembles Olesha's Kavalerov, whose envy of Andrei and Volodya is mixed with an undeniable eroticism. Simply because envy is present does not mean, however, that it can be identified as both the sole cause and the true nature of the works' homoeroticism. In both Lyutov's and Kavalerov's cases, the critic becomes complicit in the same sublimation process used by the narrators themselves. Kavalerov ascribes his fascination to envy, and thus the critics do the same. Lyutov describes the erotic appeal of the Cossacks but does not dwell on it, and the critics do the same. But if we turn our attention to the eroticism of "My First Goose," the story presents itself in a different light. "My First Goose" begins to resemble less a rite of passage than the beginning of a long and difficult courtship.[28]

Cossack beauty enthralls Lyutov before "My First Goose" and will continue to do so long after he and his five new comrades have fallen asleep at the story's end. Andrew correctly observes that "[a]ll men, or at least all Cossacks, seem to appear physically beautiful to the narrator" (74). The first Cossack to captivate Lyutov with his physical prowess and beauty is Dyakov, a former circus athlete who is now the remount officer. His dandyish appearance is reminiscent of the athletes and actors who fascinated Yuri Olesha in his youth: Dyakov is "red-faced, gray-whiskered, in a black cape and with silver stripes along the seams of his red riding breeches" (2: 15). Through skill and an almost mystic charm, Dyakov practically resurrects a half-dead nag, subduing her to his will while at the same time forcing her to call upon reserves of energy no one else thought she had. Throughout the process Lyutov never loses sight of Dyakov's dexterity and grace. He notes the ease with which Dyakov's "stately athlete's body" (*statnoe telo atleta*) dismounts from his own horse. After straightening out his "wonderful legs" (*prekrasnye nogi*), Dyakov approaches the jade "as if he were on stage." The listless horse immediately feels "the knowing strength that flowed from that gray, flourishing, and dashing Romeo." When the deed is done, the remount officer "jumped up four stairs at once and, tossing his opera cape over his shoulder, disappeared into the headquarters" (2: 16).

The example of Dyakov is applicable to all of *Red Cavalry*, perhaps even to all of Babel's work. Lyutov's observations of Dyakov have a voyeuristic quality that differs sharply from that found in the works of Olesha. Olesha's characters are incessantly scopophilic, but they interact with the objects of their gaze. Babel's voyeurs (and they are many) are transfixed by men who never once acknowledge their presence.[29] Lyutov is distant from Dyakov not only because of their undeniably different personalities and physical appearance, but also because Lyutov has no role to play in the brief incident that comprises the story. Envy and admiration aside, Olesha's narrators never let the reader forget who the protagonist is. Lyutov, however, truly does recede to the background on more than one occasion. Events are recounted according to his perspective, but often Lyutov is merely a witness. Kavalerov spends all of *Envy* trying desperately not to be a mere bystander, while the journalist Lyutov shows no resentment for his role as observer.

Lyutov's observation of Dyakov is typical in that the narrator's fascination with the Cossack's physical qualities is tinged with awe before a metaphorical display of the man's sexual prowess. Dyakov's conquest of the female horse is described in terms that could easily apply to the seduction of a woman. Lyutov calls Dyakov a "Romeo," while the jade cannot tear her "doglike, fearful, love-struck eyes" (*sobach'ikh, boiazlivykh vliubliashchikh glaz*) from the remount officer. Dyakov's treatment of the horse reads like a sadomasochistic encounter: the jade responds to the "insistent and masterful tickling" (*neterpelivoe i vlastnoe shchekotanie*) of Dyakov's whip against her belly. "Her entire body shaking" (*Drozha vsem telom*), she stands up after he yanks her mane and whips her bloody side (2: 16).

Even here, when Babel presents one of his most virile men, Dyakov's relationship with the horse contains a strong element of gender ambiguity. The bond between rider and horse is an essential part of the Cossack myth (Kornblatt 122). In this context, writers often use the masculine word *kon'* ("steed") rather than the feminine, and more common, *loshad'* ("horse"). In "The Remount Officer," the horse is initially called a nag (*kliacha*), immediately marking it as a female. The peasant who complains to Dyakov about the horse's uselessness persistently refers to it as "she." His first words to Dyakov end with the phrase, "Just try going about your business on that one" (*Khozaiistvui na ei*). Dyakov interrupts him to praise the jade's potential value to the peasant. Right after the word *ei* ("her"), Dyakov says, "You have every right to get fifteen thousand rubles for that horse from our stable" (*A za etogo konia . . . ty v polnom svoem prave poluchit' v konskom zapase piatnadtsat' tysiach rublei*). Arguing that the horse is perfectly adequate, he shifts the horse from "she" to "he." The horse, however, must prove itself worthy of such a promotion. Dyakov explains that a horse is a *kon'* if it gets back up after it falls. The peasant does not believe the horse can get up and thus refuses to grace it with the masculine pronoun that befits a *kon'*, sticking doggedly with the female pronoun. When Dyakov begins the process of rousing the nag, the horse is now referred to as an animal (*zhivotnoe*), a neuter noun in Russian. Thus the next reference to it uses the neuter pronoun *ono*. In a sense, the horse itself is going through a rite of passage. At the beginning of the "ritual," the horse is in a liminal space, neither male nor female. Only after the test is gender returned to it, whereupon Dyakov triumphantly announces that the horse is, of course, a horse (*kon'*). Dyakov has had a pseudo-sexual encounter with the horse, demonstrating his masculinity, but at the same time he has figuratively transformed the horse from female to male.

A clear parallel can be drawn between the horse's experience and that of Lyutov.[30] If Lyutov is to be successful in his attempt to be accepted by the Cossacks, he must allow himself to be changed by them, to give himself over to their power and be remade in their image. He must let their virile strength do its work on him as well. Herein lies the essence of the homoeroticism of the *Red Cavalry* stories. In comparison to the Cossacks, the passive, nonviolent Lyutov appears less manly. He finds himself in a feminine role, and admires the Cossacks' masculinity both out of envy and out of the desire to let their virility have an effect on him. Paradoxically, if he wants to become like them, he must give himself over to their influence and accept the traditionally feminine, passive position he is trying to abandon. "The Remount Officer" suggests that the road to true manhood is through a temporary, submissive femininity: Dyakov's quickening of the nag, after all, can also be seen as the masterful stimulation of flaccid flesh to proud erection.

A similar dynamic of sexual initiation is at work in "My First Goose"; here, it is the division commander, Savitsky, who now enthralls Lyutov's imagination. Like Dyakov, Savitsky is a puzzling mix of athlete and dandy. Lyutov does not hide his admiration from the reader, admitting in the story's very first sentence that "the beauty of [Savitsky's] giant body" has an effect on him (*ia udivilsia krasote ego tela*) (2: 32). Savitsky, like Dyakov, has the dashing air of a silent movie star. From Lyutov's description of him, Savitsky seems to pose rather than to move naturally. At the same time, Savitsky's body carries the promise of both sex and violence simultaneously. The reader is already familiar with Savitsky from "Crossing the Zbrucz," when Lyutov dreams of the division commander shooting the brigade commander twice in the eyes. In the earlier story, the peculiar violent intimacy of men at war immediately gives way to the unexpected physical contact of the pregnant woman's fingers on Lyutov's face (2: 7). As Andrew notes, all the verbs used in connection with Savitsky in "My First Goose" are violent: *razrezal* ("sliced"), and *udaril* ("hit") (Andrew 74). The first violent image associated with Savitsky in "My First Goose" is phallic: Savitsky's body "slices the hut in two, like a standard cuts the sky" (*razrezal izbu popolam, kak shtandardt razrezaet nebo*).

Like Dyakov's encounter with the horse, however, Savitsky's description is conspicuously androgynous. He smells of "perfume and sickeningly sweet soap," while his legs look like "girls who are bound up to their shoulders in brilliant bosphurs" (2: 32).[31] Savitsky's androgyny adds to the sexual undercurrent between Lyutov and the Cossacks. Lyutov freely admires Savitsky's manliness, at least to the reader, and yet he perceives part of Savitsky's appeal as distinctly feminine. Lyutov stops short of openly praising any particular part of the division commander's body. Rather, Lyutov's vision transforms a disturbing object of attraction into a more standard one: instead of writing that the division commander's legs are particularly noteworthy, he compares them to girls. Lyutov thus defuses at least part of the homoerotic tension of his attraction to Savitsky by turning the object of his gaze into something resembling women.

If Lyutov and Savitsky were not of the same sex, the reader would immediately see that Lyutov's description of their interactions includes a pronounced element of flirtation.[32] As it stands, Savitsky's description threatens to add new meaning to the phrase "the Cossacks' camp." If "My First Goose" is the first step in a failed courtship, Lyutov's encounter with Savitsky represents the initial coquetry that begins the relationship. Indeed, Savitsky's manner contains echoes of Dyakov's taming of the nag. Like Dyakov, Savitsky is not averse to using his whip: "He smiled at me, struck the desk with his whip, and drew the order to him." For his part, Lyutov continues to be struck by Savitsky's physical beauty: "[he] turned his gray eyes, which danced with merriment, upon me"; "[I] envied the iron and flowers of his youth" (2: 32). Savitsky, however, is as unimpressed by Lyutov as Lyutov is captivated by Savitsky. Lyutov envies the division commander's manliness, but Savitsky finds Lyutov sorely lacking in the qualities needed for Cossack military life. To Savitsky, Lyutov is a "mangy" (*parshiven'kii*) little man with glasses. Savitsky makes it perfectly clear that Lyutov does not belong and most likely never will.

Savitsky is not alone in his opinion. On the way to the Cossacks' hut, the quartermaster stops to give Lyutov advice "with a guilty smile." Men with glasses have no luck with the Cossacks, he explains, "[b]ut if you ruin a lady, the purest of ladies, then the lads will show you some affection" (*A isport' vy damu, samuiu chistuiu damu, togda vam ot boitsov laska*) (2: 33). The quartermaster's phrasing calls our attention to the erotic character of both the price and the reward of male community. Essentially, his actions would offer up the woman to the group as the price of initiation. Once again, a woman serves as a victim or a sacrifice, a commodity to be exchanged among men. The woman has little value for herself; rather, she is a means to an end. The pleasure is to come not from sex with the woman, but from the approval Lyutov will receive from the group. The quartermaster calls attention to the intimacy that is the point of "spoiling a lady": then Lyutov will "get affection [*laska*] from the warriors."[33] Here the quartermaster's words trail off, and a puzzling, mute scene follows: "He hunched over with my trunk on his shoulders, came up quite close to me, and then jumped back in despair and ran into the first courtyard" (2: 33). His conduct foreshadows the subsequent course of Lyutov's courtship of the Cossacks: each side comes close to the other, only to jump back in despair.

When he presents Lyutov to the Cossacks, the quartermaster "turns scarlet," as if he knows that the ensuing scene will be humiliating. The Cossacks, who had been shaving each other when Lyutov entered, respond to Lyutov's inappropriately official salute with a display of schoolyard wit. One young Cossack, whom, despite his conduct, Lyutov finds handsome, throws out Lyutov's trunk, whereupon he "turns his backside" to Lyutov and makes "shameful noises." To call such behavior erotic would strike most readers as a mystifying exaggeration, but the fact that the young man displays his backside to Lyutov accentuates the homoerotic elements of their interactions with Lyutov. From this point on the Cossacks give Lyutov no peace: "the Cossacks stepped on my feet, the young man made fun of me nonstop."

Here Lyutov encounters the half-blind old woman, the only female present in the story. Her description is utterly devoid of eroticism; in a camp full of handsome men she is the only ugly character (Andrew 74). In other circumstances Lyutov might have felt pity or kinship for such a woman: both of them wear glasses, and both are treated with no respect. Indeed, her words to Lyutov are one of the few instances in the novel when anyone calls him "comrade." The address is, of course, official, but in similar circumstances the local peasants and Jews address him as *pan*. Yet if Lyutov is to be accepted by the Cossacks, he must deny precisely that part of himself that resembles this woman: his passive role, his despair, his glasses, and, most of all, his compassion. Andrew finds that the woman is an "archetypal victim figure—even the weak, passive narrator pushes her around" (Andrew 75). It is precisely because she symbolizes victimization that Lyutov must treat her harshly, for the only way he can prove that he himself is not a victim is to play the role of the oppressor. Lyutov resorts to such a course of action repeatedly in *Red Cavalry*, but never to such effect as in "My First Goose." He punches her in the breast, and twice utters a curse degrading a mother: "Goddamned motherf–" (*Gospodi boga dushu mat'*) (2: 33-34). Lyutov completely rejects any sympathy he might have had for her as woman or as victim.

To become part of the Cossack community of men, Lyutov has to show that he knows how such a man should treat a woman. When he takes up the saber to kill the goose, Lyutov follows an old Cossack tradition: the sword is his bride, his true companion (Kornblatt 61). At the same time, a sword is a symbol of manhood; it is appropriate that Lyutov notes that the saber does not belong to him (*chuzhuiu sabliu*) (2: 34).[34] Only after he has proven himself to the Cossacks does heterosexual eroticism return. Asleep among the other men, Lyutov dreams of women.

In the short term, Lyutov has gained the "affection" of the Cossacks. They invite him to share their meal, one of them offers him a spoon kept in a boot, and, as consummation of the courtship, Lyutov sleeps with five Cossacks, "warming each other, our legs tangled together" (2: 34). Along with physical intimacy, Lyutov even achieves a limited spiritual communion with the Cossacks. He reads them Lenin's speech from *Pravda*, underscoring their ideological unity. Now they are all part of one big communist family, "brothers" in blood (the sacrifice of the goose) and politics (Lenin's speech). Lyutov has even made himself useful, since he is most likely one of the few literate men among them. His internal conflict has not been resolved, however; it has merely been postponed. The very structure of *Red Cavalry* highlights the fact that Lyutov is still far from being one of the Cossacks.

Lyutov cannot maintain true comradeship with the Cossacks because he is unable to take part in the peak experiences that bind them. Even when he shares the danger, he does not take part in the violence. Lyutov's problem is posed most clearly in "After the Battle," the story of the entire division's retreat and Lyutov's personal humiliation. Defeated by the Whites, the Red Cossacks run away to save themselves. Lyutov has the misfortune of running into Commander Vinogradov, who tells him to turn the troops around. Lyutov attempts to do as he is told, but he is nearly killed when he tells the Kirghiz Gulimov to turn back:

> Gulimov... grabbed me by the shoulders and began to take out his sword with his other hand. The saber rested snugly in its sheath, the Kirghiz shook and looked around. He embraced my shoulder and leaned his head closer.
>
> ... [He] lightly poked me in the chest with the tip of his extended saber.
>
> I grew nauseated from the nearness of death, from its close quarters. With my palm I pushed away the Kirghiz's face, which was hot like a rock under the sun. (2: 122–23)

As in "The Remount Officer," a violent episode is rendered with words from the realm of the erotic: Gulimov "embraces" Lyutov's shoulders and moves his own head closer to Lyutov's. When Gulimov speaks to Lyutov, it is in a barely audible whisper. It is not merely the danger, but the "nearness" and "close quarters" of death, that nauseates Lyutov. Once again he finds himself in the feminine role in the eroticized violence of *Red Cavalry*. Like the encounter between Lyutov and the old woman in "My First Goose," the scene reads like a mock rape, only this time he plays the part of the old woman. Even the actions taken against the victim are the same: both are struck in the chest by their assailant (2: 33, 123). Lyutov fights back, but his response is not the "manly" fisticuffs of a Cossack. Rather, he scratches Gulimov's face and rides off.

Back at the camp, Lyutov is once again implicitly compared to a woman. The nurse Sashka berates one of the soldiers for retreating; when asked why she herself did not pick up a gun and shoot, she points out that she has nothing to shoot with. Here she is like Lyutov, who rode off into battle with an empty gun. Akinfiev cannot understand why Lyutov will not fight back against the Poles. Once again, Akinfiev's accusation is ambiguously phrased, suggesting that Lyutov has not only failed to fulfill his military duties, but also is not holding up his side of a personal contract: "The Pole'll do it to you, but you won't do it to him" (*Poliak tebia da, a ty ego net*). Lyutov, rather than arguing, confirms Akinfiev's charge: "The Pole'll do it to me, but I won't do it to him" (*Poliak menia da, ... a ia poliaka net*) (2: 124). Matvei Pavlichenko extols the intimacy of prolonged murder, which is clearly the most intense experience available to him. Lyutov, however, cannot kill, so he misses a key element in the lives of the Cossacks who surround him. The most he can do is fight back against Akinfiev, which reaffirms his masculinity, at least to Sashka. Tending to Akinfiev's wounds, Sashka says with disgust: "Roosters just care about one thing: . . . . beating each other in the face." This time Lyutov has fought with his fists rather than his fingernails, and he earns the dubious distinction of being just as ridiculous as any other man in Sashka's eyes. Sashka's words once again hark back to "My First Goose": her complaint that "all this stuff today just makes me want to shut my eyes" (*ot delov ot etikh ot segodiashnikh glaza prikryt' khochetsia*) echoes the old woman's refrain, "all this stuff makes me want to hang myself" (*ot etikh delov ia zhelaiu povesit'sia*) (2: 33, 124). In each story, Lyutov has managed to prove himself a man in the face of a Cossack's challenge, but this time, Lyutov realizes the hollowness of his victory. At the story's end he is left begging the fates for "the simplest of abilities—the ability to kill a man" (2: 124). His unwillingness to abandon the humanistic traditions that are so important to him cannot be considered an unequivocal failing; *Red Cavalry* is replete with examples of horrific violence and injustice, yet none of them is perpetrated by Kirill Lyutov. Hence Lyutov's fundamental conflict: he is attracted to the Cossack community both aesthetically and emotionally, but he cannot accept it philosophically. In turn, Lyutov's mixed feelings for the Cossacks mirror the dilemma faced by not only Babel himself, but by so many writers and intellectuals in 1920s Russia: their attraction to both the trappings and the general ideals of revolution is mitigated by moral compunctions over the methods and policies of the regime. For the fellow travelers of the 1920s, this quandary meant that their status in Soviet society could never be anything other than tenuous. For Lyutov, it meant that as long as he holds back from complete participation in Cossack life, he can never attain comradeship with them.

In the concluding chapter of the later editions of *Red Cavalry*, Lyutov's inability to attain comradeship is examined in terms of his desire to "live without enemies." "After the Battle" suggests that Lyutov, who cannot deal with enemies in the manner required of him, can therefore never truly become a comrade to the members of the cavalry. "Argamak" takes this line of reasoning to its logical conclusion: one cannot gain comradeship without accepting the existence of enemies. Lyutov tries whenever possible to make peace with his enemies, but in his very attempts he shows how different he is from the Cossacks. Through no fault of his own, Lyutov has nearly killed Argamak, a horse who is accustomed to the roughest of riders. His experience with Argamak puts Lyutov in an unfamiliar position. Here Lyutov, precisely by being too soft, too unlike the Cossacks to whom Argamak is accustomed, causes the horse as much pain and suffering as if he had intentionally set out to torture the animal. All that the Cossacks in general, and Argamak's former owner in particular, can see is that Lyutov is the immediate cause of the horse's decline. Though Lyutov meant no harm, no one will forgive him. When Lyutov confronts Baulin to find out why the latter has set him up as an enemy, the answer is that "you're always trying to live without enemies," and life without enemies is "boring" (*eto skuka poluchaetsia*). Lyutov is forced to admit defeat and leave, and yet he has learned from Argamak and from his experience of having an enemy: now he knows how to ride like a Cossack. This in turns allows him at least a peaceful coexistence, if not necessarily comradeship, with the next group of Cossacks he joins.

As always, Lyutov's success in "Argamak" is hardly unqualified, and there is no reason to assume that the story's "happy end" will have any more global repercussions than the apparent accomplishments of "My First Goose." Lyutov's inability to effect the changes within himself that would make him a good Cossack is brought home in nearly every story in which he is featured and is set in relief by the contrast with more "successful" initiates. Again, the structure of the cycle facilitates Lyutov's characterization, for even the stories that appear to have little to do with Lyutov go a long way to define him. When Lyutov courts the Cossacks, his "initiation" amounts to little more than "maimed rites," an alien ritual carried out formalistically (and badly). The same story of group incorporation is retold numerous times in *Red Cavalry*, and when the protagonist is not Lyutov, all goes well. The mock hagiographies of Sashka Christ and Matvei Pavlichenko, so similar to each other and to "My First Goose," make Lyutov's failure more pronounced.

Lyutov's acceptance by the Cossacks is inevitably short-lived, for Lyutov is incapable of joining them on their own terms. By the time he is helplessly torturing the horse Argamak in the final story of the cycle, Lyutov at least subconsciously has lowered his sights to an attainable goal:

he dreams not of close friendship with the Cossacks, but of their benign indifference. Earlier in the book, however, Lyutov strives to win the Cossacks' friendship, and this is his fundamental error. In "Argamak," the squadron commander disparages Lyutov for trying to live without enemies, but this reproach implies an equally valid antipode: Lyutov's search for friends is in vain. Lyutov mistakes the bonds between the Cossacks for friendship, when in fact they are the less personally demanding, and thus theoretically more accessible, ties of comradeship.

Here we recall the definition of comradeship offered by J. Glenn Gray: comradeship is a collective phenomenon entailing the "suppression of self-awareness," while friendship is based on a "heightened awareness of self" and is thus intensely individual (Gray 90). Gray's analysis is virtually tailor-made for *Red Cavalry*. Lyutov, who never attains true comradeship with the Cossacks, can only marvel at their feats of bravery and impulses to self-sacrifice. Gray explains these very phenomena in terms of war's mysterious appeal. Comradeship arises when people (for Gray's purposes, men) are united for a common goal, overcoming specific obstacles. Gray theorizes that humans are characterized by "a genuine longing for community" that is difficult to achieve in normal conditions. "Some extreme experience—mortal danger or the threat of destruction—is necessary to bring us fully together with our comrades or with nature." United by common aims and common dangers, these men are "true comrades only when each is ready to give up his life for the other." Thus Gray finds that comrades, whose connection is "ecstatic" and collective, are far more likely to lay down their lives for one another than friends, whose bonds do not depend on the shared threat of death. Comrades are consoled by the feeling that after their death, "that which is real in me goes forward and lives on in the comrades for whom I gave up my physical life." Death for men united by comradeship "can be shared as few others of life's great moments can be" (45–47).

Lyutov, who in a later story would prove unable to put his mutilated comrade Dolgushov out of his misery, experiences the closeness of a shared death only in "The Rebbe's Son." In the last moments of Ilya's life, Lyutov talks to him for the first time, and yet Lyutov feels an unmistakable kinship for Ilya. Their closeness is underscored by the story's last sentence: "I took in the last breath of my brother" (*Ia prinial poslednii vzdokh moego brata*) (2: 129). Babel leaves no doubt that something of Ilya is, indeed, passed on to Lyutov in that moment. And, most important, after Ilya's death, Lyutov proceeds to write about the experience to a third party, preserving Ilya's memory and spreading the word of his demise.

Gray also helps shed light on the eroticism of Lyutov's relationship with the Cossacks. Though Gray by no means considers comradeship and sexual love to be identical, he nonetheless finds that they share the same emotional range. Comradeship demands a sacrifice of individual identity for the sake of the group, and in this it resembles erotic love: "Friends do not seek to lose their identity, as comrades and erotic lovers do" (90). Both lovers and comrades are united by a "destructive dynamic." Each relationship is "ecstatic," relying on a peak experience. Both comrades and sexual lovers attain an intimacy based on the destruction of the "walls of self" (90–93). Here we recall the erotic nature of Lyutov's "courtship" of the Cossacks. Lyutov is fascinated by the virility of the Cossacks and repeatedly finds himself in situations where he is metaphorically in a female position in relation to them. To become one with the Cossacks means to give up that part of Lyutov's self that differs from them, to surrender to their influence. The same intimacy is demanded by both comradeship and sexual love, and Lyutov, whose experience with both is apparently rather limited, feels the attraction of comradeship in erotic terms.

JEWISH MOTHERS

As a community, Babel's Cossacks are determined enemies of femininity and feminization. As Lyutov tries to prove himself "manly" enough for his fellow soldiers, he is hampered not only by his Judaism, but by the manner in which Judaism anchors him in the family and the feminine. "The Rebbe" ("Rabbi"), one of the three particularly "Jewish" stories in the cycle, begins with a speech in praise of the mother. Such a sentiment could hardly be more of a contrast to the atmosphere of "My First Goose," in which women serve only to be degraded by men. "The Rebbe" and "My First Goose" are mirror images of one another: each presents the encounter of an outsider with an all-male group, yet the characters and ideals of the communities appear diametrically opposed.³⁵ Gedali's initial speech about the mother directs us to the feature that both unites and divides the Cossack and Hasidic male communities: the function of women.

In both "The Rebbe" and "My First Goose," Lyutov is presented to a male group by another man. "The Rebbe," like the previous story, fits the pattern of a rite of passage: Lyutov is led to an unfamiliar place, passes a test, and is welcomed into the community. In many rituals the initiate is given a new name, but here Lyutov apparently loses his. The rebbe simply calls him "the Jew" (*evrei*), and Reb Mordechai addresses him as "my dear young man" (*moi dorogoi i takoi molodoi chelovek*) (2: 36). Lyutov's loss of his own name serves a dual function: it heightens the sense that he has entered a completely different world, but also shows his anonymity as one in a group that values his ethnicity above all else. Here the similarity with "My First Goose" ends. In the previous story, Lyutov had to overcome his own nature and perform a difficult task in the hope of gaining acceptance, while in "The Rebbe" such acceptance is a foregone conclusion. Lyutov earned his right to join the Hasidim at their Sabbath by the very fact of his Jewish birth. The rebbe's questions merely confirm that he is allowing a good man into his home. Rather than having to kill or rape, Lyutov is asked to prove himself on familiar ground. All he need do is show that he is a learned man, the very sort who is fair game to the Cossacks of his regiment.

Like the Cossacks, the Hasidim traditionally sublimate sexuality and redirect it according to the dictates of the male group. In an essay about Hasidic sexuality, David Biale notes the paradox of a group almost exclusively composed of married men who strive to channel their sexual impulses through prayer. Hasidism's antisexual ethic led inevitably to misogyny: "Because sexuality was so threatening, women became guilty by association, and were identified as metaphors for sexual contamination" (Biale 24). Eroticism was displaced onto the Shekhina, the female aspect of God. The founder of Hasidism, the Baal Shem Tov, wrote that "[p]rayer is a form of intercourse with the Shekhina" (Biale 88). Thus sexuality, debased as an activity in daily life, is exalted to a form of communion with the divine. By the same token, flesh-and-blood women were disdained as impure, but the abstract, fleshless female ideal was glorified.

Hasidism, then, fits the pattern of male societies featured in early Soviet fiction: a group of basically celibate men who are comfortable with women only when they are elevated to the realm of pure abstraction. Babel's Cossacks conform to this model less than the other examples in this book. Unlike Platonov's Chevengurians or Olesha's celibate Komsomol members, the Cossacks of *Red Cavalry* engage in sexual contacts with women. Women, however, are secondary to the solidarity of the male group and despised on more than one occasion as liars, traitors, and thieves. Indeed, Babel's Cossacks appear more virulently misogynistic than the men of either Platonov or Olesha, for they appear at first glance to totally lack a female ideal. Yet glimpses of such an ideal do show through on occasion, such as the respect for the fallen Cossack's mother in "The Widow." Traditionally, the Cossack myth in Russian literature features a female abstraction of its own: the fiancée-steppe, the mother-*sech'*. (Kornblatt 61). If this element is missing in Babel's work, it is perhaps because the steppe and the *sech'* themselves are absent.

Gedali's monologue, like the works of Olesha and Platonov, is a paean to the Eternal Feminine that nonetheless draws attention to the self-contradictory dynamic behind the myth: "Everything is mortal. Only the mother is destined for eternal life. And when the mother is no longer among the living, she leaves behind memories of herself, which no one has yet dared to profane. The memory of the mother fills us with compassion, like the ocean, the boundless ocean fills the rivers that cut across the universe" (2: 35). Gedali's first three sentences are a chain of contradictions. He asserts that "all is mortal," to which he allows only a single exception (the mother), only to proceed to discuss the legacy of the mother once she is no longer among the living. Talk of "the mother" quickly turns to discussion of "memory of the mother." The physical woman who was once the mother, is, like all humans, mortal, but she is not important here. Rather, it is her memory in the hearts of living men that remains forever. No mention is made of the living mother. In Gedali's monologue, the mother is both immortal and dead from the very beginning. She plays a crucial role in the lives of men, but only once she has ceased to be a physical presence and turned into a constantly felt absence. When she becomes a memory, she is transformed from an individual mother into the very principle of motherhood: she is like an amorphous, "immeasurable ocean" that continually feeds its rivers.

Gedali compares this abstract idea of motherhood, the "soul of the mother" that achieves immortality only in death, with Hasidism: "In the passionate edifice of Hasidism all the windows and doors have been knocked out, but it is immortal, like the soul of the mother . . . With dripping eye sockets, Hasidism still stands on the crossroads of history" (2: 35). Both metaphors Gedali chooses for Hasidism suggest that it is a moribund casualty of violence: Hasidism is a vandalized building and an eyeless man. But Hasidism is like the mother: no matter what happens to the physical body, the soul remains eternal. In arguing for the immortality of his faith, Gedali identifies it with a feminine principle. Here one recalls Gedali's previous characterization of the revolution, a feminine noun in Russian, which, in Gedali's description, becomes a woman whom he struggles to understand. If Gedali's understanding of Hasidism is as muddled as his conception of revolution, the description of the eternally present, abstract soul of the mother could be an idiosyncratic understanding of the Shekhina. To him, both the International and Hasidism are movements of good people, bound together by the feminine ideals of revolution and the mother.

Gedali's comparison of Hasidism to the soul of the mother raises an issue that is at the heart of Lyutov's difficulties with the Cossacks. Numerous critics see Lyutov's personal dilemma in *Red Cavalry* as the conflict between Cossack and Jew, treating the work in terms of a fundamental dichotomy.[36] One set of binary oppositions leads to another, and the Cossack-Jew dichotomy becomes the basis for an entire series of contrasting terms. Gender is invariably one of these terms. Louis Iribarne finds that the "world of the protagonist . . . is divided into two irreconcilable opposites: Jew and Cossack, the 'goat and the lion,' which stand for femininity versus masculinity, peace through violence" (67). In other words, Cossacks are masculine and Jews are feminine. The evidence of *Red Cavalry* both rejects and supports such a notion. As discussed above, the Hasidim are a male community that is structurally similar to the Cossacks. Judith Kornblatt asserts that the "surface depiction of the Jews . . . as puny, dirty, and dying" belies that fact that "Babel nonetheless endows them with much of the Cossack myth. . . . The Cossacks and the Jews of *Red Cavalry* share a vital trait: a direct connection with the elemental power of existence" (115). The Cossacks, in turn, are not totally without a feminine side, as demonstrated by the example of the perfumed Savitsky.

Nevertheless, the *Red Cavalry* stories repeatedly show Jews to be passive, domestic, and, by implication, feminine. The indoor-outdoor opposition of the cycle's first story is repeated in "The Rebbe." As in "Crossing the Zbrucz," the Jews of "The Rebbe" are shown in a domestic, enclosed setting, while the narrator's attention returns to the untamable Cossacks: "The rebbe blessed the food, and we sat down to eat. Outside the window horses neighed and Cossacks shouted. The desert of war was yawning outside the window" (2: 38). If Lyutov's attention is drawn to the Polish Jew's lack of virility, it is partly because these Jews so sharply differ from the southern Jews of Lyutov's home. The Jews Lyutov meets in his travels are "narrow-shouldered" (*uzkoplechie*), with "long and bony backs, with those yellow and tragic beards. In their passionate features, so torturously carved, there is no fat and no warm beat of blood" (2: 43). Even these weak Jews have a hidden strength, however. Their "secret hatred for the *pan* is limitless." In Lyutov's thoughts, the Galician and Volhyn Jews are both victims and, after a fashion, resistance fighters. Lyutov remembers stories of rabbis and talmudists who own taverns and work as moneylenders and of "girls who were raped by Polish troopers and for whose sake Polish magnates shot themselves" (2: 43). This last comparison is particularly telling, for it once again brings together Jews and femininity, but it presents a picture of the Jew as both victimized and triumphant.

On the surface, *Red Cavalry* seems to support the notion that Jews are essentially effeminate. Lyutov is made constantly aware that he lacks the vital strength of the Cossacks, and it is perhaps the narrator's discomfort with himself as a Jew among Cossacks that makes him see his fellow Jew as weak. This, however, is Lyutov's initial impression, one that is routinely exposed as a fallacy. The ruined, apparently matriarchal house in "Crossing the Zbrucz" holds the body of an old Jewish male of undeniable courage. The weak Galician Jews Lyutov sees on the road fought, in their fashion, the authority of the Polish *pans*. The equation of Jews with femininity was an idea with many popular spokesmen in Babel's time, but the author does not content himself with such a simple outlook.[37]

Babel's last word on Judaism and femininity was originally the culmination of the *Red Cavalry* cycle: "The Rebbe's Son." This is a man's story, in which the once-exalted feminine is relegated to a secondary role. The Sabbath, which in traditional Judaism is often equated to a bride, crushes stars with a "red heel" more appropriate to a streetwalker.[38] Only two women actually appear in the story, and these "fat-breasted typists" with "the crooked legs of uncomplicated females" (*krivye nogi nezateilivykh samok*) accentuate the indignity of Ilya's final moments by carrying his "shy body" and "dryly observing his private parts" (2: 128). Again women function as witnesses, but this time the act of gazing, rather than reducing the women to helpless passivity, humiliates the object.

It is the much-venerated mother, however, who suffers the most categorical demotion. Gedali praised the mother for her endless capacity to nurture, but Ilya, who was earlier compared to a newly apprehended escaped prisoner, sees the other side of the coin. The mother is a detaining force that prevents the son from realizing his independent destiny. Ilya had been in the party when Lyutov met him, but could not bring himself to abandon his mother. To the man of war, the mother is an obstacle that must be overcome; when Ilya is drafted, he realizes that "[d]uring a revolution, a mother is just an episode" (*Mat' v revoliutsii—epizod*) (2: 129). The contrast between Ilya's words and Gedali's is striking: in the mother, Ilya sees only an "episode" where Gedali finds "eternal life."

By relegating his mother to a secondary role, Ilya breaks the last ties he had with the family he had already rejected. For if Ilya turns away from the maternal embrace, he does not choose father over mother. The chain-smoking Ilya, who in "The Rebbe" defiles the Sabbath with his cigarettes, is, in the words of the beggar Mordechai, the "accursed son, the last son, the insubordinate son" (2: 36). In "The Rebbe's Son," Lyutov echoes Mordechai, referring to Ilya as the "last prince of the dynasty" (2: 128). Yet both utterances precede Ilya's death; Mordechai in particular could have no knowledge that Ilya would die childless. Nonetheless, Ilya is shown to be the family's last generation, as well as its antagonist, from his very first appearance. Each story hints at Ilya's sterility, or at least his abstinence: in the first, he has the "sickly face of a nun," while in the second, the typists stare at his "puny, curly manhood of a withered Semite" (2: 36, 129). As the cycle was originally conceived, *Red Cavalry* starts with the persistence of fertility in the face of death and violence and ends with the death of an entire family line. Throughout the book, Babel presents the reader with scenes of sterility and parodies of sex and fertility: the eunuchs, winking madonnas, and semen-oozing crucifixes of "The Church in Novograd"; the grotesque Deborah, who vomits on her husband during their wedding night ("Pan Apolek"); young Sashka Christ's sexual encounter with a syphilitic old beggar; the old countess in "Berestechko" who beats her son for not producing any heirs; the baby who turns out to be a bag of salt ("Salt"); and Dyakov's sexually charged conquest of the exhausted nag.[39] The death of Ilya is the final mockery of the family and the family line. Ilya breathes his last on a train full of strangers, comforted not by a mother, who is only an episode, or by a father, who embodies the unbearable weight of tradition, but by a "brother" who is no blood relation to him at all.[40] In this respect, Babel is truly a product of his time. Like the early Platonov, Babel elevates freely chosen, affiliative ties at the expense of the traditional family. Platonov lived long enough to change his stance on the family, and in Olesha's finest work the much-maligned family avenges itself on those who underestimate the value of filial bonds. Babel, however, reduces the status of the family unequivocally.[41]

The family, though dislodged from its authority, is not replaced purely by communist ideology or military comradeship, though each has its role to play. The death of a soldier in the arms of his comrade is the stuff of military legend, perhaps the most exalted intimacy among men. Lyutov inhales "the last breath of his brother," taking within himself Ilya's last vital force. Life "passes from male to male," with no need for a female intermediary (Kornblatt 115). This all-male pietà provides Lyutov with the brotherhood he looked for, but could not find, among the Cossacks and the Hasidim. The closeness of the two men transcends each category precisely because neither of them could be completely encompassed by one group or the other. Thus Ilya's death scene does more than "stress the Hasidic male's self-sufficiency" (Kornblatt 115), since neither one of them can be contented with being merely a Jew or merely a Cossack.[42] Lyutov and Ilya have taken a page from Gedali's book. Gedali refused to see the revolution in terms of Reds and Whites, longing for an "International of Good People" that transcends conventional categories.[43] When Lyutov sorts Ilya's personal belongings, he sees that Ilya has thrown together seemingly irreconcilable opposites into one small trunk. Ilya is both a party agitator and a Jewish poet, and he travels with portraits of both Lenin and Maimonides. Ilya has managed to put the Song of Songs and revolver cartridges side by side. If his personal effects are any indication, Ilya has managed to reconcile the conflict that has nagged at Lyutov from the cycle's first pages.[44]

For a man who has discovered a new, middle path, Ilya is aptly named. "Ilya" is the Russian equivalent of the Hebrew "Eliahu," or Elijah, the Hebrew prophet whose reappearance heralds the coming of the messiah.[45] In keeping with his ability to reconcile opposites, Ilya is replete with both Jewish and Christian symbolism. He dies having revealed a new way, leaving behind men who will tell of his final moments. "The Rebbe's Son" is like apostolic writings, spreading the word of Ilya in epistolary form. Alone among all the stories narrated by Lyutov, this one is a letter to a heretofore-unmentioned Vasily.[46] The reader is told almost nothing about Vasily, but what little is mentioned makes it possible to include him as another "brother" to Lyutov and Ilya. On a night almost identical to the one portrayed in "The Rebbe,"[47] Vasily accompanied Lyutov on a visit to Motale Bratslavsky, and together they saw the picture of the rebbe's son hanging like an icon over the Torah. The introduction of Vasily is jarring: suddenly Lyutov has a comrade who shares his interests and joins him in his explorations.

On the narrative level, Vasily serves as a counterbalance to Ilya. "The Rebbe's Son" begins with Lyutov recounting a story to Vasily and ends with Lyutov listening to Ilya tell his own tale. In the first half of the story, Lyutov calls Vasily by name five times, underscoring the fact that the story has a specific audience while making the narration resemble a letter to a friend or an oral tale.[48] When Lyutov sees Ilya, he refers to Vasily by name for the last time (*"Ia uznal ego totchas, Vasilii"*) (2: 129). Now Ilya dominates the story, and it is his name that Lyutov invokes three times. Lyutov's repeated use of Ilya's name, combined with Ilya's own repetitions of Lyutov's words, elevates their dialogue to the point that it resembles a prayer or a catechism:

> . . . you weren't in the party then, Bratslavsky.
> —I was in the party then, . . .

—And now, Ilya?
—A mother during a revolution is an episode. . . .
—And you were in Kovel, Ilya?
—I was in Kovel! (2: 129)

Ilya has the advantage over Vasily in that the latter is never more than an addressee, while the former can answer Lyutov's questions. These words, however, are Ilya's last, and if the dialogue is to be continued, it needs a new participant. Here Vasily is crucial, since the very fact that the story is replete with rhetorical questions Lyutov directs at Vasily begs the question of Vasily's response. As an epistolary tale, "The Rebbe's Son" opens up the narrative, directing it outward to an unseen addressee. The existence of Vasily lessens the despair of the story's end, for it implies that there is someone else besides Lyutov who can mourn Ilya's passing while finding value in his example.

The story's form also serves another function: it calls attention to the status of Lyutov's words *as writing*. The reader's awareness of this fact is critical to an understanding of Lyutov's relationship to Ilya. Ilya's belongings show that he can support the baggage of both his revolutionary ideology and his Jewish cultural background, combining the two in one small trunk. These are the signs of Ilya's spiritual kinship with Lyutov. If one sees Lyutov as merely the narrator of the *Red Cavalry* tales rather than their writer, then Lyutov is at a distinct disadvantage. In no single story does Lyutov show his own capacity to reconcile the nagging dichotomy between his Jewish past and his Cossack present. At times he appears triumphant, but his victories are fleeting and involve adaptation rather than reconciliation. As a character in *Red Cavalry*, Lyutov does not solve his dilemma, but as its "author," he is no less able to embrace duality than Ilya. Ilya's trunk is a metaphor for *Red Cavalry* itself: the contrast between "My First Goose" and "The Rebbe" is no less striking than the juxtaposition of Lenin's portrait with that of Maimonides.

If the dichotomies of *Red Cavalry*, along with Lyutov's search for community, can be said to have a "resolution," it is not because opposites have been successfully reconciled, but because the narrator has seen (and shown his reader) that the path of unqualified commitment is illusory. Ilya has taken decisive action, ultimately dying for the revolution, but not at the cost of his cultural heritage or individual identity. Lyutov, too, has made a firm political choice, but one that does not transform him into a different type of human being. For all his squeamishness and alienation, Lyutov writes for *The Red Cavalryman,* not for a White publication. The path of Lyutov and Ilya depends on the constant tension between opposites rather than on total dedication to an all-encompassing idea. Just as *Red Cavalry* contains both "My First Goose" and "The Rebbe," so Ilya and Lyutov (and perhaps Vasily) cannot be completely themselves without both *shtetl* and *sech'*.

Lyutov calls Ilya his "brother," but his choice of words is a metaphor rather than the assertion of a biological fact.[49] Like the Bolsheviks, Lyutov chooses a man unrelated to him as the object of emotions usually reserved for a biological relative. If Lyutov and Ilya are not blood relations, neither are they friends, strictly speaking; Lyutov and Ilya do not know each other well enough to be true friends. Instead, they are united by their common circumstances: both are men who straddle the line between two cultures, yet choose to fight on the side of the revolution. Lyutov and Ilya have not had the opportunity to learn about each other's personalities; all they know is that they have both come from similar backgrounds and made similar choices. The potential for friendship, which Gray believes is based on "an intellectual and emotional affinity" (89), is certainly present, but the realities of war prevent it from beginning. If death interferes with their possible friendship, however, it serves only to advance the feeling of comradeship. After all, the bond between Lyutov and Ilya cannot be subjected to further testing. Perhaps the greatest irony of Lyutov's declaration of his "brotherhood" with Ilya and his implied connection to Vasily is that Lyutov's bond to each of these two men resembles the most successful model for heterosexual ties discussed in the previous chapter: one of the objects of Lyutov's affection is distant, while the other is dead.

ARRESTED DEVELOPMENT: MASCULINITY, CYCLICITY, AND THE PROBLEM OF ENDINGS

Red Cavalry is unique in early Soviet fiction in that it approaches masculinity as more than a theme; in Babel's cycle of stories, the question of masculinity becomes a question of genre. One can, of course, argue that most war stories are inherently "masculine" tales, both for their preoccupation with male heroics and for their enduring popularity among young men and boys; hence the Russian cliché that when schoolchildren read *War and Peace,* the boys like the "war" parts and the girls like the "peace" parts. Yet stories of war do not necessarily have to posit masculinity as a problem; on the contrary, the more "heroic" and optimistic the tale, the more likely that the hero's manhood will be treated as a given. In such works, the hero has either long since "proven" himself a man, or his rugged character leaves little doubt that he will offer such proof by the story's end. Here one recalls Bakhtin's definition of the hero's image in the ancient Greek romance: the hero's identity has already been formed and is immune to change; through the course of the novel, he will be tested, but he will always pass the test (Bakhtin 86–110).

Babel's *Red Cavalry,* however, offers what might seem to be an antithetical case. The identity of Lyutov, the novel's central figure, is inherently unstable: torn between the world of his Jewish father and that of his revolutionary comrades, he is at home in neither. Moreover, if the hero of the Greek romance is bound to overcome every obstacle that the narrative throws in his path, Lyutov (a postrevolutionary incarnation of the eternal Jewish schlemiel) can be counted upon to fail every test. Yet Lyutov's propensity for failure is obscured by the structure of *Red Cavalry;* in a given story, Lyutov might appear to succeed, but subsequent stories imply that every short-term success is actually a long-term failure.

But one wonders if success and failure are even appropriate concepts within the context of *Red Cavalry.* Babel's stories simply do not work as a sequential, biographical, conventionally novelistic depiction of the narrator's life. Events in one story are not always reflected in another; inconsistencies abound, and, more important, any sense of resolution offered by a particular story is undermined by subsequent events. Lyutov's fundamental dilemma (his desire to prove his manhood and find a lasting place in the Cossack male community) is a priori unresolvable, and the proliferation of short-term resolutions only accentuates the long-term open-endedness of the cycle. At the end of "My First Goose," Lyutov appears to have gained the acceptance of his fellow soldiers, but in the very next story he is looking for companionship among the local Hasidim. At the end of "The Rebbe's Son," Lyutov has found a "brother," yet in "Argamak" we find him back at square one, replaying the battle for acceptance that he seemed to have won in "My First Goose." Equally jarring is Lyutov's retelling of the events of "The Rebbe" in the beginning of "The Rebbe's Son"; now it seems that the mysterious "Vasily" had accompanied Lyutov in "The Rebbe," although Lyutov's interrogation by the rebbe makes sense only if Lyutov has come alone (Avins 708). In *Red Cavalry*, understanding accrues not so much from story to story as from the juxtaposition of local "truths" that cannot be assembled into a thoroughly consistent narrative. Rather than being a new element of a coherent sequence, each new story is, to a large extent, a revision of the ones that preceded it, requiring that the reader view prior episodes in a new light.

This cannot help but have an effect on the outcome of any given attempt by Lyutov to "prove" himself by undergoing a rite of passage. It is appropriate that such rites are also called life-*cycle* rituals, for by moving the initiate from one state to another (boyhood to manhood, bachelorhood to marriage), they ensure their own perpetuation. Yet Babel's story cycle appears to struggle with the life cycle, even when the subject is someone other than Lyutov. If the stories of Sashka Christ and Matvei Pavlichenko have all the trappings of a tribal manhood rite (sexual initiation, physical separation and reincorporation, the endurance of pain, and the rejection of the mother), it is a rite of passage into a new, extrabiological state. The move made by Sashka Christ is implicitly a dead end, a disruption of the cyclicity of generations: he wants to join the shepherds because "all the saints came from shepherds" (2: 51). Saints, of course, are typically ascetics, who do not have families, and as Marcia Morris argues, the ascetic follows a different narrative pattern from that of the canonical hero: if the canonical hero follows Joseph Campbell's pattern of separation-initiation-return, the ascetic hero refuses to return (Morris 4). Moreover, Sashka is immediately hired by the Cossacks, a group whose literary representation is connected to the monastic tradition: "Implicitly or explicitly, several texts suggest that entrance into the Cossack community resembles tonsure" (Kornblatt 62). In a traditional society, the manhood rite does not signal freedom from the father and the family, but rather the potential for equality with the father in a family of one's own; living in the "men's hut" with other bachelors is only a stopping point on a path that leads inevitably to family life.[50]

Presumably, a wartime army also provides only a short-term separation from the domestic context, for the lucky survivors can expect to go home and start families of their own. But the affiliative structures of *Red Cavalry* have a suggestion of greater permanence to them: first, because the soldiers are Cossacks, and literary or mythic Cossacks manage to perpetuate their group without accepting the bonds of domesticity (see the introduction). Second, Budyonny's army is fighting no ordinary war; since the revolution promised to destroy the traditional family, some extreme partisans of War Communism felt that the comradely relations of war could be extended into peacetime, thus permanently cementing the warrior bond. Finally, the very structure of *Red Cavalry*, as well as the history of its composition, offers some support to the War Communist worldview by portraying a conflict that has no end in sight, a permanent war: Babel is meticulous in conveying the progress made by Budyonny's army in space, but he is not so clear about the army's progress in time. Though Bolshevik Russia's adventure in Poland would end with the Treaty of Riga on 18 March 1921, the stories themselves give little indication that the war might be coming to a close. The relatively brief Russian Civil War (and even briefer conflict with Poland) is stretched into an inexhaustible period of cyclical time, into which episode after episode can be inserted without bringing the war itself any closer to its resolution.[51] Though an endless war might hold little appeal for the civilian population, it bodes well for the continued cohesion of the warrior collective. When distinguishing between comradeship and friendship, J. Glenn Gray observes that wartime comradeship feels as though it will last forever but usually fades not long after the war is over (Gray 89). The task of the new regime in general, and of the romantic proponents of permanent War Communism in particular, was to transform comradeship from a conditional, ephemeral phenomenon into an enduring social structure. But if Babel's story cycle freezes wartime comradeship into place, it also freezes Kirill Lyutov out: the endless civil war (historical cyclicity) is mirrored by Lyutov's endless quest for belonging (personal cyclicity).

Red Cavalry frustrates both Lyutov's and the reader's expectation of lasting results, especially when the collection is viewed as a whole. Because the *Red Cavalry* stories, most of which were originally published separately in a variety of Soviet journals, are usually arranged in a specific order and deal with a recurring cast of characters, there is a strong temptation to read them as chapters in a novel rather than as short stories. Such a reading implies progression, development, and closure; yet the history of *Red Cavalry*'s composition and publication points toward the opposite conclusion. Babel was a notorious perfectionist, a rewriter who put his works through repeated drafts before allowing them to be published. Though all but two of the stories were first printed in a three-year interval (from 1923 to 1926), Babel would return to the cycle long after it was first collected in book form. If the author's motivations for his later additions to *Red Cavalry* were artistic as well as political, Babel must have felt that he could add new episodes to Lyutov's adventures without damaging the cycle's integrity. This willingness to embellish on a long-completed work even extended to the cycle's ending: the first six versions of the collection end with "The Rebbe's Son," while the seventh and eighth editions (the last to be published during the author's lifetime) conclude with "Argamak." Though the two "endings" would appear to be mutually contradictory, Babel did not replace "The Rebbe's Son" with "Argamak"; rather, he simply added another story, one whose events are difficult to reconcile with the book's chronology.

As a result, we are left with two, or perhaps even three, *Red Cavalries*: one ending with "The Rebbe's Son," the second ending with "Argamak," and the third, somewhat more problematically, ending with "The Kiss." "The Rebbe's Son" appears to be the preferred ending among Babel scholars, and it is easy to see why: it is this story that provides an illusion of closure. Indeed, I would argue that a coherent reading of *Red Cavalry* requires the reader to approach "The Rebbe's Son" initially as "the ending," if only to better understand the role of "Argamak." Stopping with "The Rebbe's Son" affords us a convenient perspective for examining the major motifs and themes with which the cycle began, including the questions of male relationships that are the primary concern of the present study.

Yet the opposition between fathers and brothers or comrades frames only one version of the cycle, and to insist on this framework as the single organizing principle would be to do violence to Babel's own unrelentingly violent text. More than a decade after Babel finished his own travels with the Soviet cavalry, the author decided to put his hero through his paces yet another time. All editions of *Red Cavalry* that have appeared since 1932 end with "Argamak," the story of Lyutov's attempts to learn to ride the uncontrollable horse that gave this story its name. Like most of Lyutov's adventures, "Argamak" is a tale of simultaneous losses and gains: his riding style, so different from that of Argamak's previous Cossack owner, all but ruins the horse, but his experience with the horse teaches Lyutov proper technique and allows him to ride like his fellow soldiers when he moves on to a new regiment. One critic has suggested that political pressure obliged Babel to make the cycle end "more optimistically," although any optimism the story contains is muted at best.[52] Certainly, "Argamak" represents a shift in thematic emphasis: where "The Rebbe's Son" focuses on creating a communal identity based partly on one's past (i.e., Lyutov's and Ilya's Jewish roots), "Argamak" is concerned with the capacity to forge bonds based on demonstrated ability and a shared warrior ethos. Moreover, if "The Rebbe's Son" develops the theme of fathers and sons, "Argamak" is a final exploration of the bond between a man and his horse, another theme that runs throughout the cycle. The Cossacks in *Red Cavalry* become far more emotional about their relationships with their horses than about those with other men (let alone women): Vasily Kurdyukov's concern over the well-being of his horse Styopa is particularly jarring when set against the story of the deaths of his brothers and father. Savitsky's expropriation of Commander Khlebnikov's beautiful stallion leads not only to a falling-out between the two men, but even causes Khlebnikov to leave the party ("The Story of a Horse" and "The Story of a Horse, Continued"). The death of Afonka Bida's horse is rightfully seen by all his comrades as a great personal tragedy: "A horse [*kon'*] is a friend," one of them declares. "A horse is a father," respond another. "He saves your life countless times. Bida will be lost without his horse" ("Afonka Bida" 2: 84). The words chosen to describe the horse's importance only emphasize the gap between Lyutov and the Cossacks, for it is both a father and a friend that Lyutov so clearly lacks. Throughout most of "Argamak," Lyutov's alienation from the bond between Cossack and horse is made painfully manifest by the open wounds his poor riding inflicts on his unruly mount. Ultimately, Lyutov learns how to ride, but there is no sense in the text's final paragraph that the horse itself comes to hold any kind of emotional meaning for him; instead, he is simply able to ride without attracting the hostile stares of his fellow soldiers. "Argamak" tells the story of a purely superficial assimilation to the ways of the Cossacks.

And what are we to make of the tale that may be the third and final ending of the cycle, "The Kiss"? Babel originally published this story in 1937, one year before his arrest. It was first included in a Czech edition of *Red Cavalry*, and the editor of the 1990 two-volume edition of Babel's works includes it as the final story in the cycle. Patricia Carden also argues for the story's role as a "third alternative ending" (Carden 196). In terms of the cycle's chronology, however, "The Kiss" seems as though it should be placed before the end: its setting, Budyatichi, is also the setting of "The Song," which immediately precedes "The Rebbe's Son." Indeed, "The Kiss" shares so many traits with "The Song" that one might call it a variation on the earlier story; in both "The Kiss" and "The Song," Lyutov and another man are billeted with a young woman and her child, and in both stories, the landlady is seduced. Here, however, all resemblance ends: in "The Song," it is Sashka Christ who sleeps with the landlady, while in "The Kiss," the eternally frustrated Kirill Lyutov finally proves his manhood in the bedroom. Here the landlady, Elizaveta Alekseevna Tomlina, is an educated woman with a five-year-old son and a paralyzed father. Lyutov quickly wins her trust by bragging of his education (precisely the same tactic that met with the Cossacks' scorn in "My First Goose"), and soon they make plans to move the whole family to Moscow once the war is over. Though she rebuffs his first attempts at a kiss, she herself kisses him right before he is commanded to return to his brigade. When he returns, they spend the night together, but his fellow soldier Suvortsev rouses him early in the morning and tells him it is time to leave. Lyutov never answers her insistent question, "When will you take us away from here?" the answer is provided by Lyutov's own actions: never.

"The Kiss" introduces a rare note of heterosexual passion into the homosocial world of *Red Cavalry*, suggesting that Lyutov can indeed "be a man" under the right circumstances. If "Argamak" is about learning to ride, "The Kiss" is about learning how to mount and dismount: Lyutov's successful seduction and subsequent disentanglement from Elizaveta Alekseevna are serious breaches of ethics for a Petersburg University graduate, but they are perfectly appropriate for a Cossack Red cavalryman. Moreover, even this individual triumph has its "comradely" dimension, facilitated as it is by Suvortsev, who hurries Lyutov away from the Tomlin family and any possible obligations toward them. And, finally, the story's ending leads us back to the cycle's beginning: Suvortsev wants Lyutov to leave before Elizaveta Alekseevna discovers that her father has died during the night. In "Crossing the Zbrucz," Lyutov inadvertently spends the night with a dead father; in "The Kiss," he runs off without seeing the corpse.

However one reads "Argamak," "The Rebbe's Son," and "The Kiss," the multiple endings only reinforce a plot dynamic inherent in the cycle: any sense of a final resolution is ultimately shown to be illusory. The plot's linear progress is impeded by the cyclical nature of the book. *Red Cavalry,* much like the folk genres of fairy tales, myths, and epics whose rhetoric Babel borrows to great effect, operates in a special time frame. In fairy tales, there is no sense of continuity from one story to the next. Kashchei the Deathless can be killed in one tale but will be back in the next; Ivanushka the Fool's adventures and marriage in one story do not preclude his subsequent adventures and marriages in another.[53]

This is not to say that the *Red Cavalry* stories are utterly lacking in continuity. Instead, they are a hybrid genre, of the sort described by Umberto Eco in his "The Myth of Superman" (1972). Eco argues persuasively that the hero of *Superman* comics exists in a time frame halfway between myth and novel. In myth, the story has already taken place, and the life of the hero is already known from beginning to end; the story must be in part predictable. In the modern novel, the events happen while the story is being told, thus reducing the distance between hero and reader while adding a previously unknown element of suspense (331–32). The comic book hero must embody the "totality of certain collective aspirations," becoming "immobilized in an emblematic and fixed nature which renders him easily recognizable," while at the same time "he must be subjected to a development which is typical . . . of novelistic characters"— that is, his story must unfold over time (333). Because his adventures (like

Babel's short stories) are published serially rather than as one coherent unit, the result is a compromise between time and stasis: in each particular adventure, Superman does, in fact, accomplish something, and yet, according to the temporal framework of the modern novel, this entails "a gesture which is inscribed in his past and weighs on his future. He has taken a step toward death, he has gotten older, if only by an hour; his storehouse of personal experience has irreversibly enlarged." For Superman to act, he must, like a novelistic hero, "consume" himself; yet Superman is also a myth, and his stories must continue ad infinitum. He must "remain 'inconsumable' and at the same time be 'consumed' according to the ways of everyday life" (333–34). According to Eco, Superman's story necessitates a temporal breakdown: "The very structure of time falls apart, not in the temporal sphere about which it is told, but rather, in the time in which it is told." The stories develop in an "oneiric climate, where what has happened before and what has happened after appear extremely hazy. The narrator picks up the strand of the event again and again as if he had forgotten to say something and wanted to add details to what had already been said" (335–36). The stories of Superman are not so much sequential as they are "iterative": "each event takes up again from a sort of virtual beginning" (338). Yet the result is not the utter lack of continuity to be found in folk genres; past stories did, indeed, happen, but their effect on the present (and their movement of the hero toward an inexorable, mortal future) is limited.

I would argue that a similar temporal compromise is at work in the *Red Cavalry* cycle. Some events described in one story are referred to in later ones, and Lyutov's store of knowledge about his fellow Cossacks does appear to grow. After Afonka Bida breaks off his friendship with Lyutov in "The Death of Dolgushov," the effect is felt in subsequent stories that feature both men. Other details, such as Sashka Christ's syphilis, are forgotten, even when they might have relevance to the events described in the story ("The Song"). In the case of minor inconsistencies involving supporting characters, one can argue that they are of little importance, but when taken together with the fundamental temporal paradox of Lyutov's own development, they point to the special logic of the *Red Cavalry* cycle. Nearly all the stories in which Lyutov acts rather than observes adhere to a basic plot structure: Lyutov's arrival, his confrontation with an alien group or individual, his attempt to fit in, and the attempt's success or failure. More often than not, Lyutov fails, but even when he succeeds, the results are local to the story at hand and do little or nothing to change his status at the beginning of subsequent stories. Here one recalls Eco's other example of the "iterative scheme" of episodic literature: the French hero Fantomas. At the end of each adventure, Fantomas evades capture, yet despite the money he makes through blackmail and kidnapping, "at the beginning of each episode [Fantomas] finds himself inexplicably poor and in need of money and, therefore, also of new 'action.' In this way the cycle can keep going" (340–41). By the same token, Lyutov gains the acceptance of the Cossacks at the end of "My First Goose," only to go searching for fellowship among the Hasidim of "The Rebbe." Lyutov's sense of belonging, like Fantomas's ill-gotten gains, vanishes between episodes, thus allowing the cycle to continue. If *Red Cavalry* ends with "The Rebbe's Son," then the reader can believe that Lyutov has indeed made a step forward in his search for community, that he has solved his dilemma. Yet "Argamak" only makes sense if the gains of "The Rebbe's Son" are as local as those of "My First Goose." "Argamak," too, ends with a triumph of sorts, as Lyutov has finally learned to ride like a Cossack. But the story's immediate proximity to "The Rebbe's Son" calls our attention to the limited scope of any possible success that Lyutov can achieve. Like the tales of Superman and Fantomas, *Red Cavalry* develops in an "oneiric climate" that provides only an illusion of the passage of time and that allows the hero to avoid "consuming" himself by rendering every possible character development local rather than global. Character development within a particular episode is essential; Lyutov does appear changed by the story's end. But character development within the cycle as a whole is impossible; like the heroes of Bakhtin's Greek romances, Lyutov's character is fixed throughout the story, even if his character's stability consists of its apparent instability. Lyutov, by definition, is unable to define himself, and every test Lyutov undergoes only serves to affirm Lyutov's unchanging lack of definition. Or, to put it another way, Lyutov is not a character at all, but a dilemma. For Lyutov to solve his dilemma is to move closer to death, or even to stop being Lyutov. Thus the appending of "Argamak" to Babel's cycle does not lead to optimism, as some critics have suggested, but, on the contrary, to the very essence of pessimism, since the triumph of "Argamak" implies the negation of the success of "The Rebbe's Son": nothing Lyutov does will improve his lot in subsequent episodes. A Soviet Sisyphus, Lyutov is condemned by the narrative to an unending, repetitive struggle whose successes are undone as soon as they are achieved.

Though the other examples that follow Eco's "iterative scheme" are traditionally masculine entertainments (adventure tales and superhero comics), one can easily imagine examples that are either "feminine" or gender neutral. If the genre of *Red Cavalry* is connected to masculinity, it is because the dilemma to which Babel's narrative inevitably returns (and the drama that is subsequently enacted) is a male rite of passage. Lyutov, the eternal outsider, is repeatedly required to pass some form of test in order to earn his place in a group of men. Two conclusions can be drawn from the redundancy of the testing. First, the initiation does not "take." Second, the cycle confirms the notion of masculinity best articulated by Margaret Mead and elaborated upon more recently by Bruno Bettelheim, Nancy Chodorow, and Elisabeth Badinter: that "girls and women 'are,' while boys and men 'do'; that feminine identity is 'ascribed' and masculine identity 'achieved'" (Chodorow 33). Or, as Mead puts it, "There is no exact moment at which the boy can say, 'Now I am a man,' unless society steps in and gives a definition" (175). Bettelheim elaborates upon Mead's contrast between the readily apparent signs that a girl has become a woman (menarche and childbirth) and the far less dramatic biological maturation of the man by speculating "whether men did not create the larger forms of society after they despaired of being able, by magic manipulation of their genitals, to bear children" (120). Badinter points to the male "necessity for tests" (68): though initiation rites might serve to mark the passage into manhood, masculinity can never be taken for granted. "Being a man implies a labor. . . . Manhood is not bestowed at the outset; it must be constructed, or . . . 'manufactured.' A man is therefore a sort of *artifact*, and as such he always runs the risk of being found defective" (1–2; emphasis in the original). Masculinity must therefore be constantly reaffirmed. The iterative scheme of *Red Cavalry* drives home the notion of the instability of the male character; unlike the incessant testing in more heroic genres (such as Bakhtin's Greek novel), Lyutov's trials always find him wanting. It is precisely Lyutov's inability to prove himself that keeps the cycle focused on masculinity, since the cycle's narrator, doomed by the laws of genre to "arrested development," will never overcome his almost adolescent fascination for those who never fail the test of manhood.

Chapter Three

THE FAMILY MEN OF YURI OLESHA

> It seems to me that the course of a man's fate and the development of the male character are, to a large extent, predetermined by whether or not he was attached to his father. — Yuri Olesha, "I Look into the Past" (1928)

Yuri Olesha wrote about fathers, sons, and brothers, but never simply about men. No matter how hard they try, Olesha's male characters cannot escape the context of the family. Indeed, story after story portrays its protagonists' attempts to extricate themselves from filial ties, but every effort only highlights its own futility. Biology itself is against them: every man is born a son, and most are destined to become fathers. But Olesha wrote in an era when biology, like all nature, was a frontier to be conquered, an elemental force to be reined in. If ever it seemed possible that the hackneyed fathers-and-sons issue could be resolved, that time was the 1920s.

As this chapter's epigraph shows, however, Olesha's protagonists are only too aware of the father's integral role in their lives. Both despising and needing a male parent, they typically escape from one father only to run straight into the arms of another.[1] If he cannot avoid fathers completely, Olesha's hero reserves the right, in the words of Elizabeth Beaujour, to "choose his ancestors" ("Imagination of Failure" 123). Thus the personal dramas of Olesha's characters find a common agenda with revolutionary ideology: affiliation, based on freely chosen alliances, is always preferred to filiation, bonds founded on blood relationships.

Nonetheless the revolution is far from a reliable ally in the generational struggle. Rather, the extent to which Olesha's characters can sympathize with the forces of revolution depends upon the time frame of the story at hand. If the work has a revolutionary or prerevolutionary context, then the communists function as destroyers of the old rather than builders of the new. Their struggle with the established order extends to the institution of the "bourgeois" family, and thus the rebellious son sees in them a natural partner. When the revolution is already a fait accompli, however, the balance of power shifts. Yesterday's rebels are today's orthodoxy, and the founders of the new world create institutions that are disturbingly reminiscent of the family structures they claim to abhor. It is one of Olesha's great accomplishments that his novel *Envy* (*Zavist'*) puts the fathers-and-sons issue in an entirely new light. If the would-be revolutionaries of pre-Soviet Russia were the avowed enemies of the family, Olesha's postrevolutionary communists are forced to admit that the father-son relationship is integral to their new world. In essence, if both fathers and sons are committed to creating a new society, there is no longer any reason to fight. The alliance between father and son is assured, for in *Envy* this relationship is not based on anything as unreliable as ties of blood; the men in question are not even relatives in the strict sense of the word. Instead, they choose each other freely, unfettered by the demands of kinship.

The postrevolutionary society of *Envy* is thoroughly a man's world, one that has little use for traditional femininity. The domestic sphere is under attack by men such as Andrei Babichev, who wishes to subsume the customarily female world of the kitchen under a hyperrational, coldly masculine plan. The new world, like the old, has a feminine idol, but it is an entity that nonetheless represents relentless, masculine efficiency: the machine.

Kavalerov's dilemma in *Envy* consists of his complete inability to enter into the new world's complex network of male relationships. Frustrated in his search for a new father, he is equally discouraged by his failure to establish a connection with the new world's younger generation. For if the novel's postrevolutionary society is characterized by a renewed partnership between father and son, it is even more marked by its general emphasis on male comradeship. Like so many of Olesha's protagonists, Kavalerov can only admire such comradeship from a distance. Unable to join them, he alternately fetishizes these men as beautiful, inaccessible aesthetic objects and envies them the comradeship he can never experience. Both Kavalerov and Ivan are in at a disadvantage: like the representatives of the new world, they have abandoned filial ties, but unlike them, they have yet to find a satisfactory replacement. Their attempt (and similar attempts in Olesha's other works) to come to terms with the family in general, and with the father in particular, is the subject of this chapter.

Though the main focus of this discussion will be Olesha's short novel *Envy*, this chapter starts with a close reading of "Legend" ("Legenda"). I will argue that "Legend," published in the same year as *Envy*, provides the key to understanding the relationship between fathers and sons in Olesha's novel. "Legend" shows how a rather mundane family conflict comes to a head when political events intrude. The narrator displays a "father complex" that elevates interpersonal and sexual problems to the realms of language, philosophy, and politics.

When we turn our attention to *Envy*, it becomes clear that the adult Kavalerov suffers from the same complex as the young Kolya of "Legend." There are, however, two important differences. Whereas Kolya is in silent rebellion against his biological father, Kavalerov both seeks out and resents a series of father figures. Perhaps more important, Kolya declares his intention to be different from his father while still a boy, but Kavalerov's memories of his own father, his interactions with Ivan and Andrei, and, finally, his humiliating sexual encounter with Anechka all serve to remind him that he is as much a failure as was his father. Such moments of realization happen when Kavalerov is looking in a mirror; all too often, the face that looks back at Kavalerov is disturbingly paternal.

The chapter closes with an analysis of the novel's only father-son relationship that can be considered "happy": that of Andrei Babichev and Volodya Makarov. As much as Kavalerov resents Andrei's other "offspring" (the sausage and the superkitchen), it is Volodya who has the truly "enviable" position in the Babichev household. Volodya and Andrei represent an important reevaluation of the very concept of fathers and sons: rather than being at odds with each other, both are united in their efforts to build a new world. At first Andrei finds himself hard pressed to defend his relationship with Volodya from Ivan's accusations of sentimentality, but ultimately Andrei manages to turn paternal feelings from a source of shame into an essential part of human relationships in the new society. That the "father" and "son" involved are not blood relatives makes their bond even more revolutionary: their feelings stem not from blind sentiment, but from ideological affiliation. This chapter will show that the new world of *Envy* is portrayed as an all-male "family" that is based on political choices rather than ties of blood.

"LEGEND": THE POWER OF PASSIVE RESISTANCE

In 1927, the year in which *Envy* first came to print, Olesha published a critically neglected short story called "Legend."[2] Along with "Human Material" ("Chelovecheskii material") and "I Look into the Past" ("Ia smotriu v proshloe"), both of which appeared the following year, this story is part of a fathers-and-sons cycle that treats in a few brief pages the domestic conflict that is integral to Olesha's novel. In *Envy*, the issue of paternity and filial responsibility is complicated not only by the longer work's greater variety of events and characters, but also by the unclear familial status of most of the protagonists. Father figures, rather than fathers per se, populate Olesha's novel. The stories, however, are narrated by sons of conventional nuclear families consisting of a mother, a father, and one child. One is tempted to see these narrators as Olesha's representation of his own childhood; certainly some biographical facts do coincide, but not enough to consider the works purely autobiographical.[3] While it is conceivable that Dosya and Kolya, the narrators of these stories, might grow up to be Yuri Olesha, their connection to Olesha's own life is obscured by the unreliability of Olesha's memoirs as biography.[4] It is far more profitable to posit that, having reached physical, if not emotional, maturity, Kolya and Dosya became not Olesha, but Nikolai Kavalerov and Modest Zand (the protagonist of "From the Notebooks of Fellow-Traveler Zand" ["Koe-chto iz sekretnykh zapisei poputchika Zanda," 1929]). The fact that they are namesakes ("Kolya" is a diminutive of "Nikolai" and "Dosya" is short for "Modest") conveniently reinforces this link, although there is no evidence that Olesha was consciously creating anything remotely resembling a coherent biography of either character.[5] Olesha's protagonists both function and perceive each other more as embodiments of worldviews than as actual personalities; whether he is named Dosya or Kolya, Zand or Kavalerov, the most commonly encountered Olesha hero is distinguished by his alienated, "underground" outlook and his persistent habit of "thinking in images." Kavalerov and Zand show the Olesha hero in his Soviet context: an alienated adult who awkwardly straddles the line between two worlds. Kolya and Dosya provide the opportunity to "look into the past" of this Soviet artist manqué, exposing the childhood traumas that form the background of his adult life. Upon encountering Kavalerov's father fixation in *Envy*, one might wonder about his biological father, yet the reader is privy to precious little information about him. Instead, it must be inferred from the stories.

A scant three pages long, "Legend" is the first-person account of the raid of a bourgeois home by a group of presumably revolutionary soldiers. The noise of gunfire two floors above awakens the narrator, who runs into his parents' room. The bulk of the story is structured like an official report: the narrator calmly enumerates four events, each described first in one sentence, then elaborated in the course of one or more paragraphs. First, Kolya finds his parents naked in their bed, making no effort to hide themselves. Second, he internally rebels against his father, asserting silently that he has no desire to continue the family line. Third, he sees his domestic surroundings with new eyes, repulsed by the collection of household objects that hold inordinate power over him. Fourth, he betrays his father. Initially he sees his father pathetically "flying" around the room like a chicken, then is horrified by his father's sudden, final attempt at dignity. Rather than calmly walking to his death with his parents, Kolya throws open the door, telling the soldiers to shoot, to free him from the power of the "legend" that has oppressed him all his life. At this point, Kolya falls "completely submissively into someone's hands" (I 101), aware that such excitement could be "catastrophic" to him while he is still sick with typhus. On this somewhat jarring note, the story ends.

The structure of "Legend" reflects the basic problems of family relationships that underlie all of Olesha's work. The story's four-part "list" describes a veritable father complex that is not at all unique to Kolya. Each item describes a clash with paternity in four separate spheres: the interpersonal, the sexual, the philosophical, and the political. Each aspect of the problem applies to a significant number of Olesha's characters, of which Nikolai Kavalerov is the prime example.

The first event in the narrator's four-part schema is an almost programmatic depiction of the Freudian "primal scene": Kolya finds himself in his parents' bedroom "at night, for the first time" (I 99): "Father appeared before me in a shameless state. Besides which, his actions caused Mother to be in a similar state. In order to get off the bed, Father, who had the place next to the wall, had to either roll or crawl over Mother. He crawled, dragging the blanket. Mother was left uncovered. She continued to lie there, making no attempt to hide, her consciousness eclipsed by fear" (I 99). Though the mother is presumably the object of desire in the oedipal triangle, here she, like most of Olesha's women, plays only a marginal role in the plot. Indeed, even the furniture in "Legend," alternately cajoling and intimidating the narrator, is more active than Kolya's mother. It is the father who displays both himself and the mother; the latter meekly allows herself to be displayed. She is merely an object or place that the father must cross (*perelezt'*) in order to be free of the bed, which, as readers of *Envy* know, is a particularly seductive and inescapable item of furniture in Olesha's world. The mother makes no attempt to hide her nudity, "her consciousness eclipsed by fear."

The young narrator finds himself in a situation that is typical for Olesha's protagonists: his narrators are obsessive spectators who have honed their powers of observation to a fine art but are themselves incapable of action. Twice in rapid succession, Kolya states that he saw his parents' bedroom at night, thus shifting the emphasis to Olesha's favorite of the five senses: vision. In Olesha's work, the observer is the man who fails to act and is thus burdened with a sense of crushing inferiority when faced with a man of action. The soccer scene in *Envy* is perhaps the most famous example of the observer's plight: Kavalerov persistently watches not only the soccer match, but also Valya and Babichev as they, too, watch the game. But when the ball is, literally, in his court, he proves incapable of the slightest movement, let alone of picking up the ball and returning it to the playing field. As a spectator, Kavalerov is *vne igry* ("out of the game"), always observing but never acting.[6]

In "Legend," Kolya is confronted with a similar problem, one that also threatens his sense of himself as a (growing) man. Though the soldiers are the initial cause of the story's events, it is the father who has put both the mother and the son in an awkward position from which they make no attempt to extricate themselves. In the introduction to his collection *The Fictional Father,* Robert Con Davis posits the "seduction of the son into relationship" as a part of a primal narrative process that exists before the onset of the oedipal triangle:

> The son faces a crisis, for subsequent to this primal seduction is an inevitable betrayal in the staging of a primal scene. Here, without warning, what was a surrender to the father (in passivity) is turned around and becomes an act of aggression by the father (directed, perhaps, in fantasy toward the mother), one that prohibits desire out of relation to the father and the seeking of narcissistic, pre-paternal (maternal) satisfactions: that is, having found the father as the route to the satisfaction the mother represents, the son may not abandon him. (Davis 9–10)

If the mother is the object of desire, she can be found only through the father and the law the father represents. In this light, Kolya's father's exposure of his and his wife's nudity does not at all undermine paternal authority. Instead, the father's power is reinforced by the revelation of his sexual relationship to the desired mother. In "Legend," however, the nudity of Kolya's parents constitutes their demotion from the status of "legend" to mere flesh. Ultimately, the effect of this "primal scene" on the father's status is determined by the story's outcome. Had Kolya meekly accepted his father's primacy, the initial revelation of the parents in bed would, indeed, only serve to underscore the father's "possession" of the mother. But the effect on Kolya is quite different: unmoved by pity, he issues a mental challenge to his father and in the end betrays him to the forces that would destroy familial authority altogether.

It is the father's actions that result in the mother's nudity, but Kolya alone shoulders the responsibility for the resulting scene. The parents have failed to console one another, and the child feels that it is his responsibility to step in. Yet he feels no pity for his parents and thus does nothing to restore his mother's dignity or "bring back his [father's] composure" (*samoobladanie*). This last word is significant, for the father has lost control over himself and thus, as we shall see, has lost his authority. The child does not submissively try to return them to their former roles, and this constitutes Kolya's initial rebellion. Hence Kolya's passivity is not only a shortcoming and source of shame, but also a means of defiance. He has none of the weapons of the adult men in the story, lacking both his father's prestige as head of a noble family and the guns wielded by the soldiers who raid the house. His only armament is that of all Olesha's protagonists: his unrelenting, imaginative vision. Thus Kolya gives us the first feature of the father complex: a sense of helplessness and passivity before the father, a status of perpetual observer behind which hide defiance and hostility. Olesha's protagonists transform their observation of their father surrogates into the main weapon of the passive, inadequate son.

With his parents' authority crumbling before his very eyes, Kolya begins to give words to his rebellion. Naturally, he does not express himself aloud: Olesha's protagonists generally prefer interior monologue to serious dialogue. Such a monologue is an integral part of Olesha's presentation of the father-son conflict in all his works. Intimidated by the authority and physical presence of the father, Olesha's narrator instead vents his rage on an internalized addressee who serves as a substitute for the father figure. Olesha's work abounds with letters to fathers that never reach the person to whom they are supposedly addressed: Kavalerov's and Volodya's letters to Babichev in *Envy*,[7] Dosya's monologue about his reading in "I Look into the Past," and the entire text of "Human Material." In "Legend," Kolya rejects the hierarchy implicit in the family structure: "It never occurred to you that you might be more stupid than I. You could never have allowed for the possibility of even discussing the equality or inequality of parents and children" (I 99). Here we find the ideological justification of Kolya's final betrayal of his father. The soldiers who are raiding the building are eradicating the old order in favor of the new one; if we presume a revolutionary context, they are theoretically liberating the oppressed from their oppressors. Kolya, as the son in the family, is at the bottom of the domestic hierarchy from the moment of his birth. His father must be smarter than Kolya by virtue of his paternal role. Until Kolya reaches adulthood, their positions in the family are fixed, and any discussion of their possible equality is impossible. The only option available to, indeed demanded of, the son is to grow up and join the oppressors: "You thought that you were my ideal. You thought that I wanted to be just like you, you thought that I wanted to continue you, your features, mustache, gestures, thoughts, bedroom, that I must also lie with a woman like you lie with Mother. You thought that this was how it must be. I don't want to be an extension of you!" The power of the father is dependent on the cooperation of the son, who is expected to look upon his parent as the model for future development. All fathers were once sons and owe their paternal status only to the existence of offspring. Fatherhood exists only in relation. Eventually, the son will become an adult and will no longer be completely subject to his father's will. At this point, the father's power is defined in different terms: the adult son need no longer obey his father; rather, it is expected that he, too, become a parent and continue the line of paternal authority into which he was born. As the epigraph to this chapter asserts, the son's character is determined in relation to his father. Kolya is expected not only to obey his father, but to want to become his father and take on his father's role.[8]

It is this continuity from father to son that the revolution disrupts, not only in Olesha's work, but in that of Babel and Platonov as well. Babel's protagonists struggle to abandon the world of their fathers only to find it has a lingering attraction. Dvanov in *Chevengur* cannot accept that his biological father is dead and inaccessible and thus repeatedly returns to his father's grave even as he collects father surrogates throughout his travels. Reverence for biological fathers notwithstanding, Platonov's characters have much in common with Olesha's: both continually search for father figures while displaying no desire to become parents themselves. Platonov was influenced by Fyodorov, who saw the very act of reproduction as a sign of disrespect for the dead biological father, whom the son must strive to resurrect.[9] Olesha's Kolya, however, views the continuation of the family line in the opposite light. The refusal to have children is a revolt against the father's power, for becoming a father requires that the son be coopted into the very hierarchy he despises. The physical father must eventually die, but he consoles himself with the survival of some of his characteristics in future generations. Olesha's passive protagonists are incapable of raising their hands against the father and thus can only attack through inaction. For Platonov, abstaining from reproduction is an expression of filial love; for Olesha, childlessness is tantamount to parricide.

Childlessness, however, is a crime that contains within itself the seeds of its own punishment. Total rejection of the father entails a denial of adult masculinity itself. Kolya wants nothing to do with the trappings of manhood, seeing in them a trick that would bind him once again to his father's power. Kolya does not want any of his father's features, including his mustache. More important, he denies that he "must also lie with a woman." In not accepting his father as a model, Kolya rejects adult heterosexuality. For Kolya, becoming a father would require him to abandon his accustomed position as passive bystander and adopt an active role, both as head of the household and as a man in bed with his wife. Again, Kolya's very passivity is his greatest weapon against his father: engaging his father in conflict would require that Kolya become active and thereby adopt one of his father's defining traits. Whereas the oedipal child actively struggles against his father for possession of the mother, Kolya realizes that he can win his battle only by having nothing whatsoever to do with the mother. In Kolya's monologue, Oedipus meets Peter Pan: Kolya's greatest act of defiance against paternal supremacy is his unspoken refusal to grow up.

The second feature of the father complex, then, is the severing of ties with paternal authority through the refusal to continue the family line. In so doing, Olesha's protagonists are obliged to reject both adult masculinity and heterosexual relations, each of which amounts to an acceptance of the paternal role through its internalization and recapitulation. The result is what Harkins terms the "sterility" of Olesha's characters, their inability (or disinclination) to engage in adult heterosexual contact. In *Envy*, this is expressed in Kavalerov's horror at the idea of becoming a father even as he continually seeks the approval of paternal surrogates. Kavalerov, as we shall see, is both attracted and repulsed by father figures. His search for new fathers is part of his rejection of filiation in favor of affiliation, a bond that is freely chosen rather than imposed by birth. But when he attempts sexual relations with a woman, he is in danger of restoring the authority of the original father by continuing the family line. Kavalerov wants sex with women only if it can be an experience completely isolated from any familial or paternal context. Inevitably, a father figure either watches over his shoulder during the act (Anechka's dead husband) or takes his place in bed (Ivan), inhibiting his pleasure and reminding him of the ever-present threat of paternal authority.

Having issued a (silent) challenge to his father, Kolya is shocked by his new comprehension of his physical surroundings: "Every object forced kinship on me. Every object ascribed something to me" (I 100–101). Here Kolya expresses that familiar antagonism between people and objects found throughout Olesha's work, summed up in Kavalerov's famous assertion "Things don't like me" (*Menia ne liubiat veshchi*). In *Envy*, Kavalerov's fear and loathing of physical objects amounts to a character trait, an expression of his insecurity and paranoia. The text does contain an implicit connection between the animosity Kavalerov attributes to the physical world and the disdain he perceives in Andrei Babichev: as Kavalerov continues to describe Andrei's morning routine, he remarks parenthetically, "Things like him" (13). At this point in the novel, however, Andrei's role as father surrogate has yet to surface before the reader. In "Legend," the world of objects is shown to be hostile precisely because it is allied with the rule of the father and the perpetuity of filial ties: "A round clock hung on the wall. 'I was born to the sound of its chimes,' said Mother on more than one occasion. 'Grandma, too.' The clock was a tradition, the clock was a legend. I don't need any legends. I don't want to die to the sound of this clock. I don't want to be a continuation. Suddenly I realized: a family council of furniture surrounded me. The furniture was advising me, telling me how to live" (I 100). Theoretically, objects such as the clock and the furniture belong to the family, but the older possessions predate the living family members. Things last longer than people, and the objects that surround Kolya are more precisely the property of the family rather than any particular family members: people are born and die to the chimes of the family clock, but the clock knows neither beginning nor end. The clock, like the rest of the furniture, symbolizes the continuity of the family, personifying it in a way that no single family member can. The father, mother, and son are merely points on the family line, but the furniture, which both predates and survives them, embodies the essence of the family, what Kolya calls the legend. Thus, when Kolya suddenly realizes that a "family council of furniture" is trying to run his life, he perceives himself as the victim not so much of the furniture itself, but of the furniture as an extension of the family. The buffet, the same household item that laughs at Kavalerov in *Envy*, makes explicit the role of objects in perpetuating the family legend: "two generations stored food in me. I'll be around . . . for your son, too, and your grandson. I will become a legend" (I 100). The tie between these family heirlooms and the past generations is in itself enough to be repulsive to Kolya, but their implicit connection with the future generations to be sired by Kolya himself is intolerable.

Throughout his work, Olesha tends to personify objects by endowing them with the traits of their owners, but "Legend" highlights a specific link between the world of things and familial authority. Such a connection is essential for any understanding of the tensions between the family and revolution in Olesha's work, since it provides a point of contact between Olesha's artistic concerns and revolutionary ideology. Following Marx and Engels, Soviet communist doctrine held that the bourgeois family unit, based on private property and domination by the father, was an exploitative entity that must be eradicated in the new world (see the introduction). The complex feelings Olesha's protagonists hold toward families are by no means a result of political ideology; rather, they are one of the emotional factors that lead to at least a limited sympathy to some parts of the revolutionary program. Kolya is more a fellow traveler than a revolutionary, cheering on the forces of change without actually pointing a gun.

Now Kolya comprehends his "dependence on all these things" (I 100). Just as the family legend dictates the future course of his life, the placement of the furniture obliges him to walk one way when he would rather walk another.[10] More than once he considers rebellion, "[b]ut Father mediated [*posrednichal*] between me and the furniture." The father receives "secret instructions" from the buffets and gramophones in order to keep Kolya from rebelling. At this point the father appears to be less the master than the emissary of the world of things, whose main purpose is to keep Kolya within the bounds of domestic order. If the father is only a middleman, then where is the locus of authority? In making his father the human representative of a more abstract order, Kolya turns his family conflict into a set of philosophical questions: Does the physical world have objective significance? If not, who determines what values are attributed to physical objects? These questions, so clearly on the surface of Olesha's short story "Liompa,"[11] are relevant to more than just the problem of physical objects in Olesha's work. They are tied to Olesha's portrayal of the world filtered through various layers of consciousness, to what R. Jones calls the "primacy of the subjective" in Olesha's literary world (3). Olesha's characters do not see the physical realm as an immutable given; or rather, if the material world is given, then it has been given by someone who has predetermined its meaning. Objects (and, by extension, people) are significant only to the extent to which they are attributed meaning. As a child, Kolya is given only a limited taste of this power of signification, and he clearly wants more: "Sometimes a curtain, terrified for the whole authority, would give me a bribe in the form of a velvet ball torn from a cord. I could swing it in all directions, breaking traditions and legends, I could give it any purpose I pleased, rudely breaking the family's conception of a curtain, and of the place [a curtain] should have in human life" (I 100). Kolya wants the power to interpret the world in his own manner, to have complete, unobstructed control over signification. In connecting his father and the family to the world of objects and their meanings, Kolya presents his family in a manner suggestive of Lacan's Symbolic Order. The father is important not merely for his concrete role as biological sire, but for what he represents: the ordered relations of signifiers and signifieds, the arbiter of all systems. The father is the symbol of signifying authority but is not authority itself. As noted above, sons grow up to take on the mantle of fatherhood, to continue the family line. The father is merely the physical representation of what Lacan terms the Name of the Father, an abstraction who is never completely embodied in any man and thus is always absent. Juliet Mitchell points out that, in Lacan's reformulation of the oedipal triangle,

> [i]t is the place of the father, not the actual father, that is thus here significant . . . The little boy cannot be the father, but he can be summoned for his future role in the name-of-the-father. The symbolic father, for whose prehistoric death the boy pays the debt due, is the law that institutes and constitutes human society, culture in the fullest sense of the term, the law of order which is to be confounded with language and which structures all human societies, which makes them, in fact, human. This symbolic law of order defines society and determines the fate of every small human animal born into it. (Mitchell 391)

It is the Symbolic Order that Kolya calls the "legend" of family continuity. In rebelling against his biological father, Kolya fights against what the father represents: a way of life that is imposed from without rather than projected from within. Control of the curtain implies limited mastery over the world of things, and thus the possession of a small piece of curtain makes Kolya giddy with his newfound power. The rest of his family is firmly attached to things, never daring to change their significance. But Kolya is only too willing to go against the family's ideas of "what a curtain is" and "what place it must have in human life." This earlier rebellion against the "legend" prefigures Kolya's eventual betrayal of his father.

This third part of the father complex in Olesha's work elevates the father-son conflict beyond dynastic struggles and issues of reproduction, reinterpreting it in philosophical terms. The material world and the father are inextricably linked: at certain times it seems that the world of objects belongs to the father, while at others it appears that he is only their representative. In either case, it is a world in which the father is at home, but the son is only a guest. Olesha's protagonists, sons all, repeatedly refuse to view the world in the "objective" manner expected of them. Rather, they reinterpret what they see, attaching new meanings to things and to people as an act of self-assertion. Much has been written about the "distorting" vision of Olesha's characters,[12] but here we see that their very tendency to "think in images" is a deliberate challenge to a symbolizing authority irrevocably linked with the father. It is the battle with the father that leads Olesha's heroes to their semiotic rebellion.

Kolya's betrayal of his father is preceded by a final conflict over the representation of paternal authority. On the first page, Kolya's father is stripped of his clothes; on the next, Kolya's gaze strips him of his humanity (*"on perestal byt' chelovekom"*). The father, according to the narrator, has turned into a chicken. The father's humiliation appears to be complete, for now all trappings of his authority have been removed, and his own son sees him as a panic-stricken, trapped, female animal.

But here the Symbolic Order reasserts itself, as the father reasserts control over his own image. His attempt to regain his composure (*"vziat' sebia v ruki"*) forces Kolya to concede that his father never really flew; it was only dizziness that led him to such an interpretation of his father's fear (*"cherez golovokruzhenie ia tak vosprinimal vneshnie proiavleniia ego strakha"*). Such an admission comes at a high cost to the pride of Olesha's narrator. If in Olesha's work the physical world belongs to the fathers, narration is the almost exclusive purview of the sons.[13] Olesha's narrators use their powers of observation and description to defuse the paternal threat. When Kolya's father ceases to provide him fodder for his narrative mockery, his son loses his only weapon.

Before the Symbolic Order reestablishes itself, the events of the story take place outside language. Of course Kolya narrates the story, but all the actions occur without speech. Thus the only voice heard is that of Kolya's rebellion. Now that Kolya has admitted to himself that his perception is faulty, his father regains the power of speech. He puts his hand on Kolya's shoulder and tells him "to be proud," saying they will die "like noblemen." The father's very manner of speech connotes mastery; he addresses Kolya three times, each time starting with a command, followed by an assertion in the future perfective.[14] Until the very end of the story, the father alone has the power of speech, and he exercises it only after he reclaims his role as master of the household. Mother and son, both passive, remain completely silent. Kolya is horrified at this sudden reversal: "In a word: the father is still in power, the council of furniture has not been disbanded, the legend exists. The father of the family, the continuation of the family line, the bearer of tradition, is performing his last trick. He will die historically. He will make himself a martyr" (I 100). Even in the face of death, the power of the father is not defeated. When his father walks toward the door, Kolya sees that "he already was a legend" (I 101). But Kolya refuses to take part in the continuation of the legend, and instead opens the door himself, shouting: "Open fire! Open fire! Shoot the bedroom! The mystery! The buffet, the legend, all the buttons! Cut me loose from him, from his mustache, from his thoughts. Free me" (I 101). Kolya's plea is pure Olesha: it makes no distinction between the ideological or thematic concerns of the story and the objects or people used to symbolize them. Kolya tells the soldiers to shoot the things that perpetuate the legend as well as the legend itself. He asks to be freed not only from his father, but from his father's thoughts and even his mustache. Legends and buttons are either equally concrete or equally abstract: either both are physical entities that can be harmed by bullets, or bullets are themselves abstract weapons in an ideological battle.

Whatever the case, Kolya perceives that he and the soldiers' bullets have a common cause and a common enemy. This conflation of the political and the domestic comprises the fourth part of the father complex. In "Legend" and the other short stories, the interests of the son and the goals of the revolution converge, a fact the narrator himself discovers during the course of the story. Kolya welcomes the invaders on impulse alone. In *Envy*, the forces of the revolution are at odds with the novel's central "son," Nikolai Kavalerov. The difference can be partly accounted for by the time frames of the two works: if "Legend" does, indeed, have a revolutionary context, it concerns a revolution in progress. *Envy*, however, presents the revolution as a fait accompli. Any new affiliation can eventually ossify into an institution just as rigid as the one it replaced; the revolution is no exception.

But even if the boy Kolya and the adult Nikolai diverge in their attitudes toward revolution, they share a trait that plays a crucial role in the drama of family and revolution: each is willing to treat the issue metaphorically. Kolya welcomes the soldiers because he sees in their cause the political counterpart of his rebellion against his father. Kavalerov — indeed, all the characters of *Envy* — persists in interpreting his essentially familial conflicts as an ideological war between opposing philosophical camps. When politicized, these family tensions are only exacerbated.

"Legend" is also consistent with Olesha's other short stories in that the family and the revolution are shown to be completely at odds with one another. The father's rule is undermined by his unmasking before the son, but the ultimate cause of the loss of paternal authority is the soldier's raid of the family's building. In *Envy*, Ivan Babichev exhorts against the "elephants of the revolution" (*slonami revoliutsii*) that threaten to destroy the domestic hearth (91). Ivan's view, however, is only one of many featured in the novel. As we shall see, *Envy* reexamines the relationship between family and revolution, discovering alliances where one would expect only enmity.

THE UBIQUITOUS FATHER

Olesha's approach to the family and fatherhood in "Legend" is, compared to that in *Envy*, remarkably straightforward: the son wants nothing to do with his father or the filial burden of the "legend" that his father would impose on him. The fact that Kolya's disdain for his father extends even to heterosexuality and male secondary sex characteristics suggests that his path to adulthood may be complicated, but the story concludes long before we can see Kolya attain manhood. In *Envy*, Kolya's namesake, Nikolai Kavalerov, is without a doubt physically an adult, but, as has been often noted in the critical literature, he has the emotional maturity of a little boy.[15] Kavalerov shares Kolya's distrust of father figures but nonetheless doggedly seeks new fathers among the ranks of all his male acquaintances who are even marginally older than he. The young Kolya wants nothing to do with fathers, but the older Kavalerov both fears and needs them. Kavalerov's contradictory impulses are symptomatic of a larger phenomenon in Olesha's novel. In *Envy*, two opposing forces continuously struggle for supremacy: the deep-seated urge to flee from fathers, reproduction, and family ties, and a contrary, inescapable pull toward the very institutions that Olesha's characters find so threatening.

In *Envy*, the only mention of Kavalerov's biological father occurs when Kavalerov suddenly notices a family resemblance: "Once, while changing my shirt, I saw myself in the mirror and suddenly discovered a striking resemblance to my father. In reality there is no such resemblance" (27).[16] Like Kolya in "Legend," Kavalerov would deny any connection to his father, preferring to be a self-contained entity rather than part of a family line. Kavalerov, however, feels pity rather than disgust for his father: "I remembered: my parents' bedroom, and I, a boy, am watching my father change his shirt. I felt sorry for him. He was never going to be handsome, to be famous, he was already finished, complete, and would never be anything other than what he already was. So I thought, pitying him, taking silent pride of my superiority. And now I had discovered my father in myself" (27).[17] As in "Legend," Kavalerov's sudden comprehension of his father's fate comes in his parents' bedroom when his father is partially unclothed. Kavalerov watches two other half-naked men in *Envy*, Andrei Babichev in the beginning of the novel and Volodya Makarov near the end, and in each case he is transfixed by what he sees. Such moments combine fascination, revelation, and shame: Kavalerov cannot take his eyes off these men, finding them sexually intimidating. He uses each of these incidents as opportunities to explore the character of the man he views. When he sees Volodya doing gymnastics "almost naked" he is "seized by a feeling of shame and fear" (97). The sight of Volodya's physical prowess exacerbates Kavalerov's sense of inadequacy. Volodya, unlike Kavalerov's father, is not a "daddy" (*papasha*); instead, his future is filled with limitless possibilities, compared with which Kavalerov's prospects look bleak. But Volodya is by no means a father figure; his role as Kavalerov's rival and sublimated object of desire will be explored in the next chapter. Andrei, however, is the first substitute father Kavalerov adopts, and thus the spectacle of his seminude body is a source of ridicule and contempt rather than of shame and fear. Kavalerov's vicious caricature of Andrei in the first pages of the novel parallels his childhood attitude toward his half-naked biological father: the pathetic limitations of the older man allow Kavalerov to "take quiet pride in his own superiority."

Andrei, like Kavalerov's and Kolya's fathers, becomes the victim of the son's mocking, self-defensive gaze discussed in connection with "Legend." But Kavalerov himself is not immune to the powers of his own vision, and it is his sight of himself in the mirror that forces him to realize he is no longer a little boy. The mirror scene begins with the admission, "I am twenty-seven years old." From Kavalerov's point of view, his youth, which, like Olesha's, coincided with the "youth of the century" (25), is already part of the past. The fact that Kavalerov now recognizes his physical similarity to his father only heightens his sense of premature aging and wasted potential. He sees his resemblance to his father as the outer manifestation of a biological imperative: "It was not a resemblance of forms — no, something else: I would say, a sexual resemblance, as though I had suddenly sensed my father's seed within myself, within my substance. And it was as though someone had told me: you're finished. Complete. There will never be anything more. Go father a son" (27). By reducing his similarity to his father to a purely sexual resemblance, Kavalerov makes his plight appear all the more hopeless. Now he has reached the stage of life that Kolya found so hateful: having achieved physical maturity, he is supposed to take on the mantle of the father and become just one more link in the chain of generations. Like Dosya's father in "Human Material," Kavalerov must now accept that his life has not lived up to his expectations. The "plan" Kavalerov had for his own life must then be passed on to his son. To become a father is to admit defeat. Kavalerov now realizes all the opportunities that have been lost to him: he will never be handsome or famous, will never be a general, a scientist, or an adventurer (27).

Nor will he ever find the true love of which he dreams. The only woman available to him is the widow Prokopovich, "the symbol of my masculine humiliation" (*simvol moego muzkskogo unizheniia*). In Kavalerov's imagination, Anechka knows perfectly well that his ambitions will never be realized and thus tries to disillusion him with one of the most threatening statements she could possibly make: "You're already a 'daddy'" (28). Kavalerov's unvoiced response to Anechka's unspoken accusation is hostile and self-defensive: "I'm no 'daddy' . . . ! I'm not a match for you, reptile!" (28). At this point Anechka is exactly what Kavalerov has termed her: a symbol. Kavalerov manipulates her image, first making her offend him, then insulting her for the words he mentally puts in her mouth. In the critical literature, Anechka has been typically viewed as a mother figure.[18] But if Anechka is a mother, she is implicitly connected to the father. Kavalerov uses her as the mouthpiece for his fear of fatherhood the very first time she is mentioned in the novel, suggesting that Kavalerov links the widow with the threat of paternity.

Rather than accept Anechka as a lover, Kavalerov prefers to imagine himself her little boy (84). He fantasizes the childish joy he would have exploring the expanses of her fantastic bed.[19] It has been suggested that the bed symbolizes Kavalerov's "retreat from active sexual competition" (Harkins 451), but such an interpretation can be supported only by ignoring a salient detail found in the sentence immediately following the bed's initial description: the bed was won in a lottery by Anechka's husband (83). It is, without a doubt, connected with its owner, but Anechka is neither its initial nor its sole possessor. Kavalerov would like the bed to represent an asexual childhood, but this is merely another attempt to redefine a threatening object on his own terms. Later in the novel, however, Kavalerov is forced to see that the bed remains the father's territory. Kavalerov's sudden realization of his resemblance to his biological father was spurred by looking at a mirror; the discovery of the bed's original owner is also connected with a reflection. The morning after Kavalerov finally sleeps with Anechka, he is dumbfounded by a curious spectacle:

> He saw a fantastic reflection of himself in the mirror, with his soles forward. He was lying there splendidly, one arm bent behind his head . . . He was lying on Anechka's bed.
> "You remind me of him," Anechka whispered hotly as she bent over him.
> A portrait under glass hung above the bed. A man was hanging there, someone's young grandfather, solemnly dressed. . . . One could feel that the back of his head was strong and sinewy. A man of about fifty.
> Kavalerov remembered: his father was changing his shirt. (107–8)

Where before Kavalerov saw his father reflected back at him in the mirror, now he looks in a mirror and sees a portrait of a middle-aged man whom he is told he resembles. Kavalerov makes the connection between the two events instantly, again recalling his father putting on his shirt. As a child, Kavalerov considered his father a pathetic sight and thus reveled in his superiority even as he pitied him. The image of the man changing the shirt is that of the father defeated. The man in the portrait is another matter entirely: "solemnly dressed," Anechka's husband seems the master of all he surveys. He is the father triumphant.

The portrait of Anechka's husband, like Volodya's picture in Andrei's apartment, reminds Kavalerov that he is only a replacement for an absent loved one. Like Volodya, Anechka's husband appears proud, self-confident, and masculine: "One could feel that the back of his head was sturdy and sinewy." Though both Volodya and Prokopovich serve as rivals in Kavalerov's love triangles, the threat each presents is markedly different. Volodya is younger than Kavalerov, but the fifty-seven-year-old Prokopovich is just the right age to be Kavalerov's father. Indeed, he is more than a father, for he looks like "someone's young grandfather" (108), even more firmly grounded in the continuation of the family line. The father has turned into the grandfather at a particularly appropriate moment, for Kavalerov has consummated a sexual attraction for the first time in the novel. In "Legend," Kolya rejects sexual ties with women precisely because he does not want to follow in his father's footsteps and perpetuate the family line. Kavalerov has fallen into the trap that Kolya resolved to avoid: by sleeping with Anechka, he allows the possibility that he, too, will become a father.[20] Kolya refused to be a "continuation" of his father and his father's features, but Kavalerov has allowed himself to be precisely that. When the young Kavalerov sees his father changing his shirt, he is given a glimpse of what the future has in store for him; at that time, Kavalerov's father was probably about the same age as Kavalerov is when the action of *Envy* takes place. Only when he sees himself in the mirror, years later, does Kavalerov understand that he and his father are cut from the same cloth, that he is just as "finished" and unsuccessful as his father. Now another "mirror" image affords Kavalerov one more look into his future, showing him a portrait of Kavalerov as an old man. Oedipus' horror came upon finding that he had unknowingly taken his father's place. Kavalerov, on the other hand, is appalled not only to find out that he has taken on the father's role, but also that he has fulfilled the father's will. Prokopovich's picture humiliates Kavalerov on two levels: first, it shows him that he is only a replacement, a usurper; second, it marks Kavalerov's surrender to the march of family generations.

Anechka makes matters worse by commenting on Kavalerov's resemblance to her dead husband. She does so twice, whereupon she tells him that the two men even make love in a similar fashion. It is at this point that Kavalerov beats Anechka, for he has found that he cannot escape the father even in bed. As a widow, Anechka already serves as a reminder that men are replaceable. By telling Kavalerov he looks like her husband, she only exacerbates his resentment at being a mere interchangeable part. Kavalerov lashes out at her because she is the sole target he is capable of beating, yet even here he cannot be an independent, isolated individual. Anechka smiles through her tears and tells Kavalerov, "He used to beat me, too" (108).

Kavalerov's feelings of replaceability are confirmed by the appearance of Ivan. First he sees Ivan standing over the bed during his fever dream, then again three days later. Ivan's second appearance is ideally timed to reinforce Kavalerov's fears that he is only one in an endless chain of men and generations.[21] Upon awakening from his illness, Kavalerov notes that his suspenders have a new loop. He immediately decides that Anechka has taken it from her husband's old clothes, a thought that sends him into complete despair. He leaves the house, only to return later and put on the very suspenders that had disgusted him. He leaves again, and again comes back, this time deciding that he will be firm and "put the widow in her place" (112). But upon his return he finds Ivan lying in the bed that he himself had once occupied. Anechka tells him not to be jealous, since she is sorry for both of them, and they are both equally lonely. Now she has verbally confirmed that Kavalerov is only one of many.

The fact that it is Ivan who has taken Kavalerov's place in the bed only makes matters worse, for Ivan is the second father substitute Kavalerov turns to in the novel. Even more appalling, Ivan, lying in bed, looks like his brother (111), the inaccessible surrogate father from the novel's first half. In "Legend," Kolya knew that sex with women means repeating the act that inaugurated the father's reign. In *Envy*, Kavalerov discovers that when he sleeps with Anechka, he is never alone with her. Every significant father figure in the novel is in bed with Kavalerov and Anechka, if only symbolically. First, two of the novel's absent fathers appear: Anechka's dead husband smiles down at Kavalerov from the ceiling, reminding Kavalerov of his own father. Then Kavalerov discovers Ivan in the bed, looking like his brother Andrei. Ivan's proposal to share Anechka equally could scarcely please Kavalerov, though the novel ends before he can respond. Kavalerov attempts to have a sexual encounter that is completely isolated from the surrogate family that has rejected him, only to hear his second substitute father suggest a *ménage à trois*. Kavalerov's miserable liaison with Anechka confirms what little Kolya in "Legend" seems to know instinctively: sexual contact with women only cements the bonds between fathers and sons, strengthening the power of the family over the individual.

Kavalerov's desire to escape from paternal authority is matched only by his need for a surrogate father. That the two "fathers" Kavalerov adopts in *Envy* are brothers renders all filial ties in the novel convoluted, if not incestuous, for the Babichevs' views on the family are no less paradoxical than those of Kavalerov. Though Ivan and Andrei are at opposite ends of the ideological spectrum, they share a number of traits that would attract Kavalerov. Both are self-made men who have broken with the world of their fathers; both substitute projects and inventions for children (the sausage and the Quarter vs. Ophelia), at the same time replacing the family unit with ideologically determined affiliations (the toiling masses vs. the "vulgarians" [*poshliaki*]).²² As Victor Peppard notes, both are builders, and both are concerned with the family, which one wants to preserve and the other hopes to transform (*Poetics* 79). Despite Ivan's cult of womanhood, neither he nor his brother has any emotional ties to adult women. The novel contains not a single reference to Valya's mother, almost as though Valya, like Ophelia, had sprung forth asexually from Ivan's imagination. Indeed, each of them is the perfect father for a man who abhors filial bonds, since they have detached themselves from their own hereditary past. Finally, they share one characteristic without which the very plot of *Envy* would be impossible: both are willing to "adopt" stray young men whom they do not even know. When Kavalerov turns to Ivan for a mentor, he is deliberately choosing the path that opposes Andrei's. Yet it is the similarities of the two estranged brothers that make the transition possible.

Ivan in particular makes a paradoxical father figure. He espouses an ideology based on a cult of womanhood and reverence for the family, yet his own family life is in shambles. Kavalerov is fascinated by Ivan from the moment he first sees him, as he writes in his letter to Andrei. Despite this genuine interest in such a puzzling man, Kavalerov's original motive for crossing over to Ivan's camp is merely to ally himself with Andrei's enemies. He senses that Ivan has a weapon with which to defeat his brother, writing that Andrei is afraid of Ophelia. When Kavalerov claims that Andrei might try to put him in an insane asylum, he justifies his fear by noting that Andrei said his own brother should be shot (45). Kavalerov knows nothing of Ivan, yet he already identifies with him so much that he is willing to fight for him. Before he even meets Ivan, Kavalerov has already created him in his own mind, seeing a kindred spirit in this strange man with a bowler hat. At this point, however, there is no guarantee that Kavalerov and Ivan will be on the same side. In the same letter, Kavalerov sees Volodya as a fellow victim of Andrei's condescension and thus an ally. When this proves not to be the case, Kavalerov is deprived of all potential allies but one: Ivan Babichev.

The initial meeting between Ivan and Kavalerov has all the familiar hallmarks of Olesha's father-son recognition scenes. Kavalerov admits his resemblance to his father when glimpsing his own reflection in the mirror and later mistakes the portrait of Anechka's husband, another father figure, for his own reflection. Each case forces Kavalerov to admit some sort of resemblance to the father in question. Now Kavalerov identifies his newest father when Ivan appears before him in the mirror: "The man approached the mirror, appearing from somewhere to the side. I got in the way of his reflection. The smile he had prepared for himself came to me" (58). He appears as if from nowhere, as though he himself were a trick of the mirror. The mirror immediately forces the two men together, for Kavalerov becomes the receiver of a smile Ivan had directed at himself. For one moment, they serve as mirrors for one another.[23] Kavalerov has yet to identify Ivan; recognition comes only after Ivan's puzzling pronouncement, "I invented myself" (*Ia sam sebia vydumal*) (58). Only after Kavalerov looks at Ivan twice, first in the mirror, then when Ivan answers his question, does he understand the significance the other Babichev holds for him: "I realized immediately: here is my friend, and teacher, and comforter" (58). Now Kavalerov has completely shifted allegiances, and the next half of the novel will be dominated by Kavalerov's new father, Ivan, rather than by Ivan's unattainable brother Andrei.

Having accepted Ivan as his new guide, Kavalerov surrenders himself completely to Ivan's authority. On the textual level, Kavalerov even abdicates his privileged role as sarcastic narrator; for most of the second section, the (third-person) narrative focus is on Ivan. Thus the reader's access to Kavalerov's perceptions has been sharply limited, allowing a view of Ivan that is presumably undistorted by Kavalerov's perspective. The reader, like Kavalerov and the police interrogators, listens intently to Ivan's monologues. Kavalerov is remarkably silent as Ivan speaks, saying almost no words aloud and revealing few of his thoughts through the narrator. After four pages of invective that would do Kavalerov himself proud, Ivan urges his new disciple toward a revenge and subsequent downfall that will be colorful enough to shake the new world and ensure his everlasting fame. Kavalerov thinks: "He is reading my mind" (*On chitaet moi mysli*) (79). Though Kavalerov's observation refers to his personal situation, it can be applied to the narrative as well: Kavalerov no longer needs to express his feelings in histrionic monologues because

Ivan is expressing them for him. Kavalerov has finally found a mentor who shares his ideals and his resentment and thus allows himself, for a time, to be almost completely under Ivan's spell. Where before Kavalerov despised Andrei for sending him on errands, now he willingly lets Ivan lead him from place to place.

At first glance, Ivan would seem to be the perfect father for Kavalerov. Ivan's life story, like that of all the Babichev brothers, is one of resistance to paternal authority. The stories Ivan chooses to tell of his childhood recount his imaginative triumphs over his literal-minded father. Despite his rhetoric about the sanctity of the family as an idea, in reality Ivan is hostile to most filial bonds. The narrator relates a rumor that Ivan interrupted a wedding to harangue the bride and groom: "Don't love each other. Don't join together. Groom, abandon your bride! What kind of fruit will your love bear? You'll produce your own enemy. He'll gobble you up" (69). Though Ivan extols the virtue of the old-world family, he sees the appearance of the "new people" as the end of true filial ties. He speaks from his own experience, for his own daughter Valya leaves him for the representatives of the new world. Ivan's ideology is necessarily self-contradictory: he worships the family, but finds that the new world has made the family part of the problem. Any attempt to bear children under present conditions will only lead to the production of more enemies. Ivan is a father who sees an entire nation of children that have broken with the world of their parents and can only conclude that producing more offspring is self-defeating. Ivan's ideological rejection of reproduction echoes Kavalerov's more personal distaste for fatherhood: for Ivan, the new generation sounds the death knell for the world of its parents, while for Kavalerov, having children amounts to admitting that one's life is finished.

In moving away from the biological family, Ivan, like his brother and the protagonists of the other authors discussed in this book, searches for satisfaction in an ideological conglomeration of people who have no biological connection to him. He establishes himself as the "king of the vulgarians" (*korol' poshliakov*) (65), who will lead the representatives of the old world on their last crusade. His "conspiracy of feelings" (*zagovor chustv*) is just as fanciful as Gedali's "International of Good People" in Babel's *Red Cavalry:* each movement opposes the new revolutionary order with a conglomeration of romantics, and each movement exists only in its founder's imagination. Lacking a family, Ivan attempts to become the leader of a ragtag group of outcasts. But Kavalerov is the only "representative of the old world" to join Ivan's cause, and Ivan's extended family consists only of Kavalerov and his creation Ophelia.

Ivan, however, cannot be a satisfactory father for long. He is too much like Kavalerov to be a satisfactory substitute father (Harkins, "Theme of Sterility" 451). He also shares yet another trait with his brother Andrei that comes between him and his "children": he treats all his offspring, both literal and figurative, as embodiments of ideas. Ivan comes close to seeing this failing in his brother, telling him that "symbolizing the new world in the image of an unremarkable youth [Volodya] . . . is nonsense" (68). Here Ivan argues with Andrei's choice of symbols, not with the action itself. Ivan has his own blind spot in that regard, having been sure that his daughter Valya was the embodiment of the old world's feminine grace (74–75). Valya wants no part of her father's fantasy; she leaves him, shedding her excess symbolism like an ill-fitting hand-me-down. Ivan substitutes for Valya a new daughter, his imaginary creation Ophelia, but she, too, is angry at her treatment by Ivan. As Ivan freely admits, he has "disgraced" (*opozoril*) the machine (86) and fears that Ophelia will not forgive him: "I'm afraid of her . . . She hates me . . . She's betrayed [*izmenila*] me . . . She'll kill me" (88). At one point Ivan may have been at the bottom of the familial hierarchy, but now that he has reached adulthood, he has proved the rule that little Kolya deduced in "Legend": when boys grow up and have children, they turn into the enemy. Despite his personal rebellion against his own parents, Ivan is another in Olesha's long series of manipulative fathers.[24] His attitude toward Kavalerov reveals his tendency to see his children, both biological and spiritual, as instruments for his cause. Kavalerov has found a "teacher" (*uchitel*), a "friend" (*drug*) (58), while Ivan has found the bearer of a feeling (73).

Though Kavalerov calls Ivan his friend, the two were never friends in the sense that J. Glenn Gray defines the word (see the introduction and chapter 1). Instead, the two "coconspirators" were comrades, a relationship that, though often intense, is notoriously fragile. Ivan's and Kavalerov's relationship is grounded in a shared ideology and thus cannot last when one of the two forsakes his long-held beliefs. When Ivan renounces his conspiracy, Kavalerov abandons him, hurling an insult that is particularly appropriate to this novel of fathers and sons: "Ivan Petrovich, you son of a bitch!" (*Sukin vy syn, Ivan Petrovich!*) (99). Even as he attempts to carry out the mission Ivan originally assigned him, however, Kavalerov shows that he and Ivan are truly kindred spirits. Just as the vision of Valya induces Ivan to give up his dreams, the sight of the triumphant Volodya forces Kavalerov to realize that he will never succeed. Later, when Ophelia slaughters Ivan in Kavalerov's nightmare, Kavalerov shouts, "My place is with him!" (110). This turns out to be truer than he could know, for in the end he is left with nothing but parodies of his original goals (Peppard, *Poetics* 79): instead of Valya, he has Anechka, and in place of the successful, famous Andrei, he is left only with the defeated Ivan Babichev.

REVOLUTION AS MEN'S CLUB

It is fitting that the second half of the novel should be dominated by Ivan, for Ivan is only Kavalerov's second choice for an adoptive father; it is Andrei's function as surrogate father, both for Kavalerov and Volodya, that is the key to Olesha's treatment of masculinity in *Envy*. His brief mentorship of Kavalerov aside, Ivan is the father of daughters, not sons: both Ivan's motherless child Valya and his imaginary invention Ophelia are embodiments of femininity gone astray. Though they partake of the novel's pervasive androgyny, Andrei's children are all essentially masculine in nature. Volodya, the engineer and star athlete, is the most "manly" of the novel's characters. The "Quarter," the superkitchen to which Andrei wants to "give birth," is a masculine, industrial reorganization of feminine, domestic space. Andrei's prized creation, the perfect sausage, merits its own discussion.

Andrei's phallic sausage is one of the great clichés of Olesha criticism. Certainly, anyone even vaguely acquainted with Freudianism would tend to see a suspiciously male organ symbolized in this tube-shaped piece of meat. But like most of Olesha's symbols, the sausage is ambiguous, representing different things at different times. A number of objections can be raised to seeing the sausage as a culinary representation of male genitalia, not the least of which is the gender of the word "sausage" (*kol-*

basa). In Russian, *kolbasa* is a feminine noun, the antecedent for repeated uses of the pronoun "she." Indeed, the sausage is even said to be Babichev's bride: when Andrei first sees the fruits of his labors, he is shy, "like a groom, who sees how beautiful his young bride is and what a charming impression she makes on the guests" (34–35). Earlier, Andrei calls the sausage a kratsvitsa, or beautiful woman. In *The Conspiracy of Feelings* (*Zagover chuvstv*), the feminine side of the sausage is developed further in a phone conversation between Andrei and Shapiro, the butcher: "Andrei: Listen, Solomon Davidovich, how is my beauty? Under lock and key? I'm in love with her. What? There's nothing on earth dearer to me. What? Yes, yes. When do I get to see her? On Wednesday or Thursday? Send her my regards. Yes. I dreamed of her. So pink, so shiny, so tender" (P 46). Here Andrei actually confesses his love for an inanimate deli item of his own devising. The sausage is a bride who must be kept safe from other men before her wedding.²⁵ A culinary Pygmalion, Babichev is so taken with his creation that "she" even appears in his dreams.

What, however, makes "her" so beautiful? When Andrei calls the sausage of his dreams "pink" (*rozovaia*), "shiny" (*siiaiushchaia*), and "tender" (*nezhnaia*), he chooses epithets that by no means contradict its phallic nature. By the same token, these very words could easily be applied to Babichev himself: in the morning, Andrei is the color of an "egg" or an "opal," he exercises in a room full of "sunshine" (*siianie*), and he inadvertently reveals to Kavalerov his "tender" (*nezhnyi*) groin (13). The sausage will bring Babichev glory, allowing him to shine (*siiat'*) (35). Kavalerov's physical descriptions of Andrei and the sausage reveal a marked resemblance:

> [The sausage's] *sweaty [vspotevshaia]* surface, the *yellowish [zhelteiushchie]* bubbles of subcutaneous *fat [zhira]*. Where it was cut that very lard looks like white dots. (32; emphasis added)

> His body's oil was a *tender yellow [nezhno zheltelo]* . . . Babichev's great-grandfather took care of his skin, rolls of *fat [zhira]* were situated on his great-grandfather's trunk. Babichev inherited this fine skin . . . on the small of his back I saw a birthmark—that very same blood-filled, transparent, *tender [nezhnuiu]* thing. (19; emphasis added)

Like Andrei, the sausage is "sweaty" (*vspotevshaia*). Both Babichev and his creation have a yellowish coloring (*zhelteiushchuiu zheltelo*). Each one has spots on his skin—Babichev his birthmarks and bullet wound, the sausage its "white dots." The sausage is, indeed, flesh of Andrei's flesh. When the reader first sees the sausage, Babichev proudly displays his creation as it is lying in Babichev's pink palm "like a living thing" (*kak nechto zhivoe*). Babichev's love affair with his sausage is a displaced autoeroticism: he treasures his "beautiful" sausage as a sign of his own achievement.

As their physical similarity implies, the sausage is an extension of Andrei's own being. The androgyny of Babichev's offspring stems from both wordplay and family resemblance. One critic argues that the sausage is actually an excremental symbol, associated with images of birth and male envy of reproduction (Harkins, "Theme of Sterility" 447). While this interpretation does lead to cogent observations about production and reproduction in Olesha's novel, it does not preclude the possibility that, despite all evidence to the contrary, the sausage is stubbornly phallic.[26] The sausage's shape and mode of production do, indeed, suggest feces, but the ritual that follows its "birth" connotes something else entirely. Presented with his creation, the first thing the proud father of the new sausage does is to have Kavalerov take it to the butcher Solomon Davidovich Shapiro, an old man whose name could not possibly sound more Jewish to the Russian ear. Shapiro then "carefully cut[s] off a small slice with a penknife" (*perochinym nozhom ostorozhno otrezal malen'kii lomtik*). Babichev's new child has just been circumcised.[27]

It is the tension between the sausage as a phallic symbol of achievement and the sausage as a piece of meat that confounds Kavalerov. At first glance, the threat posed by the sausage seems inordinate for a mere inanimate object. But Kavalerov makes clear from the novel's first chapter that he and the physical world are in a constant state of war. In "Legend," physical objects conspire with the hated father against the hapless son. Making peace with the world of things is tantamount to accepting paternal supremacy: objects belong to the father, and the father belongs to the objects. Andrei Babichev is at home in the physical world and has even managed to create something materially useful. Besides Mr. Kovalevsky from "Human Material," Andrei is the only father figure in all of Olesha's work who has a successful career; the parents of Dosya and Kolya, as well as of Olesha himself, are unhappy failures who place all their hopes on their sons. Olesha's other protagonists are unable to live up to the expectations of their frustrated fathers; all the more hopeless is Kavalerov's attempt to be "adopted" by a man who is an unqualified success.

Though a product of the previous century, Babichev firmly establishes a place for himself in the new order by contributing to its development. For his part, Kavalerov can offer no such accomplishment as a ticket into the coming world. Kavalerov envies Babichev's accomplishment at the same time that he admits his incomprehension of its significance. The sausage, both an extension of Babichev and an artificial "son," exerts a tremendous power over Kavalerov, controlling his very movements (*"Kusochek parshivoi kolbasy upravliaet moimi dvizheniiami, moei volei"*) (36). When he considers tossing the sausage away, he involuntarily imagines the huge bulk of Babichev heading menacingly toward him. The sausage, both as symbol of access to the new world and as icon of virility, is a challenge that Kavalerov simply cannot meet. As Babichev's "son," the sausage is the perfect child of an ambitious father: it fulfills its proud parent's design simply by its very existence. As Harkins tells us, Andrei, like his brother Ivan, prefers artificial children to flesh-and-blood offspring. Unlike Dosya and Kolya (or, for that matter, Valya), the sausage cannot suddenly announce that its goals are different from those of its creator. Kavalerov has achieved nothing and, in himself, does not represent a father's accomplishments. He can neither be nor produce a better "child" than the sausage. In comparison, Kavalerov is hopelessly weak and impotent.

If Kavalerov is rendered powerless by an inanimate object that functions as Andrei's son, he is all the more threatened by the young man who fulfills the same role on a more personal level. In the literal sense of the word, Volodya Makarov is no more Andrei's son than the sausage or the Quarter. In his excellent schema of the "family" relationships in *Envy,* Andrew Barrat observes that "in each case the relationship is one of adoptive, rather than natural parentage, and one which, moreover, displaces that natural, fraternal bond between the Babichevs" (*Yurii Olesha's "Envy"* 41). The new world of *Envy* values freely chosen affiliations over the filial ties forced upon the individual through an accident of birth. In

Olesha's novel, such biological mistakes are corrected. Because she cannot share her father's vision, Valya, in a Shklovskian "knight's move," chooses the protection of her uncle over her father. Volodya apparently has no need to completely deny his natural father; indeed, Volodya's absence, indispensable for the novel's plot, is necessitated by a visit to his hometown.[28]

Andrei is at pains to describe his relationship with Volodya in sufficiently revolutionary terms. As noted above, Babichev's unconventional living arrangements have raised a number of critics' eyebrows. It has been suggested that Andrei, in denying that he and Volodya form a family unit, is inventing a "rationalization to hide from himself the homosexual implications of their relationship" (Harkins, "Theme of Sterility" 447–48). It would be far more logical, however, to assume the contrary: if Andrei were truly concerned that his ties to Volodya are homosexual, claiming a paternal bond would help defuse this anxiety and deflect any veiled accusations. Instead, Andrei is deeply disturbed when Ivan accuses him of harboring a fatherly affection for young Volodya. Paternity is a stigma that Olesha's characters fear but cannot escape. Homosexuality does have a role in the novel, but its place is elsewhere. Fatherhood, not homosexuality, is the love that dare not speak its name.

In *Envy*, as in the other works discussed in this study, filial bonds have been weakened and condemned by the new Soviet order. Thus Andrei's "fatherhood" of Volodya must be ideologically justified in order to be acceptable. Andrei claims that his attachment to Volodya is based on irreproachably revolutionary grounds. The only apparently direct glimpse into Andrei's thought processes is a response to Ivan's accusation that Andrei keeps Volodya not because the latter is a "new man," but out of a typically bourgeois desire for a son.[29] Ivan takes this opportunity to attack his brother's hypocrisy and argue the case for his own ideology simultaneously: "You're just getting old, Andryusha! And you just need a son. It's just fatherly feelings. The family is eternal, Andrei! And symbolizing the new world in the form of an unremarkable youth who is famous only as a soccer player is nonsense" (68). As so often occurs in the novel's philosophical debates, this "insult" could just as easily be applied to the accuser as to the accused. In a different context, Ivan's allegation would be of little consequence, but in Olesha's novel it challenges Andrei's basic assumptions about himself. Since Ivan sees himself as both the champion of the family and the standard-bearer for outmoded romantic abstractions, his words would cause him little harm even if he saw that they were applicable to himself as well as to his brother. For Andrei, however, accepting the truth of Ivan's accusation is tantamount to joining the enemy: "Maybe Ivan is right? Maybe I'm just an ordinary philistine and family feeling lives in me as well? Is he dear to me because he has lived with me since he was a child. . . . Have I just grown accustomed to him, to love him like a son?" (80). Even pseudo-familial bonds are unacceptable to a true revolutionary: if Andrei's love for Volodya is "nothing more" than paternal affection, he is just a "philistine" (*obyvatel'*). Andrei, who is technically too old to be a "new man," is painfully aware of his tenuous connection to the new world: "What I live for is concentrated in him. I've been lucky. The new humanity's life is still far off. I believe in it. And I've been lucky. He's fallen asleep right near me, this wonderful new world. The new world lives in my house" (80). Here Andrei reveals the cardinal mistake to which his generation of Babichevs is prone: like Ivan, he treats those he loves as embodiments of abstract ideals rather than individuals. Young Volodya embodies what Andrei, because of his more advanced age, can never hope to represent: the spirit of the new world. Andrei makes this perfectly clear in his monologue: "he is dear to me, like the embodiment of a dream" (81). Volodya is not Andrei's son, he is the personification of Andrei's most cherished ideals. Andrei is not cohabiting with an "unremarkable youth," but rather sharing his house with the new world itself. Such ideological self-deception protects Andrei from both his brother's accusations of bourgeois inclinations and any unspoken fears of homosexual tendencies.

Andrei renounces fatherhood in terms reminiscent of Kolya's rebellion in "Legend": he rejects any continuity between generations. He does not need someone to "close his eyes," nor does he want to die "on pillows," as Ivan fantasizes in his "fairy tale." He replaces the family unit with an affiliative bond that is too large and amorphous to resemble a family: "I know: the masses, not the family, will take my last breath."[30] In lofty words, Andrei denies the nature of his connection to Volodya by replacing individuals with more abstract groupings: "We are not a family, we are humanity" (81).

At this point Andrei is forced to bring his antifamily values to their harsh, logical conclusion, giving voice to a revolutionary mentality that puts ideology above any emotional tie. Andrei will not allow any bourgeois emotions to govern his conduct and thus claims that Volodya's place in his life is guaranteed only as long as the "young Edison" fulfills Babichev's expectations: "I'll throw him out if I'm wrong about him, if he is not new, not utterly different from me, because I'm still up to my belly in the old and will never get out" (81). Despite his claims that "I don't need a son, I'm not a father, he's not a son, we're not a family," readers familiar with Olesha's other works will note that Andrei protests too much. Though Andrei disdains any desire for a son or heir, his expectations of Volodya are no different from those of Dosya's father in "Human Material" and "I Look into the Past": the son must make up for the shortcomings of the father. No matter what his achievements may be, Andrei's roots are still in the old world. He can, as Barratt would have it, cut himself off from the family tree, but he will never be reborn as a young man in the new world.[31] Both Kavalerov and Ivan rejoice at any visible traces of Andrei's prerevolutionary upbringing, and here we see that Andrei, too, is aware that he cannot escape from his past. Thus Andrei, like any other of Olesha's dissatisfied fathers, looks to the next generation to forge ahead where he can only watch. Albeit voluntarily, Volodya bears the same sort of paternal burden as Kolya and Dosya. Nowhere else, however, is this paternal attitude expressed so baldly: "I am the one who believed in him, and he is the one who justified that belief" (*Ia tot, chto veril v nego, a on tot, chto opravdal veru*). Andrei's monologue highlights the substantive difference between a father and a father figure: no matter how much a son may disappoint his father, the filial tie remains. But the affiliation of Volodya and Andrei, at best an imitation of the filial bond, is based on choice rather than blood and can presumably be annulled at any time by either party. Thus the threat of rejection by the father can become all too real in a pseudo-familial relationship, thereby enhancing the pressure on the "son" to achieve.

Since the reader follows the thought processes of Kavalerov rather than Volodya, the latter gives the overall impression of a self-assured young man who is secure in his position. It is Kavalerov who constantly frets that he will always be an outsider, yet the one glimpse we have of

Volodya's consciousness belies his confident manner. Kavalerov's and Volodya's letters are remarkably similar, enough perhaps to raise the point that the letter comes to the reader through the perceptions of Kavalerov. Whether or not the entire action of the novel is, as one scholar asserts, nothing more than the delineation of the progressive breakdown of Kavalerov's personality is beyond the scope of this study.[32] Kavalerov's and Volodya's letters reveal that they suffer from the same basic anxiety to varying degrees. Their insecurities are not identical, but rather mirror each other. Kavalerov, the envier (*zavistnik*), covets an unattainable bond with Andrei, while Volodya, who admits, "Yes, I'm jealous" (*Da, ia revnuiu*) (52), possessively protects that very tie that he fears to lose.

Given Andrei's insistence that love be justified ideologically rather than bestowed unconditionally, it should come as no surprise that Volodya is so protective of his privileged position. Before seeing Volodya's letter, the reader could assume that Kavalerov has built up a purely one-sided rivalry with this "new man." But by the time Kavalerov has written his letter, he has come to identify with Volodya as a fellow victim of Andrei's oppression. For his part, Volodya reveals a fierce antagonism toward Kavalerov, while the latter has only begun to see Volodya as an enemy. What begins in a half-joking tone ends with threats of violence: "And what if, when I arrive, it turns out that Kavalerov is your best friend, I've been forgotten, he's replaced me . . . Maybe he's actually a wonderful guy, much nicer than I am . . . Has that Kavalerov of yours married Valya? . . . Then I'll kill you, Andrei Petrovich . . . For betraying our conversations, our plans" (53). Volodya, like Kavalerov, fears that he is replaceable. If Andrei's love is based only upon a dispassionate appraisal of Volodya's personal qualities, there is always the threat that Andrei will find someone even more spectacular than Volodya. Particularly noteworthy is the way Valya plays a role in Volodya's insecurity. Just one paragraph earlier, Volodya appeared to take Valya completely for granted: "What about Valka? Of course we'll get married! In four years" (53). Now he sets up Kavalerov as a potential rival for Valya's hand, albeit in a humorous tone. If Kavalerov really does turn out to be a better "new man" than Volodya, the latter might stand to lose his place with both his fiancée and his "father."

In his letter Volodya walks a fine line between insecure son and jealous lover. His anxiety is perhaps based on more than the fears of inadequacy of a son before his father, and the novel's ubiquitous homoeroticism will be treated in due course. Here, however, Andrei's androgyny once again becomes an issue. Every time Volodya writes about Andrei as a parent figure, the latter appears to be more mother than father. Volodya mocks Babichev's "tenderness" and his all-encompassing pity, yet it is these qualities that he finds so endearing. He recalls when he was injured on the soccer field and brought home to lie on the couch under the watchful eye of Andrei: "I look at you—suddenly you look at me; I immediately close my eyes—like with mama" (53). Yet at the same time, he declares that Andrei is his role model, much like a father is for a son: "I imitate you in all things" (52). For Volodya, Andrei plays any number of roles: mother, father, object of desire. None of these ties, however, is based on bonds of blood. Instead Volodya must always rationalize his feelings in the same materialistic terms that Babichev himself prefers: he thanks Andrei for giving him such a good life, then immediately mocks himself for appearing to write a love letter. He continually brags about his glorious future as the "Edison of the new age" (*Edison novogo veka*) (53), always following his claims with the nervous, self-mocking assertion that Andrei must be laughing at him. Volodya's letter, for all the insecurity it reveals, is an extended self-advertisement aimed at an audience of one. At all costs Volodya must prove that he is not only intrinsically worthy of Andrei's affection and admiration, but better than any challenger who could possibly threaten his station.

Volodya, however, has little to fear from Kavalerov or from any other rival for Andrei's attention. Though Babichev professes to base his love for Volodya on idealism and gratitude, he reveals his true fatherly feelings when caught off guard. When Kavalerov first asks Andrei about Volodya, the sausage maker immediately lauds his protégé as a "wonderful young man" (*zamechatel'nyi chelovek*). Kavalerov refuses to take such a general statement at face value (*"Chem zhe on zamechatelen?"*), in effect requiring Andrei to justify his appraisal of Volodya much as Volodya himself has to constantly prove his worthiness to himself and Babichev. Andrei beats a hasty retreat, admitting that Volodya is "simply a young man" (*"Da net. Prosto molodoi chelovek"*). Failing to sense any sort of ideological challenge (Kavalerov says that Andrei does not notice the spite in his voice), Andrei provides a simple, unadulterated explanation of his connection to Volodya: "The thing is that he is like a son to me" (*Delo v tom, chto eto kak by syn moi*) (22–23). Soon after he proceeds to explain how Volodya once saved his life, giving yet another rational justification for his affection. But even this fact, he claims, is not essential. The important thing, according to Babichev, is that Volodya is a "new man" (*sovershenno novyi chelovek*), like no one else in the world ("*Eto sovershenno ni na kogo ne pokhozhii iunosha*"). Such a statement is consistent with a worldview that denies the continuity of generations. Andrei, however, does not retract his claim to fatherhood; he merely embellishes it with an ideological gloss. Andrei himself has tacitly admitted that fatherly love and admiration of the new world can coexist, establishing in the novel's first pages a connection between the new world and male relationships.

Only when challenged to provide a full accounting of his bond with Volodya does Andrei at last land upon the proper rhetoric to explain the dual nature of his feelings. Returning to Andrei's monologue, we see that he actually goes beyond the call of duty, redefining the new world specifically in terms of fathers and sons: "Does this mean the human feeling of fatherly love doesn't have to be destroyed? But why does he love me, this new one? Does this mean that there, in the new world, the human feeling of love between father and son will flourish? Then I have the right to rejoice; then I have the right to love him like a son and like a new man. Ivan, Ivan, your conspiracy is worthless. Not all feelings will die" (81). Having first rejected fatherhood as such, Andrei reverses himself, turning paternity from vice to virtue. He was able to rationalize his paternal feelings away but incapable of devising a comparable explanation for Volodya's loyalty to him. Volodya is a new man, and he displays filial affection for Babichev. The new man cannot be wrong; therefore, the father-son bond lives on in the new world. In an impressive feat of circular logic, Andrei has beaten Ivan on the latter's terms. That this conquest takes place only in the mind of one of the struggle's participants is consistent with a novel where most arguments and battles occur only in the realm of the imagination.

Andrei sees the ideological rehabilitation of paternal ties as a satisfactory rebuttal to Ivan's charge that all feelings are dead in the new world. Andrei's conclusion that "not all" feelings have been destroyed does not deny that some feelings have indeed been eradicated. The only emotion that earns a revolutionary seal of approval is the bond between father and son. Here Olesha turns a decades-old Russian literary cliché on its head: from Turgenev's Bazarov to Bely's Ableukhovs, the revolution has been depicted as a force that sets fathers and sons against each other. Much of Olesha's novel, replete with broken families and new pseudo-familial structures, fits this well-established pattern. But now, in a masterful stroke of irony, Olesha puts forth the proposition that, despite the ubiquitous generational conflicts of the 1920s, it is the loyalty of father and son that survives the upheaval of revolution. The substance of the father-son bond is not subject to change; rather, the nature of fathers and sons themselves is different. Babichev speaks of fathers and sons, but he is referring to a relationship that has nothing to do with biology. Andrei does not retreat from the antifamily stance implicit in his plans to revolutionize the kitchen; rather, he wants to replace these filial ties with freely chosen, affiliative substitutes that, once established, essentially recapitulate the "bourgeois" relationships the revolution has rendered obsolete. Babichev, who "gives birth" to kitchens and sausages, who provides shelter to young men, repeatedly demonstrates a desire to free biological relationships from nature. As Harkins notes, he creates asexually, adopting his children rather than creating them naturally.[33] He embodies both the early Soviet rhetoric of "conquering" nature and the male "quarrel with nature" that Camille Paglia sees as the basis of Western art and culture (Paglia 28). When Babichev does without the natural, he does without women. Birth and creation become the solitary act of a solitary male. When he finds that his postrevolutionary utopia has room for emotion, it is a bond of a purely masculine sort. His father and son choose each other, love each other, and establish a connection that needs neither mother nor wife. Hence Andrei's joy at his findings: he has proven Ivan wrong without having to accept his brother's woman-centered rhetoric. The old world's Eternal Feminine, it would seem, has been replaced by the Eternal Masculine.

Chapter Four

THE OBJECT OF *ENVY*

Androgyny, Love Triangles, and the Uses of Women

"Who is Jocasta?" — Andrei Babichev, *Envy*

By revising the received wisdom that the revolution always pits father against son, Olesha presents in *Envy* a picture of the new postrevolutionary society as a man's world. As in the works of Babel and Platonov, femininity in *Envy* becomes a nagging, potentially subversive threat to the male order that must be kept at bay at all cost. Though femininity is consistently marginalized by the forces of the new society, the outright misogyny of Babel's Cossacks is nonetheless absent. Waving a bloody knife as she stands ankle-deep in entrails, Anechka may evoke castration anxiety, but the threat she presents to Kavalerov is more personal than ideological, however blurred the distinction between the two categories may become. Indeed, the only tendentious pronouncements about women and their place come from Kavalerov and Ivan, who profess to exalt women even as the new world degrades them. Andrei has neither the patience nor the inclination to debate the problem of women in the new world. It is Kavalerov who describes Andrei's plans in terms of women's liberation; Andrei does not discuss women at all. His new world, filled with superkitchens and ready-to-eat food, has no room for women as women, for the traditional femininity that Ivan so bombastically champions. Though Andrei himself never characterizes his project as an attack on the feminine, his efforts to incorporate the preparation of food into the public sphere amounts to an assault on one of the pillars of domesticity. His "adoption" of three stray "children" — Volodya, Kavalerov, and Valya — allows him to accumulate "offspring" without any recourse to women. The new world, it would appear, has little use for the feminine.

To accept that the feminine has been effectively banished by the new society, however, is to repeat the mistake of Ivan Babichev. Ivan's diatribe on the disappearance of womanhood is at best a self-fulfilling prophecy:

his identification of Valya with the incarnation of femininity drives her to his brother and ideological enemy, thus depriving Ivan of the only woman in his life. Far from being absent, femininity assumes new forms and functions in the novel. Paradoxically, the masculine world of *Envy* repeatedly shows itself to be androgynous. When the domestic sphere is assimilated into the public, the formerly clear boundaries between masculinity and femininity begin to fade. By trying to take on both traditionally masculine and feminine tasks, the men who do so themselves acquire feminine traits. The very triumph of masculine values leads to the partial feminization of the victors. The assault on traditional femininity and the resulting feminization of the conquerors is the subject of the first part of this chapter.

Femininity, like masculinity, is an abstraction. One can deny the importance of the feminine and still have to come to terms with the roles of individual women. For both the self-appointed representatives of the old world and the members of the new, women serve to bind men together. Valya is an object of exchange for all the men in her life, a "prize" for Kavalerov, a lost ideal for Ivan, a convenient mate for Volodya, and a ward for Andrei. By becoming a bone of contention, Valya facilitates the interactions among the men in the novel. Here René Girard's theory of triangular desire is crucial for understanding the fundamental dynamics of *Envy:* Valya is a pretext for the male rivalries that drive the plot. The triangular structure of the relationships in *Envy* will be treated in the second part of this chapter.

Valya herself straddles the line between concreteness and abstraction; she is such an ethereal, underdeveloped figure that she exists in the novel more as an idea than as a character. It is appropriate that her "sister" Ophelia is nothing but a concept, the perversion of old and new feminine ideals. Just as the traditional feminine sphere has been coopted by the masculine, so too does *Envy* present the *machine* as a male reimaging of the Eternal Feminine. The end of this chapter examines the fate of the feminine ideal in the masculine world and the persistence of femininity in the face of social change.

ANDROGYNY AND THE WAR AGAINST WOMEN

In the critical literature, Andrei Babichev has been described as a parody, a eunuch, a hermaphrodite, a failed attempt at a rugged Bolshevik ideal, and a possible pederast.[1] At first glance Andrei presents an appearance that is anything but masculine: enormously fat, he himself notes that his breasts shake in rhythm with his steps (12). Andrei's very name has *baba* at its root, a word rich in connotations. When used by a member of the urban population, it is usually a pejorative term for woman, along the lines of "broad" or "dame." Andrei is thus set up as an easy target for Kavalerov's derision. William Harkins provides the most extensive analysis of Andrei's sexuality, finding him a conglomeration of masculine and feminine traits. He notes that Babichev is "fussy as a housekeeper" (17) and makes copious use of eau de cologne ("Theme of Sterility" 444). In accordance with the prevailing attitudes of the time, Harkins equates homosexuality with effeminacy and describes gluttony as a character trait appropriate to a eunuch ("Theme of Sterility" 444, 445). After discussing Andrei's masculine and feminine characteristics, Harkins comes to the conclusion that the youngest of the three Babichev brothers is a "hermaphroditic figure." His explanation of Andrei's "hermaphrodism" contains a number of cogent observations, but none of them supports his overall interpretation of Andrei:

> As hermaphrodite he combines masculinity with femininity, but a masculinity and femininity which tend to neutralize one another: for masculine sexuality Andrei substitutes an intense career drive, while his feminine sexual tendency satisfies itself as latent homosexuality through the adoption of young men. He combines in himself the roles of provider (father) and nourisher (mother) and this is the inner reason why he is characterized as hermaphroditic. For he seeks to win for the utopian state which he represents the same fusion of both parental roles, and he identifies himself with that state. ("Theme of Sterility" 445)

One can certainly argue that Andrei sublimates his sexuality (whether it be masculine or feminine) in the service of his career, though the culturally conditioned equation of homosexuality with feminine sexuality is a proposition that can no longer be accepted at face value. When Harkins asserts that Andrei Babichev is emblematic of a state that is trying to replace the family, he has discovered an essential feature of Olesha's novel: the new world in *Envy* is a masculine society that is encroaching on a traditional female realm. Like Babichev, the new society is an imposing, somewhat comical male figure who attempts to replace the feminine, domestic sphere by incorporating it into the masculine, public order. It is essential, however, to differentiate between social conceptions of gender and the physical differences between the sexes. Bouncing breasts notwithstanding, Andrei's body presumably does not contain both male and female sexual organs. Rather, it is more accurate to follow George Nivat in calling Andrei "androgynous" (241), which refers to an ambiguity of gender rather than of physical sexuality.[2] Andrei can be accepted as a hermaphrodite only in the sense used by Marie Delacourt, who defines androgyny as a "pure concept, pure vision of the spirit, adorned with the highest qualities," whereas the hermaphrodite, by physically embodying this Platonic ideal "in a being of flesh and blood," is a parody or "a monstrosity" (Delacourt 45, qtd. in Hoeveler 211). Andrei's androgyny, however, is neither romantic nor Platonic. Rather, it is a phenomenon appropriate to the time in which Andrei lives. During an age when the family is in ruins and both male and female roles are subject to reexamination, men and women adopt personal characteristics usually associated with members of the opposite sex. This phenomenon has nothing to do with the physical traits of either men or women, entailing instead a confusion of the qualities society attaches to each sex.

Hence Andrei is only one of a set of androgynous figures who characterize the new world. Even Volodya and Valya, who appear to be the perfect male and female ideals, are at times portrayed in a distinctly androgynous light.[3] Volodya, the great soccer hero and "Edison of the new age," writes a letter to Andrei whose tone recalls nothing more than a "kept woman" guarding her place.[4] Indeed, were it not for the telltale masculine suffixes, Volodya's language could be lifted from a nineteenth-century tale of a "fallen woman" rescued by a noble-minded benefactor: "You raised me up, Andrei Petrovich! Not all Komsomol members live like this. And I live with you, with the wisest, most amazing personality ... I know: many people envy me."[5] Volodya's repeated objectification in the eyes of male observers, as well as his envy for the (feminine) machine, is discussed below. Valya is both a vision of feminine beauty and a budding athlete: when Kavalerov sees her and Volodya exercising, he notices that Valya's shoes give her a "masculine or childish" posture (97). As the similarities of their names might imply, Volodya and Valya are mirror images of one another, respectively embodying masculine and feminine ideals that contain an admixture of the opposite gender. The same holds true for the novel's inanimate "children," Andrei's sausage and Ivan's Ophelia, who are described in alternately masculine and feminine terms. Andrei's more obvious combination of gender traits is hermaphroditic or grotesque only to the extent that it takes the general confusion of male and female roles to a greater extreme.

The presence of both masculine and feminine characteristics in one person does not, however, connote neutrality. To Kavalerov, though Babichev is laughable for his feminine traits, he is nonetheless a particularly masculine threat. When Kavalerov contemplates throwing the sausage away, he is prevented by his fear of Babichev's reprisal: "I saw Babichev bearing down on me, an awe-inspiring, wide-eyed, invincible idol. I'm afraid of him. He stifles me. He doesn't look at me—and sees right through me" (36). Kavalerov is like a small boy who feels threatened by the sheer size of his father. His only defense is to turn the source of the threat into an object of satire, as Kolya does in "Legend." Many of the early descriptions of Babichev consist of Kavalerov's attempt to undermine Babichev's intimidating masculinity. He repeats Babichev's observation about his breasts, says he washes his face "like a boy," and calls him a dandy (*shchegol'*) (14). When Kavalerov calls Andrei a "model male being" (*Eto obraztsovaia muzhskai aosob'*) (12), his statement can only be interpreted ironically. Yet the targets Kavalerov chooses for his irony strongly suggest that he is compensating for feelings of inferiority. He lavishes a great deal of description on Andrei's groin, calling it "magnificent" (*velikolepen*), comparable only to that of an antelope buck. "Women, his secretaries and office workers, must be pierced with amorous shock from his gaze alone" (13). By directing so much venom at Babichev's apparently large genitalia, Kavalerov only draws attention to his own feelings of inferiority.

While it is true that Andrei's "present and past . . . are seemingly devoid of sexual companionship" (Harkins, "Theme of Sterility" 447), to suggest that Andrei should be seen as a neutral figure is to misinterpret his relations with both men and women.[6] Despite his incursion into the primarily female realm of the kitchen, Andrei Babichev lives and functions in a world of men. If Ivan laments the decline of womanhood, Andrei is the bearer of the opposite ideology, creating a new world that is defined almost exclusively in terms of male relationships.

The source of Andrei's androgyny, then, lies not in an essentially feminine nature, but is rather part and parcel of his attempt to draw the feminine into the masculine sphere. He strives to reorganize the traditionally feminine kitchen by removing it from the private, familial world of women and transforming it into something akin to industry. His entire life's work consists of subsuming the feminine within a totalizing masculine order. Either he chooses such a project because of his own gender ambiguity, or the work itself leaves its mark on his personality. As Volodya writes his mentor, "It's the sort of work you do that makes you so sensitive" (51). Instead of treating Andrei as a eunuch, one should consider him a man trying to usurp the role of a woman. Harkins insightfully notes that "by assuming for himself the role of mother as well as father, [Andrei] seeks to eliminate these functions and relationships in private life. The state itself shall become mother and father" ("Theme of Sterility" 446). What Babichev wants, however, is not to become less masculine, but to appropriate the female capacity for creation. Andrei's obsession with food and the rearing of young men indicates that Kavalerov and Ivan are not the only victims of envy in the novel: as Milton Ehre notes, Andrei covets the female capacity for reproduction (Ehre, "Olesha's *Zavist'*" 603).[7] Since biology will not permit him to get pregnant, he presses forward on another front. "War," Kavalerov tells us in an appropriately masculine metaphor, "has been declared on the kitchens" (15). Babichev cannot be female, but he can recreate the female in a masculine image. As Kavalerov puts it, Andrei "would like to give birth to food. He gave birth to the Quarter" (15). His "child" is a huge industrial superkitchen that is intended to render the private kitchen outmoded.

In his work, Andrei repeatedly attempts to give the food business a masculine character. In his memo dealing with the wrapper for a new candy bar, he rejects the name "Rosa Luxemburg" for the new product (it has already been used), directing his subordinate to look elsewhere for inspiration: "Maybe something from science (poetic—geography? Astronomy?) with a serious name and an enticing sound: 'Eskimo'? 'Telescope'?" (16) The name he dismisses belongs, of course, to a woman, whereas the only female names he suggests as a replacement are the grammatically feminine terms for scientific disciplines.[8] For Andrei, the candy bar's name must be "serious," and the appellations he chooses all reflect a preoccupation with the traditionally male sphere of science.

In "subjugating 1,000 kitchens" (16), Andrei battles a decidedly female enemy. In a world of men, Andrei might seem effeminate by contrast, but in the kitchen, in the eyes of suspicious housewives, Babichev is completely out of place. It is his maleness that makes him an unwelcome intruder when he visits the local kitchen like Harun-al-Rashid inspecting his harem. Andrei is in everybody's way, "huge, taking up much of their space, light, and air" (16). The housewives take one look at him and decide that he must be a "member of some committee." They shout accusations at him, blaming him for ruining their work with his very presence. He comes from a male world of briefcases and committees that is completely irrelevant to the domestic kitchen. Kavalerov calls these women, who aggressively defend their territory against the male interloper, "furies" (*furii*), connecting them with the Greek spirits of female vengeance. Babichev has lost this battle and is forced to leave without saying a word.

In Kavalerov's opinion, Babichev's lack of imagination prevents him from swaying these women over to his cause. Indulging in a sort of narrative masochism, Kavalerov spends much of the first half of the novel putting words into Andrei's mouth, usually finding a personal affront in every one of Babichev's unspoken utterances.[9] Here he supplies Babichev with an entire speech, most likely to demonstrate his own intellectual and oratorical superiority. His "ghostwriting" of Andrei's social program reveals nothing about his own views on the subject; rather, it is a purely rhetorical exercise, a bravura display of Kavalerov's way with words. Kavalerov provides the reader with the ideological justification of Andrei's project, employing the rhetoric that Babichev "should have" used. He talks in terms of liberation, of returning "the hours that the kitchen has stolen" from women: "half your lives will be returned to you"

(16). Kavalerov speaks of a liberation conferred upon women by men; Babichev was supposed to say that "we" (the men who are building the new world) will give "you" (the housewives) back your lost time. Even here, the women are only passive recipients of a gift bestowed by men of action. Women are not consulted in the development of this plan; rather, Babichev's work is to be presented as an inevitable part of the transformation of society.

In an equally imaginary speech, Andrei's brother Ivan also issues an appeal to women. Ivan, however, views Andrei's project in terms of violence and violation. The kitchen is not a thief of women's time, but the source of female pride and power: "*The horses of revolution, thundering along the back stairs, crushing your children* and your cats; *breaking* your beloved stoves and bricks, will *break into* your kitchens. Women, your pride and glory is threatened—the hearth! *The elephants of revolution want to crush your kitchen,* mothers and wives!" (91) (emphasis added). Here the revolution is a purely disruptive force, a wild animal that wants to destroy the home. The verbs Ivan uses all suggest extreme violence: "thundering" (*gremia*), "breaking" (*lomaia*), "breaking in" (*vorvutsia*), "to crush" (*razdavit'*). What Ivan describes is nothing short of a pogrom against the (female) old world, a rape of the bourgeois home. Thus he adds: "What do they want to push out of your heart? Your home—home, sweet home! He wants to make you wanderers on the wild fields of history" (91). For Ivan, the destruction of the home is an event of near-apocalyptic proportions. Indeed, the phrase "horses of the revolution" calls forth a host of associations in the mind of the Russian reader, from the four horsemen of the apocalypse to the heavily symbolic horses that abound in Russian literature.[10]

Though Ivan describes Andrei's plans in apocalyptic terms, he presents women's ultimate fate in a different light. The apocalypse is, by definition, the end of history, and yet the female victims of Andrei's project are condemned to become part of history rather than stand outside of it. For Ivan, women and the home comprise a world that does not function in historical time. His words recall the ancient Greek view that the world of women is cyclical, ahistorical. Women maintain a home that is untouched by the passage of time and world events, while men address the task of making history. Thus women are removed from the historical, linear time of men. The destruction of the home will force women to become "wanderers in the wild fields of history." Such a displacement will deal a fatal blow to the already dying old world. The family is destroyed, woman has lost her place, and the only human ties of any value are those among men.

THE TRAP OF TRIANGULAR DESIRE

With the exception of the handsome, athletic Komsomol members of his 1934 film script *A Strict Youth,* whose Aryan beauty and celibate camaraderie would bring a lump to the throat of a Hitler Youth organizer, the main protagonists of Olesha's works always observe male communities from an unbreachable distance. Their longing for masculine companionship, however, remains unabated. If anything, their desire only increases along with their frustration; the outlet it takes, however, appears on the surface as comradeship's opposite. Olesha's heroes have only one way of establishing ties with other men, hostile and unsatisfying as these ties may be. They are left with the poor man's substitute for male comradeship: the peculiar combination of intimacy and rivalry known as the love triangle.

If one were to judge only on the evidence of Olesha's works, love triangles would appear to be an inevitable and ubiquitous part of everyday existence. *Envy* alone has as many triangles as characters, with the Kavalerov-Valya-Volodya triangle being the most obvious.[11] The plot of *A Strict Youth* revolves around the love triangle of Grisha-Masha-Stepanov but also includes Tsitronov-Masha-Stepanov and Tsitronov-Masha-Grisha. "Aldebaran" (1931) presents the rivalry between the older Bogemsky and the younger Sasha over Sasha's girlfriend Katya. "The Cherry Pit" (1929) hinges upon the triangle Fedya-Natasha-Boris Mikhailovich, but also includes casual references to triangles throughout the story: while Fedya is out walking with Natasha and Boris Mikhailovich, two young women are off on a boat with Natasha's brother Erast, who shares a name with "Poor Liza"'s unfaithful lover. The narrator travels through his "invisible land" accompanied by "two sisters": Attention (*Vnimanie*) and Imagination (*Voobrazhenie*).[12] "Legend" hints at the oedipal triangle even as the mother is accorded less and less of the narrator's attention. The title character of "Natasha" (1936) is both the jealously guarded daughter of a respected professor and the adventurous girlfriend of the skydiving Stein. The fragments of the Modest Zand plays ("The Death of Zand" ["Smert' Zanda," 1930] and "The Black Man" ["Chernyi chelovek," 1932]) are built on love triangles, sometimes between a husband, a wife, and the wife's ex-husband, at other times between the married couple and Zand, and at still others between the couple and Dr. Gurfinkle. *The Conspiracy of Feelings,* Olesha's stage adaptation of *Envy,* features a scene in which Ivan tries to convince a cuckolded young man to kill his wife's lover and then congratulates the man for killing his wife instead. On a more abstract level, *A List of Assets* can be seen as a triangle in which the old and new worlds, each represented by a man, struggle for the conscience, if not the heart, of the actress Lelya Goncharova. In "The Chain" (1929), the narrator reduces the triangle to a fetish, stating, "Here was a triangle: the bicycle, the student, and I" (PR 247). When the bicycle is ruined, the triangle metaphorically begins to resemble more conventional love plots: "It can be put more strongly: the student had a wife, and I poked out her eye" (PR 249).

As "The Chain" demonstrates, the usually female object of desire is prone to substitutes and abstractions, creating triangular relationships involving two men when no human woman is present. "Summer" ("Letom"), one of the "Three Stories" ("Tri rasskaza") Olesha printed as one unit in 1936, centers on the bond formed between an intellectual older author (ostensibly Olesha himself) and a younger worker-turned-author who knows the names of the stars but is unable to recognize their poetry. In the first line of the story, the narrator tells us he dislikes the man from the very start. But after the narrator finds that the man is making a serious, though amateur, study of the stars, and, more important, that he remembers Olesha under the byline of "The Chisel" ("Zubilo") from *The Whistle* (*Gudok*), he warms to the younger writer. The two are erotically united by their fascination with a particularly feminine star:

> One had to see the rapture with which this charming young man gave me his explanations. He positioned me first one way, then another. All the while he lightly touched my shoulders. He stood behind me and raised my head . . .

> He said that he would call me when *she appeared [poiavitsia ona]*. Suddenly he stopped. I felt that—without looking backwards—he was looking for my hand. I extended my hand to him, and he led me forward.
>
> In silence, above the sleeping world, hung a star—greenish, plump, fresh, almost moist.
>
> "Capella?" I asked quietly. (PR 301; emphasis in the original)

After the narrator's initial distrust of the younger writer, the two men feel a closeness that extends to physical contact. This bond is based on their common susceptibility to the star's spell. The star connects them, but the relationship it creates is not one of equals: admiration of the star blends with admiration of the worker-writer, and the narrator blissfully accepts a passive role. The younger writer stands behind the narrator, lifting his chin, searching for his arm. Their stance could be a metaphor for all of Olesha's triangles: two men, standing in the dark, discover an intense bond with each other while turning their gaze toward a distant, aestheticized object.

The star itself is distinctly feminine, "almost moist," and almost sexual. Here Olesha takes the idealization and elevation of the feminine love object to its logical, if bizarre, extreme: the woman in question is no longer even a human being, having been replaced by a point of light in the sky. As we shall see in our discussion of *Envy*, Valya, though physically human, is scarcely more real to the desiring subject than the star in "Summer." Valya is in turn replaced by two ill-suited female substitutes (Anechka and Ophelia), who are respectively more and less concrete than she. The woman in the triangle serves a functional rather than a substantive role: she is the excuse for bringing the men together.[13]

Triangular desire is the engine of so many of Olesha's plots that its source and function must lie at the heart of his poetics. If the memoirs of Valentin Kataev are to be trusted, such triangular relationships were a recurring motif in Olesha's life as well. Olesha's friendship with Kataev dates back to their youth in Odessa; it became strained when both would later take up residence as writers in Moscow. Though *My Diamond Wreath* recounts their continuing friendship in the 1920s, by 1933 Kataev had attacked Olesha as "decadent," "provincial," and "lacking in culture" (Sobolev). Alexander Gladkov poignantly recounts Olesha's reaction to the official celebration of Kataev's sixtieth birthday in the late 1950s. The two authors, according to Gladkov, "had much to connect them, but something came between them." Olesha could not stop talking about Kataev's birthday, his reactions running a wide gamut of emotions. Nor could he make up his mind whether or not to pay a visit to Kataev. "In further conversation Y[uri] K[arlovich] called K[ataev] his "brother," but then immediately began making "malicious, paradoxical statements about brotherly love." Clearly envy, Olesha's recurring theme, played a role in their relationship: suddenly Olesha asked Gladkov whether he or Kataev was the better writer. Gladkov, naturally, could not bring himself to answer this question immediately, whereupon Olesha made a pronouncement that Kataev would repeat in his memoirs: "I write better, but . . . his demon is stronger than my demon!" (Suok-Olesha 275). For his part, Kataev professed to agree with Olesha's appraisal even while admitting he never would know what Olesha meant by "demon" (Kataev 89).[14]

Kataev writes that he and *kliuchik* ("little key"), as he nicknames Olesha, "were fated to become the closest of friends—closer than brothers" (Kataev 11). The two were "connected by some sort of mysterious thread," predetermined "to become eternal friends/rivals, or even enemies who are in love with each other" (Kataev 89). The force that Kataev identifies as the source of their relationship seems to come right out of an Olesha story: "Basically, mutual envy bound us together stronger than love, starting in our youth and lasting our entire lives" (Kataev 98). Like the Victorian poets whose mutual affection extended to the point of marrying each other's sisters, Kataev confesses that he "always was in the habit of falling for [his] comrades' sisters." This custom extended to Olesha's younger sister, who "resembled [her brother], but was better looking." He kept his love a secret but claimed that Olesha told him his sister called out for Kataev on her deathbed (Kataev 89). With the benefit of hindsight, even Kataev places his infatuation with Olesha's sister in the context of his strong bond with Olesha himself; the description of her death is immediately followed by one of Kataev's frequent meditations on the nature of his and Olesha's friendship.

When women began to play a greater role in both their lives, Olesha's friendship with Kataev began to revolve around their mutual attraction to the same women. According to Kataev, Olesha was "devilishly successful with women," a fact his closest friends "secretly envied" (Kataev 95–96). Kataev admits that he envied the effect Olesha had on women (Kataev 98), but his friendship with Olesha was only strengthened by the latter's relationship with the woman Kataev calls *druzhochek* ("little friend"): "His love for his little friend didn't change our relationship. But now we were no longer two, but three.... We lived as a trio" (Kataev 102). Rather than become rivals, the two friends were united in their resolve to keep Olesha's "little friend" away from other men. This proved no easy task: she twice abandoned Olesha for other men. Curiously, each time it fell to Kataev to attempt to "steal" Olesha's girlfriend from his rivals.[15] Olesha, writes Kataev, was too "well raised" (*vospitanyi*) to be "given to adventures," and thus Kataev "took on the abduction" of Olesha's girlfriend himself, since he was "in greater despair" than Olesha (Kataev 103). After her first "abduction" by Kataev, Olesha's "little friend" seems only too glad to return to her beloved. When she is "stolen" for a second time, Olesha himself, at Kataev's urging, attempts to recapture her, but this time he is unsuccessful. Once again it is Kataev who attempts to negotiate between the two rivals. When it becomes clear that she has left Olesha for good, the ever-flexible triangle widens to include the man who won her heart: "But our relations with [the rival] and 'little friend,' strangely enough, remained unchanged. We continued to be friendly and got together often" (Kataev 130). This predilection for sharing a woman and abducting her from a rival becomes permanently associated with Olesha in Kataev's memoirs.[16] In *The Holy Well*, Kataev reports a dream in which he and Olesha abduct, of all people, Nadezhda Mandelstam as part of a lighthearted joke on her husband (6: 157–59).

The ability to defuse rivalry and turn it into an even stronger friendship may have been a motif in Olesha's life, but in his art, triangles rarely bring Olesha's protagonists anything but frustration.[17] The only exception is *A Strict Youth,* in which the athlete Diskobol acts upon Grisha Fokin's desires for Masha while the latter can only watch passively.[18] Much as Kataev abducted "little friend" for the overly timid Olesha, Diskobol casually informs Masha of Grisha's feelings, displaying not the slightest concern that he has done so in the presence of Masha's husband. *A Strict Youth* contains a love triangle centered on rivalry (Grisha-Masha-

Stepanov), but it also allows for two friends (Grisha and Diskobol) to be allies in the battle for Masha's heart. The heroes of Olesha's film, however, differ from the typical protagonist of his prose: instead of alienated dreamers, they are the author's conception of the ideal Komsomol youth. Unlike Olesha's earlier characters, these men are capable of friendship (Grisha and Diskobol) and comradeship (the Komsomol) and thus experience a bond that Kavalerov or Fedya from "The Cherry Pit" can never know.

Yet despite Kavalerov's inability to make either friends or comrades, the desire for a connection with other men is still at the heart of the novel's triangles. Here I would argue that René Girard's reinterpretation of the classic love triangle provides a particular useful model for understanding intersubjective dynamics of Olesha's novels and stories. Although Girard acknowledges no debt to Lévi-Strauss and polemicizes with Freud, his hypothesis of mediated desire has much in common with cultural theories based on the exchange of women. Like Lévi-Strauss and Irigaray (see the introduction), Girard approaches a well-known human phenomenon as an interaction between men through women. Though Girard would later expand his theory to encompass all of civilization, it is his first exposition of his ideas in *Deceit, Desire, and the Novel* that is applicable to Olesha. Girard considers desire a phenomenon whose source is intrinsic to the desiring subject; one does not simply desire something for its own sake, but rather because it is coveted by someone else. Hence triangular desire: first the subject finds a model, or "mediator," whereupon the subject's desires grow out of the desires of his chosen idol. If the two men (and Girard talks almost exclusively of men in these situations) are separated either by physical distance or social status, the result is external mediation, in which the "hero . . . proclaims aloud the true nature of his desire. He worships his model openly and declares himself his disciple" (*Deceit* 9–10). Of greater relevance to *Envy* is internal mediation, which arises when the distance between the two men is reduced, resulting in rivalry. The "hero of internal mediation, far from boasting of his efforts to imitate, carefully hides them. . . . The subject is convinced that the model considers himself too superior to accept him as a disciple." Thus the subject "no longer wants to see in his mediator anything but an obstacle" (*Deceit* 10).

Girard identifies two "triangular" vices whose source is internal mediation: jealousy and envy, each of which involves an object, a subject, and a third person who bears the brunt of the subject's hostility. Both the jealous person and the envier see their desire as spontaneous, the former seeing his rival as "an intruder, a bore . . . who interrupts a delightful tete-à-tete." Such a conviction is delusional: "true jealousy . . . always contains an element of fascination with the insolent rival" (*Deceit* 12). Analogously, envy can only be explained by rejecting "the object of rivalry as a starting point and [choosing] the rival himself, i.e. the mediator, as both a point of departure and its conclusion." Rivals are trapped in a never-ending loop of mediation, since competition for the desired object only "increases the mediator's prestige and strengthens the bond which links the object to this mediator" (*Deceit* 13).

Though Girard's analysis grows more problematic when it makes claims to universality,[19] his approach is almost tailor-made for Olesha's works.[20] Most important is the break he makes with traditional definitions of desire and love triangles: for Girard, the mediator or rival always takes precedence over the object. Dethroned from the pedestal on which each rival so tenaciously places it, the object of desire is reduced to a mere symptom of the rivalry, its official excuse for existence. Traditional approaches to *Envy* operate on the assumption that Kavalerov's rivalry with Volodya is based on a true desire to "capture" Valya. Girard's theory suggests a radically different reading: Kavalerov's desire for Valya is secondary to the attraction exerted by Volodya.

The Kavalerov-Valya-Volodya triangle is embedded within the novel's other major triangles and is thus difficult to isolate from the rest. Kavalerov's competition with Volodya for the paternal affection of Andrei Babichev is at least as intense as the desire for Valya, and it takes chronological precedence in the story's sequence of events. Yet it is the struggle for Valya that is most clearly identifiable as a love triangle, and it is this rivalry that Kavalerov himself would prefer to see as the driving force of the plot. Indeed, it is far more comfortable to imagine oneself in a rather traditional competition for the affections of a beautiful woman than to admit that one is jealous of or attracted to the qualities of another man. Kavalerov's very name, whose root, *kavaler,* means "cavalier" or "gentleman caller," implies that he was born to participate in civilized contests for a lady's favor. From the very beginning, Kavalerov tries to turn his admiration for Valya and Volodya into an old-world romantic tale, but any control he exerts over the novel's narration has no effect on the events of the plot, and thus *Envy* resolutely transforms itself into another story altogether. In his attempt to deceive both himself and the reader as to the nature of his aspirations, his unspoken goal is much the same, as in his urge to avoid the ubiquitous father: Kavalerov wants to escape from mediated desire. Kavalerov desperately needs his sexual encounters to be untouched by the presence of a father, because he yearns to be free from the pattern set up by paternal authority. He wants his desire to be a sign of spontaneous self-expression, rather than a factor that would chain him to the path of family continuity shown to him by his father. Similarly, Kavalerov does not acknowledge that his designs on Valya are the result of mediation; after a quick reading of the novel, one could be left with the impression that Valya's appeal is purely based on her beauty. Closer scrutiny reveals that Kavalerov's desire for Valya could scarcely be more mediated.

The initial mediator of Kavalerov's desire for Valya is Ivan, rather than Volodya. Ivan mediates in a profoundly different way from Volodya, one that poses no threat to Kavalerov's pride. Ivan is part of an older generation, Valya's father and Kavalerov's father figure, and thus he is not in romantic competition for Valya. Theoretically, Ivan and Kavalerov could share Valya, as presumably only one of them is seeking a sexual bond with her.[21] As a freely chosen substitute father, as a "teacher," Ivan is Kavalerov's external mediator. Where the subject of internal mediation would deny any desire to imitate his mediator, the subject of external mediation quite openly proclaims himself his mediator's disciple, the Sancho Panza to the mediator's Don Quixote.

It is Ivan who unwittingly draws Valya to Kavalerov's attention. Kavalerov catches his first glimpse of Valya while following Ivan, who has fascinated him since his first appearance under Andrei's window. So strong is the immediate kinship Kavalerov feels with Ivan that he almost acts under the assumption that the two men share the same thoughts. When Kavalerov thinks that the bird both he and Ivan are observing looks like a half-moon, he almost says as much aloud, for he is "convinced that the resemblance occurred to [Ivan] as well" (30). Later the two serve as each other's reflections in a mirror, and Kavalerov thinks that Ivan is reading his thoughts.

Before Kavalerov approaches Valya, he listens to Ivan's impassioned pleas for her to return. Only after watching this drama unfold does Kavalerov tell Valya, "You passed by me like a branch covered with flowers and leaves" (31). His words appear romantic and spontaneous, but they mask a desire that has deeper roots. Kavalerov has met Valya while following Ivan, and it is Ivan who has shown that he, at least, considers Valya worthy of his attention. Throughout the novel, Ivan unwittingly encourages Kavalerov's desire for Valya. Ivan tells Kavalerov that Valya, who he had thought was the embodiment of true womanhood, has deserted to the other side. Kavalerov's unspoken response uses a verb more appropriate for a plant than for a living woman: "I'll pluck [*vyrvu*] Valya from them" (67). It is Ivan who has supplied the motivation for a desire upon which Kavalerov is expected to act. If Kavalerov idealizes Valya's ethereal beauty, his feelings are in part due to Ivan's own conception of his daughter. In praising Valya as the symbol of old-world femininity, Ivan encourages Kavalerov to see in Valya the woman of his dreams.

When Kavalerov declares war on Babichev in his letter, he is only beginning to comprehend the family structure of the people who surround him. Based on his extremely limited knowledge of Ivan and Valya, he has decided that he will "defend" them from Andrei (38). But Kavalerov chooses his allies before truly understanding the nature of the conflict. The triangle Ivan-Valya-Andrei is part of the background of the novel, having begun long before Kavalerov entered the scene. In his letter, Kavalerov admits that he is intrigued with Andrei's brother, whereupon he accuses Andrei of having sexual designs on his own niece. Even Ivan never accuses Andrei of such an offense, perhaps because he knows that Valya is romantically involved with Volodya. Kavalerov sides with Ivan in part from fascination, in part from the conviction that the enemy of his enemy is his friend. All he really knows about Ivan is that Ivan is against Andrei, and that is enough. As a result, Kavalerov, who is already predisposed to see Ivan as the keeper of a "mystery" (*taina*), is mediated not by Ivan, but by his conception of Ivan: he takes Ivan's side in the battle as he understands it.

Kavalerov's gravest error concerns Volodya. For once, Kavalerov's first impression proves more accurate than subsequent reevaluations. Before Kavalerov becomes aware of Valya's existence, he has already started to feel hostility and envy for Volodya, whom he knows only from a photograph in Andrei's apartment. His first "acquaintance" with Volodya immediately presents the soccer player as a threat, for Kavalerov realizes that he will have to give up his place on Andrei's couch when Volodya returns. Naturally, Kavalerov uses all the sarcasm in his vast arsenal, first ironically referring to the "greatness" of soccer players, finally stooping to name-calling. But Andrei does not hear Kavalerov, and the insults never reach their target. At this point represented only by his portrait, Volodya remains completely unharmed. The "plebeian face" in the portrait continues to smile, showing his "particularly manly, shiny teeth" (*osobenno, po-muzhski blestiashchie zuby*) (25). As yet no tie has been established between Volodya and Valya in Kavalerov's mind, but the former is already an object of envy and scorn.

By the time he writes his letter, however, Kavalerov has completely reversed himself. Carried away by his own invective, he divests Andrei of every potential ally, enlisting even Volodya in his faction. In life, Kavalerov is deprived of close relationships, and only in his letter does he achieve his cherished dream of belonging. Having failed to establish a relationship with Andrei, he turns to Andrei's brother, "son," and niece. Valya will be his bride, Ivan will be his friend, and Volodya will be his brother. Kavalerov admits that his knowledge of Volodya is limited ("I only know that he is a soccer player"), but he "has no doubt" that Volodya "has fled" from Babichev, "fed up with [his] mockery." Earlier Kavalerov had been offended that Babichev brought him home only because of a fleeting resemblance to the absent Volodya; now he assumes that Andrei's unstated comparison was justified, and that Volodya is just as much a victim as Kavalerov. Unable to raise himself to Volodya's status in the Babichev household, Kavalerov instead pulls Volodya down to his level, deciding that they are both "jesters and freeloaders" in Andrei's court. While writing about Volodya, Kavalerov slowly builds a closer and closer relationship with him. By the end of the section, they have forged a firm alliance: "But I assure you, neither he nor I—we will never come back to you" (44).

Before they meet, Volodya is a figment of Kavalerov's imagination, a "comrade in misfortune" (49) superimposed by Kavalerov on the sketchy information available to him. Just as he fantasizes a happy-go-lucky folk hero named Tom Virlirli upon hearing the sound of church bells ("Tom-vir-lir-li! Tom-vir-lir-li! Tom-vir-lir-li!"), Kavalerov concocts a Volodya Makarov all his own. Both are the products of Kavalerov's brief stay with Andrei Babichev, and both are ideal men whom Kavalerov can never equal. Tom Virlirli is a romantic image of lighthearted youth: unlike Kavalerov the "daddy" (*papasha*), Tom Virlirli lives a life of pure potential: "He can do everything. He personifies the haughtiness of youth, the secret pride of daydreams" (49). It is a boy's fantasy of total freedom, and Kavalerov imagines that the bell's song of Tom Virlirli is actually a melody sung by little boys who dream of such a carefree existence. The name "Virlirli" itself suggests manliness, containing the Latin root *vir*, or "man."[22] Immediately prior to his first (and only) direct encounter with Volodya, Kavalerov feels he is taking an action worthy of Tom Virlirli: like this imaginary hero, Kavalerov is gathering his meager possessions and preparing a journey into the unknown. But it is Volodya who fits the profile of Tom Virlirli. When Kavalerov opens the door to Volodya, he sees Tom Virlirli, complete with a backpack. Their meeting is a disappointment for both. Volodya smiles "as though he has already seen a dear, cherished friend through the closed door," only to be thrown off balance by the presence of Kavalerov. For his part, Kavalerov makes a fool of himself by talking to Volodya as if the latter truly were a fellow "jester and freeloader" in Babichev's court. Only now does Kavalerov realize that Volodya will never be his ally. This realization is a great blow, for Volodya has proved to be Kavalerov's superior on two levels: not only is he the "favored son" (*barchuk*) of Andrei Petrovich, it is he, and not Kavalerov, who approaches the ideal of Tom Virlirli. From this point on, every time Kavalerov sees Volodya, he will feel humiliated and inferior.

Kavalerov's fascination with Volodya, who is both his physical superior and the rightful occupant of Andrei's spare couch, takes on erotic overtones in the novel's second half. It is in this section that Ivan becomes Kavalerov's "teacher" and assertive mediator, fanning the flames of Kavalerov's infatuation with Valya by continually singing her praises. The specter of Volodya, however, is ever present, for Ivan blames the soccer player for Valya's betrayal. Still unaware that Kavalerov's enemies are

Ivan's blood relations, Ivan finally decides to acquaint Kavalerov with his daughter. The acquaintance is to be a one-way affair, as Ivan's words suggest that Valya is a sight to be seen rather than a person to introduce: "Today I want to show you Valya" (95).[23] The task is not so simple, however. Just as Ivan took Kavalerov on a journey through deserted lots and broken fences to see Ophelia, now the two of them embark on a tour of downtown Moscow. The suspense is built up over three pages, as the two of them search for Valya and her companions. Finally, having reached their destination, Ivan whispers to Kavalerov: "There she is . . . Look." The reader would be perfectly justified to expect an extended description of Valya's ethereal beauty, but Kavalerov's gaze falls on an entirely different object:

> Everyone shouted and clapped. The high-jumper, almost naked, walked off to the side, slightly leaning on one leg, most likely out of an athlete's coquetry.
> It was Volodya Makarov.
> Kavalerov felt lost. He was overwhelmed by shame and fear. Volodya smiled, revealing an entire shining mechanism of teeth. (97)

Ivan continually directs Kavalerov's attention toward Valya, but, at this point, the latter sees only Volodya. This vision of Volodya combines all the necessary elements to inspire "shame and fear" in Kavalerov. Kavalerov sees Volodya during a moment of personal triumph and public acclaim: "everybody" is applauding and cheering him, while he smiles his perfect smile. Through his high jumps, Volodya has proven his physical superiority, while Kavalerov can only stand by and watch.

Kavalerov's shame is also connected to Volodya's eroticism. Though Kavalerov is no longer the narrator, the entire scene is framed by his vision. There is an element of voyeurism involved that he himself cannot help but notice; when he gazes at Volodya through the hole in the stone wall, he thinks that it would be "very stupid to be caught peeping behind the wall" (97). The fact that Kavalerov has to struggle to hide in order to see the half-naked Volodya suggests a forbidden sexual attraction.

At the soccer match, where Volodya further proves his superiority as both a physical specimen and a team player, Kavalerov's gaze once again lingers on Volodya's eroticized body as well as Valya's: "A body flew up over the crowd, exposed, naked skin flashing... One of his socks had slid down his leg, becoming a green bagel around his pear-shaped, slightly hairy calf. His torn shirt barely stayed on his body. He chastely crossed his arms over his chest" (105–6). Here Volodya assumes the classically feminine, languid pose of the embarrassed woman vainly trying to hide her nudity. At this point Kavalerov's voyeurism is shared by the 20,000 soccer fans in the stadium, but it is Kavalerov's eyes that frame this particular scene. Twice Kavalerov is humiliated by watching Volodya, and each time because he sees first Volodya's superior physical prowess, then his strong erotic appeal. Each scene hits Kavalerov on two fronts simultaneously, inciting feelings of both personal and sexual inferiority.

The soccer match is the perfect vehicle for the resolution of the novel's ideological struggle: what better metaphor could there be for a male system than a sporting match? The game pits the Soviet team against a German one. The juxtaposition is classic, for the Germans had long been the epitome of "foreignness" in Russian literature and culture. Each team is, in turn, represented by its star player, and thus much of the description of the game focuses on the contrast between Volodya Makarov and the German Getske. Long before the game, the reader is aware that Volodya exemplifies the collective ideal: "His strongest feeling was that of comradeship" (81). The soccer match gives Volodya the chance to demonstrate this characteristic in action: "As a soccer player, Volodya was the complete opposite of Getske . . . For Volodya, the most important thing was the general outcome of the game, the common victory. Getske strove only to show his own artistry. He was an old, experienced player who had no intention of supporting his team; he valued only his own success" (102). Getske functions as Kavalerov's "wandering id," fighting the battle against Volodya that Kavalerov himself could never hope to join. The narrator's criticism of the German is equally applicable to Kavalerov, who, like Getske, is concerned only with personal, rather than collective, glory. But Kavalerov finds himself in a situation far more loathsome than Getske's: neither is a team player, but at least Getske knows how to play the game. When the ball comes flying into the stands and lands at Kavalerov's feet, Kavalerov can no longer rely on Getske to act for him. He must abandon his passive role-playing and take direct action if the game is to continue. But when faced with the prospect of actually participating, he is paralyzed by the knowledge that thousands of people are looking at him, waiting for him to throw the ball. The narrator notes that such events make spectators laugh by forcing them to confront the absurdity of their own rapt interest in the game; all the more ridiculous is Kavalerov's role as perpetual voyeur. To add insult to injury, it is Andrei, the unattainable father, the man who defines the new world in terms of father-son ties, who throws the ball back onto the field.

Kavalerov's failure to attract the attention, let alone the affection, of either Valya and Volodya, the two other members of the love triangle, or Andrei, the substitute father, prompts him to leave the game before it is finished. Because the game's outcome is never revealed, LeBlanc finds that the ideological conflict the game represents is thus left ambiguous and unresolved (66–67). The soccer game is left before it ends, however, precisely because the results of the battle no longer hold any interest for either of the underdogs who claim to have joined it. Ivan has admitted the total irrelevance of his "conspiracy" (88), and now Kavalerov has proven his inability even to participate in the game. Thus Kavalerov has stopped even trying to play. Ivan's toast to indifference in the novel's final lines implicitly explains why the results no longer matter: the challengers have quit before they can be defeated.

When Kavalerov leaves the soccer match, he abandons not only the battle of worldviews, but also any hope of a connection with either Valya or Volodya. His subsequent sexual encounter with Anechka can easily be seen as a mockery of Kavalerov's unconsummated love for Valya, but Anechka is only one element of the parody: even with Anechka, Kavalerov finds himself in a triangle. Kavalerov is left with the repulsive, middle-aged Anechka instead of the beautiful young Valya, and Kavalerov now has to share a woman with the ridiculous, middle-aged Ivan instead of the beautiful young Volodya. Like Valya, Anechka also brings men together, even if only as rivals. She salvages the tie between Ivan and Kavalerov, replacing a bond of ideology with one of sex. But the resulting *ménage à trois* brings together both the younger generation's love triangle and the oedipal triangle of the son and his parents, for both Anechka and Ivan are significantly older than Kavalerov. The novel has come full circle: the father is once again the rival, and the mother is still the object of desire, albeit an ironic one. The result is the closest thing to a family to which Kavalerov can ever belong. Ivan's lurid proposal to take turns with the widow is consistent with the internal logic of the novel: love in *Envy* is always triangular. No encounter with a woman can have any value in the novel unless it involves another man.

THE RETURN OF THE FEMININE IDEAL

Women in *Envy* are left with the thankless task of facilitating the connections among the novel's various men. Their role is purely relational: the only qualities they have are the ones men choose to attribute to them. In creating Ophelia, Ivan takes this tendency to its extreme, for he invents a "woman" who exists only in his own mind. But it is Valya whose image is most manipulated by the men in her life. Valya is established from the very beginning as an empty vessel to be filled by the desires and ambitions of the men around her. Her first appearance associates her metonymically with a vase (*vazochka*), a noun phonetically similar to her name. When Kavalerov first looks up at Valya's balcony, he sees only a vase with a flower. He assumes that it is this vase that draws Ivan closer to the apartment ("Chelovechka privlekaet vazochka"). For a moment Valya and the vase are merged in the narrative: "He called out to the vase, 'Valya!'" When Valya does, at last, appear, she knocks over the vase. Even so, the vase continues to function as her double: "The girl lay face down on the window sill, hanging her disheveled head. The vase rolled beside her" (30). When Valya leaves the apartment to pursue her father on the street, Olesha does not strain his readers' credibility by having her take the vase with her, but the narrator still manages to draw one last comparison between the girl and her pottery: "A tear flowed down the curve of her cheek, as on a vase" (31). Even Valya's own father, Ivan, recognizes that his daughter serves as the vessel of men's aspirations, though he fails to see his own complicity in her exploitation. He accuses his brother of trying to use Valya as part of a communist eugenics program: "You want to bring forth a new breed. My daughter is not an incubator" (88). Though the charge is specific to Andrei, the basic idea behind Ivan's accusation has broader implications. Most of the male characters in *Envy* have designs on Valya, and yet she has little more substance than her imaginary "sister" Ophelia.

It is Ivan who first defines his daughter in terms reminiscent of the Symbolist Eternal Feminine: "woman was the best, most wonderful, purest flower of our culture . . . The feminine was the glory of the old era" (66). He had searched for a woman who embodies these qualities and thought he had found her in Valya. But she abandons him, apparently convinced by Volodya that her father is insane. *Envy* repeatedly presents family relationships that have been rendered unnecessarily complicated by the imposition of ideology. Andrei and Volodya must rationalize their pseudo-filial bond through revolutionary rhetoric, while Ivan estranges his daughter by treating her as a metaphysical phenomenon rather than an ordinary human being.

Through a combination of physical beauty and an apparent absence of any views of her own, Valya becomes a pawn in a family drama that is viewed by its participants as an ideological struggle.[24] She takes the central place in two opposing triangles: as Andrei's niece and Volodya's girlfriend, she is a token of the closeness between the two men, but as her father's lost ideal and Kavalerov's unattainable goal, she serves as a symbol for their aspirations. Valya is seen by Kavalerov as part of a "package deal" received by the young man fortunate enough to have won Andrei's favor: Volodya gets Andrei's couch, his attention, his respect, and his niece. Ideologically, she has joined the camp of the new world and its builders, exercising together with Volodya and accompanying Andrei to Volodya's triumphant soccer match. Andrei never expresses the desire to use Valya "to bring forth a new breed," as Ivan would have it, but Volodya's attitude toward his girlfriend would hardly reassure her father. He takes for granted that they will marry, subsuming her under his own and Andrei's ambitions. He speaks not of love, but of the "union" (*soiuz*) he has established with Valya (45). Their first kiss will take place at the opening of Andrei's "Quarter," the colossal kitchen designed to render the family obsolete. Here sexuality, marriage, and the unstated promise of offspring are regulated in terms of male ambition and social engineering.

Valya also serves as the cement between Ivan and Kavalerov: one has lost her while the other seeks to "steal" her as a "prize." Though Kavalerov is fascinated by Valya from the moment he first sees her, he sets out to win her only after discovering her relationship with Volodya. It is Ivan, the old world's "ideologist" (Barrat, *Yurii Olesha's "Envy"* 41), who establishes Valya as a symbol of the lost romantic age. Ivan had hoped Valya would serve as a hypostasis of his feminine ideal, thus functioning as the ideological glue that would hold his conspiracy together. Though Ivan's plans never come to fruition, his idealization of Valya fuels Kavalerov's growing obsession with the image of a woman he barely knows.

As the example of Valya shows, women pose a particular problem for the new world. Traditional femininity is to be either eradicated or coopted by the communist future; the new world offers no individual woman as a symbol, no equivalent to the French Marianne: "Mother Russia" was only rehabilitated during World War II (Bonnell 275).[25] In rejecting her father's delusions, Valya does land firmly in Andrei's and Volodya's camp, but she never becomes an emblem of the new society they are trying to build. She is an example of the "new people" rather than their symbol.[26] Andrei and Volodya do not speak of her in anything approaching idealized terms. Indeed, they barely speak of her at all. It is Volodya who is exalted by Andrei as the symbol of the new world, showing that he is no less prone to hyperbole than his brother. As the phonetic similarity between their names suggests, Valya is the female counterpart to Volodya, but she actually functions as a symbol of the new only to the extent that her youth suggests the promise of the future. The future is precisely what Kavalerov sees in her as she exercises with Volodya: "But, higher, beneath her black shorts, the purity and tenderness of her body showed how wonderful its owner would be upon reaching maturity and becoming a woman" (98).

Despite the pretenses to pure rationality, the new world is the heir of the old, and traces of the romantic era championed by Ivan have their distorted counterparts in the evolving revolutionary society.[27] As discussed in the previous chapter, Volodya, the new man, worships a feminine idol: the machine.[28] The word "machine" (*mashina*) is feminine in Russian, a fact that Olesha exploits to great effect in *Envy*. When Ivan describes his "universal machine" to Kavalerov, his words continually suggest seduction and rape: he has dishonored (*opozoril*) and debauched (*razvratil*) the machine (76–77). Yet the machines Volodya so admires are barely recognizable as feminine. They are "proud and dispassionate," functioning with impeccable logic and skill. These machines are the perfect "women" for new men such as Volodya, and it is not for nothing that Volodya devotes a paragraph to his envy of and passion for machines while disposing with Valya in a few curt lines. Like Eve created from Adam's rib, the machine is a new "woman" who owes her existence only to men. The machine, brought forth into the world asexually by men, is the result of production rather than reproduction: it is woman recreated in man's image. Volodya envies the machine because it has proved more efficient and cold-blooded than its creators (44). Once again the masculine drive to subsume the feminine leads to a strange brand of androgyny. Volodya wants to be more efficient and cold, a goal that would create a further distance between him and traditional femininity. Yet his chosen model is the machine, an object whose essential femininity is reinforced throughout the novel.

Ivan, who recognizes that the machine is the "idol" (77) of the new men, wishes to exploit the machine's femininity in his struggle with Andrei and Volodya. He superimposes his romantic ideal of the Eternal Feminine onto Volodya's sleek, efficient machine, and the result is a travesty of both. The machine Ophelia is a parody of the Eternal Feminine, a "cheap, sentimental good-for-nothing" (*poshliachkoi, sentimental'noi negodiakoi*) who can "sing the silly love songs and gather the flowers of the old era" (87). As a machine she is a disgrace, for her potential as the "highest creation of technology" is ruined by her acquisition of "the most vulgar human feelings" (86). Volodya extols the machine's ability to work "without wasting a single digit" (52), but Ivan tells Andrei in his "fairy tale" that Ophelia "will turn every one of your digits into a useless flower" (93). Ophelia, it is true, is only a figment of Ivan's (and later Kavalerov's) imagination, but the same can also be said for Ivan's conception of Valya.[29] Just as Anechka is poor compensation for Valya in the novel's love triangles, so, too, is Ophelia Ivan's second choice as ideological symbol. Ophelia is the monstrous synthesis of the novel's two opposing feminine ideals, and Ivan meets with little success in his attempts to build a movement centered around such a creature.³⁰ Instead, she terrifies even her own creator, who is convinced that she hates him and wants to kill him (88).

Ivan's attempts to find a substitute for his daughter only emphasize the futility of his cause: how can Ivan claim to be the champion of femininity and the family in the abstract if this crusade has estranged him from every one of his blood relatives? Ivan sacrifices practice at the altar of theory and loses his daughter in the process. Andrei asserts that Ivan's conspiracy is worthless (*nichtozhen*) because fatherly feeling, having shed its dependence on ties of blood, survives in the new world. Andrei "wins" the contest with his brother by being a better father to an adopted son than Ivan can ever be to his natural daughter. After Andrei's unspoken declaration of victory in *Envy*'s chapter 5, Ivan celebrates his own imaginary triumph in the "Tale of the Meeting of Two Brothers" in chapter 6. He can defeat his brother only in fantasy, with the assistance of an artificial "daughter" who exists only in his imagination. Chapter 7 recounts Ivan's final and total defeat, an event that happens with almost inexplicable rapidity. When examined in the light of filiation, this puzzling scene reveals itself to be completely consistent with the workings of the novel. Unlike Kavalerov, Ivan is unmoved by the sign of Volodya's and Valya's gymnastic skills. He noisily calls for Kavalerov to stop running away, for he is ready to use his only real weapon: Ivan wants to make a scene. For all his apocalyptic bluster, Ivan's fight with Andrei never amounts to more than a game. It is Kavalerov who brings Ivan down to reality by revealing an unexpected family tie: the man Ivan has been encouraging Kavalerov to kill is Ivan's brother.

> "You said that I must kill your brother . . . What am I supposed to do? . . ."
> Valya was sitting on the stone wall.
> "Papa!" she shouted with a gasp.
> Ivan grabbed her legs as they hung down from the wall.
> "Valya, gouge out my eyes. I want to be blind." (98)

Suddenly, Ivan finds himself in a twisted version of *Oedipus Rex*. Oedipus discovers that he has killed his own father and married his mother, but Ivan learns that he has been plotting the death of his brother. Parricide is the cardinal sin of the old world, but in the new world of comradely relations, fratricide is the crime Ivan so blithely flirts with. The road to this Sophoclean recognition scene has been paved throughout the entire novel. Not only does Kavalerov refrain from revealing his enemy's identity, but Andrei himself refers to the Greek tragedy that is parodied in this scene. Andrei, whose role here is brother rather than father, is not connected to any mother: who, he asks Kavalerov, is Jocasta? In *Envy*, Jocasta is not mother, but daughter.

Having spent the entire novel lauding the virtues of the family, Ivan is suddenly confronted with the reality of the filial bonds that he has put in jeopardy. His discovery that he has been plotting the murder of his brother is immediately followed by the appearance of his daughter, who destroys his resolve with one word: "Papa." Ivan's alienated family has returned with a vengeance. No explicit explanation of Ivan's surrender is present, but the scene is replete with hints to Ivan's motivation. Like Oedipus, Ivan has discovered forgotten filial ties, and he demands a punishment that is appropriate to the Greek subtext: "Gouge out my eyes." Ivan is guilty of the very sin he identifies with his ideological opponents: he has underestimated the value of the family.

Ivan's last words to Valya, when taken together with his toast to "indifference" on the novel's last page, constitute a total reversal of the entire ideological program for which he had been agitating since chapter 5. He admits that feelings have not died, that "love and devotion and tenderness . . . remain, but not for us, all we have is just envy and more envy" (98). His response is not to change sides, however, but to want to be blind to the "truth" now revealed to him, and to abandon the ideological struggle in favor of "indifference" (112). The novel's second half refutes Ivan's program point by point. First Andrei salvages the love between fathers and sons for the new world, despite the fact that the "fathers" and "sons" involved are not blood relations. Such love is the only feeling Andrei identifies as appropriate to the new world, and it rests specifically on the ties between men. This is consistent with both Andrei's project and the general character of the new world as described in the novel: the new society is both masculine and masculinizing, striving to bring the feminine world of domesticity under its totalizing vision.

Then Ivan is forced to admit that the very feelings he champions will survive the construction of the new society but will no longer be shared by die-hard romantics such as himself. Valya is still beautiful, but she has become part of something different. When she is exercising, her stance looks "not feminine, but more masculine or childlike." Her legs are tan and covered with scratches, but her body still promises purity and future womanhood (97). Valya will have a place in the new world, but not as its emblem or ideal; for Andrei, that ideal is Volodya, and for Volodya himself, it is the machine. Valya will simply be a part of the new society.

Finally, Kavalerov is forced to see how a talented man can gain glory as part of a team. Getske, like Volodya, is a good player, but Volodya both leads in the game and wins the acclaim of his teammates and fans. It would be a mistake to agree with hard-line critics who, following Pertsov (*My zhivem*), assert that the author satirizes Kavalerov while presenting Volodya as a role model. By the same token, Volodya and the ethic of comradeship he embodies cannot be dismissed as a mere caricature of the "new man." The novel is entitled *Envy* precisely because the self-styled representatives of the old order, even as they profess their inability to conform, find something in this new world they consider worth coveting. The reader last sees Volodya reaping the fruits of good comradeship, acclaimed by both his team and a stadium full of spectators. Kavalerov, however, is left with nothing but poor substitutes for all his goals. Instead of Andrei, the father who never accepted him, he has Ivan, the father whom he himself rejected. Instead of Valya, the ethereal beauty, he has Anechka, the slovenly cook. His desire for Valya had bound him, however distantly, to Volodya, whereas Anechka serves to connect Kavalerov and Ivan by the simple fact that she "feels sorry" for both of them. A love triangle is an unsatisfactory means to bring together two men, and Kavalerov is left with a parody of a love triangle. Ivan's call for indifference and blindness is a strategy for survival: the only way to pretend they are enjoying their isolation is to pay no attention to the larger world being built around them.

Chapter Five

PURITANS AND PROLETARIANS
Andrei Platonov's Asexual Revolution, 1919–1923

> Man can't live—he's afraid of his own soul and releases it into woman. If a woman is beautiful, his soul will leave and go into her immediately. He just has to copulate with her once and his soul will flow away with his seed.—Andrei Platonov, "A Story about Many Interesting Things" (1923)

"Communist society," wrote Andrei Platonov in a 1920 issue of *The Voronezh Commune*, "is essentially a society of men . . . Humanity is courage (man), and not the embodiment of sex (woman). He who desires the truth cannot desire a woman."[1] With the aphoristic confidence that characterizes so much of his early writing, Platonov's pronouncements in "The Future October" appear to resolve a variety of potential conundrums in a few short sentences: both women and sexuality can be found in his present-tense depiction of the future social structure only through their negation ("and not"). On the textual level, they are invoked only to be denied. If the text is a blueprint for the future, then women and sexuality become the paradigmatic other against which the communist utopia can be defined. Indeed, the primary question addressed in the above passage is one of agency and subjectivity: the story of communism will be (or perhaps is) a tale by and about only men. Where the fiction of Babel and Olesha reflects mixed feelings about the struggle between filiation and affiliation, Platonov's early works preach the gospel of revolutionary male bonding.

Nonetheless, the author's all-male utopia would be continually haunted by the return of what it appears to repress: desire and femininity.[2] This principle finds its most striking illustration in *Chevengur* (1929), where the architects of a naive, all-male "socialism in one town" are confronted by their newest members' demand for women. Having built communism through the exclusion of the "bourgeoisie" (who have been either exiled or slaughtered), Chepurny and his closest comrades are obliged to allow their town's recontamination by the potentially disruptive presence of women. Platonov's critique of his own earlier antisexual dogmatism is all the more poignant for its ambiguity; one senses that the author is hesitant to part with the utopianism that he so skillfully satirizes. Though the separatism of Platonov's heroes proves untenable, it does not change the fact that *Chevengur* is still a man's story; even such relatively developed characters as Sonya appear in the novel only when they intersect the lives of the male protagonists. In the collective bildungsroman of *Chevengur,* the women play their parts in the (de)formation of the novel's heroes, only to disappear when they are no longer needed. Only in Platonov's post-*Chevengur* period would female protagonists become more prominent.[3]

From the beginning of his career until the turning point of 1925–1926, Platonov's fictional and political writings constitute an all-out assault on sexuality and the family. In the mid-1920s he begins to moderate his views, even satirizing them in "Antisexus," a sketch purporting to advertise a new device that relieves its users of the atavistic desire for sexual contact.[4] The final stage of his career is a "compromise with happiness" (Semenova, " 'Tainoe tainykh" 113): Platonov makes a decisive break with his earlier hostility to the family, if not with his antipathy toward sex. His short story "The Potudan River" ("Reka Potudan' ") comes to a "happy end" when the husband and wife finally assume their expected sex roles and set up a conventional household, while his much-maligned "Ivanov's Family" ("Sem'ia Ivanova," later entitled "The Return" ["Vozvrashchenie"]) is not the attack on the Soviet family seen by Stalinist critics, but rather a story that both begins and ends with the protagonist's return to his family.[5]

For reasons of chronology as much as ideology, however, Platonov's later work falls beyond the scope of this book. It is the Platonov of the 1920s who provides the most fruitful material for the analysis of comradeship, sex, and the family. Platonov is hardly the only writer of the time to make these issues central to his work, but he is perhaps the only one to examine them from two fundamentally opposing points of view. Though it would be an exaggeration to say that Platonov has turned his back on male relationships by the end of the 1920s, one can make the case that he nonetheless spends the second half of the decade slowly dismantling the edifice of fratriarchy he so carefully built in the first. Such a metaphor, however, simplifies Platonov's complex philosophical system. Platonov's approach is deconstructive rather than destructive: instead of merely refuting his earlier views, Platonov recasts them in such a way that they refute themselves.

Exactly how the radical proletarian contributor to the *Voronezh Commune* and the *Smithy* became the unconventional proponent of the conventional family is unclear to this day. Scholars of Platonov's work often look to the author's disenchantment with NEP and his withdrawal from the communist party as a possible explanation, and yet one can easily argue that each is less a cause than a symptom of a crisis of faith. Though information about Platonov's life is scarce, one suspects that a rather banal factor might have played no small role: his wife and children.[6] Platonov may well have found it difficult to continue his ideological war on the family as he grew more and more involved in the care and raising of his son and daughter.

In order to understand both this transformation and the later work itself, however, an examination of Platonov's earlier ideological pronouncements is in order. In the early 1920s, Platonov articulates the worship of male comradeship and contempt for sexuality more thoroughly than any other author of this period, yet even in his nonfiction he manages to discuss these issues with no small amount of verbal artistry.[7] The author of these early essays would warrant a place in this study even if he were not the same man who wrote *Chevengur*. That Platonov *is* the writer of both the essays and the novel enhances our understanding of his work as a whole. The concepts that lie at the heart of his utopia were expressed long before the author began his novel; one cannot determine the extent to which Platonov's views had changed without first becoming acquainted with the ideas in their original form. Close readings of the early writings also reveal that the standard division of Platonov's career into three parts depends on a simplification of his attitudes about sex and gender. While there can be no doubt that there is a marked shift in his outlook, the contradictions inherent in the author's early philosophy cannot be ignored.[8] Careful study of Platonov's 1919–1923 writings shows that the seeds of his reevaluation of his sexual philosophy can be found in the very articles that seem to be such a striking contrast to his later works.

The bulk of Platonov's journalistic writing is so reassuringly schematic that one is tempted to speed past the more confusing points in order to return to familiar territory. In his early essays, sex is seen primarily as an enslavement to the material, animal world, an impediment on the road to revolutionary awareness; woman, the "embodiment" of sex, comes to represent everything that must be overcome in order to lead a truly human life. After an overview of Platonov's antisexual thought, this chapter will focus more on his early paradoxes than on his oversimplifications. Though the young Platonov appears to be rigid and dogmatic, the binary oppositions that form the foundation of his philosophy have a disconcerting tendency to reverse polarities and take on paradoxical meanings: the natural suddenly turns into the mechanical, noblemen reveal themselves to be true proletarians, and even men are, on occasion, transformed into women.[9] Since these procedures are metaphorical rather than surgical, they are relatively painless for Platonov's subjects, if not for his audience. In any event, the facility with which Platonov effects such metamorphoses will enable us to understand how the author's fratriarchal, antifamily rhetoric could eventually turn on itself.

The rest of the chapter will treat Platonov's attempts to find a constructive role for women even as he continues to argue that the world of conscious communism is masculine by definition. Svetlana Semenova, in the most comprehensive study of sexuality in Platonov's early essays written to date, concludes that woman in the early Platonov can take one of three forms: the embodiment of sexuality (and thus a threat to man's progress), mother (a positive role despite the author's distaste for reproduction), and the Eternal Feminine (whose sublime sublimation of the erotic drive draws man "to the heights of a new, transformed nature" ("'Tainoe tainykh'" 81).[10] All three of these hypostases rely on abstraction and synecdoche: a specific aspect of woman's "nature" comes to define her. Indeed, we are not far off from the traditional "three faces of Eve": the trinity "maiden, mother, crone" has become "maiden, mother, whore."[11]

Semenova's typology works quite well, but for the purposes of this book, it must be expanded and revised. Platonov allows not two loopholes for women, but three, and all of these seeming concessions to the author's masculinist ideology involve treating women as a sign of something other than herself. His 1920 review of a theatrical production of Dostoevsky's *Idiot* is a rare instance in Platonov's work when it is a woman rather than a man who is torn between the extremes of sex and consciousness; in most of Platonov's pre-*Chevengur* fiction, women are scorned because they embody (for men) the regressive threat of sexual temptation. Here Platonov spares Nastasya Filippovna his customary scorn for femininity, but only because he sees her as transcending gender altogether. In Platonov's reading, Nastasya Filippovna is not a woman at all, but rather the soul of a confused and ambivalent man (Dostoevsky himself). Platonov turns Nastasya Filippovna into a soul at the expense of her body; he treats the woman as subject rather than object, but only by seeing her as the abstraction of a fundamentally male dilemma.

If Platonov's "rehabilitation" of Nastasya Filippovna virtually deprives her of a body, his paean to mothers is rooted in biology: through the very process of giving birth, the mother redeems the "abomination [*bezobrazie*] and horror of the earth" (*Chut'e* 67). In his article "The World Soul" ("Dusha mira," 1920), Platonov extols mothers for the feature that elsewhere renders women execrable: their connection to nature and matter. If at times Platonov portrays women as almost animallike, here the very "fact" that they are closer to the natural world makes it possible for them to serve as the consciousness of matter itself. Ironically, this focus on woman's biology once again leads to her idealization as a spiritual entity: if Nastasya Filippovna is the soul of Dostoevsky, mothers are the "soul of the world."

In his fiction, Platonov presents the third and final variation on ethereal womanhood: the chaste and uplifting eternal feminine. In "A Story about Many Interesting Things" ("Rasskaz o mnogikh intersnykh veshchakh," 1923), Platonov's Bolsheviks are bound together by their love of the Caspian Bride, a virtually bodiless woman who, like the mother in "The World Soul," represents the hope for the future. The Caspian Bride's femininity escapes censure precisely because of her ties to an as yet unrealized order; virginal and chaste, she is pure potential. And yet she is abandoned by the story's hero for that very reason: her time has not yet come. Thus, even when Platonov showers his female characters with praise, ambivalence remains. "A Story about Many Interesting Things," though artistically flawed, is the summit of Platonov's early work, recapitulating his antisexual ideology while weighing the possibility that the world of the future might have a place for women.

SOCIALIST DARWINISM

Though his works bear the distinctive traces of Lenin, Fyodorov, and Bogdanov, Platonov develops his ideas in a different genre from that of his precursors. Lenin wrote a series of political-philosophical tracts of varying length, Bogdanov authored books and lengthy articles, and Fyodorov spent his entire adult life writing, expanding, and revising a voluminous magnum opus that he made no effort to publish. By contrast, Platonov's political and philosophical writings were printed as journalism. Republished in book form only in recent years, the average length of these essays is two to three pages, the longest one ("The Culture of the Proletariat" ["Kul'tura proletariata"]) reaching a scant ten. The fact that the fundamental expressions of Platonov's early thought appeared in bite-sized form both restricted and liberated their author: on the one hand, Platonov was forced to encapsulate complex ideas using the least amount of ink possible, thus leading to some inevitable oversimplification; on the other, he was spared the political philosopher's onerous task of explaining not only his ideas, but also their source, development, and consequences. In other words, the limited space for publication relieved Platonov of the burden of proof.[12] The result is an extremely schematic, if not axiomatic, "solution" to the various problems that Platonov discussed, as well as numerous instances of apparent contradiction of views he expressed only a month or two before.

Platonov's early thought is firmly rooted in a dialectic that, if not recognizable as orthodox Marxism or even orthodox Leninism, is clearly connected to Bolshevism. In his 1902 tract *What Is to Be Done?* Lenin elaborated the distinction between "spontaneity" and "consciousness" that arose in Russian Marxist circles at the end of the nineteenth century. Spontaneity and consciousness are seen as the two opposing forces present in humanity from its earliest days. In primitive society, spontaneity, the lack of political awareness and discipline, is the dominant mode, while consciousness exists only in potential. As history marches toward communism, "conscious" elements arise to direct humanity along its proper path. After the revolution, the dichotomy between spontaneity and revolution is to resolve itself in a new synthesis: the interests of individuals will no longer conflict with the interests of organized society.[13]

The spontaneity-consciousness dialectic is central to Platonov's work from the very beginning, albeit in idiosyncratic form. As Katerina Clark observes, the dichotomy of spontaneity and consciousness is easily conflated with more recognizable binary oppositions: Slavophiles and Westernizers, the subject-object distinction, and the nature-culture opposition (Clark 20). Though all are important, it is the last of these dichotomies that has the most relevance to Platonov's work. Nature is a distinctly hostile force in Platonov's thought, as it is in mainstream Bolshevism and the works of Bogdanov. The classic myth of early Soviet ideology is the scientific triumph of humanity over the harsh, inhuman conditions of nature.[14]

Platonov's early articles explore this mythic confrontation between science and nature, attacking the latter with two closely linked weapons. The first involves a deliberate lack of subtlety: Platonov exhorts his readers to embrace science as opposed to nature, employing the simplistic rhetoric of war and liberation. In "About Science" ("O nauke," 1920), he calls science the "eternal companion and devoted friend of man [*cheloveka*]" whose enemy is nature: "To conquer the madness of nature, to turn master into slave and use her [nature's] powers to grow and outgrow oneself—is there any greater happiness for the radiant consciousness of man?" (*Chut'e* 52). In "The Battle of the Brains" ("Bor'ba mozgov"), written in the same year, Platonov reaffirms this struggle as the essence of proletarian existence: "Our purpose is all humanity's conquest of nature" (*Chut'e* 91). Such statements, which can be found throughout Platonov's early nonfiction, all amount to the same thing: nature is our enemy, while science is our trusted ally.[15]

Platonov's second strategy is more subtle and thus requires more attention. At the same time that Platonov attacks nature, he is forced to admit that humanity, too, is part of the natural order (*Chut'e* 53), and that the triumph of science cannot mean nature's utter annihilation. Thus his second approach, whose repercussions are felt well after *Chevengur*, is to coopt nature by using the language of industry to describe it. Platonov's secret weapon in the battle against nature is metaphor: Platonov's language depicts natural phenomena as if they were manmade. This tendency is expressed in both the content and the title of Platonov's 1920 essay "Repairing the Earth" ("Remont zemli"), in which the noun *remont* ("repair" or "remodeling") is removed from its customary realm of apartments, cars, and machines and attached to the feminine noun *zemlia* ("earth"), which encompasses all of nature. Platonov asks his peasant readers to join in "remodeling" the planet, a project that Platonov has already begun on the level of language. In order to remodel the earth, Platonov first redefines it: "[The earth] is the means of production of bread, feed grass for cattle, and so on; that is, a machine like any other, except that it manufactures human food like, for example, a mechanical loom manufactures fabric for clothes" (*Chut'e* 49). Once the earth has been reclassified as a machine, it is as subject to human control as any other device. The men who must fix the earth are the peasants, who thus become the equivalent of factory workers. Platonov's rhetorical trick succeeds on more than one level: not only does the earth become a machine, but he is able to force the identification of the peasants with the workers, performing a metaphorical *smychka* (alliance) between town and country that is just as tenuous as its historical counterpart.

Platonov's recasting of the nature-culture debate, however, has other implications. As categories, nature and culture are themselves often represented by other sets of binary oppositions, most notably femininity and masculinity. Certainly, the representation of nature as a woman is a classic trope of literature and folklore; though such an identification is in itself a culturally determined concept, it is a relatively benign phenomenon as long as nature is seen to have some advantages over culture. The cult of nature was a more than adequate background on which to place woman's pedestal. The valorization of the two sexes, however, changes dramatically once nature is reinterpreted as inherently hostile and antihuman. If woman is not extricated from her identification with nature, then she becomes guilty by association.

With the exception of two essays that will be discussed below, Platonov's articles amount to a rejection of both the cult of nature and the cult of woman. In their place he erects a new idol, one that can symbolize the accomplishments of male culture and yet still be the object of revolutionary romanticism. As in Olesha's *Envy*, woman and nature are replaced by the (female) machine.[16] "Repairing the Earth" only gives a glimpse of this new cult, which is developed in more detail in Platonov's other works. In "May Your Name Be Blessed" ("Da sviatitsia imia tvoe," 1920), Platonov calls the machine "a miracle of human work" that "both produces labor and is created by it." Just as the machine worshiped by Olesha's Volodya is both a feminine ideal and a symbol of masculine labor, so is Platonov's machine distinctly androgynous: "She [the machine] is not only our brother; she is equal to man, she is his living, surprising, exact image" (*Chut'e* 61).[17] In his 1923 article "Proletarian Poetry" ("Proletarskaia poeziia"), he writes, "Every new machine is a real proletarian epic" (*Chut'e* 198). In 1920, Platonov asserted that bourgeois art was a "prayer in the name of woman" (*Chut'e* 107); in "Proletarian Poetry," woman is replaced by the machine: "Machines are our poetry, and the work of machines is the basis of proletarian poetry" (*Chut'e* 198). If revolutionary man has a female ideal, she is the rational, industrial product of his own labor, a superhuman entity whose origin lies in man rather than woman: the machine as Adam's rib.

By superimposing gender onto the dichotomies of nature-culture and spontaneity-consciousness, Platonov creates a complex network of associations that leads him far afield from Marx and Lenin. Platonov's essays revolve around a set of binary oppositions: spontaneity, nature, sexual reproduction, the bourgeoisie, and women, versus consciousness, culture, machine production, the proletariat, and men.[18] Such a laundry list of philosophical categories is too awkward for any casual reference, let alone for a two-page article in *The Voronezh Commune*. They are therefore represented in Platonov's writings by a single, overarching dialectic: sex and consciousness.[19]

From 1920 to 1922, Platonov published a series of articles that explicitly formulate the sex-consciousness dialectic in terms of class and historical development: "The Battle of the Brains," "The Culture of the Proletariat," "On the Culture of Harnessed Light and Apprehended

Electricity" ("O kul'ture zapriazhennogo sveta i poznannogo elektrichestva"), and Platonov's review of a staging of *The Idiot,* published under the title "But Man Has Only One Soul" ("No odna dusha u cheloveka"). In these essays, Platonov identifies sex (*pol*) as the driving force of the bourgeoisie, a power that is immanent in that most counterrevolutionary creature, woman.[20] In the opposite camp is the proletariat, the hero of history, guided by consciousness rather than sex, and gazing at machines rather than at women. "The Battle of the Brains" states the conflict baldly, though leaving its implications unexplored: "Even before rising up the proletariat knew that its main force, its soul, was consciousness, and contrasted this force to the old soul of the bourgeoisie: sexuality, the passion to live in the name of oneself, for the sake of false goals" (*Chut'e* 90). Platonov treats the bourgeoisie and proletariat less as two opposing classes than as two different species. Not only do they represent "two different worlds," but the bourgeoisie's retreat from labor has led the part of their brains that holds consciousness to atrophy: "the very possibility of developing their brain [the instrument of consciousness] in their body has been destroyed" (*Chut'e* 91). Evolution has rendered the bourgeoisie a backward ancestor of the proletariat: "The history of the bourgeoisie is the history of the contraction of the brain and the development of the jaws and sex organs" (*Chut'e* 92). The superiority of the proletariat has inexplicably become a matter of genetics rather than social forces; their "consciousness" is "like a natural force, born from centuries of labor" (*Chut'e* 91).[21] Platonov is, of course, speaking figuratively; his flirtation with genetic imagery predates the Stalinist doctrine of the "hereditary proletarian" by several years. All the same, his phrasing is striking. Platonov demonstrates a marked propensity to ignore the distinction between discrete categories of discourse: rather than being the material base for cultural development, biology becomes a function of class. Now that the revolution has come to pass, Platonov writes of the bourgeoisie as a feature of the past — Neanderthals who served their function during a bygone stage of social evolution. Though Platonov refutes social Darwinism as a reflection of the bourgeoisie's preoccupation with the individual's struggle for success ("The Culture of the Proletariat," *Chut'e* 102), he tacitly endorses a view of evolutionary biology that concerns classes rather than species.[22] In essence, Platonov has invented his own "socialist Darwinism," in which social progress is indistinguishable from biological evolution.

In "The Culture of the Proletariat" (1920), Platonov further develops his approach to the bourgeoisie and the proletariat, begun two weeks earlier in "The Battle of the Brains": as in the earlier essay, the bourgeoisie are, if not another species, an embarrassing distant ancestor, a skeleton in the evolutionary closet. Having dismissed the bourgeoisie for being frozen at an earlier, "idealist" stage of development, he returns to the formula that provided the fundamental distinction between the bourgeoisie and the proletariat in "The Battle of the Brains." What is the "essence," the "soul" of the bourgeoisie? The question is so central that Platonov answers it twice: "Sexuality. Sex is the soul of the bourgeoisie" (*Chut'e* 106).

According to Platonov, bourgeois culture arises after man has gained limited mastery over his surroundings, when the world no longer presents a constant threat. Thus the senses most essential for the detection and avoidance of danger (vision and hearing) atrophy, to be replaced in priority by the mind, or consciousness. However, consciousness does not become the bourgeoisie's "soul," for the bourgeois remains obsessed with continuing his existence after his own death through the only means available: "Reproduction, the replacement of oneself with one's children—these are blows against death and the flight to immortality" (*Chut'e* 107). Now sex becomes the "central sense" (*tsentral'nym chuvstvom*) in the struggle for existence, even managing to subjugate consciousness to its needs. As a result, women gain a new importance in human culture—since, for Platonov, the desiring subject is always male.[23] Platonov, too, sees woman and sexuality as an unsatisfactory compensation for mortality. Sex is the illusion of advancement, a weapon whose power over death is only illusory (*Chut'e* 108).[24]

True to his Fyodorovian roots, Platonov does not deny the validity of the struggle with death; rather, he argues with the bourgeoisie's choice of weapon. Implicit in his treatment of consciousness is the belief that consciousness can conquer mortality. Consciousness will conquer death, "destroy" sex, and take arms against the "Mystery" ("Taina") of existence (*Chut'e* 108). This does not mean that man will grow cold and emotionless; in a feat of revolutionary sublimation, Platonov redirects the language of sexuality to the realm of consciousness. The bourgeois "sexual passion" (*strast' pola*) is to be replaced by the proletariat's "passion of thought and consciousness" (*strast' mysli, soznaniia*) (*Chut'e* 109).

"On the Culture of Harnessed Light and Apprehended Electricity," the last of Platonov's programmatic articles on sex and consciousness, appears in the beginning of 1922. By this point, Platonov has taken his philosophy of sex to its logical extreme, reducing both sexuality and class distinctions to a stark biologism that stands out even in the context of his earlier writings on the subject.[25] Though he excludes class distinctions from most of his discussion of sex, Platonov intensifies the evolutionary rhetoric found in his earlier articles. Even in "The Culture of the Proletariat," his most detailed assault on sexuality, Platonov concedes that the central organ of prerevolutionary man was his brain, even if it was subordinated to the interests of reproduction (*Chut'e* 106). Now, however, Platonov has found a different biological approach to drop "unconscious" man several notches down the evolutionary ladder. The "undisciplined band" of "feelings, moods, and neural sparks" is controlled not by the brain, but by the spine, the "area of unconscious physiological human activity." Primary among these instincts is the reproductive drive, or "love," which Platonov reduces to "swarming semen" (*koposiashcheesia semia*) (*Chut'e* 191).

"On the Culture of Harnessed Light" shows Platonov at his most cynical. Though consciousness was slowly developing even before the appearance of the revolutionary proletariat, humanity was nonetheless only "a little more valuable than any species of plants." Humanity was nothing more than a "sexual seed factory" (*zavod polovykh semian*), while the essence of culture could be "reduced to the production of two sex cells and to their necessary transportation to their destinations." Answering a question he himself poses, Platonov proclaims that it is time to "put a stop to this ancient production" (*Chut'e* 191).

Platonov's language is particularly noteworthy in this article. Like many of his contemporaries, he implicitly contrasts the virtues of production with the redundancy of reproduction. Where Olesha uses the language of reproduction to characterize the work of industry (Kavalerov's assertion that Babichev wishes to "give birth" to his superkitchen), Platonov describes basic biological processes in terms of factories and the production line. At the same time, Platonov's call for a halt in reproductive labor contains wording that reveals the weak spot in his antisexual crusade: when Platonov writes that it is "high time" to abandon sex, the Russian words he uses are *smertel'naia pora* (literally, "it is deadly time"). Though Platonov is a long way from the reexamination he would give his ideas in *Chevengur*, his choice of words foreshadows one of the novel's basic premises: the connection between death and the denial of sex.

If "On the Culture of Harnessed Light" points the way to *Chevengur*, however, it is not because the article represents a change in the author's views. Instead, the essay is the summation of the very philosophy that *Chevengur* puts to the test. Platonov presents his argument in a formula that is ready-made for *Chevengur*:

> [Just as] labor-love began as the combined warmth of two bodies, and ended as Beatrice and the "beautiful lady," so work began as a stone thrown at a beast, and will end as the reconstructed universe, where the concepts of work, resistance, matter, man, etc., are finished, gone. And the highest form of work will not be human movement, not even the movement of his thought . . . , but rather his renunciation of the world, for the reconstructed world will discipline itself in relation to man automatically. Man will have nothing to do, an eternal Sunday will begin for him. (*Chut'e* 191–92)

Platonov completes his conflation of the languages of sex and labor with the unusual phrase "labor-love" (*rabota-liubov'*).[26] This allows him to draw parallels between proletarian labor and old-fashioned sexuality that will be brought into play in his later novel. Stepan Kopyonkin, Bolshevism's chivalric knight, manages to combine both a love for communism and the cult of the beautiful lady in the (dead) body of Rosa Luxemburg, while the denizens of Chevengur take the arrival of communism as a signal to abandon all constructive activity. Both love and labor reach their apotheosis when they abandon the features that most clearly characterize them: sex and motion. Kopyonkin's preference for a dead abstraction over a living woman and the Chevengurians' ideologically justified inertia are expressions of the highest forms of sex and labor that Platonov establishes in his 1922 article. Platonov, the harsh enemy of idealist philosophy, elevates both love and labor to pure abstractions.

COMRADE MYSHKIN

Of all the apparent contradictions in Platonov's nonfiction, perhaps the most puzzling is the role of women. In his identification of woman with sexuality, Platonov establishes a connection between women and the old, bourgeois world that should be familiar to readers of Olesha's *Envy*. "Woman," he writes in "The Culture of the Proletariat," was the center of the world for the bourgeoisie" (*Chut'e* 107). But whereas Ivan Babichev exalts woman as the embodiment of the old world, Platonov appears to reject her unconditionally. And yet Platonov's condemnation of woman as sexual object does not necessarily amount to an attack on woman as a human being. True, Platonov's tendency to link the very word "feminine" (*zhenskii*) with semantically negative adjectives is less than flattering to his female reader, whom he, in any case, never addresses.[27] Yet even Platonov's stark declaration of the impossibility of sexual equality contains a hint of potential redemption: "Equality between men and women is a noble gesture on the part of the socialists, but not the truth, and it will never be the truth ... He who desires the truth cannot desire a woman, and now all humanity is starting to desire the truth. This is not woman's doom, but something else." Upon closer examination, what appear to be Platonov's most antifeminist statements actually criticize man's attitude to woman rather than woman as an ontological category. It is woman as the object of male desire who is the enemy of proletarian society. Certainly Platonov disparages woman as the "embodiment of sex" (*voploshchenie pola*) in "The Future October," yet she embodies sex only for men.[28] A product of his times, Platonov always treats the thinking subject as male: "He who most feared death most loved women" (*Chut'e* 107). The new communist man is not supposed to be interested in women, and thus, in the articles dedicated to sketching this man's portrait, women are absent.

If Platonov's diatribes against women and sexual relations sound suspiciously reminiscent of religious sermons on chastity, this is perhaps because Platonov, like any preacher, is concerned above all with one thing: saving man's "soul." In Russian, the word for soul (*dusha*) is feminine, a grammatical accident that Platonov takes quite literally. We have already seen him assert in "The Culture of the Proletariat" that "sex is the soul of the bourgeoisie"; in the same essay, sex itself (a masculine noun) is seen to be equivalent to "woman," who is the "center of the world" for the bourgeoisie. In terms of grammatical gender, the triumph of the proletariat becomes the neutering of the soul: the masculine "sex" and the feminine "woman" are replaced by the grammatically neutral "consciousness" (*soznanie*) (*Chut'e* 106–8).

Yet Platonov is either unable or unwilling to let go of the metaphorical possibilities suggested by the feminine soul. Two years later, in "On the Culture of Harnessed Light," Platonov takes up his familiar lament that the "soul of the man of the past [*proshlogo cheloveka*] (and of the majority of men of the present) manifests itself only in relation to woman, in sex" (*Chut'e* 191). Later in the same essay, he exhorts his readers to improve this pathetic state of affairs: "Let the soul of man reveal itself not in relation to woman, but in relation to matter — not in love, but in work" (*Chut'e* 191). We have already seen that this appeal to labor-love is compared to the sublimation of eros in the chivalric passion for Beatrice and the beautiful lady. By extension, labor-love becomes a new feminine ideal, one that provides a far more appropriate form for the soul than does any physical woman.

If women and femininity are to be even partially rehabilitated in Platonov's early writings, it can only be through their connection to the soul. In 1920, Platonov devotes two articles to women: "But Man Has Only One Soul" and "The World Soul." Despite the fact that these articles precede "The Culture of the Proletariat" by two months,[29] one cannot dismiss the different portrayal of women in the former essays as merely an earlier stage of the thoughts presented in the latter. Though it purports to be a review of a theatrical production of *The Idiot*, "But Man Has Only One Soul" recapitulates the familiar litany of Platonov's early-1920s nonfiction: "The bourgeoisie produced the proletariat. Sex gave birth to consciousness. Sex is the soul of the bourgeoisie. Consciousness is the soul of the proletariat" (*Vozvrashchenie* 72).[30] As he demonstrates the urgency of the battle against sex, Platonov's language is typically violent: both the bourgeoisie and sex must be "destroyed," and the "ancient, hot voices of sex in our blood" must be "crushed."

To readers of Dostoevsky, such statements might seem curiously out of place in any discussion of *The Idiot*; at best, the emphasis on class struggle is an anachronistic imposition of Soviet ideology on the works of an author whose hostility to revolutionaries is well known. If one approaches Platonov's deliberate misreading of Dostoevsky's novel merely as bad criticism, then the essay is of little value; it becomes merely an early and rather peculiar precursor of orthodox Soviet "ideologically correct" interpretations of the Russian classics. But Platonov does not practice literary criticism in the standard sense of the word; indeed, despite the occasion of his Dostoevsky essay (his attendance at a play), Platonov is not engaging in "criticism" at all. Rather, the plot of *The Idiot* affords Platonov the opportunity to test his ideas on sex and consciousness in fiction without having to produce a new fictional work of his own. Platonov's transformation of *The Idiot* into an allegory of sex and consciousness is best treated as a miniature adaptation of Dostoevsky's novel. Indeed, the fact that Platonov chooses to approach the story of Prince Myshkin through a response to a stage version of the novel reveals Platonov's own method: after seeing one adaptation of *The Idiot*, Platonov offers the reader his own. To paraphrase Akhmatova and Tsvetaeva, Platonov has created "My Myshkin." The genre of this new work straddles the line between fiction and essay, between originality and appropriation: the plot of "But Man Has Only One Soul" is a given, but the form and approach are the product of its author's imagination.

Once Platonov begins to impose his concepts of sex and consciousness on Dostoevsky's *The Idiot,* the article turns into a series of paradoxes whose internal contradictions reveal much about Platonov's apparent castigation of women. As readers of either Dostoevsky or René Girard will certainly recall, the plot of *The Idiot* is based on love triangles.[31] Platonov's "plot" of sex and consciousness, however, is one of binary oppositions, allowing Platonov to view any given phenomenon as a struggle between opposing forces. Platonov's dualism cannot enter into Dostoevsky's world of triangular desire without being transformed. The result is a highly idiosyncratic reading of *The Idiot* that tells far more about Platonov than it does about Dostoevsky. In "But Man Has Only One Soul," Platonov's customary oppositions between male and female, bourgeoisie and proletariat, and even sex and consciousness are destabilized. Platonov's basic terms drift free from their standard denotations, resulting in a view of class and gender that lacks a fixed referent.

In discussing Dostoevsky's novel, Platonov cannot simply turn Nastasya Filippovna into the embodiment of sex and Myshkin into the symbol of consciousness, since this arrangement would beg the question of Rogozhin's role. Instead, Platonov reshuffles his cards, according Nastasya Filippovna the primary position in the struggle between Myshkin and Rogozhin. The result is that the burden of binary opposition is placed on two men rather than a man and a woman: "Myshkin and Rogozhin: these are the two elements, the two centers, the two driven devils of the heart of Dostoevsky. And Nastasya Filippovna is the merging of the two worlds, of Myshkin and Rogozhin, into the most dangerous, deadly, unstable moment, hanging over the abyss on a blade of grass" (*Vozvrashchenie* 73). Sexual dualism is still at work in this article, but it has been transposed. According to Platonov, the stage version of *The Idiot* expresses the battle of the sexes. Yet he follows this statement with a puzzling characterization of Rogozhin: "Rogozhin is the earth herself, her black, powerful depths, the still-unconscious life, breaking loose" (*Rogozhin—sama zemlia, ee chernye, moshchnye nedra, vyrvavshaias' eshche bessoznatel'naia zhizn'*). Identified with both the (feminine) earth and "unconsciousness," the biologically male Rogozhin has become the incarnation of all that Platonov disparages in femininity.[32] Myshkin, who in Dostoevsky's novel appears passive and almost effete in contrast to the "manly" Rogozhin, turns out to be a virtual model of masculinity: "Myshkin is our brother. He has escaped from the power of sex and entered the kingdom of consciousness" (*Myshkin—rodnoi nash brat. On vyshel iz vlasti pola i voshel v tsarstvo soznaniia*). Platonov's only reproach to Myshkin does seem to involve a lack of warriorlike masculinity: Myshkin has yet to rid himself of pity. He must still learn that such feelings should be channeled away from love of weakness into the struggle to transform weakness into strength, into "the construction of iron palaces of power on the swampy ripples of powerlessness" (*Vozvrashchenie* 73). Platonov frees gender from biological determinism, paradoxically discussing the battle of the sexes in terms of two men. Platonov's treatment of gender in this essay is reminiscent of feminist and Lacanian arguments that the apparent biological determinism of Freud is actually metaphorical rather than physical. Just as the Freudian phallus is not necessarily a physical penis, Platonov's "femininity" can be incarnated by a man.

Though jarring, such a reinterpretation of sexual difference is the apotheosis of Platonov's all-male revolutionary philosophy: even women are represented by men.

Once Platonov's sexual dichotomy has been successfully implanted within Dostoevsky's triangle, the other concomitant binary oppositions quickly fall into place. Hence the most paradoxical sentence in the entire article: "Prince Myshkin is a proletarian: he is a knight of thought, he knows much; within him is the soul of Christ, of the king [*tsar'*] of consciousness and the enemy of mystery" (*Vozvrashchenie* 73). The connection between Christ, consciousness, and Myshkin makes sense in the context of Platonov's idiosyncratic reinterpretation of Christ's teachings in his earlier essay "Christ and Us."[33] In class terms, however, Platonov's statement was bound to raise the eyebrows of its Marxist readers. Platonov underscores the apparent contradiction of his assertion that Myshkin is a proletarian by using the title "prince" for the first and only time in the article. Just as he disconnects gender from biological sex, Platonov has separated the concept of class from the everyday factors that would seem to determine it. As a result, "But Man Has Only One Soul" turns Dostoevsky's novel into a rather eccentric collection of female men and proletarian princes.

Though the disassociation of sex and class from their everyday meanings might render Platonov vulnerable to charges of idealism (a term that is consistently negative in Platonov's lexicon), it provides for the possibility that individual women can escape Platonov's censure as long as they eschew his definition of femininity. Though Nastasya Filippovna represents the "merging" of the dichotomy of Rogozhin and Myshkin, she is not a Hegelian synthesis of the two worlds. The third, extra figure that turns a binary opposition into a triangle, Nastasya Filippovna embodies the absence of stable characteristics; she is the incarnation of liminality itself. Because she cannot decide between "the devil (Rogozhin) and God (Myshkin)," her "soul is a child of a third, unseen kingdom, where no one reigns, where there is nothing, where there is freedom, emptiness, and the whirlwinds of dead deserts" (*Vozvrashchenie* 73).

This does not mean, however, that Nastasya Filippovna has no identity: "Nastasya Filippovna is Dostoevsky himself" (*Vozvrashchenie* 73). Like Nastasya Filippovna, Dostoevsky is trapped on the margins, "writhing on the border of the world of sex and the world of consciousness. Each one at times gained the upper hand in his weary martyr's soul" (*Vozvrashchenie* 72–73). Both Nastasya Filippovna and Dostoevsky are characterized by a Gogolian series of contrasts: "neither living nor dead, mixing up death with life, the ally of both God and the devil, terrified and mortally wounded by doubt." The satanic connotations of such a description are not lost on Platonov; Dostoevsky, unable to "get out of his state of chaos" and "be Myshkin or Rogozhin," is "neither this nor that, the most frightening and real Satan, his own enemy, an uncertain spirit" (*Vozvrashchenie* 73).

In the hands of a less dualistic thinker, the identification of Nastasya Filippovna with a "third kingdom" would perhaps allow her to forge a middle path or third way that reconciles the contradictions between sex (Rogozhin) and consciousness (Myshkin). Yet here Platonov exploits the triangular structure of Dostoevsky's novel to its full potential: as in most traditional love triangles, Nastasya Filippovna must choose between two rivals; compromise is out of the question. Forced to decide between sex and consciousness, she has the same options available to her as any of Platonov's male protagonists: she can choose sex (Rogozhin) or brotherhood and comradeship (Myshkin). Indeed, her situation corresponds so fully with Platonov's conception of the male dilemma that he accords Nastasya Filippovna as little femininity as possible, viewing her instead as a stand-in for the male creator. Ironically, she is bereft of both the sins and the virtues of femininity in Platonov's philosophy: she escapes being equated with the incarnation of sexuality for men (which would deprive her of her subjectivity), but she also has no recourse to the redemptive powers of motherhood. Instead, she is making a man's choice and has only a man's options.

The identification of Nastasya Filippovna with Dostoevsky demonstrates that a woman can represent something other than femininity in Platonov's eyes and thus can potentially escape the author's familiar scorn of sex and "woman." Though the same essay that identifies Nastasya Filippovna with Dostoevsky also contains one of Platonov's many antisexual and misogynist statements, the sentiment has no bearing on either Nastasya Filippovna or, by extension, her creator and double. Caught in the middle of opposing forces, Nastasya Filippovna/Dostoevsky appears to transcend gender. Platonov's treatment of Nastasya Filippovna's femininity—what little there is of it—is remarkably traditional. As in his later work, Platonov, the enemy of sex and woman, flirts with the idea of the Eternal Feminine, describing Nastasya Filippovna as the "very possibility of eternity itself." Nastasya Filippovna is not only Dostoevsky; twice Platonov calls her Dostoevsky's "soul" (*dusha*) (*Vozvrashchenie* 73). This definition would seem to elide the problem of sexual difference, since the feminine "soul" does not clash with Nastasya Filippovna's own gender. Any gender confusion would then reflect not on Nastasya Filippovna, but on Dostoevsky, the man whose soul is a woman.

"But Man Has Only One Soul" tells us much about Platonov's vacillations over sexuality and gender during the very height of his antifamily crusade. If anything, Nastasya Filippovna represents not Dostoevsky's ambivalence, but Platonov's. Though Dostoevsky was intrigued by Fyodorov's doctrine of positive chastity, it is Platonov who, in 1922, would find himself writing antisexual articles for proletarian newspapers at the same time he was courting his future wife. As early as 1920, Platonov provides a loophole for women, suggesting that, at least in fiction, they can overcome their biology through a kind of spiritual androgyny: like Platonov's beloved *mashina* (machine), Nastasya Filippovna can be feminine in body and masculine in soul.[34] At the same time, it is important to remember that Platonov ascribes these qualities to a fictional character not of his own creation, a heroine whom he identifies firmly with her author. Nastasya Filippovna escapes the horrors of femininity only because she is, literally, not herself; rather than being an independent agent, she is the "soul" of her author. Platonov's interpretation of *The Idiot* saves Nastasya Filippovna by imagining that she is not the author's idealized object of erotic desire, but rather the feminine receptacle of Dostoevsky's own (male) struggle with sex. If Nastasya Filippovna is a "good" woman, it is only because she is Dostoevsky in drag.

THE WORLD SOUL: MOTHER AS MEDIATOR

Platonov returns to the idea of woman as soul in the article he publishes the very next day: "The Soul of the World." Most scholars who have given Platonov's early nonfictional writings thorough study pass over this article in silence.³⁵ Both in his introduction to a collection of Platonov's fiction and in his notes on Platonov's articles, Chalmaev notes that the appearance of "The World Soul" is "sudden" (*Gosudarstvennyi zhitel'* 14; *Chut'e* 439). No biographical explanation is available to us; the essay predates his courtship of Maria Aleksandrovna by two years, and little is known about Platonov's personal life at the time. Indeed, the ideas presented in this essay seem to come from nowhere, vanishing without a trace in the nonfiction that immediately follows it.³⁶

The crux of the apparently positive portrayal of women in "The World Soul" is motherhood and birth, both of which are treated with surprising respect and sympathy in the article.³⁷ While it is unclear whether or not Platonov was familiar with Fyodorov in 1920, Platonov's other articles of the same year resonate with Fyodorovian concerns about reproduction and immortality. Even "But Man Has Only One Soul," printed on the previous day, features Platonov's typical depreciation of sexuality and reproduction as an insufficient weapon against death. For Fyodorov, the birth of a child is yet another in a long series of betrayals against one's dead ancestors. But Fyodorov rejected all forms of progress, including the succession of generations, on the same grounds. At this time, Platonov, following Bogdanov, was a firm believer in progress. Though this conviction did not usually express itself in reproductive terms, Platonov's faith in the evolution of classes could conceivably be transferred to a more individual level: the child as the next step of "evolution" after the parents. In "The World Soul," the child (or the son; typically, Platonov uses the two words interchangeably) is the only one who can complete the tasks his parents have left unfinished. Platonov calls the child "the master of humanity" because life is "ruled by the future, expected, but yet-unborn pure thought." The "purpose of life" (*smysl zhizni*) of woman as mother is the same as that of all humanity: "the future" (*Chut'e* 66). The child is valued because he is the embodiment of progress.

Platonov's strategy is reminiscent of his rehabilitation of the natural world in "Repairing the Earth." In that essay, Platonov transforms the earth into a "machine" for the production of bread, a tool to be harnessed by the peasant. In "The World Soul," Platonov performs a similar operation upon women: now woman is valued as the mechanism that brings forth a product that is vital to the common cause—the child.

Woman is still not engaged in the same struggle with matter that is so central to the life of the conscious man, but is instead providing man with the means to advance his cause. In this regard, woman is far superior to the earth, which provides only consumer goods (food), while the mother, who gives birth to a child destined to remake the world, creates the very means of production themselves: the son, and hence the man of the future. The child produces hope (66), while the mother produces the child; feminine labor is now on a par with heavy industry.

Though such a view of the child's importance is not reflected elsewhere in Platonov's journalism, it is central to much of his later fiction. In Platonov's 1926–27 tale "The Ether Tract" ("Efirnyi trakt"), Mikhail Kirpichnikov dies before his grand scientific experiment can be realized; it is completed years later by his son Egor. In *Chevengur,* the death of a child is a blow to the Chevengurians' hopes for the future. In *The Foundation Pit* (*Kotlovan,* 1930), the workers identify the foundling Nastya with the radiant future that they strive to build, only to watch helplessly as she dies before their very eyes.[38] Though Platonov would continue to portray reproduction in a negative light throughout the 1920s, the identification of the child with the future would become a frequent counterpoint to his antisexual views, paving the way for his eventual "compromise with happiness."

Even more jarring than the praise of the child is that of its mother.[39] From its very first sentence, "The World Soul" sets itself apart from the rest of Platonov's nonfiction: "Woman and man [*muzhchina*] are two faces of the same creature: the human being [*chelovek*]; the child is their common eternal hope" (*Chut'e* 66). Not only does Platonov implicitly give his approval to reproduction, but he also places the sexes on an equal level. This is not to say that he abandons his customary dualism; "man" and "woman" still form a binary opposition. Now, however, Platonov emphasizes their common membership in the human race. Woman's basic humanity would be considered self-evident in the work of nearly any other author, but in an article by Platonov, such an admission becomes part of a counterargument to Platonov's own philosophy.

Platonov does not stop at merely admitting woman's humanity; "The World Soul" inaugurates a virtual cult of womanhood that is particularly at odds with the rest of his nonfiction. From a historical point of view, however, Platonov's article is more derivative than groundbreaking, for it recapitulates the myth of the Eternal Feminine, which by the beginning of the twentieth century had been transformed from a complex, philosophical teaching to something akin to a fad. Even the article's title is a Russian rendition of the mystical term "World Soul" that played a significant role in the writings of Solovyov and the later idiosyncratic Sophiology of Blok and Bely. A number of commonplaces in the cult of the Eternal Feminine find their way into Platonov's essay: woman as the embodiment of creative force, her connection to the earth, her potential to redeem earthly existence. Were it not for the article's anomalous place in Platonov's nonfiction, "The World Soul" would not stand out from the dozens of similar hymns to womanhood that appeared in the decades preceding the revolution.[40]

Unlike Solovyov (or Blok and Bely), Platonov does not hesitate to examine the physiology of woman's existence even as he elevates her from body to soul. Here Platonov shows his debt to Rozanov, whom he would discuss with such hostility three months later in "The Culture of the Proletariat." Like Rozanov, Platonov focuses on the physiology of childbirth in his elevation of the woman as mother: woman brings forth her child "with her blood and flesh," with which she also "feeds humanity" (*Chut'e* 66).[41] Forms of the word "blood" appear four times in this three-page article, each time connected with woman's maternal function. Yet Platonov is neither parroting nor refuting Rozanov's discussions of women and blood.[42] The fixation on the physical aspect of woman's existence in "The World Soul" is perfectly consistent with the mainstream of Platonov's philosophy, which is itself opposed to everything Rozanov stood for. Woman in Platonov's articles personifies nature, the physical world that has yet to be transformed by man's consciousness. The difference between "The World Soul" and Platonov's other pronouncements on the same subject is a matter of value judgment. Elsewhere, the association of woman with nature and physicality is inherently negative, but in "The World Soul" that same connection is shown to be both the key to human happiness and the justification of woman's existence.

In "The World Soul," woman is in a constant liminal state, yet, unlike Nastasya Filippovna of the *Idiot* review, she is capable of reconciling the two worlds she straddles. It is she who "brings heaven down to earth," at the same time raising "man" (*cheloveka*) to new heights. Unlike the men of Platonov's other essays and early fiction, she builds the future not by struggling with nature, but by embodying nature in a conscious form. It is in her body that nature and consciousness meet: "within woman lives the highest form of human consciousness: the consciousness of the worthlessness of the existing universe, the love of that far-off image of the perfect creature—the son, who does not yet exist, but will, whom she carries within herself, conceived by the conscience of the dying world, guilty and repentant" (*Chut'e* 66–67). Here woman is not merely the incarnation of the forces of nature so hated by Platonov, but rather a vehicle for the redemption of the natural world through its own self-consciousness. "But what is woman?" Platonov asks. "She is the living, effective incarnation of the world's consciousness of its sin and crime." Woman is the "redemption of the universe's madness," the "awakening conscience of all that is." Woman's "higher consciousness" is in her "eternal birthing" and "eternal passion of motherhood" (*v vechnom rozhdenii, v vechnoi strasti materinstva*). Rather than denying the physicality of woman in order to praise her, Platonov finds that the very "shamefulness" of female biology serves to elevate the matter to the realm of consciousness: "Woman distills the ugliness and horror of the earth through her own blood" (*Chut'e* 67).[43]

The identification of woman as the world's soul in physical form allows Platonov to present in a sympathetic light the phenomena he disdains elsewhere in his work. For Platonov, the agony of childbirth is not simply a result of the sin of Eve but is linked with the sinfulness of the entire material world. Not only reproduction but sexual desire itself is reevaluated in terms of the redemption of matter. Thus Platonov makes the only positive statement about physical passion to be found in his early work: the desire that "moves a man closer to woman is not what people think." Both pleasure and prayer, sexual desire is a "breach in the stone walls of the world's inertness and hostility" (*Chut'e* 67).

It is in this seemingly positive treatment of sex, however, that one sees the first sign of a motif that will reach its peak in *Chevengur, The Foundation Pit,* and, to a lesser extent, "Dzhan" ("Dzhan," 1934). In all of these works, the womb and the grave are conflated, suggesting a link between sex, woman, and, death.[44] Solovyov, Berdyaev, and Rozanov all share Freud's contention that the sexual instinct is an expression of the will to live,[45] but Platonov sees sexuality in terms of death and the end of the world. Sexual desire, which serves as a vehicle for creating a child, is yet another way in which man expresses his preference for the future over the present, his desire that the existing world be destroyed and replaced by another one: "It is the supreme moment when all the black snakes of the earth are covered by the ice of death. In the silence of the illuminated tenderness of the mother-woman, worlds die along with their suns. There arises a new, silent world of the unity and love of the mingled streams of all lives, of all enlightened beings" (*Chut'e* 67). By equating sex and reproduction with the negation of the present and past, Platonov shows that he has not strayed as far from Fyodorov as it might otherwise seem. But where Fyodorov sees this aspect of sex as an interference with the cult of the dead, Platonov finds that the very forces of reproduction conspire to destroy the existing order and hasten the arrival of the future.

Thus woman, in her role as both mother and soul of the world, serves to "bring the suffering life to the end of its path." Her reproductive function renders her the embodiment of both life and death simultaneously:

> Woman is a woman when the conscience of the dark world, its hope to become perfect, its moral anguish, lives within her.
>
> Woman is truly alive when the desire for torment and death within her outweighs the desire for life. For the earth breathes, moves, and becomes green only through her death.
>
> Not to see heaven, but to fall dead at its gates—this is the purpose of woman, and, with her, of humanity. (*Chut'e* 68)[46]

Here the argument of "The World Soul" reaches full circle. Woman is valued because she is the living vessel for the linkage of nature and consciousness, but her ultimate function is to negate the natural world by using its own laws (sexual desire and reproduction) to replace the present with the incarnation of the future. The very "fact" that woman is more firmly rooted than man in the realm of biology and matter is what renders her so important. Man's struggle to transcend matter is, as Seifrid argues, complicated by a dual heritage: "Embodied—literally—in man are both the principle of consciousness, whose advent will ultimately enable transcendence of the physical world, and the principle of matter, whose dominance is the root of cosmic suffering. Though he yearns to rise above them, man must suffer his origins in the base, primordial matter of the earth, a circumstance which repeatedly leads Platonov toward apprehension of what might be called the 'dilemma of chthonic origin'" (Seifrid 37). If this dilemma is felt so keenly by Platonov's men, it does much to explain their ambivalence toward women. In the first section of *Chevengur*, Prosha Dvanov's mother churns out new offspring with horrifying regularity, exacerbating the family's poverty. Yet despite Platonov's early antifemale rhetoric, he is acutely aware that woman, however less politically conscious than her mate, is far more conscious than a cow or ewe. As a member of the human species, she, like man, is aware of the horror and senselessness of nature; indeed, because her own body is the material base for the creation of a thinking, conscious son, she is all the more cognizant of the "worthlessness of the existing universe" (66).

As in "But Man Has Only One Soul," woman is valued only when she is presented as something other than herself: "And woman knows that the world and the sky and she are one, that she gave birth to everything, and this is why she has no identity, this is why she is so elusive and unfathomable, because she has given herself to everything" (68). Platonov uses the process of birth to turn woman into a vessel not only of her own child, but of the surrounding world into which her child is delivered. Just as Platonov's Dostoevsky "writhes on the borders of the world of sex and the world of consciousness" (*Vozvrashchenie* 72–73), so does the mother provide human self-awareness to birth, the most animal of processes to which humans are subject. The natural world is itself unconscious and thus can have no soul. But woman, who is less able than man to escape the strictures of nature, can become the world's soul precisely by being conscious of the horrible process that she undergoes.[47] Woman is still without subjectivity (she has "no identity"), lending her consciousness to the "world and the sky." In "But Man Has Only One Soul," Platonov exempts Nastasya Filippovna from his misogynist scorn by rendering her nearly bodiless; in "The World Soul," he provides a loophole for mothers by initially focusing on maternal physiology, only to use the biological process of birthing in order to render her once again ethereal and abstract. Small wonder that Platonov extols the mother, since for him woman is only of value if she is pregnant with something other than herself, whether it be a child, an idea, or a soul.

THE BRIDE TO BE

With the exception of mothers, Platonov's early stories have few female characters; for their part, the mothers, while portrayed sympathetically, play only limited roles. Ilya Bratslavsky's words at the end of *Red Cavalry* apply equally well to Platonov's fiction: "A mother during a revolution is an episode" (Babel 2: 129). Platonov's idiosyncratic reading of *The Idiot* is the closest thing we have to a developed female character in Platonov's fiction of 1920. It was only in 1923 that Platonov would write a work of fiction that addresses the issue of asexual male utopianism at the same time that it introduces a significant female character, the Caspian Bride in "A Story about Many Interesting Things."

"A Story about Many Interesting Things" is, like many of Platonov's better works, a hodgepodge of genres and styles, a fairy tale for grown-ups in which the son of a werewolf saves his dying village, travels the country with a band of Bolsheviks, visits a laboratory that uses electricity for the production of "immortal flesh," and flies away to a distant star on a ship powered by "electromagnetic dust," all in the course of twenty-six short chapters. From the very beginning of the story, sex is portrayed as, quite literally, animal desire: the pockmarked Glashka, despairing of ever finding a husband in her native village of Surzha, leaves home for the forest and conceives a son with Yakim, who looks like a wolf but has the heart and eyes of a (human) wanderer (*Starik* 44). Her neighbors are startled when she returns "eleven months and eleven days" later with a small boy and no husband; when the priest asks if she claims to have produced a child through immaculate conception, Glashka laughs off the comparison. Indeed, there is nothing exalted about motherhood or childbirth in this story; after Yakim sleeps with Glashka, he feels more exhausted than ever in his life: " 'I'm dead,' thought Yakim. 'Death comes from the girl' " (*Starik* 45).

As the boy, Ivan Kopchikov, grows older, he becomes aware of the inherent hostility of nature to man. Through an imaginative feat of false etymology, Ivan determines that the ravine (*ovrag*) bordering Surzha is actually the enemy (*O vrag ty nash!*) of the town and develops a scheme to prevent the ravine from "eating up" the entire town (*Starik* 49–50). Thus even in this fairy tale, Platonov manages to include yet another appeal for land reclamation, for "repairing the earth." Ivan's subsequent experience during the famine that ravages his village leads him to the conclusion that everyday life must be changed radically. When he is told that one of the women is about to give birth, he responds that "[a] new nation must be born . . . the likes of which have never been" (*Starik* 57). Even the woman's husband is forced to conclude that sex alone cannot repopulate their dying village: "We've gotta herd some people over here" (*Starik* 59). In a move that prefigures the arrival of the new, "miscellaneous" people in Chevengur, Ivan brings a band of twenty Bolshevik wanderers to Surzha, along with one girl, the "only property" of the men: the Caspian Bride (*Starik* 61). So captivated is Ivan by the beauty and purity of the Caspian Bride that he soon takes her with him as he wanders the countryside so that he can "show [her] to everyone" (*Starik* 68).

In the course of their travels, they come to the "Workshop of Sturdy Flesh," the laboratory of a scientist who is trying to conquer death with the help of electricity. Subsequently they encounter another amateur researcher, a "twilight man" (*sumrachnyi chelovek*), who has constructed an electromagnetic spaceship. Ivan and the engineer fly off to another star while the Caspian Bride is still asleep. On a distant planet they encounter strange, headless (but Russian-speaking) creatures who have "instituted heaven" (*Starik* 90) by dedicating their lives to "feeding and copulation" (*pitanie i sovokuplenie*). The story ends abruptly when the two earthmen encounter an old creature who is "neither man nor woman" (*ne to muzhik, ne to baba*) (*Starik* 91) and the sun is suddenly extinguished.

Though Platonov's rather uneven tale is, as the title declares, about "many interesting things," one of the most striking aspects is the pervasive rhetorical dissonance on the subjects of women, sex, and love. If birth is an animal function when a "new person" crawls out of a woman as she "squeals like a bitch being murdered" (*Starik* 59), erotic desire can be channeled into useful activity as long as it is divorced from reproduction. Not long after his victory over the ravine, Ivan becomes ill: his body itches, his appetite is gone, and he cannot sleep. One feature does, however, redeem Ivan's condition: he experiences this awakening of desire as a drive to further labor. He repairs a friend's hut, adjusts a fence, and feels as though he could dig a pit to the center of the earth with his bare hands. But there is no task that can satisfy his need to work (*Starik* 51). His neighbor tells him he needs a woman, while a visiting doctor informs him that his body is tormented by the bacillus "amo," which the narrator translates for his simpler readers as the "louse of love" (*liubovnaia vosh'*) (*Starik* 52). When Ivan does find some satisfaction with the peasant Natasha, their affection appears to be the opposite of the destructive passion of sex and reproduction: thanks to them, the "love louse" spreads throughout the entire village, "[b]ut these caresses brought neither children, nor languor, but only joy—and people worked with fervor" (*Starik* 52). The "love louse" is a form of eroticism that exists on the edges of expression and sublimation: when it finds its object in the opposite sex, it does not disrupt the body's delicate economy by expending the energy needed for labor on reproduction, an act that constitutes an almost fatal drain of one's bodily reserves. Even after he finds Natasha, Ivan is still tormented by the thought that he cannot see this invisible "love louse," and his inability to capture and control it leads him to "grow mildewed, like a leaf from bad dew" (*Starik* 52–53). Ivan is saved from his obsession by the very bodily economy that sexual passion threatens to disrupt: famine comes to the village, and "if you have no grub, you'll forget about even a boot louse, let alone a love louse!" (*Starik* 53). Natasha, like Ivan's mother, disappears from the text, never to be mentioned again.

Ivan's early erotic experience begins to make sense only after he begins his travels with the Caspian Bride. Ivan's encounters with numerous wise men throughout the countryside display a surprising uniformity; no matter how far he travels, the people he meets all seem to argue for the same antierotic philosophy—it is as though every landowner met by Gogol's Chichikov were different incarnations of the miser Plyushkin. First Ivan finds himself in the Workshop of Sturdy Flesh run by the Sturdy Man (*Prochnyi chelovek*), a scientist who is attempting to conquer death. Ivan (as well as Platonov's readers) passes the time with the Sturdy Man's book, a tract on the "construction of the new man" that bears a remarkable resemblance to both Fyodorov's *Philosophy of the Common Cause* and Platonov's own early essays. The Sturdy Man defines civilization as "chastity," a word common to the lexicon of both writers: "Chastity is man's conservation of that inner, powerful bodily strength that is spent on the production of progeny, and using this work for labor, for invention, for the creation within man of the ability to improve what already is or create what never was." All civilizations were made by men who were "only somewhat chaste," but now the time has come to create a completely new man, the chaste communist, who will create both himself and the world anew (*Starik* 73). The Sturdy Man's theory provides a valuable context for understanding Ivan's own prior erotic experience. Ivan is not yet a man of the future and thus is "only somewhat chaste." According to the Sturdy Man, when men gain a respite from wars and the struggle for survival, they go back home to their women, but such men are no longer the same. This new type of husband "becomes more chaste, and although he lives with his wife, he sleeps with her less, and plows more, builds higher and sturdier houses" (*Starik* 73). Both this passage in the Sturdy Man's essay and the "love louse" episode are rare instances of moderation in Platonov's early writing; each implies that a man can lead a useful, creative life without living up to the ideal of complete chastity.

This voice of moderation, however, is drowned out by the more extreme rhetoric of the rest of the Sturdy Man's essay and of the story as a whole. When Ivan overhears a different man reading another tract ("On the World and on the Souls of the Creatures That Inhabit It"), the case against sex is made once again. Here the author, Johann Pupkov, addresses himself to an unnamed, generalized man who wastes his life on eating and sex. When this man's son comes of age, he has the potential to develop a truly human soul, but "the child became a husband, went off with a woman, and emitted all his spiritual, star-creating power into her" (*Starik* 79). As a result, the child "has forever perished for the stars that were awaiting him." Pupkov's addressee, "like the star, pined for a child and expected from him miracles and the accomplishment of that which perished within you during your youth from contact with woman" (*Starik* 79). Pupkov's castigation of any sexual contact with women is phrased in terms that seem to be directly polemicizing with Platonov's "The World Soul": sexual intercourse has no positive value whatsoever, and the long-awaited son, rather than fulfilling his parents' hope for the future, will be even more venal than his father.

Ivan is thus faced with a chorus of voices, each of which in turn takes up the antisexual theme. A man on the street tells Ivan to be careful, or someone might steal the Caspian Bride: "Man can't live—he's afraid of his soul and releases it into a woman. If a woman is beautiful, his entire soul will go into her immediately. All he has to do is copulate with her once, and his entire soul will flow away with his seed" (81). Here we recall Platonov's earlier identification of women with souls, either as the negative embodiment of the essence of the bourgeoisie or as the vessel that contains the confused spirit of Dostoevsky. But what is perhaps most significant about this line of reasoning is that it is immediately recapitulated by the narrator: "People worked . . . in order to release everything they had stored up during the day as liquid ashes in the depths of a woman, . . . in order to dry up the soil with her, out of which future salvation will be propagated" (82). The narrator sounds a note of regret that is absent in the previous quote, but that resonates with Pupkov's address to his generalized reader: reproduction has the potential to lead to salvation, to a son who, like the son in "The World Soul," will transform the world. But as things stand now, such activity is merely a waste of precious energy.

When the argument is recapitulated for the last time, it is placed as an epigraph to the crucial twenty-fourth chapter, in which the engineer convinces Ivan to abandon the Caspian Bride and join him in his journey to the stars. Presumably, there are no more intermediaries; the words are identified as belonging to the "authors" of the story. (Of course, this still does not mean they can be thoroughly identified with Platonov's own view, if for no other reason than that we know that the very notion of the story's plural "authors" is fictive: Platonov wrote "A Story about Many Interesting Things" alone.) The passage appears to be a comment on the story as a whole: "We are telling about those who are making the future, about those who are now tormented by weighty thoughts, who are themselves nothing but the future and aspiration. Such men are few, they're lost. There may be no such men at all. We are telling about them, and not about those who extinguish the life within themselves with their passion and women, and who keep their souls at zero" (*Starik* 84). Despite any apparent concessions to the natural order, "A Story about Many Interesting Things" is only about the man of the future, the man who avoids women for the sake of higher things. How, then, are we to explain the exalted role of the Caspian Bride?

The Caspian Bride is initially a perfect example of "Bolshevik chivalry": she unites the men around her into a close-knit group rather than provoking rivalry (see chapter 1); her "magical force" causes them to change, bringing them new thoughts and a "tender spiritual strength." Ivan is initially puzzled by her effect on him and the other men: "What is this? . . . there shouldn't be anything besides thoughts and machines. Some hidden power is at work within the Bride that makes her so necessary to us" (*Starik* 65). Soon he realizes that she has the potential to bind together the entire universe, including the sun and the stars: "Everywhere . . . will be brotherhood. . . . There will be a brotherhood of stars, of beasts, of grasses and man" (*Starik* 65). When Ivan and the Caspian Bride set out on their journey, it is because Ivan has become convinced that she is the only instrument he needs in order to give the world "silence and thought." Ironically, his very quest shows the dangers of obsession with women, since it leads him away from comradeship with his fellow Bolsheviks in a manner that suggests selfishness as much as altruism: "I will get to know her power and take possession of it myself" (*Starik* 65). Readers of *Chevengur* will recognize this impulse as the very reason the residents of Platonov's all-male socialist ghost town will offer for excluding women: the collective will fall apart into smaller units.

Like the mother in "The World Soul," the Caspian Bride is valued for her vagueness and lack of identity: in terms reminiscent of the Eternal Feminine of Solovyov and the second-generation Symbolists, she is described as having a "lunar body—pale, firm, and calm, like the mute radiance of the midnight bread moon" (*Starik* 63). Her thoughts are not her own, but were produced instead "by the sun." She is "an empty and pure pitcher" into which is poured "the solar force of the world, [which] makes her thoughts, and soul, and words" (*Starik* 65). Yet despite all the "magic" attributed to her by the narrator, the Caspian Bride is revealed to be the final female distraction that the hero must overcome. When the engineer invites Ivan to join him on his interstellar journey, he tells him, "Leave your girlfriend here—so she won't fence your eyes off from the world and tear your soul in two" (*Starik* 85–86). Though the engineer reassures Ivan that the Caspian Bride will be found, the narrator tells us that she will "disappear without a trace" (*Starik* 86). When one reads the engineer's words in conjunction with the "authors'" epigraph to the chapter, the story's message about men's relations with women seems to be clear: women have no place in the struggle to create the new world.

Were that the case, "A Story about Many Interesting Things" would add little to what we already know about Platonov. And yet the Caspian Bride cannot be dismissed casually, even if Ivan and the engineer appear to do precisely that. The narrator, at least, must say his good-byes:

> Farewell, Bride! May all your roads on this earth be short ones and may your soul be filled with the lightest gas of joy. You were born at the wrong time. The time for your birth will never come. You are a member of that humanity which is not born, but which remains on the edges of the maternal womb. You are the scrawny seed that is not fertilized and does not swell into a person. Your accidental, dying initial seed stuck together with another such doomed seed and out hatched a person who never exists, and if he does exist, then he blinds people's eyes and perishes without a trace, like wind against a mountain. (*Starik* 86)

Each of the "loopholes" we have seen Platonov provide for women has been abstract, but none so much as the circumstances surrounding the Caspian Bride: with no characteristics of her own, she exists as pure potential and makes sense in the present only as a premonition of the future. It would be too simple to say that Platonov is simply recasting a common respect for virgins; her purity is not exclusively the result of her sexual inexperience. She is called not "virgin," but "bride" (*nevesta*), a term that has a special meaning in Platonov's world.[48] A bride is a virgin who is about to become a wife, a woman who is almost accessible to her beloved, but still distant. Like the horizon, she seems attainable but always recedes. In the early 1920s, Platonov repeatedly invokes the metaphor of the brides in order to make his point, from "But Man Has Only One Soul" to his 1921 "Notes" ("Zametki") to his only recently published letters to his wife.[49] By using the bride as a symbol of the unattainable future, Platonov allows for a love of a traditionally feminine woman, but only if she is kept at enough of a distance that she is no longer a threat.

The farther away she is, the easier she is to worship, and the less likely it is that she will distract the hero from the task at hand. From the Caspian Bride to Kopyonkin's beloved Rosa Luxemburg is only one small step: death. In *Chevengur*, Platonov will satirize his earlier admiration for such distant women by presenting the perfect bride as a woman who is already in the grave.

At this point in his career (when he has already met his own bride, Maria Kashintseva), Platonov is clearly struggling to reconcile his masculinist utopian worldview with a passion for women, however circumscribed by ideology that passion may be. "A Story about Many Interesting Things" presents a much more difficult choice between women and consciousness than was previously seen in Platonov's work, for here the deck is not stacked so heavily against women. Yet Ivan Kopchikov's decision begins to seem inevitable when one looks at the examples of the men who guide him on his journey: almost none of them has a wife.[50] Again and again, Ivan is told that it is women who prevent men from "reaching the stars": in the case of his conversation with the engineer, this advice is literal, but Johann Pupkov's essay describes the miserable lot of the stars who await man's arrival in vain while man expends his energy on sex and reproduction (*Starik* 79–80). Only the narrator recognizes that leaving behind the Caspian Bride is a real loss, necessary though it may be.

In "A Story about Many Interesting Things" and in Platonov's non-fiction we see nearly all the essential components of *Chevengur*: the masculinist utopian ideology and the disdain for sex and femininity are already tempered by a love for a distant feminine ideal, an almost mystical respect for mothers, and an identification of (male) children with hope for the future. In these early works, Platonov is able to balance his fervor for male society with a wistful longing for women precisely because he keeps women at a distance.[51] The beloved Bride has no place in man's world just yet, which is exactly why she can be portrayed with such fondness. *Chevengur*, however, will force the issue of contact between the two sexes: when the men finally rid themselves of the women, the distant, abstract bride is not enough. The author who gave the ideology of communist masculinity its most forceful expression ultimately concludes that a world without women is a world without a future.

Chapter Six

CHEVENGUR

Buried in the Family Plot

> [W]hat will we do with fathers and mothers in the future communism? — Andrei Platonov, *Chevengur* (1929)

If the ideology of "men without women" has either a bible or a book-length rebuttal, *Chevengur* is both. Most of the recurring motifs of all-male utopianism are taken to their extremes in *Chevengur:* Fyodorovian father worship becomes necrophilia; the manly, ascetic builders of the new world are forced to face the social and sexual consequences of their misogynist exclusivity; the ethereal female object of desire, already little more than an excuse for male rivalry in Olesha, has become so abstract that she has passed on into the next world; the implicitly male masses are shown in their daily reality, ultimately balking at the sexless order to which the ideologues of the new world think they are so well suited. While rendering the attraction of fratriarchal ideas with the understanding of an insider, Platonov shows that they, like the men who represent them, are doomed to vanish without issue.

With the benefit of hindsight, it is all too easy to see in Platonov's novel, which was first printed in Russia during the height of *perestroika,* the very "counterrevolutionary" elements that had so long rendered the book unpublishable. *Chevengur,* however, is not a conventional satire; though certain plot similarities suggest *The History of a Town* (*Istoriia odnogo goroda,* 1869) as a possible model for *Chevengur,* Platonov's novel is not suffused with the biting irony of Saltykov-Shchedrin's parody of Russian history. Certainly, irony has a place in *Chevengur,* particularly in the descriptions of the labors of Zakhar Pavlovich at the beginning of the novel and the Chevengurians near the end.[1] Irony, however, is tempered with sympathy for the novel's "fools" (*duraki*), whose childlike sincerity is proof against the distance irony usually creates between character and reader, between character and the authorial persona.[2] Nor is *Chevengur* the realistic rendition of an earnest attempt at the creation of "socialism in one town," although it does bring Platonov's utopianism down from the disconnected heights of his early science fiction to the more familiar world of revolution and civil war. Science fiction provided the young Platonov a controlled laboratory environment for the implementation of his ideas; his "Descendants of the Sun" ("Potomki solntsa," 1922) allowed him to depict the result of centuries of humanity's march toward collectivism while leaving him free to avoid describing the actual historical events leading up to socialism's apotheosis.[3] By contrast, *Chevengur* places its characters firmly in a contemporary setting even as they do their best to leave history behind.

Platonov's novel, however, is no less a test site for his utopianism than was his science fiction. Mikhail Geller rightly calls the genre of *Chevengur* "menippean satire," which Bakhtin defines as the "universal genre of the last questions," whose goal is "to test an idea and the man of the idea."[4] Platonov populates *Chevengur* with the adherents of his revolutionary philosophy, tacitly enjoining them to construct in history what his science fiction heroes had created outside of history. Unlike the protagonists of more traditional "novels of ideas," Platonov's Chevengurians are not educated or intelligent enough to argue with any sort of rigor; they embody theories rather than espouse them.[5] The philosophies of Dostoevsky's heroes are filtered through the personality and reasoning of the characters themselves, but Platonov's Chevengurians represent the unmediated idea let loose in an attempt to transform the world.[6] Rather than examine the philosophy behind the idea, Platonov displays the world that results from it. Like Sasha Dvanov, Platonov "thinks two thoughts at once and finds consolation in neither" (357). This approach does not require that the authorial stance be freed from all sympathy to the idea's proponents or the idea itself. On the contrary, *Chevengur* is the wistful leave-taking of an idea that has dug its own grave.

Chevengur is easily Platonov's densest and most difficult work and may well be the most complex novel in the twentieth-century Russian canon. The book has little that can be considered a plot in the traditional sense, and the closest approximation of a hero in *Chevengur,* Aleksandr (Sasha) Dvanov, is repeatedly lost within the meandering narrative. Like the original version of Babel's *Red Cavalry, Chevengur* begins with a dead father and ends with a dead son. Here the similarities between the two frames ends, however. Babel's unrelated father and son are both victims of violence, and both can be said to have died a heroic death; in Platonov's novel, the two men do actually constitute a biological family, and each voluntarily causes his own demise. When we meet Sasha Dvanov, he is a small boy who watches as his father's coffin is placed in the ground. Sasha's mother is long since dead, and his father (who is never named) was a fisherman who died of curiosity: "he saw death as another province" and drowned in Lake Mutevo in order to "live in death and return" (28). Zakhar Pavlovich, an eccentric peasant inventor whose accomplishments include a wooden pot for boiling water on an open fire, arranges to have Sasha live with the Dvanovs, a large, impoverished family that grows larger and poorer each year. Sasha's foster brother Proshka (Prokofy) resents the orphan as an extra mouth to feed and eventually convinces his parents to drive Sasha out to forage for himself. By day Sasha begs for food, and by night he sleeps on his father's grave. Meanwhile, Zakhar Pavlovich, who has been working as a railroad engineer, finds that his fervor for machines is waning in favor of a new interest in people. Zakhar Pavlovich pays Proshka a ruble to bring Sasha to him, whereupon he adopts the boy as his own. Like his latest "father," Sasha develops interest in machines and engineering, but not to the same extent. After the revolutions of 1917, Zakhar Pavlovich convinces the seventeen-year-old Sasha to join the Bolshevik Party; soon Dvanov begins to work on the railroad, is nearly killed in an accident, and develops typhus. When he recovers, he is sent by a local party official out into the countryside to see if the common people have developed socialism on their own. Before he departs, he says goodbye to his neighbor Sonya, a young girl who is about to become a schoolteacher.

At this point the novel undergoes a change of genre: from now until Sasha's arrival in Chevengur, his journey takes on a vaguely picaresque character. Dvanov is shot by anarchists, and, clutching the bloody leg of a horse, he thinks of Sonya and experiences his first orgasm. The anarchists plan to finish him off, but he is saved by Stepan Kopyonkin, the quixotic Bolshevik knight who rides a horse called Proletarian Strength and worships the memory of Rosa Luxemburg. Kopyonkin brings the wounded Sasha back to Sonya and allows his soldiers to return to their wives. Sasha wanders off in a delirium, moves in with a peasant woman he has just met, and then abandons her to ride off with Kopyonkin. As they travel, Dvanov and Kopyonkin meet a bizarre collection of people, including a man who has changed his name to Dostoevsky, a nameless man referred to only as "Incomplete" (*Nedodelannyi*), and the armor-clad Pashintsev, who lives in a "revolutionary national park" (147). Dvanov and Kopyonkin part ways temporarily, and Dvanov meets a locksmith named Gopner and a man named Chepurny, who comes from the communist town of Chevengur. Dvanov sends Chepurny to find Kopyonkin and take him to Chevengur. When they arrive, Kopyonkin finds a town where all constructive labor has been abolished in the name of communism; he sends for Dvanov. The inhabitants of Chevengur include Dvanov's estranged foster brother Prokofy and an acquisitive woman named Klavdyusha Klobzd, the object of both Chepurny's and Prokofy's desire. All the town's bourgeoisie have been shot, and soon the communists rid themselves of the "semi-bourgeois" as well. Now the town has only twelve inhabitants, and Prokofy repopulates the town with the starving and destitute "miscellaneous" (*prochie*), whose miserable lives have left them with no individual identity. One of the new arrivals, a small boy, dies, causing the Chevengurians to doubt that true communism has been built. Dvanov and Gopner arrive in Chevengur just as the now-sated miscellaneous demand wives and families for themselves. Reluctantly, Chepurny accedes to their request, sending Prokofy on a mission to bring back the most unfeminine women he can possibly find.

Abruptly, the scene changes to Moscow, and we are introduced to a new character, Simon Serbinov, a communist who has been unable to overcome his own sense of individuality. Serbinov has fallen in love with Sonya, who also now lives in Moscow. When Serbinov discovers that his mother has died, he convinces Sonya to come with him to the cemetery, where they have sex on his mother's grave. Serbinov is sent to Chevengur to investigate the disappearance of the region's arable farmland and writes a report suggesting that the town has been taken over by either a minority nationality or itinerant beggars. He arrives not long before Prokofy brings the women, whom the men take as mothers and sisters rather than wives. Their arrival heralds the downfall of the Chevengurian experiment: the community separates into smaller "families," and soon a mysterious "machinelike enemy" (*mashinal'nyi vrag*) arrives and kills nearly all the town's inhabitants, including Kopyonkin and Chepurny. Dvanov escapes on Proletarian Strength and returns to Lake Mutevo, where he drowns himself to join his father. Zakhar Pavlovich arrives at the ruins of Chevengur, where he finds Prokofy, alone and crying. Zakhar Pavlovich offers Prokofy a ruble to bring him Sasha, but Prokofy promises to do it for free. Here the novel ends.

"THE MYSTERIOUS RELATIONS BETWEEN COMRADES"

Few works of the early Soviet period are as self-consciously dedicated to specifically male experience as Platonov's *Chevengur*. Babel's *Red Cavalry* comes close, if for no other reason than that the wartime ordeal of an intellectual in a Cossack regiment is inherently tied to questions of masculinity and initiation. While it would be a mistake to reduce Babel's focus on male relationships to the exigencies of plot, the very fact that *Red Cavalry* is a cycle of war stories leads the reader to take this masculine emphasis for granted. Platonov's novel, however, lacks the "extenuating circumstances" of Babel's stories; there is nothing in the basic plot of *Chevengur* that requires the work to pay special attention to men as men. The attempt of a group of enthusiasts to build communism (or at least a project that is a metaphor for communism) could easily include women, as any number of socialist realist novels demonstrates. In *Chevengur*, however, the masculinist worldview of the early Platonov is the point of departure; one can argue that male authors often use men to stand in for all humanity, but Platonov places such vast distance between male and female experience as to make such generalization impossible. In attempting to remove sex from the life of men, Platonov isolates sexuality, relegating it to the realm of women. The irony of Platonov's antisexual strategy is that it results in a world based on sexual difference. When Platonov's characters consistently exclude women from the social structures they create, they no longer have the luxury of being generalized "people": they are forced to be men, and only men.

The masculine focus of Platonov's novel is so pervasive that it verges on self-parody; even the weeds and grasses of Chevengur are said to grow together "like brothers" (*bratski*) (274). As in the earlier essay "The World Soul," the words "child" and "son" are virtually synonymous.

There are no daughters in the novel, only sons; when a child is born, it is always a boy.[7] Even the oath shouted by an anarchist early in the novel is based on a highly inventive male anatomical metaphor: "By the scrotum of Jesus Christ, by the rib of the Mother of God and the entire Christian generation, fire!" (*Po moshonke Iisusa Khrista, po rebru bogoroditsy i po vsemu khristianskomu pokoleniiu—pli!*) (104). One can safely assume that few novelists have even mentioned Christ's testicles, let alone have a character swear by them. The subsequent reference to the Virgin Mary would seem to balance out the overtly masculine tone of the oath, and yet the part of the body invoked is the rib, which, according to Judeo-Christian tradition, was taken from the first man to create woman. Only Platonov could call upon Christianity's most powerful feminine symbol and still allude to men.

Even more than in the works of Babel and Olesha, many of the male relationships of *Chevengur* display an unmistakable homoeroticism. Men in *Chevengur* kiss on several occasions, an act that is less jarring in the Russian and European cultural contexts than it would be in America. Nonetheless, more than one of these kisses evokes awkwardness and shame in the men involved. Dvanov and Kopyonkin first kiss before parting ways in the first half of the novel, after which "both of them felt pointlessly ashamed" and Kopyonkin bursts into tears (169–70). When they are reunited, their second kiss is even more emotional: having approached Dvanov from behind, Kopyonkin stares at Sasha "with the greed of his friendship for him" (*s zhadnost'iu svoeiu druzhby k nemu*). For his part, Dvanov is also moved:

> Dvanov . . . was ashamed of his excess feeling for Kopyonkin and afraid to express it and make a mistake.
>
> Kopyonkin also had a conscience for the mysterious relations between comrades, but he was encouraged by his neighing, merry steed.
>
> "Sasha," said Kopyonkin. "You've arrived? . . . Let me kiss you a little, in order to stop suffering." (315)

The entire scene is characterized by shame. After the kiss, Kopyonkin can no longer face his comrade, turning his back on him to pretend to talk to his horse. He turns away again when Dvanov confirms that Rosa

Luxemburg is long dead. Sasha is forced to shed his tears out in the open, "since he had no place to turn away from Chepurny and Kopyonkin" (316). Kopyonkin berates Chepurny for staring at them, but Chepurny himself is embarrassed by what he sees.

The eroticism of the moment is reinforced by the behavior of Kopyonkin's horse, which, like the mounts of Babel's Cossacks, is repeatedly associated with virility and sexuality. It is the task of Proletarian Strength to bring Kopyonkin closer to the objects of his desire; he is the vehicle that allows Kopyonkin always to move in the direction of his dead Rosa. In this scene, Proletarian Strength seems to embody Kopyonkin's libido: the horse prompts Kopyonkin to reveal feelings he might otherwise hide. Kopyonkin is on horseback when he finds Dvanov and is so distracted that he forgets to climb off. It is Proletarian Strength who announces Kopyonkin's presence to Dvanov with the same neighing that encourages Kopyonkin to kiss him. After the kiss, the horse seems to mock its master, appearing to know that Kopyonkin's conversation with Proletarian Strength is only a cover for his feelings. Proletarian Strength refuses to stop staring at Kopyonkin.[8] Of all the observers of the scene, only the narrator displays enough sensitivity to "turn away" as the two men embrace: though Kopyonkin himself draws extra attention to the kiss by referring to it in words, the narrator never actually depicts the act itself. First Kopyonkin proposes the kiss, and then the narrator writes, "Having kissed Dvanov, Kopyonkin turned away" (315).

If this were an isolated incident, or if the language of the passage were less emotionally charged, one could counter that Kopyonkin and Dvanov are merely good friends who happen to be unusually sentimental. Yet the narrator repeatedly chooses words throughout the novel that seem deliberately suggestive of homoeroticism. Certainly the phrase "the mysterious relations between comrades" (*tainye otnosheniia mezhdu tovarishchami*) begs the question of the nature of comradely ties.[9] On two other occasions the novel's characters all but link comradeship and homoeroticism, through either ellipsis or wordplay. The first is when Zheev kisses Prokofy and enjoins him to find women (see chapter 1). The second occurs when Chepurny and Sotykh lie together in the barn. Chepurny is glad for the company of "any proletarian person" (*liubomu cheloveku-proletariiu*), even if only to lie by his side and "hear the formulation of his own feelings" (248). As Sotykh dozes fitfully, Chepurny "straightens his legs and folds his arms, so that [Sotykh] could rest better." Sotykh gives Chepurny's actions a different interpretation: "Don't caress me, don't shame a man. . . . It's good with you already" (*Ne glad' menia, ne stydi cheloveka . . . Mne i tak s toboi khorosho*). Chepurny tells his companion to go back to sleep, but Sotykh persists in his reproach: "You just won't let me sleep at all . . . We have an activist like you in our settlement; he won't leave the [peasant] guys alone. You're also an activist, devil take you!" (249). Rather than tell Sotykh that he was merely trying to make him more comfortable, Chepurny asks, "What am I supposed to do, if I can't sleep?" Both Sotykh's reprimand and Chepurny's defense are the stuff of heterosexual situation comedy: one spouse wants sex while the other prefers sleep. This sexual connotation is bolstered by the name Sotykh calls Chepurny: "activist" (*aktiv*). Literally, *aktiv* does mean "activist" in the political sense, and yet the Russian word contains more of a suggestion of an "active-passive" opposition than does the English. Sotykh calls Chepurny an *aktiv* in response to an apparent caress rather than a political harangue. The comparison of Chepurny to the *aktiv* in his village is phrased in a way that increases the scene's suggestiveness: like Chepurny, that *aktiv* would not leave the peasant men alone. Sotykh uses the lexicon of politics in a dialogue structured to resemble a more intimate moment.

Such revealing scenes are few, but they do help set the novel's tone. For the most part, however, the homosexual undercurrent of *Chevengur* is developed in ways familiar from the previous discussions of Babel and Olesha: the men of *Chevengur* appear unusually preoccupied with the bodies of other men.[10] As in *Red Cavalry* and *Envy,* the gazes of Dvanov and Kopyonkin often linger on male naked bodies. Unlike Lyutov or Kavalerov, Platonov's protagonists have no qualms about revealing their own nudity. After being shot by anarchists, Dvanov readily agrees to undress in order that his clothes will not be spoiled by his impending execution. When Dvanov runs into difficulty undressing because of his wounded leg, Nikita, the man who shot him, helps Dvanov "like a comrade" (tovarishcheski).

Though the focus on male nudity is reminiscent of Babel and Olesha, Platonov's approach is fundamentally different. His protagonists stare at naked men or simply encounter them in unexpected places, but they never aestheticize the male body. At times naked men are simply taken for granted, as when Dvanov comes across two men in a hut, sitting on the Russian stove and mending their clothes (115). Dvanov can never be said to be sexually aroused by the nude men he encounters; indeed, he only experiences sexual excitement of any sort during illness and a near-death experience.

Kopyonkin's fascination with male nudity comes closer to overt homoeroticism, as this aspect of his character is developed more fully than in Dvanov.[11] When he and Chepurny go swimming in the river, Chepurny's body catches Kopyonkin's eye. Naked, Chepurny appears "pathetic" (*zhalkim*) but has "a warm smell of some long-ago healed, coagulated motherhood that Kopyonkin barely recalled" (221). Motherhood is the only positive expression of sexuality postulated by Platonov in his earlier works, and mothers will continue to evoke tender feelings throughout Platonov's later novels and stories. The naked Chepurny viscerally reminds Kopyonkin of birth and thus the maternal bond, which Kopyonkin fondly recalls.

Soon after dressing, Kopyonkin encounters another naked man, whose nudity Kopyonkin transforms from a sign of comic humiliation to a statement of male solidarity. When Kopyonkin first met Pashintsev, Pashintsev was as clothed as he could possibly be, hiding within a medieval suit of armor in which he could barely move. Now he is naked, and his "weak body" with "protruding ribs" presents a picture of utter defenselessness (223). After his defeat by the Whites, Pashintsev is left only with the one-piece helmet and breastplate of his armor, which cannot defend his body either from bullets or from prying eyes. Though Kopyonkin expresses sympathy, Pashintsev feels that he is being stared at: "why are you looking all over my naked body?" (*chego ty menia sharish' po golomu telu?*) (224). Here the verb Pashintsev uses (*sharit'*) conveys an unwelcome visual examination, but it literally means to "grope" or "feel." Kopyonkin responds to this reproach by once again examining Pashintsev's nude form.

Kopyonkin convinces Pashintsev that the helmet and breastplate are enough clothing for him, and the two walk toward town. After Kopyonkin discovers that Pashintsev's defeat was due to female treachery, he warms to his "naked comrade," telling him, "You didn't bare yourself; it was the semi-Whites who hurt you" (*Ty zhe ne sam obnazhilsia—tebia polubelye obideli*) (224). Now Pashintsev feels he is walking naked "for the sake of poverty-communism, and thus was not embarrassed by the possible female passers-by." But when they encounter Klavdyusha, she covers her eyes and remarks to herself that Pashintsev's body is weak and pathetic. Her reproach is phrased as a denial of all-male community: "This, citizens, is not the front: it isn't quite proper to walk here naked." Kopyonkin tells his comrade to pay no attention to this "bourgeois" (*burzhuika*), who interferes with "naked proletarians." But Pashintsev nonetheless puts on his breastplate and helmet, saying that people will think he is expressing a "kind of new policy" (*forma novoi politiki*) (225). Though the scene is comic, it has allowed Kopyonkin to use Pashintsev's nudity as a weapon against Klavdyusha. The implication is that if Chevengur were relieved of its only woman, men could walk naked as they please.

Male comradeship is also emphasized by another motif familiar from Babel's works: the persistence with which the men of *Chevengur* sleep side by side and huddle together for warmth. For Lyutov in *Red Cavalry*, sleeping next to another man is a sign of acceptance, the reward for his struggle to fit in. For Platonov's characters, sleeping with other men is a source of comfort that is not won, as is the case with Babel, but taken for granted. On the conscious level, the motivation of both Babel's and Platonov's characters is pragmatic and physical: they sleep together for warmth. Unlike Babel's cavalrymen, the men of *Chevengur* often remark on this fact, issuing verbal invitations to join one another in makeshift beds. The miscellaneous of Chevengur take this sleeping habit to its extreme: they sleep together not in twos or threes, but in entire heaps of people (276).

The nature of the ties among these miscellaneous, however, is less personal than those among the other Chevengurians. Collectivist ideals to the contrary, those men who are not miscellaneous tend to interact with each other on an individual level. Their choice of sleeping partners is thus more personalized than that of the miscellaneous. The conversation between Chepurny and Sotykh that I have just cited exaggerates the homoeroticism present in similar scenes. When Dvanov is lying alone by the road, he is awakened by the weight of a man's body next to his. The stranger proposes that they sleep with their arms around each other for warmth. When they awake the next morning, they cannot find a common language. Dvanov is at a loss to understand his companion's sudden touchiness. "You warmed yourself with me all night," Dvanov tells him, "and now you get offended!" Like Dvanov's reproach, the stranger's response resembles the words of a lover after a brief encounter: "Yesterday it was evening. . . . After all, I got cold during the night, not the morning" (96).

It is such intimate sleeping arrangements that give the reader the first clue of the intensity of the relationship between Dvanov and Kopyonkin. Kopyonkin has only just been introduced in the novel, appearing at Sonya's doorstep with Dvanov and three other men. When all five go to sleep in the kitchen, they arrange themselves with military orderliness: "Five men lay down in a row on the straw." There are none of the usual discussions of human warmth that Platonov includes in such scenes, nor do the men's legs intertwine as in *Red Cavalry*. Soon, however, two men move closer together: "and soon Dvanov's face turned pale from sleep; he burrowed his head in Kopyonkin's stomach and grew quiet, while Kopyonkin, sleeping with his saber and in full uniform, put his arm around him for protection." Almost immediately upon his introduction in the novel, Kopyonkin identifies himself as a protector, raising a toast "in order to gather strength for the defense of all the babies on earth" (110), but here Kopyonkin shows that his concern extends to a grown man. The image of Kopyonkin lying with his arm around Dvanov as the latter rests his head on Kopyonkin's stomach is reminiscent of both mother and child, and warrior and (female) beloved. That Kopyonkin is still in full military garb — and with his saber, no less — surrounds their relationship with decidedly masculine imagery.

Convinced that women are an ideological threat, Kopyonkin himself takes on a maternal, comforting role with the men who are closest to him. When Dvanov stands alone on the outskirts of a strange village, the night is described as "one of those nights that children fear" and from which they seek the protection of their mothers. Dvanov, however, has no mother: "Adults are orphans, and Dvanov stood alone on the outskirts of a hostile village." It is Kopyonkin who steps into the place of the absent mother, telling Dvanov that he had been looking everywhere for him: "Did you miss me? Now you'll drink some milk" (167). Kopyonkin is not the only man in Chevengur who acts as substitute mother. When Dostoevsky, the leader of an idiosyncratic communist village, is faced with the task of including the documentless local known as "Incomplete" in his official list, he manages to find a suitably bureaucratic formula to describe the man. As a result, Dostoevsky "firmly secures [Incomplete's] existence: he sort of gave birth to Incomplete for Soviet power" (*kak by rodil Nedodelannogo dlia sovetskoi vlasti*) (134).

As in Olesha's *Envy*, the combination of hypermasculine traits with motherliness in *Chevengur* is rooted in the drive for total male self-sufficiency. At the same time, such male "mothering" reinforces the homoerotic character of some of the relationships. When examining the male relationships in *Chevengur*, it is tempting to fall into one of two equally unsatisfying extremes. One can attempt to explain the entire novel in terms of homosexuality, as does Boris Paramonov: "*Chevengur*," he writes, "is a *gnostic utopia resting on homosexual psychology*" (334; emphasis in the original). By contrast, Eric Naiman asserts that homosexuality in Platonov's work is the "perversion of the utopian ideal (brotherhood/filial desire)" (Naiman, "Andrej Platonov" 357). Ultimately, it is a question of priority: which comes first, utopian comradeship or homosexual desire? Paramonov's Freudian reading assumes that homosexual impulses are transformed into "homosocial" ones through a process of sublimation, and, indeed, it is difficult to accept that the pervasive homoeroticism of the novel is purely an ideological phenomenon.[12] Both Naiman's and Paramonov's approaches are open to charges of reductivism (does all homosexuality have to be "explained away" as the sign of something else?), yet Paramonov is clearly more liable, for homoeroticism becomes the driving impulse not only of Platonov, but of a large part of the Russian religious philosophical tradition.[13] Here Paramonov does an injustice not to the philosophers (whose sexual orientation in any case has no bearing on the value of his writing), but to "homosexual psychology," which Paramonov connects to the hatred of nature, women, and life itself (339, 342).[14]

Homosexuality is not the central meaning of *Chevengur*, nor is it purely a symptom of an ideological problem. Only a few of the male relationships in the novel are markedly homoerotic; the ties that bind the miscellaneous are, as we shall see, a special case. Instead, Platonov places homoeroticism and comradeship even closer on the spectrum of male relationships than do Babel and Olesha. Overt homosexuality is inadmissible in Chevengur, for sex itself is incompatible with the continuing survival of the utopian community, which, as Naiman argues, is fundamentally opposed to all sexual desire ("Andrej Platonov" 319). If Kopyonkin's relations with other men have homoerotic overtones, this may well be simply an aspect of his characterization. Yet the conjunction of homoeroticism with Kopyonkin's passion for comradeship also allows for the possibility of viewing homoeroticism as the logical consequence of a Whitmanesque dedication to exclusively male attachments.[15] While I do not wish to reduce all instances of homoeroticism in the novel to a function of ideology, I would suggest that the issue is best addressed in the context of the "woman question" and the bonds between fathers, sons, and comrades.

ANSWERING THE WOMAN QUESTION

The function of women in *Chevengur* is even more complex than in Platonov's earlier writings: women in the novel are either a threat to male community, or the tie that binds two or more men together, or even both at once. They are the exalted embodiment of Russia (Sonya) and the incarnation of bourgeois acquisitiveness and betrayal (Klavdyusha). The difference between these two types of women, however, is not reducible to issues of individual personality; when women are either criticized or praised in the novel, it is as representatives of their sex rather than as unique human beings. Chevengur's ideologues debate woman's capacity to be a comrade rather than merely a sex object and never resolve the issue to their satisfaction. The arrival of women heralds the end of the male utopia, and yet the decision to bring them to the city is nearly unanimous. The inclusion of women in Chevengur does not lead to an unqualified acceptance of femininity and sexuality, but is rather the acknowledgment that antifemale, antisexual ideologues are unable to come up with a viable alternative to biology and tradition.

Despite emotional attachments to his dead mother and to the decaying corpse of Rosa Luxemburg, Kopyonkin has no use for living females. The only concession to women and sex he is willing to make is to allow his soldiers (such as they are) to see their wives as much as possible. Kopyonkin's plans to create a "family army" (*semeinaia armiia*) are purely pragmatic: he believes that armies lose battles when the soldiers are distracted because they miss their wives (110). Kopyonkin is spared anything as distasteful as actually observing his men together with their wives; rather, he lets them go to rejoin their families elsewhere, with the assumption that his men will be more dedicated upon return. Kopyonkin's soldiers, however, never do return during the course of the novel, though none of the characters seems to notice their absence. It is possible that Kopyonkin's soldiers are only imaginary, but it is also likely that they, like the Chevengurians at the novel's end, have chosen family life with women over the exclusively male community offered by Kopyonkin's army.

On the whole, women in *Chevengur* are a disruptive force that men must try to ignore. Sasha Dvanov is a worthy comrade for Kopyonkin precisely because he is nearly immune to women's charms. Kopyonkin "respectfully became fond of" (*s uvazheniem poliubil*) Dvanov for his "youth," an attraction that was "enhanced by his indifference to girls" (220). When the first women arrive in Chevengur "to be hired out as wives" (*v zheny . . . nanimat'sia*), both Chepurny and Dvanov are taken by surprise: even Dvanov has "tears of excitement" in his eyes (344). Soon, however, Dvanov regains his self-control and returns to his work "so that Gopner wouldn't think he was interested in women" (345). Indeed, the two gypsy women meet with little success, for Dvanov's attitude is shared by all the men they initially encounter. When they approach the miscellaneous Karchuk with their businesslike proposal of "sharing bread and dividing love" (*khleb vmeste i liubov' popolam*), they find only shock and rejection. Karchuk has only recently awakened from the mass torpor of his miscellaneous existence and has discovered the importance of individual comradeship. When the gypsies find him, he is constructing a man-sized box for Kirei, hence his response, "I don't need that, I'm fine as it is, I'm thinking about a comrade." The older gypsy challenges Karchuk, "What do you need a comrade for? . . . When you share your body with me . . . you'll forget your comrade, that's the truth!" (346).[16] Karchuk thinks only of his comrade and his box, and chases them away.

Though Karchuk rejects both the woman's advances and her words, her assertion is accurate: contact with women causes men to forget their comrades. The builders of communism seem to know this instinctively and thus do everything in their power to keep women at a distance. Women are seen as the antithesis of comradely relations; even before Chevengur, Pashintsev describes his own city as "the commune of new life," rather than a "woman's city" (*babii gorodok*) (158). Gopner later echoes this sentiment in Chevengur itself: "As if women understood comradeship: they'll saw communism into petit-bourgeois pieces with their wooden saws!" (239). Gopner is extrapolating from his own wife, who has "five *poods* [180 pounds] of petit-bourgeois ideology . . . for every *pood* of living meat" (240).

Women in *Chevengur* repeatedly interfere with the bonds between men. Even Zakhar Pavlovich, who could never understand how "talking about a woman like one talks about men" could bring anything but boredom, who "did not see any great joy" in life with his first wife (36), allows a second wife to come between him and other men. His source of comfort at home was Sasha, but "[h]ere, too, his constantly unsatisfied wife prevented him from concentrating on this comfort" (64). When Kopyonkin was a boy, his older brother went to visit his girlfriend every evening, leaving his younger brothers alone and lonely. They had each other for comfort, but it was the older brother's passion for a woman that led him away from the company of his younger brothers.

When women in *Chevengur* are portrayed as a threat to male community, they are cast in the familiar terms of Platonov's early essays: tainted by their association with nature, women are also the embodiment of bourgeois acquisitiveness. Gopner's harsh condemnation of his wife could just as well have been addressed to Chevengur's sole female resident, Klavdyusha. Kopyonkin distrusts her from the very beginning, warning Chepurny that Klavdyusha and Prokofy, the man who satisfies both her sexual and her materialistic needs, are "the bourgeoisie" (*burzhuaziia*) (214). Indeed, it is the close association of such a woman with the commune's chief ideologue that leads Chevengur down the path to self-contradiction. The city's ideology is determined by Prokofy, who in turn "formulated all the revolution as he wished, depending on Klavdyusha's mood and objective circumstances" (250). Note that "circumstances" are a distant second after Klavdyusha's whims. Even the massacre of the "semi-bourgeoisie" plays into her hands, for she is the one who reaps the material benefits of the villagers' demise. By the end of the novel, Klavdyusha, who understands that "things are essential to her," has left for her aunt's, taking with her as much property as Prokofy can give her.

The coming of the miscellaneous initially supports the male order of Chevengur, but it is ultimately the miscellaneous themselves who insist on introducing women into the city, thus replacing comradeship among men with something approaching conventional family life. Before they came to Chevengur, the miscellaneous had neither families nor the desire to start them, "because each one had lived with such difficulty and such concentration of all his powers, that no one had any bodily excess for reproduction" (318–19). In order to begin a family, one needs to have "seed" (*semia*) and the "power of ownership" (*sila sobstvennosti*). In the pre-Chevengurian existence of the miscellaneous, comrades were valued because they provided warmth during the night, helped find food, and because they were "good . . . to have beside you, if you didn't have a wife or property and there was no one with whom to satisfy and expend the constantly accumulated soul." In Chevengur, the miscellaneous find easily accessible food and a more stable way of life, causing them to lose interest in each other: "they paled for one another and each looked at the other without interest: they had become useless to themselves." His basic needs satisfied, one of the miscellaneous, for the first time identified by name, announces that he wants a family: "any reptile supports itself on its seed and lives peacefully, while I live on who knows what" (319). The inclusion of the miscellaneous in an all-male utopia proves paradoxical: while they live in poverty, they exemplify male comradeship, but as soon as their basic needs are satisfied, they prove as "counterrevolutionary" and "unconscious" as the bourgeoisie.

Though the arrival of women signals the fall of Chevengur, their inclusion in the city is made to seem physiologically inevitable. As Titych, the de facto spokesman of the miscellaneous puts it, "[B]ring us women, the people have rested" (320). The leaders of the commune acquiesce out of necessity, since the ties among the male miscellaneous are no longer strong enough to keep them together in the town. Several miscellaneous have already left to find wives on their own; the narrator tells us that they then plan to return with them to Chevengur, but the very fact that the masses are starting to scatter is a serious threat to the town's cohesion. Rather than sacrifice the town itself, the leaders of Chevengur attempt to replace the no longer satisfactory bonds of male comradeship with the more traditional family structure. Affiliation begins to yield to filiation.

The acceptance of women is the triumph of praxis over theory, a significant shift in the theory-driven approach of both Platonov's early writings and the worldview of *Chevengur*'s main characters. It is Prokofy, the town's ideologue and the character whose own behavior most brazenly contradicts his theory, who initially objects to the idea of bringing women to Chevengur. His speech could just as easily describe himself and Klavdyusha as it does the consequences of women's inclusion: "You'll start family units here and give birth to a petit bourgeoisie" (*Razvedete vy tut semeistva i narozhaete melkuiu burzhuaziiu*) (321). Prokofy himself advocates the creation of "one large family unit" that would turn the city into "one household" (*odin dvor*), though his words can be dismissed as either hypocrisy or sentiment brought on by the arrival of his foster brother. Titych's objection bypasses ideological discipline, appealing instead to the experience of the individual: why should they want communism "with all their bodies" (*vsem tulovishchem*) if they will not live to see it realized? "Better to live by a mistake" (*luhchche zhit' na oshibke*) if that will bring more happiness than truth. Prokofy himself soon takes up Titych's line of reasoning, asserting that the Chevengurians are unhappy because man can live with only "a little bit of truth, and only at the very end." Truth alone is not enough: "Why is it that everything here is correct, there are no bourgeois, everywhere is solidarity and justice, but the proletariat is sad and wants to get married?" (323). Chepurny rationalizes the turn of events by deciding that, if the proletariat wants love, that means "he wants to tame all the elements in Chevengur," but one can just as easily argue that the elements have tamed the proletariat (324). The miscellaneous have rejected a highly theoretical male culture in favor of heterosexual relations, the family, and "nature" and have dragged their leaders down the same counterrevolutionary path to a policy that resembles nothing more than NEP on the domestic front.

The triumph of the "natural order" is not so straightforward, however. The ideologues still insist on minimalizing the sexual component of their new social policy. Chepurny tells Prokofy to bring women who are "barely" women, the "raw element" without any excessive sexual attraction (see chapter 1). Prokofy follows Chepurny's instructions faithfully, introducing to Chevengur not women but "comrades of a special construction" (*tovarishchi spetsial'nogo ustroistva*) (377). These emaciated females, like the miscellaneous men who preceded them to Chevengur, cannot appreciate the intricacies of Chevengurian theory and are frightened by these men who "make speeches" rather than immediately "getting down to business" (377). The beggar women brought to Chevengur are accustomed to "exchanging their body . . . for food," but their appearance seems calculated to extinguish rather than spark sexual desire. In their oversized men's coats, these women look "more like girls or old women, like mothers or younger, underfed sisters" (377–78). Though they have come prepared to earn their keep through sex, their skeletal bodies feel only pain at a man's touch.

Prompted by Dvanov, the men of Chevengur take the women as mothers and sisters rather than wives. The Chevengurians do not part with their collective views easily, and thus even the first kisses between the men and the women are performed as a group function. Though the arrival of women does not introduce adult eroticism to the presexual world of Chevengur, the female presence does spell the end of the town as "one family of orphans" (*odna sirotskaia sem'ia*) (323). By the time the city is destroyed by its "mechanical enemy," comradeship has been supplanted by these new relationships: "This existence with mothers was enough for them, and no one gave of their bodies to their surrounding comrades by means of labor to create gifts" (390). Male comradeship has been rejected in favor of something more faithfully approximating the nuclear family.

FATHERS AND COMRADES

The rejection of Chevengurian asceticism in favor of new families underscores the roots of Platonov's comradeship. Whereas Babel and Olesha implicitly contrast the family with the revolutionary male collective, Platonov renders this opposition explicit. This dichotomy is a constant throughout Platonov's work of the 1920s, but by the time of *Chevengur*, the relationship between the two institutions has changed. Platonov's characters still praise comradeship over family ties, but now the rise of the male collective is not so much the result of an ideological choice as a compensation for a fundamental lack. Unlike the heroes of Babel and Olesha, the men who form the affiliative groups of *Chevengur* are not rebellious sons, but orphans: they have no family to reject. *Chevengur*'s revolutionary "apostles" continue to mourn their lost parents, fathers as well as mothers, long after they have entered adulthood. The miscellaneous inhabitants of Chevengur are an even more pathetic lot, permanently crippled by the absence of paternal guidance, example, and even opposition. As the narrator of *Chevengur* puts it, they lack that "first comrade" to show them their path in life, remaining the aimless victims of their fatherlessness (*bezotsovshchina*) instead of engaging in oedipal struggle.[17] Rather than a difficult stage of development, fatherlessness in Platonov becomes a permanent existential state.[18]

Inspired by Fyodorov yet sharply differing with him on substantial philosophical points, Platonov embarks on nothing less than a radical redefinition of fatherhood itself. Writers as diverse as Vasily Rozanov and Adrienne Rich have pointed to the essential temporal difference inherent in the words "to mother" and "to father";[19] indeed, the latter verb's description of a one-time, completed action as opposed to the former's never-ending process make the two terms resemble nothing more than a Russian aspectual pair of imperfective and perfective verbs, whose semantic difference is a function of their complementary temporal status. Though he does not completely erase the difference between mother and father, Platonov partially negates the distinction between the two by portraying fatherhood as a process no less extended than motherhood. Rozanov, with whom much of Platonov's work can be seen as a polemic, prefigured Platonov by advocating a more active view of fatherhood, and yet Rozanov's approach can be reduced to mere regular repetitions of the act of conception until the fetus comes to term or is weaned.[20] Platonov's "fatherhood" ceases neither with conception nor with birth, instead becoming an essential component of human development.[21] A fatherless man is, like the Platonov character, "incomplete" and doomed to remain so for the rest of his life.

The father's loss is an irreparable blow to the development of the son, and yet it is felt only later in life, after coping with the deprivation of the mother. The "first grief" that the orphaned miscellaneous suffer in their lives is the "forever lost warmth of the mother." The mother serves to insulate her child from the harsh "outer world," first by carrying the child in her womb, then by holding and comforting him after birth. The abandoned miscellaneous, however, feel nothing but the "flickering warmth of [their] insides" (*krome svoikh tepliushchikhsia vnutrennostei*); the miscellaneous baby is left alone, surrounded by the outer world, with no one to console him for the loss of uterine warmth. The narrator presents this "homesickness" for the uterus as a universal phenomenon, but one with which the miscellaneous in particular are unable to cope. Those who are fortunate enough to be "settled people of stable statehood, living in the coziness of class solidarity," are able to create "something similar to the maternal womb around themselves"; the miscellaneous have no such consolation, "immediately sensing the world as cold, as the grass that bears the damp traces of the mother, as loneliness, because of the absence of the continued protection of maternal forces" (282). The miscellaneous bear no ill will to the mother who abandoned them, but the mother's absence is a permanent handicap to their ability to join society. Once again Platonov shows society to be a compensation for the lack of one's parents, but one that is available only to those who have been through what Shklovsky calls the "first factory" (*pervaia fabrika*) of life: the family. The family is the training ground for the child's inevitable entrance into society, which is itself only a substitute for parental care and guidance.

According to the logic of *Chevengur*, however, mothers fade into the background after their children are born. For neither the orphaned Bolsheviks nor the existentially fatherless miscellaneous is the loss of the mother as crucial to the development of the child as the loss of the father. Sasha Dvanov enters the novel with the death of his father rather than his mother; his mother is long gone, and, though vaguely missed, does not become an object of obsession and grief like Sasha's father. The same holds true for the miscellaneous, who, as a rule, lose their fathers long before their birth, only to be abandoned by their mothers soon after delivery. "The child," says the narrator of *Chevengur*, "demands nothing from his mother; he loves her, and even the miscellaneous orphans never felt hurt by their mothers, though they were abandoned by them immediately and irrevocably." It is the father, not the mother, who is essential as the child grows older: "As he grows, the child awaits his father, . . . even if he was abandoned immediately after leaving [his mother's] womb; the child turns his curious face to the world, he wants to exchange nature for people, and his first friend-comrade after the obsessive warmth of his mother, after the inhibition of life by her tender hands, is his father" (282–83). The roles of the father and mother continue the dichotomy Platonov developed in his earlier work: the mother is nature, and the father is culture. As the child (in almost all cases, the boy) grows older, he rejects nature in favor of culture, and yet there is no one to help him make the transition. Once again we recall Lacan's Symbolic Order: it is the father who is the key to the child's entry into culture. Yet, as the works of a number of anthropologists and feminist critics suggests, the question of "role models" is key to specifically male culture. Margaret Mead argues that the development of the male psyche is more complicated than that of women, since the girl can conceive of herself as being like the mother, whereas the boy must always define himself in opposition to the parent with whom he spends most of his time. Thus the boy must reject the mother in favor of the father and his male peer group, jealously guarding his place in culture through repeated attempts to prove himself a man.[22]

Platonov's conception of parenthood and infant psychological development, while sharing Mead's emphasis on the alienation from the mother, attributes far more importance to the role of the father. It is the father who can "lead [the boy] by the hand to other people, in order to leave his children other people as their inheritance, as a replacement of himself" (283).[23] In Said's terms, the boy's filial relationship with his father is the key to his ability to forge affiliative, or social, bonds later in life. Thus even children who come from relatively stable families, who benefit from paternal guidance during their critical early years, are eventually forced to exchange the family for society. Everyone is doomed to become an orphan eventually and therefore must be prepared to find consolation in the social sphere. Society is what the individual gains in exchange for the lost father.

The miscellaneous and the more individualized heroes of *Chevengur* (Dvanov, Kopyonkin, and the revolutionaries who "build" Chevengur before the arrival of the masses) represent two kinds of fatherlessness that yield two distinct models of male comradeship. In his study of the effects of the industrial revolution on the family and society, Alexander Mitscherlich identifies "fatherlessness of the first degree" as "the loss of the physical presence of the working father," which leaves the child functional but emotionally crippled (Mitscherlich 278). While this definition does not require the literal orphaning of the son, the resulting effect on a boy's psyche has much in common with the loss of a model and guide suffered by Platonov's orphans. These men have been introduced into the Symbolic Order before being abandoned to their fate.

The second degree of fatherlessness "dissolves the personal element in power relationships; one is as aware of authority as ever, but it cannot be visualized." The resulting "anonymous" or "mass" personality is strikingly similar to Platonov's depiction of the "miscellaneous": "The fatherless... child grows up into an adult with no visible master, exercises anonymous functions, and is guided by anonymous functions. What his senses are aware of is individuals similar to himself in large numbers" (Mitscherlich 279). Mitscherlich's characterization of this fatherless "mass" resonates with the initial presentation of the miscellaneous in *Chevengur;* when Chepurny first sees them on the mound outside of the town, the miscellaneous are called by the collective singular term *narod* ("the people"). The component parts of this anonymous mass look like the "black, ancient bones of the scattered skeleton of someone's huge and perished life" (276). Without a father to give them a fixed place in the social order, the miscellaneous are, in Prokofy's words, "even worse than the proletariat." They are "no one" (*nikto*). Chepurny cannot believe Prokofy's "formulation," insisting that the miscellaneous must have had a "class father" (*klassovyi otets*) and that Prokofy found them "in a social place" (*v sotsial'nom meste*) rather than in "the weeds." Prokofy responds with the most devastating word in Platonov's vocabulary, one that explains the miscellaneous's anonymous, asocial state: "They are the fatherless" (*Oni bezotsovshchina*) (279).[24]

Though both the boys who lose their parents later in childhood and the eternally fatherless miscellaneous can be said to have been deserted by their fathers, the timing of this abandonment is crucial to both the child's subsequent development and his feelings for his father. It can be argued that Sasha Dvanov was consciously abandoned by his father, who chose death over his responsibility to his son in order to satisfy his curiosity. One could imagine that such a deliberate desertion would inspire hatred on Sasha's part, yet Dvanov spends his entire childhood mourning his father, pitying him rather than despising him. Sasha has suffered a loss, but his absent father is a distinct person with a face and even a smell. Sasha remembers loving his father and continues to love him long after the latter's death. The miscellaneous cannot attach a face or a name to their missing fathers, who most likely have no idea that their sons were ever born, much less conceived. Sasha had enough contact with his father to be able to forge emotional ties with other human beings, weak as those ties may be. His experience with his father, though abruptly cut short, is sufficient to allow him, if not to enter society, then to find other, temporary fathers who can continue to help him develop. The miscellaneous are permanently crippled by their unalterable fatherlessness, forced to. "build their own lives" without any paternal help. Lacking any reason to feel positively about his anonymous father, the miscellaneous boy grows to hate him: "if his mother gave him birth, his father failed to meet him on the road, already born and alive; therefore the father turned into the enemy and despiser of the mother—always absent, always dooming his powerless son to the risk of life without help—and therefore without success" (283). The boy who remembers his father can grieve for the man who was of at least limited help, but the man who never met his male parent can only despise him for leaving him without the benefit of paternal counsel and example. One recalls the words of Telemachus in *The Odyssey*: "It is a wise child who knows his father."[25]

The predicament of Platonov's miscellaneous and, to a lesser extent, of his Chevengurian apostles is that they have been deprived of paternal guidance before they are ready to enter society. Chevengur's ideologues replace their fractured families with an equally crippled utopian social order, but the miscellaneous are incapable of creating any social structures without first being pushed in the proper direction. Though the miscellaneous have little interest in ideological debates, the description of their asocial existence resonates with Marxist theory. The alienation of the miscellaneous from the everyday world of families and governments is rooted in their lack of property. Just as Platonov's prose consistently describes the soul in terms of the body, so too does the family become indistinguishable from its property, at least in the eyes of Chepurny: "Chepurny felt that, in exchange for the steppe, houses, food, and clothes that the bourgeois obtained for themselves, the proletarians on the mound had each other, because everyone needs to have something; when there is property between people, then they calmly expend their energies on caring for that property, but when there is nothing between people, they start to cease parting and to protect one another from the cold as they sleep" (277–78). Later Chepurny watches as the miscellaneous kill flies for each other, and concludes that "[p]erhaps . . . these proletarians and miscellaneous served each other as their only property and possessions in life," which is why they "carefully guarded their comrades from flies, like the bourgeoisie guarded their own houses and livestock" (280). Thus even as Chepurny prepares himself to praise the miscellaneous and welcome them to his all-male utopia, he realizes that the bonds among the miscellaneous are based on substitution: instead of both property and family, the miscellaneous have only each other.

Deprived of any experience with families, the miscellaneous cannot be said to have built pseudo-familial ties. Affiliation resembles filiation only when the former can serve as a model for the latter, and the miscellaneous have only the vaguest conception of family life. If the goal of Bolshevik revolution is to create a mass society where all are equal and the family is abolished, the miscellaneous are the sorry embodiment of this ideal. The revolutionaries of Olesha and Babel could never escape family metaphors, but Chevengur finally presents a group to which such imagery is inapplicable. Prokofy, whose actions in Chevengur always belie his communist rhetoric, claims that the city has made them all "brothers and a family, since our housekeeping has been socially united in one courtyard" (280). Chepurny, however, recognizes that the family as a category is inapplicable to the miscellaneous: "Comrades! . . . Prokofy called you brothers and a family, but this is a bald-faced lie: all brothers have a father, but many of us have been absolutely fatherless since the beginning of our lives. We are not brothers, we are comrades, since we are the merchandise and price for each other, since we don't have any other real estate or personal property" (281). In the works of Olesha and Babel, brotherhood is the most common metaphor for comradeship, and the two words are often used interchangeably. *Chevengur* places brothers and comrades on the opposite ends of the spectrum of human relationships: no matter how much brothers might reject their parents, they are related because they have a common father. Comrades come together precisely because they have nothing at all, fathers included. Chepurny's false etymology for the word *tovarishch* ("comrade") claims *tovar* ("goods" or "merchandise") as its root, demonstrating, perhaps inadvertently, that the bonds among the miscellaneous take place at an almost subhuman level. The miscellaneous value each other as objects or possessions rather than individuals.

In *Chevengur*, each type of fatherless man seeks the company of other men as a substitute for this basic loss, but both the impulses that guide them and the relationships that arise vary drastically between the two types. The orphaned man who knew his father has benefited from the paternal model and thus knows what he is missing. When he forms male relationships, they are based on preference and desire and are marked by a distinct homoeroticism that always threatens to come to the surface. The man who has never known his father, however, also knows nothing of desire. The miscellaneous of Chevengur do find solace in their ties with men, but these bonds are impersonal and indiscriminate. Trapped on a more primitive stage of development, have no capacity for preferential love, and thus one miscellaneous is as good as any other.

Platonov's fatherless men demonstrate a physical and psychological need for other males in nearly every aspect of their daily existence. To call them all homosexual, as Paramonov does, would be a gross oversimplification. Once again, the miscellaneous must be examined separately from the other Chevengurians. Not only is eroticism largely absent from their interactions, but the need for male comradeship displayed by Platonov's fatherless miscellaneous is equated with a drive even more basic than sex: the need for warmth. Lacking a father, the miscellaneous live without consciousness and without desire. Indeed, desire as a category is inapplicable to the miscellaneous in their pre-Chevengurian state; the lives of the miscellaneous are wholly dictated by needs.[26] Thus homosexuality, which implies desire, is too developed a notion for the miscellaneous, who, never having had fathers or a home, have not been shown how to live or to desire.[27] The indiscriminate need of the miscellaneous treats other human beings as objects of warmth and comfort that can be both obtained and replaced. Unlike the homoerotic desire of the Chevengurian Bolsheviks, the needs of the miscellaneous are eminently satiable. It is the very satisfaction of these needs that leads to their defection from the Chevengurian ideology.

Purely ideological interpretations of the ties among the miscellaneous prove to be inappropriate. Indeed, the miscellaneous know nothing of ideology until they encounter the "explanations" of Prokofy and Chepurny. Thus, when Chepurny greets them "with the banner of brotherhood in his hands," the newly arrived "proletariat" is left unmoved. While the miscellaneous do seem to offer potential raw material for proletarian collectivism, such a view is a projection onto the miscellaneous by Chevengur's ideologues rather than an accurate description of their existence. Not even Sedgwick's catchall term "homosocial" can fully describe their relations, since the miscellaneous bond on a level that is lower than the social or psychological. Their need for men is a matter of reflex that is as much vegetative as animal.[28] Indeed, Platonov describes their attempts to "turn themselves into people" without the help of a parent in terms of plants and seeds: most people grow like algae on a puddle, secure in the safety provided by others and the constant source of nourishment found in the water. The miscellaneous, however, are a "strange and rare" phenomenon, "when seeds of nameless weeds tossed by a storm fall on bare clay or wandering sand; these seeds yield a lonely life that is surrounded by the empty countries of the world and is able to find nourishment in minerals" (283). The miscellaneous grow wildly and unconsciously like the weeds with which Platonov surrounds them, and their tendency to huddle together as much resembles the unconscious pull that water or light exerts on a plant. Thus the neologism most appropriate for the comradeship of the miscellaneous has its roots in the vegetable kingdom: the miscellaneous exemplify not homosexuality, but homotropism. If no obstacles are put in their path, the miscellaneous will "naturally" drift together with other miscellaneous, who are by definition exclusively male.[29]

ADULT CHILDREN OF DEAD PARENTS

The miscellaneous represent only the more extreme of the two kinds of fatherlessness that are present in the novel: the orphaned and the existentially fatherless. Whereas the miscellaneous suffer a vague sense of absence and betrayal on the part of a male parent they can barely imagine, the orphaned are fixated on the father they have tragically lost. Though the miscellaneous come to see their father as an enemy who has abandoned them to seek life elsewhere, the son who remembers his father has been forsaken for death. The child's perception of a parent's death as abandonment is literalized in the case of Sasha Dvanov, whose father makes the conscious choice to die in order to satisfy his curiosity. If fathers in Platonov serve to guide their sons and help them construct their sons' psyches by example, Sasha's father points him toward an unconventional object of desire: death and the dead. Those characters who can recall their lost parents (Dvanov, Kopyonkin, Serbinov) become obsessed with attractions that can only be described as necrophilic. Though these men, like the miscellaneous, want the company of the (male) masses, they do not need it like their existentially fatherless counterparts. In their daily interactions, these men are drawn toward a more individualized comradeship that, involving an element of selection and affinity, contains no small amount of homoeroticism. More central to their psychological makeup, however, is their overwhelming fixation on dead objects of desire. In Olesha's work, the family is threatened with extinction only after the human feeling that binds its members together starts to weaken. In Platonov, the opposite is true: the proverbial post-revolutionary "death of the family" is literalized, but the bond between parent and son is only strengthened by death.

It is those characters who most keenly feel the loss of their dead fathers and mothers who in turn look to exclusive relationships with people who are still among the living. Whereas the miscellaneous replace an unknown father with their anonymous, nameless comrades, these men develop attractions for individual human beings. Like Olesha's Kavalerov, Sasha Dvanov continually seeks substitutes for his biological father. The very fact that he is able to find such substitutes indicates that he is better able to develop emotional attachments than are the miscellaneous; Sasha has had the benefit of a "first comrade" to guide him and lead him to the company of others. Nonetheless, Sasha, too, is "incomplete"; he has been abandoned to fend for himself before his father has given him enough strength to develop. According to Zakhar Pavlovich, Sasha's status as an orphan who knew his father makes him a perfect candidate to join the Bolsheviks and create a new world. Unburdened by family ties, Sasha can devote his life to helping others: "Sasha, . . . you're an orphan, you got your life for nothing. Don't spare any of it, live the main life" (*Sasha . . . ty sirota, tebe zhizn' dostalas' zadarom. Ne zhalei ee, zhivi glavnoi zhizn'iu*). The following day Zakhar Pavlovich reinforces the connection between orphanhood and the opportunity to help humanity: "Remember: your father drowned, your mother is lord knows who, millions of people live without a soul—this is a great task here . . . A Bolshevik must have an empty heart, so that everything can fit in it" (76). Zakhar Pavlovich's revolution is to be made by orphans like Sasha, who can love the nameless millions without having to spare any feeling for their parents.

Sasha understands the revolution differently, yet his interpretation is also that of an orphan. Sasha is convinced that the revolution is "the end of the world" in which his overcurious father will "find that for which he drowned of his own accord" (77). This statement is noteworthy if we recall exactly what led Sasha's father to drown himself: the desire to know death. Though "the end of the world" in Christian thought implies the impending kingdom of heaven, in the context of *Chevengur* the apocalypse is reduced to a morbid curiosity about death and the afterlife.[30] From the very beginning of the novel, Sasha conflates the revolution with death, loving both for their connection with his lost father.

Though Sasha is capable of finding temporary living substitutes for his father, it is the dead who ultimately hold a greater power over him than the living. Zakhar Pavlovich had suggested that Sasha is uniquely qualified to help the living, yet Sasha is capable of sustaining a long-term, loyal interest only in the dead. The various living people who play a role in his life—Zakhar Pavlovich, Sonya, even Kopyonkin—cannot hold his attention indefinitely; easily distracted from the people closest to him, Sasha wanders away from each of them at various points in the novel. Only his father can expect constancy from Sasha, exerting an almost gravitational pull on his son from his grave.

Sasha's case is not the most remarkable example of necrophilia in *Chevengur* (Kopyonkin's love for Rosa Luxemburg, dead, buried, and decaying thousands of miles away, is far more striking), but it is the one that helps place the entire novel in a necrophilic framework. Numerous objections to the term "necrophilia" can be anticipated when it is used in reference to *Chevengur*, although the phenomenon has been examined in other treatments of the author's work.[31] "Necrophilia" here is used in a wider sense than the clinical designation, though sexual desire for corpses can certainly be inferred from Kopyonkin's obsession with Rosa. For the purpose of the present study, Erich Fromm's approach to the phenomenon in his *Anatomy of Human Destructiveness* provides the most incisive definition of necrophilia, since Fromm examines the issue in a social and philosophical context.

Fromm explores a variety of accepted definitions of necrophilia before settling on his own. He uses as his starting point the standard notion that there are two types of necrophilia: sexual necrophilia, where the erotic impulse culminates in actual sexual contact with corpses, and asexual necrophilia, which is "the desire to handle, to be near to, and to gaze at corpses, and particularly the desire to dismember them" (325). In offering his own definition, Fromm relies on the characterological outlook he developed in his previous works—that is, Fromm is more interested in identifying the character of the necrophile rather than the methods of clinical treatment. Fromm's definition allows for necrophilia's sexual expression without focusing on sex exclusively: necrophilia in the characterological sense is described by Fromm as "the passionate attraction to all that is dead, decayed, putrid, sickly." Fromm's original contribution is found in his elaboration of this description: "[Necrophilia] is the passion to transform that which is alive into something unalive; to destroy for the sake of destruction; the exclusive interest in all that is purely mechanical. It is the passion to tear apart living structures" (Fromm 332).[32] When *Chevengur* is examined in terms of necrophilia, a number of disparate aspects of the novel turn out to be connected: the denial of sex and nature, the attraction to graves, the fascination with machines, and the very attempt to bring everyday domestic life to a halt and replace it with ideological bonds forged among men.

A reading of Fromm in the light of Platonov underscores a feature of necrophilia that Fromm himself seems to accept as a given. Whether a perversion or an expression of "character," necrophilia in Fromm's work is an exclusively male phenomenon. His clinical examples do not include a single instance of a woman who has sexual relations with a male corpse, nor do his more abstract examples treat women as the subject of necrophilia rather than its object. While one could charge Fromm with sexism by omission, his masculinization of necrophilia resonates with Platonov's own presentation of the issue. By treating the necrophile as exclusively male, Fromm does not challenge the common identification of woman with the family and with life itself. One could generalize that necrophiles are not interested in sex with the living, but Fromm's presentation of necrophilia states the question differently: "biophiles" love women, whereas "necrophiles" do not. Perhaps unintentionally, Fromm firmly grounds necrophilia in the traditionally male world: necrophiles love not only corpses, but war, destruction, commerce (349), and machines. If Fromm's definition of necrophilia is reevaluated in terms of gender and taken to its logical extremes, necrophilia becomes the apotheosis of an exclusive, self-absorbed masculinity that denies both women and the family.

Fromm's linkage of an "increasing attraction [to] mechanical, non-alive artefacts" with the "necrophilous character" does much to explain a motif in *Chevengur* whose roots are found in Platonov's early works (Fromm 342). Though inclined to criticize the present age as overly mechanistic, Fromm reserves his diagnosis of necrophilia for "those individuals whose interest in artefacts has *replaced* their interest in life," the same people who themselves live "in a pedantic and unalive way" (343; emphasis in the original). Fromm cites two examples that are relevant to *Chevengur*. The first is the Western men who "feel more tender toward, and are more interested in, their automobiles than their wives," for whom "life without a car seems . . . more intolerable than life without a woman" (342). Though Fromm could be accused of exaggerating the significance of this example (it might not signify something "perverse," as he suggests), he reinforces his argument with his second case study, taken from an ideological proclamation rather than a fact of everyday life. Analyzing the 1909 manifesto of the Italian futurist Marinetti, Fromm is on steadier ground when he asserts that Marinetti's proclamation contains unambiguous signs of what Fromm terms necrophilia, including worship of machines and hatred of women, as well as the representation of trains and airplanes as living things (344–45). This very cult of machines and scorn for women was a prominent feature of both Platonov's early work and the avant-garde art that Platonov was surely exposed to during his literary apprenticeship.

In *Chevengur* it is Zakhar Pavlovich who passes through such a stage of machine worship only to reject it for contact with other human beings. When Zakhar Pavlovich is introduced in the beginning of the novel, we are told that he had "never made anything — neither a family, nor a home." Both people and nature leave him cold; Zakhar Pavlovich is only interested in the various "useless things" (*nenuzhnye veshchi*) he made for his own pleasure during the winter evenings (24). So disconnected is Zakhar Pavlovich from the rhythms of "normal" domestic life that he makes a frying pan out of oak. Like many of the social inventions of the novel's male theorists, the frying pan "works," but only in abnormal circumstances: Zakhar Pavlovich can boil water in his pan only on a low flame. Constitutionally unsuited to inactivity, Zakhar Pavlovich soon creates a "full set of agricultural inventory, machines, instruments, enterprises, and everyday devices — all made of wood." The only thing about this accomplishment that the narrator finds "strange" is that there was "not a single thing" among Zakhar Pavlovich's creations that "repeated nature" (26); Zakhar Pavlovich shows no interest in anything living.

Zakhar Pavlovich's infatuation with the nonliving is given greater focus when he meets the train foreman and starts to work with locomotives. Before this, Zakhar Pavlovich had merely dabbled in "machinophilia" (Bethea 172); now he encounters a man whose fondness for the mechanical is nothing less than passionate. The foreman is an old man who "distrusts living people" and "painfully and jealously" loves locomotives. His views on people and machines could serve both as a parody of the early Platonov and as a necrophile's credo: "He felt that there are many people and few machines; people are alive and can take care of themselves, but the machine is a tender, defenseless, breakable creature: in order to ride her properly, you first have to dump your wife, throw all concerns out of your head, dip your bread in machine oil—then you can let a man up close to a machine, and even then after ten years of waiting!" (36). As in Olesha, the machine as presented by the foreman is a substitute for women, an improvement, in fact, on an inferior design. The machine must be perfect and virginal; as the foreman instructs one of his workers, "a machine, brother, is a young lady . . . A woman isn't good enough: the machine won't start with an extra opening" (*mashina, brat, eto—baryshnia . . . Zhenshchina uzhe ne goditsia—s lishnim otverstiem mashina ne poidet*) (35). Living people cannot hope to match the machine for grace or beauty.

The foreman finds a quick study in Zakhar Pavlovich, who learns to love trains and engines with no less passion than his mentor. Even during his lunch breaks Zakhar Pavlovich "couldn't take his eyes off the locomotive and silently experienced his love for it within himself" (52). At home he spends his spare time staring at nuts and bolts, "never feeling lonely." Indeed, "Zakhar Pavlovich wasn't lonely—machines were people for him and constantly excited in him thoughts and desires." At night he is troubled not by thoughts of his own mortality, but by the possibility that the universe might not have enough work for wheels to do (52–53).

The foreman recognizes Zakhar Pavlovich's "loving work" (*liubovnuiu rabotu*) but never compliments him on his diligence. The foreman is convinced that "machines live and move more according to their own desire than from the intelligence and skill of people; people have nothing to do with it" (53). Instead of allowing himself to feel a bond with Zakhar Pavlovich based on their mutual interests, the foreman simply yells at him less than at the other workers. When Zakhar Pavlovich asks his mentor "why people are only all right, neither bad nor good, but machines are always equally magnificent," the foreman's first reaction is one of anger and jealousy. Only later, after allowing himself the joy of staring at one of their trains, does the foreman get carried away and forget Zakhar Pavlovich's "low qualifications," answering him "like an equal friend." The foreman asserts that people are "nonsense" (*chush*), their only value being in their ability to make machines (54–55).

Now Zakhar Pavlovich and the foreman have found that they think "identically," though they still do not talk much about their views. Each sees the world in terms that contradict standard human perceptions about animacy and inanimacy: "For both of them ... nature, untouched by man, seemed unremarkable and dead.... But any wares, especially those made of metal, on the contrary were animate and, in their construction and strength, more interesting and mysterious than man" (55). So great is Zakhar Pavlovich's concern for his mechanical charges that when he cannot find a bolt of the right size, he meticulously files down another. His diligence earns him the awkward nickname "Three-Eighths-Thread-Stock" (*Tri os'mushki pod rez'bu*), which refers to the size of the bolt. The nickname is meant as mockery, but Zakhar Pavlovich "liked it better than his Christian name: it resembled the responsible part of any machine and somehow bodily joined [him] to that true country, where iron inches conquered earthen miles" (56).

Zakhar Pavlovich's unqualified enthusiasm for the machine does not last long. His reevaluation of the importance of machines is sparked by his realization that nothing will change after his death, and after watching the pathetic demise of the foreman (Bethea 173). In addition to these factors, Zakhar Pavlovich is distracted from machines by his responsibility and affection for a living person: his foster son Sasha Dvanov. Sasha, too, has necrophilic tendencies, but his love for machines is tempered by a greater interest in people.[33] Zakhar Pavlovich substitutes machines for people, while Sasha treats the machine as "a living being like everything else" (Bethea 174).

Though Zakhar Pavlovich's adoption of Sasha marks the conclusion of his machine worship, it does not signal the end of the novel's necrophilia. Indeed, necrophilia characterizes their relationship, for it is the grave that links father and son in *Chevengur*. Not only does the grave of Sasha's biological father exert an inexorable pull on him, but graves link him to his foster father as well. Sasha's first encounter with Zakhar Pavlovich is at the funeral of his father; though Zakhar Pavlovich initially passes the boy on to another family for shelter, Sasha has nonetheless found the man who will eventually raise him next to the corpse of his drowned parent. When Sasha is already a young adult and falls sick with typhus, Zakhar Pavlovich builds his foster son a coffin—"sturdy, marvelous,... as a last gift to a son from his craftsman-father [*mastera-*

ottsa]." Zakhar Pavlovich's plans for his departed son share the fetishistic character of Sasha's own obsession with his biological father's corpse: "Zakhar Pavlovich wanted to preserve Aleksandr in such a coffin—if not alive, then intact for memory and love; every ten years Zakhar Pavlovich planned to dig up his son from the grave, in order to see him and feel himself beside him" (89–90). Just as Sasha first becomes conscious of his individual identity upon entering the cemetery where his father is buried, so too is Zakhar Pavlovich's idea of exhuming Sasha associated with self-awareness: Zakhar Pavlovich wants to expose his foster son's remains in order to "feel himself beside him." *Chevengur*'s heroes feel their own existence most acutely when they are in physical proximity to the dead.

When Sasha surprises both his foster father and his neighbor, Sonya, by remaining alive, Zakhar Pavlovich swiftly adapts. He disassembles the coffin and decides to turn it into a child's rocker, in the hopes that Sasha and Sonya will someday have children. In *The Foundation Pit*, Platonov further develops the image of the child who uses a coffin for a cradle, but in *Chevengur*, the significance of this association is already clear.[34] The grave is where the living son can always find his dead father, or where the living father can always find the dead son. Death is no longer abandonment if the bereaved survivor has constant access to the remains of his departed relative. Hence *Chevengur*'s protagonists are more conscious of their relatives when they are dead or dying than when they are living. Dvanov himself feels more kinship to a dead man than to anyone else. Indeed, much of *Chevengur*'s "necrophilia" is actually "necrofilia"—the strong sense of family ties with the dead.

The dead in *Chevengur* thus exert a doubly compelling hold on their living admirers: they are both lost relatives and objects of desire. The result is a decidedly incestuous fascination with corpses and graves.[35] At one point Zakhar Pavlovich "suddenly felt like digging up [his mother's] grave and looking at his mother—at her bones, her hair, and at the last, fading remains of his childhood motherland. Even now he wouldn't mind having a living mother" (57).[36] The physiological details of Zakhar Pavlovich's fantasy show that his impulse to exhume his mother is more than just a son's sense of maternal loss. Zakhar Pavlovich has no illusions that he will find his mother as he left her; rather, he makes a fetish out of his mother's corpse, moved by the desire simply to see his mother's body in the last stages of decay.

Zakhar Pavlovich's fantasy also highlights the repeated connection made in the novel between mothers, wombs, and graves. Here Naiman's argument that the heroes of *Chevengur* are moved by an impulse to return to the womb is particularly apt; Zakhar Pavlovich wants to exhume his mother in order to regain access to the remains of the womb that carried him. In an earlier dream, Zakhar Pavlovich watches his father die as his mother squeezes milk from her breast in order to revive him (34).[37] The foreman's death early in the novel is described in terms of birth: he imagines he is once again trying to squeeze his way out through his mother's cervix but is now too big to push his way through (68).

The fascination with mothers in their graves and the conflation of the womb with the tomb corresponds with the incestuous aspect of necrophilia discussed by Fromm. Fromm asserts that for the necrophile, the mother becomes not only the symbol of the earth, home, and life, but also the representation of "death and chaos" to which all life must eventually return. The desire of the necrophile to return to his dead mother's grave resembles "magnetic attraction, or the attraction of gravity," rather than warmth or love (363). Though this side of the necrophilous character is found in Zakhar Pavlovich, it is exemplified most strikingly by Stepan Kopyonkin. Kopyonkin is obsessed with his image of the physical remains of Rosa Luxemburg, interred far away in her native Germany. Rosa is referred to as Kopyonkin's "bride" (*nevesta*), in whose name he is prepared to kill any and all enemies (111). Like Fromm's description of the incestuous necrophile's attitude toward his mother, Kopyonkin sees Rosa as a symbol: "[Kopyonkin] considered the revolution to be the last remains of Rosa Luxemburg's body" (126). Just as Zakhar Pavlovich wants to exhume his mother, so too does Kopyonkin wish to "dig up Rosa from her grave and take her away with him to the revolution" (146).

The connection between Rosa and Kopyonkin's dead mother is made explicit by a series of dreams Kopyonkin has before coming to Chevengur. Kopyonkin had first dreamed of his dead mother the night before getting married; he saw her turning her back to him and leaving, though "not reproaching her son for anything" (170). But when his mother appears to him for the second time, she is jealous and outraged. Apparently, no living woman can be as much a threat to the mother's memory as can another dead woman: "Once again you've found yourself another slut, Styopushka," his mother tells him. "Again you've left your mother alone." Kopyonkin is well aware that Rosa is "the continuation of his childhood and mother": he "loved his mother and Rosa identically, because his mother and Rosa were one and the same being for him, like the past and the future living in his life" (171).

While the connection between death and the womb is self-evident in *Chevengur* (the word, according to Naiman ["Thematic Mythology" 210], means "womb-grave"), the novel's fascination with death cannot be reduced to this classic Freudian principle. As shown above, the impulse to return to graves is associated with the father as often as it is with the mother. In *Chevengur*, necrophilia is integral to both the oedipal pull toward the mother and the homotropic impulse to return to the father. If, in *Chevengur*, the family is truly dead (a proposition the city's ideologues do their best to support), necrophilia is the form taken by the desire for both dead parents. The novel's protagonists, however, lost their parents early in life, and this obsession with their dead bodies thus has deep roots. The miscellaneous, who do not remember their parents, are incapable of forging meaningful ties with the living but are also unburdened by such a strong bond with the dead. The characters who do remember losing their parents are able to form relationships with others as they grow older, but these ties are colored by their necrophilic orientation. For them, bonds with their dead relatives take precedence over any feelings for the living.

It is Sasha Dvanov, the novel's central character, who demonstrates that comradely ties are only a short-term substitute for the primary relationship with the dead father. Sasha's behavior at his father's funeral establishes a pattern for his later departures from and returns to his father's grave. First Sasha lies down next to his father's corpse, smelling the "living sweat" on his father's shirt; next he touches his father's hand, sensing the "fishy dampness" (*rybnoi syrost'iu*) of his drowned flesh (29). At this point he turns his head to the people surrounding him, and, afraid, hides his face in his father's shirt. One again recalls that it is the father who introduces the son "to people" in exchange for his own company; the young Sasha is not prepared to trade his father for the society of others and turns to his parent's corpse for solace.

As Sasha grows older, he repeatedly attempts to forge bonds with others, only to seek the consolation of his father's grave. Forced to leave his adopted home to beg on the streets, Sasha stops at the cemetery to leave his staff on the earth that covers his father's coffin. He compares his own loneliness with that of his father, who must surely be suffering alone in his grave, and decides that he will soon join him. Sasha's choice of words is revealing: *Ia teper' skoro umru k tebe*. Literally, Sasha informs his father that he will soon die *to* him, that is, death will be Sasha's means of transportation to be reunited with his father. If, as Geller asserts, the primary chronotope of *Chevengur* is the road, then dying, when turned into a verb of motion, becomes the shortcut to the characters' final destination.

Deprived of house and father, Sasha finds comfort in replacing them with a grave and a corpse: he will dig himself a home next to his father's grave and lie alongside him. That his father is dead is no obstacle: "his father may be dead and may not say anything, but he will always lie nearby, his shirt is covered with warm sweat . . . his father may be dead, but he is whole, identical, the same as ever" (43). Soon Sasha returns home, but eventually he is evicted again, this time forever. Almost automatically, Sasha goes back to his father's grave, where he falls sound asleep.

During those times when Dvanov has a satisfactory substitute for his lost father (Zakhar Pavlovich, Kopyonkin, Chevengur itself), his longing for his true father is restricted to dreams. But when the city of communism is destroyed, Dvanov discovers that the only destination that remains for him is to join his father in death. It is Kopyonkin, his fellow necrophile, who points the way. Kopyonkin had long felt that Chevengur was a mere distraction from the true communism embodied by the corpse of Rosa Luxemburg, and he reaffirms his conviction moments before his death: "I got sidetracked in Chevengur and now I'm dying, and Rosa will suffer in the earth alone." Kopyonkin's last words once again show death to be a destination: "But they're expecting us, Comrade Dvanov!" (396). With Kopyonkin dead, his horse, Proletarian Strength, for whom all paths led to Rosa's grave, now belongs to Dvanov. On its own accord, the horse brings Dvanov back to the town surrounding Lake Mutevo. Having changed masters, Proletarian Strength changes his ultimate destination, yet the nature of his journey remains the same; Proletarian Strength has replaced the grave of Rosa Luxemburg with that of Dvanov's father.

Back at Lake Mutevo, Dvanov once again recalls his dead father and, all substitutes exhausted, chooses to rejoin him once and for all. As before, Dvanov's recollection of his father's corpse is sensual: "his father still remained—his bones, the once living matter of his body, the decay of his sweat-dampened shirt—all the homeland of life and friendliness." Dvanov knows that there is a place for him with his father, "where they expect the return by means of eternal friendship of that blood, which had once been separated from the body of the father for the son" (397). Ashamed to be still among the living, Dvanov chooses the same path to death selected by his father, for "Aleksandr was one with the not-yet-destroyed, glimmering trace of his father's existence" (398). After Dvanov disappears into the waters, Proletarian Strength once again journeys to the land of the dead, this time returning to Chevengur, the site of unrealized dreams and mass slaughter.

It would be too much to expect from the author of "The Battle of the Brains" and "The Culture of the Proletariat" to end his novel on a note of unequivocal acceptance of family ties and rejection of comradeship, although Platonov's later work would move further in that direction. Nonetheless, all the inhabitants of Chevengur embrace some form of the family before they die: Sasha returns to his dead father, while the miscellaneous set up house with their newfound mothers and sisters. In both cases Platonov describes "families" that look backward rather than forward; like Fyodorov, Platonov emphasizes the relations between present and past generations rather than the creation of children and the future.[38] In the sense that both Fyodorov and Platonov stress responsibility to the dead rather than reproduction, both fit Fromm's definition of necrophilia.[39] In *Chevengur*, Platonov steps back from his own Fyodorovian heresy; Fyodorov would have seen comradeship as only a pale excuse for brotherhood. Both comradeship and brotherhood fight an upward battle, going deliberately against the grain of nature. Chaste and theory-driven, the heroes of *Chevengur* rush headlong toward their sterile goal, only to find that they have been moving away from life all along.

Dvanov's decision to join his father in death appears inevitable, given his earlier returns to his father's grave; if the novel ended with Dvanov's suicide, this would be an affirmation of family ties above all else, affiliative relations included. Yet the end of this apparently cyclical novel closes one circle even as it opens up another: the story closes not with Sasha's corpse, but with the arrival of the one man who most consistently played the role of Sasha's living father, Zakhar Pavlovich. Zakhar Pavlovich is now an old man, and unlike Sasha's nameless biological father, he is impatient: he has come to bring Sasha home from Chevengur. There Zakhar Pavlovich finds Prokofy, whom he has not seen in decades, "crying among all the property that had now settled upon him." Zakhar Pavlovich takes pity on Prokofy and once again offers him a ruble to find Sasha. " 'I'll bring him back for free,' promised Prokofy, and he went to look for Dvanov" (398). Without knowing it, Zakhar Pavlovich has set Prokofy an impossible task, inaugurating a journey that can have no end. Prokofy has no reason to drag Lake Mutevo for Sasha's corpse; only if he rode back on Proletarian Strength could he hope that the well-trained horse would automatically take him to Sasha's resting place, but Prokofy has set off on foot. Sasha's embrace of his biological family led him to underestimate the value of the adoptive brother and father he has left behind.[40] In *Chevengur*, the heroes' fanatical dedication to either family or affiliative ties does not free them from the "bad infinity" of mortal life, but only delivers them into its grip: Dvanov dies without seeing the accomplishment of communism and condemns his survivors to waste their lives on an impossible quest of their own.

Conclusion

FATHERS AND FURIES

> "Comrades! Last night I couldn't sleep, and I thought about women." — Boris Pilnyak, *The Volga Flows into the Caspian Sea* (1929–30)

Completed in 1929, *Chevengur* ends with a massacre that leaves few survivors. While it would be too facile to connect the ending of Platonov's novel with the mass murders that would become all too common under Stalin, the dating of the novel is, at the very least, fortuitous.[1] The dreams of male utopian collectivism survived both War Communism and NEP, but they could not adapt to the industrial literature of Stalin. Though one must be careful of accepting the standard historiographic assessment of the First Five-Year Plan as a "great break" with the culture and policies of the previous decade, there can be little doubt that the symbols and metaphors prominent in the 1920s would be deployed in entirely new fashions in the 1930s, if not transformed to the point of being unrecognizable. Appeals to brotherhood and comradeship would continue long past the 1920s, but in a context of implacable hostility toward the values of the utopian fratriarchal collective. With the onset of the First Five-Year Plan and the new emphasis on female labor both in industry and on collective farms, women would finally be identified with the forces of progress rather than symbolizing all the evils of the bourgeoisie. Meanwhile, Stalin's authority was consolidated on the symbolic as well as the political level, resulting in an image of the Leader as the ultimate father figure. Here, too, *Chevengur* proves prophetic. The commune is disrupted by the intrusion of women, while its survivors return to the comfort of patriarchal authority: Dvanov returns to his dead biological father in Lake Mutevo and Proshka willingly accepts Zakhar Pavlovich's repetition of his initial offer to pay him to find Dvanov. Of course, the word "authority" might seem to be an exaggeration in either case, but the lure of the father-son bond remains strong. In the Soviet imaginary, fratriarchal communism fell in a two-front war, unable to resist the onslaught of the industrialized woman and the autocratic father. When each of these forces laid claim to the mantle of "brotherhood" and comradeship, an exclusively masculine utopia became unthinkable.

THE RETURN OF THE SISTERS: PILNYAK AND THE *BABII BUNT*

Female solidarity appeared as a counterweight to male separatism almost immediately after *Chevengur* was finished. Indeed, it is only fitting that the male collective would be laid to rest by the work that at least one critic considers the first of the five-year plan novels, Pilnyak's *The Volga Flows into the Caspian Sea* (*Volga vpadaet v Kaspiiskoe more*) (Browning 171).[2] The history of this novel, which is an expansion of his earlier novella "Mahogany" ("Krasnoe derevo"), is one of the more visible examples of an author's capitulation to the demands of the new era.[3] Yet one of the most striking differences between the novel and the novella is its center of gravity: in "Mahogany," the only collective is that of the all-male *okhlomony* (a slang term applied to men of very low social status), "for whom time stopped with the era of War Communism" (Pil'niak, *Povesti* 657; Pil'niak, *Romany* 487–88). The *okhlomony* "have created the strictest brotherhood, the strictest communism, having nothing of their own, neither money, nor things, nor wives — and in any case, their wives left them long ago."[4] "Mahogany" was written in 1929, not long after Pilnyak spent approximately eight months working with Platonov on a variety of literary projects, including "Che-Che-O" (1928), a satirical portrait of provincial communist bureaucracy that provoked the wrath of hardline critics. Platonov had already begun work on *Chevengur* in 1926 and had sent the completed manuscript to Gorky by the summer of 1929; it is more than likely that Pilnyak was familiar with the novel (Tolstaia-Segal, "'Stikhiinye sily" 99). Certainly, any reader familiar with *Chevengur* (and at the time of "Mahogany's" publication, these were certainly few in number) could see the *okhlomony* as a parody of Platonov's Chevengurians. Like Platonov's anarchic communists, the *okhlomony* long for the heyday of War Communism and reject contact with women (Tolstaia-Segal, "'Stikhiinye sily" 98–99).

If there is an implied critique of Platonov in Pilnyak's depiction of the *okhlomony* in "Mahogany," it is only heightened when Pilnyak expands the story into a novel. Though they are present in the novel as well, the *okhlomony* in *The Volga Flows into the Caspian Sea* play a much smaller role. As a force for collectivism, they have been upstaged by the women who work at the construction site; the *okhlomony* as a group appear in the novel only on one occasion, but the procession of angry women is described repeatedly throughout the novel. It is a hallmark of Pilnyak's fiction that the action progresses through repeated motifs rather than chronologically; the unifying motif of *Volga* is the striking women workers. Nearly every character in the novel observes the event, which must be described from the point of view of each of its witnesses.

On the factory whistle's signal, the seventy-one women ("seventy-one female griefs" [*sem'desiat' odno bab'e gore*], 491, 564) put down their tools to accompany the body of Maria, whose suicide they blame on her insensitive and cruel second husband Edgar Laslo. Though this death might appear to be an isolated incident, the women, whose miserable existence is described with great sympathy by the narrator, insist on seeing Maria's plight as something of larger social significance: "Maria's death became a symbol of woman's fate" (564). The women's action is strangely resonant with the events of a novel of an utterly different sort: Kuprin's *The Pit* (see chapter 1). In that novel, all the residents of the local brothels take to the street and accompany the body of their twice-fallen comrade Zhenka. Zhenka was also a suicide, and also a victim of men, though she was never content to be passive: after discovering that she had contracted syphilis from one of her clients, she decided to take revenge on all men by infecting them; her resolve fades, however, when she is faced with the prospect of infecting an "innocent" young boy. The lot of "working women" has not changed so drastically in the twenty-five years that separate *The Pit* and *Volga*.[5]

There is one decided difference: the suicide in *Volga* now takes on political overtones. Just as Ozhogov had identified the decadent, old-world lifestyle of his brother and the Bezdetovs as "counterrevolutionary" in "Mahogany," the strike's instigator, Darya, sees Maria's death as a failure of the revolution itself: "Comrades! Brothers! Women [*baby*]! . . . What are we afraid of? Or was the revolution all for nothing?" (*Tovarishchi! brattsy! baby! Chto zhe, nam boiatsia, chto li, i revoliutsiia zria byla?*) (555–56). Though the protest itself at first appears to be a spontaneous, emotional response, a correspondent for the newspaper *Komsomolskaia pravda* later declares: "The women's mass protest must be considered the awakening of class consciousness" (567). And indeed, the women insist on seeing the Bolshevik Revolution and the sexual revolution as inextricably linked. Like a good communist, Darya formulates her plan in an announcement for the bulletin board newspaper (*stengazeta*): "Comrade women! ... Revolutionary law has equalized all laborers, both men and women, but in practice this is not the case, and women must finally stand up for themselves. ... How many female tears have been shed because of men (after chewing on her pencil for a bit, Darya crossed this last phrase out)" (556). Thus Darya turns a single incident into an offense committed by men as men against women as women. The narrative itself justifies her conclusion, however, for the news of Maria's suicide is preceded by a report of gang rape. Like Darya's appeal, the news is first reported on the bulletin board: "In the second article the rape of the woman worker by three unskilled workers was analyzed and condemned" (412). This particular rape is clearly modeled on the notorious Chubarov case (see chapter 1), and the narrator denounces it in no uncertain terms: "The rape of the woman worker, this Chubarovism, was loathsome" (413). Immediately after Pimen Sergeevich reads this report, Darya enters the room and gives the news about Maria. Thus the two events are connected not only in Darya's consciousness (she refers to this rape in her own announcement on the bulletin board), but in the mind of the reader as well. Maria is technically only Laslo's victim (though the strict code of conduct of her first husband has also played a role), and yet Maria is meant to stand for all female victims, just as Laslo represents the victimizers. Again, the "objective" voice of the press puts the events in their proper perspective: after the confrontation between Laslo and the seventy-one avenging furies at Maria's funeral, the *Komsomolskaia pravda* correspondent writes: "The cause of this protest was not only the death of Laslo's wife, but a whole series of other episodes, including: the rape by the three men from Penza (who were convicted today), the harassment of female workers by clerks and soldiers, their casual affairs with their female co-workers, the many cases of a supervisor's favoritism toward a lover from among the workers and the administration" (567).

Though Pilnyak at other times revels in ambiguity, there can be no doubt where the reader's sympathies are supposed to lie, for the newspaper echoes the sentiments of all the novel's true communist heroes.

The introduction of the authoritative voice of journalism serves another function as well: it grounds Pilnyak's fictional tale in the news of the day. The newspaper's explicit context is actually somewhat out of date: by 1929–30, Chubarov-style gang rape, horrible though it may be, was old news. Pilnyak's contemporary readers would surely have made an entirely different connection to his depiction of collective female protest: the *bab'i bunty*, or women's riots.[6] These riots, which began during the spring of 1929, the period during which Pilnyak wrote the novel, represented the spontaneous but concerted opposition of peasant women to the policies of grain requisitioning and forced collectivization.[7] As Lynne Viola notes, these riots, though characterized as hysterical and irrational, "revealed a relatively high degree of organization and tactics." Moreover, they were usually reactions to specific policies and were a relatively safe outlet for opposition to collectivization, since the women were much less likely to face serious reprisals for their actions (Viola 38–39). The *babii bunt* is important for both Pilnyak's novel in particular and the problem of male collectivism in general: the decade began with the rhetoric of male comradeship (War Communism) and ended with the image of anarchic female collective protest. If the male comrades held themselves up as models of revolutionary consciousness, the *bab'i bunty* were characterized as the spontaneous outpouring of a counterrevolutionary *un*conscious: the party and the press repeatedly characterized the riots' participants as backward and politically ignorant (Viola 27). Moreover, the initial *bab'i bunty* took place at precisely the same time that local party organizations discussed the possible liquidation of the Zhenotdel, the women's section of the Communist Party (Goldman, "Industrial Politics" 60). Symbolically, the party would liquidate the Zhenotdel in the first days of 1930, "jettison[ing] its commitment to a revolutionary vision of women's liberation" at the very dawn of a decidedly different era (Goldman, "Industrial Politics" 77). The irony surrounding this chain of events is almost palpable: the party abandoned its attempts to organize women from above at precisely the moment when non-party women had spontaneously begun to organize themselves.

Pilnyak appropriates the symbolism of the *babii bunt* for his own purposes; the women's protest in *Volga* is not directed at collectivization (an issue that is simply not addressed in the novel). Indeed, though the historical *bab'i bunty* were by definition an agrarian phenomenon, Pilnyak (perhaps deliberately) transports the women's riot to a more industrial (i.e., masculine) setting. Pilnyak also manages to strike a balance between the emotional impact of the women's actions, the almost metaphysical horror their procession evokes in its male witnesses, and the relative sobriety and orderliness that actually characterized the *bab'i bunty* in spite of their negative press. The women who call for the work stoppage are, without a doubt, motivated at least in part by emotions, yet their language is that of disappointed communists. And while the linkage between their procession and the ancient female fertility symbols scattered throughout the construction site gives their protest an almost mythic dimension, the women themselves are relatively calm and rational as they follow the body to the graveside. Though the novel itself is chock-full of political overtones, the event that prompts the women's actions is a personal one, a case of individual abuse that comes to stand for all the injustices women have suffered. But why does this event become so crucial to this novel, whose main plot line has very little to do with the death of Maria? Here Pilnyak's tricks with time are particularly important. The women's protest accrues significance with each new description of it, as though it (and, by extension, the crime to which it is a response) happened not once but several times. Furthermore, Pilnyak uses the funeral procession to conflate two distinct historical events: the Chubarov gang rape of 1926 and the *bab'i bunty* of 1929. Thus the women's march is both linked to a specific event and transcends time altogether. Here I would suggest that the target of the women's protest is more than just the particular incident of abuse in the novel, and also more than the author's belated attempt to jump on the anti-Chubarov bandwagon. Rather, this literary portrayal of female indignation at the twilight of the revolutionary decade is aimed at the abuse of women *on the level of literature and discourse* rather than in reality: the novel's target is the motif of female victimization and, by extension, the male solidarity that encourages it.[8] Again, Pilnyak's idiosyncratic depiction of time supports such a conclusion: this entirely new type of female collective action coexists with the anachronistic *okhlomony*, an exclusively male group who cannot bear to admit that the heady days of War Communism are never to return. In *The Volga Flows into the Caspian Sea,* the decade comes full circle, as the men representing the beginning of the 1920s meet the women who enthusiastically greet the period's end. But the women are doing more than bidding farewell to a miserable decade; the reader might wonder why the narrator insists on emphasizing the fact that the women number seventy-one in all, but when that figure is added to the year in which the novel takes place (1929), we are faced with the implicit suggestion that these women represent the remainder of a century that has only just begun.

The women's encounter with Laslo, the man they blame for their comrade's death, points to an even broader temporal context: the ancient world of myth. Even before the confrontation at the grave site, one of the observers of the procession states that the women are "ancient" (*Oni drevni, eti babishchi*) (477). Moreover, they are burying not simply an individual woman, but "antiquity" itself (*Poniatno, chto eti zhenshchiny khoroniat drevnost'*) (477). When Laslo himself meets the seventy-one women, their silence strikes him as "leaden," while the women themselves give off the "leaden smell of the earth." Their faces are "bronze," and the clothing worn by these "bronze-leaden women is like the pictures of medieval Russian processions of the cross" (564–65). Once again, they are explicitly identified with the ancient world: "Laslo understood both the cemetery and the minutes above the grave as antiquity." At this point, the women represent the elemental forces of unrestrained vengeance, crying for blood: "Let's shove him into the pit, to hell with him!" (565).

The scene at the graveside, with its bloodthirsty, vengeful women and the narrative's repeated appeals to antiquity, points to another ancient context: the *Oresteia* and the story of the Furies. We recall that in the *Oresteia,* Orestes is obliged to kill his mother, Clytemnestra, as revenge for her murder of his father, Agamemnon. But before she dies, Clytemnestra curses her son, calling down the wrath of the Furies, the female spirits responsible for avenging crimes against blood relatives. Orestes is spared only when Athena establishes a court to try him for his crime. When Orestes is found not guilty, Athena calls upon the Furies to temper their vengeance with mercy, whereupon the spirits are transformed into the Eumenides, or the "kindly ones."

The parallels to the *Oresteia* are clear. Laslo is held responsible for the death of a member of his own family, and though the seventy-one women are never explicitly identified as the Furies, the repeated invocations of myth and antiquity, along with their initial demand for a rather basic form of justice, allow us to make the connection. Yet with the benefit of historical hindsight, the connection between the *Oresteia* and the First Five-Year Plan novel might seem almost grotesque. The *Oresteia* is usually treated as an allegory for the triumph of justice over blood vengeance, as well as a mythological representation of the creation of the first recognizable court of law. *The Volga Flows into the Caspian Sea*, like the *Oresteia*, is situated on the cusp of two different eras, but six decades after the Great Terror it is difficult to say that the end of NEP and the beginning of high Stalinism marked the restoration of the rule of law. Yet within the context of the novel, this is precisely what takes place. The women briefly entertain the idea of collectively murdering Laslo, but they are interrupted by an old woman who calls on her comrades to "boycott" Laslo rather than killing him: "We don't need to throw him into the pit! . . . We will try him in an organized fashion, as we discussed last night, comrade women, we will show him our consciousness" (566). Whereupon the seventy-one women file into the factory office and file a resolution to boycott Laslo (569). Revolutionary consciousness and party discipline prevail over elemental rage. The Furies have been tamed.

As the 1920s come to a close, Pilnyak's novel exorcises a number of the demons that had been haunting Russian literature since the revolution. The antifeminine rhetoric of War Communism has been rejected once and for all, paving the way for the enforced optimism of the coming decade. As Eric Naiman argues, the First Five-Year Plan was quite similar to War Communism in its treatment of sex (sublimation over expression), but different in its approach to gender. Femininity is no longer treated with hostility, and women take prominence of place in Soviet iconography (Naiman, *Sex in Public* 290). They are no longer used as symbols of backwardness: the policies of industrialization and collectivization meant that women were expected to be conscious builders of socialism. The discourse of the 1930s had no patience for sexual separatism, whether of the male or the female variety (again, we recall the liquidation of the Zhenotdel just five days into the new decade). Thus the women in *Volga* organize only to vent specific grievances; ultimately, they defer to the existing party structures, lodge their complaints, and, as a group, are never heard from again in the remainder of the novel.

And what becomes of the men? In *The Volga Flows into the Caspian Sea*, the female collective has so thoroughly displaced its male counterpart that the most heartfelt speech in praise of the women workers is delivered by Ivan Ozhogov within the *okhlomony* stronghold itself. In "Mahogany," Ozhogov tells his comrades that they (the *okhlomony*) are the only true communists left. In *Volga*, this same speech is reproduced almost unchanged; but after midnight, Ozhogov delivers a second speech, one that begins with a startling admission: "Comrades! Last night I couldn't sleep, and I thought about women." This is not, however, an admission of anything as counterrevolutionary as sexual desire; rather, Ozhogov is calling his comrades' attention to the misery of the women workers in their barracks. The entire constellation of female suffering is invoked: the terrible working conditions, the death of Maria, and the gang rape, all of which Ozhogov condemns. In addition, he is outraged that because of the small ratio of women to men at the construction site, these women end up providing sexual services for the entire male labor force: "Our workers . . . live in *artels* [cooperative associations], and you can be sure that for them, the cook isn't just a cook, but the whole *artel*'s wife" (491). By this point, the narrator has already made clear that the *okhlomony* are the representatives of a recent past (War Communism) that seems no less remote than the patriarchal antiquity represented by Ozhogov's brother Yakov Karpovich. The repudiation of group male violence has thus reached its apotheosis: even the leader of the War Communist collective condemns the ill treatment of women by men.

In the literature prior to this novel, the murder of a woman was a symbolic or ritual act: Katka's death allowed the Twelve to continue their march; the woman shot by Balmashev is the very embodiment of counterrevolution; the rape of a "pure lady" is the price demanded of Lyutov for acceptance by the Cossacks. A similar symbolic network is at work in *Volga*, but with a new twist: the woman will not stay buried. Maria's funeral, which takes place at least five times in the course of the novel, is counterbalanced by the repeated discoveries of mysterious Scythian figurines (*kamennye baby*), whose large breasts, bellies, and legs suggest matriarchal fertility goddesses. While one woman is being placed in the ground, countless others are returning from the grave. The seventy-one women themselves are conflated with these figurines on more than one occasion: "these ancient women, these female proletarians. I looked: they are made of stone, these women [*babishchi*].... It was a procession of Scythians" (476).[9] When Darya nearly convinces her comrades to throw Laslo into the grave along with his victim, the sex war is once again portrayed as a battle between a group and an individual, but with the tables turned: "The women's faces showed the horror of collective hatred, collective resentment for themselves, for their fate" (567). The women do not make good on their threat to inter Laslo with Maria, but they have managed to bury something else: a vision of female sacrifice and exclusive male collectivism that would find little resonance in the decade to come.

STALIN AND SONS

Pilnyak's novel does away with fratriarchal communism rather efficiently, yet, on the surface, there appears to be no reason why the male comradeship of the 1920s could not continue into the next decade, with the appropriate adjustments made for the new times. After all, the Soviet hostility to nature would only intensify during the industrialization and collectivization drives of the 1930s, while heavy industry and factory labor would continue to be characterized by specifically masculine images. Here Vera Mukhina's famous statue of the worker and collective-farm woman, designed for the 1937 Paris Exhibition and displayed in Moscow to this day at the former VDNKh (Exhibit of the Accomplishments of the People's Economy), is particularly instructive. This gargantuan sculpture, which dwarfs everything in its surroundings, consists of two rugged and muscular human figures, one male, the other female. Like so many of the showpieces of Soviet propaganda art, it is a study in contradictions. On the one hand, it would appear to be a representation of equality, with the man and woman each stepping toward the future, each extending one arm to display a symbol of Soviet power. On the other hand, the traditional gendered hierarchy remains. Elizabeth Waters argues that "the couple in one important sense undermines rather than affirms sexual equality because a secondary role is assigned to the woman, not by the arrangement of the figures, but by the allocation of symbols—the sickle to the woman, the hammer to the man" (240). Agriculture, always the lesser partner in Soviet economic planning, is relegated to a female standard-bearer, while industrialization, the sine qua non of Stalinism, is championed by the man. Moreover, though both the worker and the collective-farm woman are stepping forward, the man is stepping a bit farther ahead.

Of course, the very deployment of a female image for these particular propaganda purposes represents a departure from the 1920s. Victoria Bonnell notes that before 1930, the peasantry was symbolized by a male figure—the *muzhik,* or peasant man.[10] This reinscription of the feminine is antithetical to fratriarchal communism in its pure form, even as it reinforces a dominant role for men and masculinity. Such attempts at inclusion might be less charitably considered tokenism, given the continued masculinity of Soviet iconography and the leading role played by the male hero in both art and fiction. Yet when combined with another central feature of the 1930s, Stalinist paternalism, the inclusion of women in a strong yet subordinate role suggests a process that reinforces male dominance at the same time that it destroys the fratriarchal collective: a restoration of classical patriarchy in Soviet discourse.

By "patriarchy" I do not mean the generalized institution of male dominance cited and critiqued by feminists, but rather the more traditional notion of "rule of the father." By the same token, this "Stalinist patriarchy" does not constitute a return to the Slavic traditions of the medieval *Domostroi,* the book that laid out the rules and relationships in a home where the father's authority was supreme. Instead, I have in mind the importance of the father as a symbol in the 1930s, as well as the emphasis placed on the father-son relationship in Soviet fiction, art, and film. Central to this father-son dynamic was, of course, the figure of Joseph Stalin himself. Stalin was often portrayed as a "wise father" in Soviet propaganda; one of his many epithets was "father of peoples" (*otets narodov*), while one of the most notorious slogans of the era was supposed to be issued, as it were, from the mouths of babes: "Thank you,

Comrade Stalin, for our happy childhood." In her study of the Soviet political poster, Bonnell finds that the identification of Stalin as father served a number of purposes, from implying a family tie between him and his people to aiding in the Soviet assimilation of certain aspects of the Russian Orthodox tradition (as in the Catholic Church, Russian Orthodox priests are also addressed as "father") (164–65).

While the use of paternal imagery to describe Stalin has been widely recognized for years, it was Katerina Clark's groundbreaking study of socialist realism, *The Soviet Novel: History as Ritual,* that provided the most detailed analysis of the dynamics and function of Stalinist patriarchy. When turning her attention from proto-socialist realist classics of the 1920s to the novels and stories of the 1930s, Clark notes that by this time, "the Soviets focused on the primordial attachments of kinship and projected them as the dominant symbol for social allegiance. Soviet society's leaders became 'fathers' (with Stalin as the patriarch); the national heroes, model 'sons'; the state, a 'family' or 'tribe.'" The resulting "great family" not only lent a "spurious organicity" to the hierarchical structure of the state, but also reinforced the "symbolic legitimization of the actual leadership" by applying the family metaphor to Stalin's "inheritance" of Lenin's powers (114–15). Part of the appeal of Clark's argument is that it is both sophisticated and economical, since it can be used as a framework to discuss not only Soviet fiction and myths of political legitimacy, but even the apparent return of the traditional family to its lost primacy. In 1930, the Zhenotdel was abolished; in 1934, male homosexuality became a criminal offense; in 1935, divorce became more difficult to obtain, and, finally, in 1936, nontherapeutic abortions were outlawed. The Stalin-era reversal of the previous decade's liberal family policies and renewed emphasis on the family's productive capacity would appear heretical to the utopian visionaries of the early revolutionary period, but Clark points out that the nuclear family "was to be strengthened because it was regarded as a microcosmic auxiliary to the state ... [t]he state was prior" (115). The well-known story of Pavlik Morozov, who supposedly turned in his own father for crimes against the state in 1932, drove home the message that whenever ties of blood came into conflict with political allegiance, the biological family had to give way.

According to Clark, the initial years of the First Five-Year Plan saw a renewed emphasis on "brotherhood" or "fraternalism," one that fit in well with a parallel metaphor of society functioning as a well-oiled machine. But after Stalin's 1931 speech on the value of expertise, new emphasis was placed on the need "not for mere experts but for good leaders and managers" (118). In fiction and biography, particularly in those texts concerning the Stakhanovite "shock-worker" movement and the heroes of Soviet aviation, readers encountered tale after tale of model "sons" mentored by their more politically conscious "fathers," whether these fathers were managers, teachers, or even Stalin himself.

This new Stalinist rewrite of the age-old Russian theme of fathers and sons is too large a topic to be broached in the pages of a conclusion, and it certainly deserves to be the object of further study. I have raised it in order to suggest, however provisionally, that high Stalinism's discursive emphasis on the family in general and the father-son bond in particular can be viewed as more than simply a retreat from revolutionary idealism and egalitarianism. In the 1920s, fratriarchal communism certainly had a utopian appeal, but it also meshed quite well with both the political climate and the situation "on the ground": as we saw in the discussion of *Red Cavalry*, the chaos of the Russian Civil War could easily be understood as the struggle for power among "sons" now that the father was gone, while the political intrigues following Lenin's death in 1924 can also be viewed in a similar light. When one adds to this the skyrocketing divorce rate and the unprecedented problem of homeless orphans (*besprizorniki*), the 1920s was a "fatherless" time, in the sense used by Mitscherlich (see chapter 6). Fratriarchal communism was, at least in part, an optimistic response to an inherently unstable situation, an attempt to see something positive in the destruction of longstanding institutions. Though the 1930s are remembered for the Great Terror, in the Soviet imaginary they brought a sense of reassurance: yes, the sons must be praised for their worthy endeavors, but society needs (and has) an older, wiser man to lead it. The father has come back home, and all is right with the world.

NOTES

INTRODUCTION

Epigraphs are from the following sources: Osip Mandel'stam, *Sobranie sochinenii v chetyrekh tomakh,* tom vtoroi (Moscow: Terra, 1991), 258; and Iurii Olesha, *P'esy* (Moscow: Iskusstvo, 1968), 149.

1   Though the author of the present book came upon its title independently, credit must be given to those scholars who used Hemingway's example in a similar context. The chapter on *Chevengur* in Tatiana Osipovich's 1988 dissertation "Sex, Love, and Family in the Works of Andrei Platonov" is entitled "Utopia Realized: Men without Women." Boris Paramonov also makes use of the phrase in his 1987 "Chevengur i okresnosti": "Men without women: this is the image of the world discovered in 'Chevengur.' " Paramonov finds the usage of the title of Hemingway's collection of war stories appropriate to Soviet literature, since "war is perhaps the most comprehensive image of Soviet reality" (Paramonov 367).

2   The works of James Fenimore Cooper and Herman Melville immediately come to mind in this connection. For comprehensive treatments of masculinity in the American literature of the twentieth century, see Peter Schwenger's *Phallic Critiques: Masculinity and Twentieth-Century Literature,* Jopi Nyman's *Men Alone: Masculinity, Individualism, and Hard-Boiled Fiction,* and Donald J. Greiner's *Women Enter the Wilderness: Male Bonding and the American Novel of the 1980s.* The first chapter of the last-named work establishes Cooper's *Leatherstocking Tales* as the model for "male bonding" in the American literature that followed it (Greiner 6-28). Masculinity in British literature is analyzed in Graham Dawson's *Soldier Heroes: British Adventure, Empire, and the Imagining of Masculinities,* and David Rosen's *The Changing Fictions of Masculinity,* while Barbara Spackman's *Fascist Virilities,* draws on a great deal of literary material in order to discuss the rhetoric of masculinity in fascist Italy. For a more international perspective on literary masculinity, see Peter F. Murphy's collection *Fictions of Masculinity: Crossing Cultures, Crossing Sexualities.*

3   In her article "The Strong-Woman Motif," Vera Dunham takes this point further: where "Russian womanhood" is extolled throughout the history of Russian literature, "it is impossible to speak as emphatically of a binding motif extolling the heroism of men" (462). The place of the hero is preempted by the heroine, and "[s]trong men seem to be punished for their masculinity and self assertion with early death ... Men *qua* men are disappointing" (462-63). The masculinization of postrevolutionary literature can be said to overcompensate for the weak heroes of the Russian classics, and the passive heroes of Babel and Olesha appear even more ineffectual against the backdrop of revolutionary heroics.

4   Heldt argues that in the works of Turgenev and Dostoevsky, the female character is "a mere foil for the male and his larger preoccupation, not a true heroine on whom the events of the plot center" (13). Joe Andrew's study of women in Russian literature

takes an even dimmer view of the heroine's role in early-nineteenth-century fiction; its premise is that the Russian novel "helped in the general process of policing women, of persuading them to consent to their own subordination" (Andrew, *Women* 4). Carolina de Maegd-Soëp takes a different view, arguing that a number of novels written by Russian men in the nineteenth century played a crucial role in the movement for women's emancipation (23). For an excellent overview of these three approaches, see Rosenshield (116–21).

5   Their treatment is perhaps a testimony to the lack of concern given domestic matters in such works. When the young Korchagins and Pavel's mother move in together under one roof, the potential for the sort of family conflict that was grist for the mill in the nineteenth century is passed over in two casual sentences: "The three of them now lived together. Taya [Korchagin's wife] and the old lady lived as friends" (Ostrovskii 322). Thea Margaret Durfee argues that Ostrovsky's Taya and Gladkov's Dasha represent two distinct ideals of Soviet womanhood: Dasha is the strong, liberated heroine of the 1920s, while Taya is much more traditionally feminine (101).

6   Cf. Sheila Fitzpatrick's "New Perspectives on the Civil War": "Politics, comradeship, and drink—all recognized by the Bolsheviks as typically proletarian attributes—belonged to the male sphere. Family and domestic economy, which the Bolsheviks saw as 'petty-bourgeois' concerns, belonged to the female" (13).

7   In translating the authors treated here, I have decided to render *chelovek* as "man," though I always provide the Russian in parenthesis to distinguish it from *muzhchina* ("man," in the sense of "adult male"). Here I must agree with Lynne Attwood, who chooses to use male nouns and pronouns when translating Russian sources, because to "attempt to rectify the male bias in the Russian language . . . would be totally misleading" (14). It would be a mistake to neuter the language of these authors, since what is often taken for discussions of the human condition in their works is, I argue, actually a treatment of specifically male experience. At times I extend the male pronoun beyond translations of the text, using it to refer to the reader. This is a conscious choice, although not a political statement. Though the works discussed here were, of course, read by women and men alike, their implied reader, whom the text manipulates into either empathizing with or taking a stand against the network of male relationships in these novels and stories, is male.

8   The masculinity of the idealized "new man" extended throughout the culture. In her study of women in the Komsomol, Anne Gorsuch finds that "young men and the masculine were defined as revolutionary in contrast to the supposed backwardness of the feminine, and young women were defined as overly adult in contrast to the idealized male adolescent" (Gorsuch 638). Frances Bernstein's analysis of posters from the "sexual enlightenment campaign" of the 1920s argues that these images had a "masculine orientation," relying on the use of male subjects to appeal to male viewers (Bernstein 147). Particularly noteworthy is a poster for the physical culture movement that depicts "Soviet society as an all-male world"; the single woman in the bottom corner

of the poster no longer poses a threat to collectivism now that the male group has successfully sublimated its libido through exercise (Bernstein 141).

9   Cf. Eric Naiman's discussion of the Chubarov Alley gang-rape case in Leningrad (1926), which he places within the context of a particular strain of Bolshevik idealism: "Influenced by misogynistic thinkers like Nikolai Fyodorov, some early extremists such as Andrei Platonov had envisioned Communism exclusively as a society of men" (Naiman, *Sex in Public* 274).

10 It has become customary in gender studies to refer to multiple and varying "masculinities" rather than a monolithic and invariant "masculinity." Though I applaud the impulse behind the coinage of such plurals ("feminisms" being another prominent example), I have chosen to use the more standard singular forms for purely stylistic reasons. My use of the term "masculinity" is not meant to imply that I consider it a universal or essential concept. Similarly, when I invoke "manliness," I have in mind traditional, stereotyped notions of courage and boldness that I consider social constructs rather than absolutes or universals. For discussions of the construction of "masculinities" in various ethnic, cultural, and social contexts, see Harry Brod's and Michael Kaufman's collection *Theorizing Masculinities*.

11 Halfin bases his argument largely on a 1926 essay by Nikolai Gredeskul, as well as on a close reading of one of Alexei Gastev's more famous poems. He notes the consistent use of phallic imagery to describe the proletariat, all the while noting the feminine nouns that repeatedly stand in for the grammatically feminine intelligentsia. The offspring of this violent union is, according to Halfin, none other than the New Soviet Man. Eric Naiman extends this comparison to include the "old world" and the "West" as other feminized victims of revolutionary rape (*Sex in Public* 62).

12 Russia's restrictive family code had long been a particular target of radicals' scorn and thus was among the first laws to be changed when the communists came to power. The new regime passed laws on civil marriage and divorce in Dec. 1917, further strengthening these reforms in the legal codes on the family in Sept. 1918 (Heller 168). The Family Code of 1926 avoided any definition of the family, according de facto recognition to unregistered unions. Abortion was legalized in 1920, though this action was seen as a health measure rather than family policy (Lapidus 60). The most detailed study of Bolshevik family policy can be found in Goldman (*Women,* passim).

13 Not all of the changes in sexual behavior could be attributed to revolutionary ideology. Some of the relaxation in social mores can be seen as the sexual equivalent of War Communism: the exigencies of war became reinterpreted as official doctrine. Fitzpatrick notes that "the men who had learnt their ideology in the Red Army . . . regarded casual sex as a Communist rite of passage"; demobilized soldiers "brought back a casual macho attitude toward sex which young brothers worked hard to imitate" (*Russian Revolution* 79; *Cultural Front* 68). The adoption of specifically masculine wartime mores will be discussed in chapter 1.

14 Kollontai is perhaps one of the most misunderstood figures of the early revolutionary

period. Both a champion of sexual equality and a confirmed enemy of "bourgeois" feminism, Kollontai published numerous books, pamphlets, and essays calling for a new "socialist" approach to the family. Her 1918 treatise *The Family and the Communist State* (*Sem'ia i kommunisticheskoe gosudarstvo*) called for the end of "indissoluble marriage based on the servitude of women," to be replaced by a "free union" founded on "the love and the mutual respect of the two members of the Workers' State" (Kollontai, as quoted in Schlesinger 68–69). Her public lecture course of 1921 condoned premarital sex while condemning alimony and the concept of illegitimacy.

Unfortunately for Kollontai, the very articles that she wrote to critique "vulgar" and "soulless" libertinism were seen as endorsements of the phenomenon she opposed. Her 1923 "Make Way for Winged Eros" ("Dorogu krylatomu Erosu") was an uncompromising attack on casual sex, whose origins she saw in bourgeois society. Yet her advocacy of a more meaningful eroticism based on "love-comradeship" (*liubov'-tovarishcestvo*) was mistaken for the "wingless Eros" she despised. Similarly, the belief that Zhenya of "Love of Three Generations" was merely expressing the views of her creator led to the misconception that this story is the origin of the glass of water theory. Aron Zalkind, whose theory of "revolutionary sublimation" took a dim view of Kollontai's "free union," dismissed such an attitude toward sex as "a disease, not an idea" (Farnsworth 332). For a concise study of Kollontai's complex role in the rise and fall of the "new morality," see Stites (*Women's Liberation* 348–58); for a more detailed look at Kollontai's life and work, see the three English-language biographies by Clements, Farnsworth, and Porter.

15 Fitzpatrick, whose examination of four sex surveys from the 1920s depicts a rather frustrated student body, concludes, "[I]t is difficult to argue that the Revolution encouraged students to be promiscuous (though no doubt the aftermath of war and civil war had this effect in the early 1920s)." One factor that contributed to the creation of "an image of student promiscuity was the popularity of this subject in contemporary fiction" (Fitzpatrick, *Cultural Front* 88).

16 On the unexpected side effects of the liberalization of family law, see Goldman (*Women*, especially chapters 2, 3, and 6), Lapidus (87–88), and Stites (*Women's Liberation* 358–62, 385–90).

17 Under Stalin, access to divorce was again restricted, homosexuality was once again declared a crime, and, in 1936, abortion was outlawed. In the 1930s, the family was officially recognized as an essential part of society. Wedding rings, New Year's trees, and female charity work came back in style, along with a general acceptance of traditional family values (Fitzpatrick, *Russian Revolution* 150–51). For a discussion of the official glorification of motherhood in Soviet times, see Goscilo (32–36).

18 The transition to "middle-class values" observed by Vera Dunham occurred only after World War II (*In Stalin's Time* 4–5), but the way had already been paved in the 1930s by the wholesale curtailing of personal freedoms and sexual experimentation.

19 The "sexophobia" of the Soviet Union has received a great deal of critical attention, especially in recent years. Eric Naiman (*Sex in Public*) and Mikhail Zolotonosov have

explored the links between "official" sexual discourse, literary texts, and everyday life in the 1920s, while Naiman has also traced the roots of revolutionary asceticism in the context of turn-of-the-century Russian religious philosophy ("Historectomies"; *Sex in Public*). Broad sociological overviews of sexuality in the Soviet Union have been provided by Kon, Popovskii, and Mikhail and August Stern; Popovskii's and the Sterns' works are largely anecdotal, while Kon's *Sexual Revolution in Russia,* though much more thoroughly researched, is aimed at a popular audience. For an overview of more recent trends in Russian sexual culture, see Borenstein ("Slavophilia"), Costlow et al., Gessen, Goscilo (135–70), and Kon.

20 Marcia Morris has traced the development of asceticism and the ascetic hero from medieval Russian literature through the socialist realism of the 1930s, arguing that asceticism in Russia is usually linked to an "apocalyptic" mindset (26), to the need to purge oneself in preparation for the end of the world and the coming millennium. According to Morris, the resurgence of the ascetic hero in the late nineteenth and early twentieth centuries can be at least partially attributed to the "millenarian" character of Marxism (130).

21 According to Naiman, revolutionary asceticism "would continue to plague the Party" throughout the 1920s: "Communists would, in fact, be cautioned against excessive asceticism even as the campaign against dissolute behavior made asceticism a more likely reaction" (*Sex in Public* 214).

22 The novel's contemporary admirers and detractors alike readily admit its stylistic weakness. The rumor that its publication was permitted in order to ruin Chernyshevsky's reputation began circulating almost immediately after the book's appearance (Paperno 27) and is asserted as a fact by the narrator of Nabokov's *The Gift* (*Dar*) (Nabokov 3: 247).

23 For a discussion of the vogue for fictitious marriages and nonexclusive unions inspired by the novel, see Matich ("Dialectics of Cultural Return" 60–66), Paperno (29–36), and Stites (*Women's Liberation* chapter 3). For speculation as to the possible historical models for the Vera Pavlovna–Lopukhov–Kirsanov triangle, see Paperno (133–41). George Sand's influence on Chernyshevsky's treatment of the marriage plot has been explored by Eidelman (48–63).

24 For examples of the attraction Rakhmetov's ascetic model held for many of the novel's readers, see Paperno (29–31).

25 Katerina Clark examines the relationship between hagiographic texts, socialist realist novels, and the "positive hero" of prerevolutionary fiction, coming to the conclusion that prerevolutionary borrowings from the hagiographic tradition were "novelistic" and "individualized" when compared to similar borrowings in Soviet canonical works (48–50). For this reason, she finds that even the story of Rakhmetov, whose biography is patterned after that of the popular saint Aleksei, cannot be considered true hagiography (50). The connection between Chernyshevsky and the hagiographic tradition is also explored by Morris (130–45) and Ziolkowski (192–95).

26 Rakhmetov's self-denial is implicitly contrasted to the "endearing" weaknesses of Vera

Pavlovna, such as her fondness for clotted cream and her habit of "luxuriating" (*nezhit' sia*) in her soft bed (Costlow et al. 14). Indeed, the introduction of Rakhmetov adds a distinctly masculine counterpoint to what has been thus far a woman-centered model for living: "In a novel that seems more centrally about *women's* work . . . , [the Rakhmetov chapter] glorifies masculinity and male labor" (Costlow et al. 13).

27   Petr Vail' and Aleksandr Genis see in Rakhmetov the answer to Dobrolyubov's call for "the real day to come"; that is, though Chernyshevsky "sincerely sympathizes" with all his heroes, it is Rakhmetov who is the true model for the future (127–28). The narrator himself supports this approach, saying that Rakhmetov, by being so clearly superhuman, serves to show that the novel's main characters are really ordinary people who exist in the everyday world (Chernyshevskii 292–94). Morris sees the contrast between Rakhmetov and the novel's main characters as an example of a cultural conflict that dates back to Kievan Rus': Vera Pavlovna, Kirsanov, and Lopukhov "engage in moderate asceticisms" like Kievan cenobitic monks, but "these ascetic acts are important primarily because of their significance as models of behavior for others to follow. They are never extreme . . . these heroes create their own self-contained social institutions . . . in order to create a model in the here and now of the beautiful society which will come into being with the advent of the millennial kingdom." Rakhmetov is a "proud, aloof ascetic," while Vera Pavlovna is a "social reformer, who is personally involved in society's woes" (Morris 142–43).

28   At this point I am mainly concerned with the role Chernyshevsky's novel had in the development of radical leftist approaches to the family structure. *What Is to Be Done?* also had a profound influence on the turn-of-the-century symbolists, including such confirmed anti-Bolsheviks as the poet Zinaida Gippius. For a discussion of the symbolist transformation of the Chernyshevskian model, see Matich ("Dialectics of Cultural Return" 60–66; "Symbolist Meaning of Love" 41–50). The role of love triangles in the symbolist movement is also discussed in chapter 1.

29   For a comprehensive study of women's movements in Russia, see Lapidus and Stites (*Women's Liberation*).

30   Kollontai's choice of words is telling: The "Communist fatherland" (*otechestvo*) would not "tear the baby from its mother's breast" (Farnsworth 148); one is left with an opposition between the biological mother and the ideological father(land).

31   At the Eighth Party Congress in 1919, Kollontai tried to convince Lenin to include a "statement of intention to abolish the bourgeois family" in the party platform, but Lenin felt that it was early for such talk, since there were as yet no alternatives to child rearing; Clements suggests that Lenin was afraid of alienating less radical party members (Clements 159–60).

32   Zalkind's crusade for chastity had its antecedents on the opposite end of the political spectrum; Nikolai Fyodorov's *Philosophy of the Common Cause* was, in part, an argument for total abstinence (see below), while Tolstoi's *Kreutzer Sonata* (*Kreitserova sonata*, 1889) inaugurated a decades-long debate on the merits of chastity and the evils

of marriage. For an excellent study of Tolstoi's role in the development of public sexual discourse in Russia, see Moller (passim).

33 Mark Popovskii sees Zalkind's preoccupation with the conservation of sexual energy as the sociological reflection of the Soviet government's call for a "regime of economizing" (*rezhim ekonomii*) (Popovskii 72). For more on Zalkind, see Kon (57–58). Frances Bernstein finds a similar fixation on "energy" in the sexual hygiene literature of the 1920s: "As in other areas of society, an obsessive concern with energy—where it came from, how it might be channeled and harnessed—lay at the core" of the pervasive advice that Soviet youth abstain from sexual "excess" (Bernstein 231).

34 In his *Total Art of Stalinism*, Boris Groys links the "demiurgic" impulse of high Stalinist culture with the avant-garde rejection of the external world as "black chaos" that must be completely recreated by the artist (19–32, 56–74). Though the literature and social policy of the 1920s do not fall under the scope of Groys's study, his analysis is germane to the topic at hand: after the revolution, nature could no longer be accepted as given.

35 For more on the anxiety over the "proper" sex roles in Soviet and post-Soviet Russia, see Attwood (125–26) and Kon (149–52).

36 Here as elsewhere, one finds some similarities between the early Soviet experience and the cult of masculinity in Nazi Germany and fascist Italy (a topic that is discussed in more detail below). In her analysis of the Italian fascist rhetoric of "virility," Barbara Spackman notes that "[i]n the fascist topography of gender and sex, stepping out into the public sphere 'masculinizes' and 'sterilizes' women, while the loss of a position in the public sphere necessarily 'devirilizes' men. Production and reproduction are strictly, and asymmetrically, linked for men and women: only men involved in economic production are figured as capable of sexual reproduction, whereas involvement in economic production is presumed to destroy the woman's ability to reproduce" (35). At the same time, fascist women were expected to be involved in political and public life. One "fascist feminist," Teresa Labriola, argued that the fascist woman should overcome this contradiction by having a "maternal heart" with a "virile mind" (41–43).

37 Indeed, femininity was so scorned in some Bolshevik literary circles that it becomes a trope for everything that is excessive, unnecessary, or detrimental in the old world. Naiman argues that "throughout the 1920s the unspoken equation beneath society's hostility toward this ontological category was '*byt* [the everyday] = woman'" ("Historectomies" 270; see also *Sex in Public*, chapters 5 and 6).

38 For a socialist realist heroine, Dasha is an unusually complex character. Though she repeatedly proves herself to be far more politically conscious than her estranged husband Gleb, her grief and guilt over her daughter's death suggest that her approach to the family is too extreme. For more on the ambiguity of Dasha's characterization, see Durfee (92–96).

39 The attempt to form a "family" and even produce offspring without recourse to women is a standard trope of utopian and anti-utopian literature. The motif can even be found, albeit in a much less developed form, in the genre's founding document, Thomas More's

Utopia. More's traveler describes the agricultural habits of Utopia's citizens: "Men, not hens, hatch [chickens'] eggs by keeping them in a warm place at an even temperature. As soon as they come out of the shell, the chicks recognize the men, follow them around, and are devoted to them instead of to their real mothers" (More 44-45).

40   Both the monastery and the barracks are important sources of Soviet male utopianism: Russian soldiers' experiences in the civil war played a large role in the new collectivist spirit of the early 1920s and provided the background for Babel's *Red Cavalry;* the antisexual and antifemale ethos of the monastery can be felt in Platonov's *Chevengur.* To the best of my knowledge, neither the monastery nor the army has been analyzed as a specifically "utopian" institution, although utopias from Plato to Campanella have tended to be organized on quasi-military lines. David F. Noble has, however, traced the connection between monasticism, the military life, and secular science, arguing that all are attempts to create a "world without women." Noble sees the Catholic Church's tenth- and eleventh-century campaigns to eradicate "double monasteries" (in which male and female ascetics lived side by side), as well as the subsequent imposition of sexual renunciation upon the clergy, as a retreat from the earlier Christian model of androgyny. Ultimately, monasticism in the Middle Ages took on a "military orientation," with monks becoming "soldiers for Christ" (53-54). Since modern science descends from monastic scholarship, Noble sees the exclusion of women from science as a continuation of homosocial asceticism.

41   Virgilio Martini's 1926 *The World without Women* describes the apocalyptic consequences of an infectious disease that wipes out the entire human female population at the dawn of the twenty-first century. The contagion is actually a biological weapon created by a Philadelphia-based "Misogynists' Club," a group of 687 homosexuals whose "divine purpose" was "destroying women" (47). Writing under the pseudonym "Cordwainer Smith," Paul Linebarger recounts his hero's battle with a group of "bearded homosexual" space pirates "with rouged lips" in his 1964 short story "The Crime and Glory of Commander Suzdal" (Linebarger was in the habit of choosing Russian names for his characters) (Mann 209). The cause of the women's demise in Linebarger's story is remarkably similar to the plague described in Martini's novel, although it is not the result of terrorism; colonists on an unknown world find that all earth females, from fish to humans, have developed a mysterious cancer: "*Femininity itself became carcinogenic*" (Mann 207; italics in the original). One female doctor discovers a radical "cure" consisting of massive testosterone injections of every woman and girl on the planet, changing them into men: "They became strutting cockerels, who mixed their love with murder, who blended their songs with duels, who sharpened their weapons, and who earned the right to reproduce within a strange family system that no decent Earthman would find comprehensible" (Mann 209). Like Martini's homosexual misogynists, these "men," who still have legends of the women of old earth, see all females as "deformities, who should be killed. The family, as they recalled it, was filth and abomination which they resolved to wipe out if they should ever meet it" (Mann 209). Linebarger's story is an oblique cautionary tale about men's attempts to manage without women; the

first three pages consist of Suzdal's insistence that he needs no female companionship on his millennia-long journey into space, while the enemy he encounters is a nightmarish parody of his claims to self-sufficiency. It is the mentality behind these claims that leads to Suzdal's twofold "crime": first, he exposes all mankind to the danger of these altered colonists; second, in order to fight them off, he creates an entire race of cat people with the aid of bioengineering and time travel.

In "Planet of the Rapes" (1977), one of Thomas M. Disch's less successful attempts at outré satire, human society of the future is divided into two segments: the earth belongs to women, who live in "utopias" scattered across the globe, while the men form a "warrior culture of Space Marines" who live completely separate from the women (147). Men and women meet on "Pleasure Island," where the women are dressed up to resemble the sex toys to which the men have become accustomed. William Golding's *Lord of the Flies* (1954) shows how shipwrecked schoolchildren, when left to their own devices, inevitably descend into savagery; the children, of course, are all boys. In his *War with the Newts* (1936), Karel Čapek invents a race of intelligent salamanders who breed in groups rather than individually; male newts fertilize the females by providing a "Sexual Milieu" thanks to their very presence en masse (157). In addition, the males have a "strange ritual" dance under the full moon, which is interpreted as "an instinctive desire to perceive oneself as *the Collective Male*, a Collective Bridegroom, and the Great Copulator" (158–59; emphasis in the original). One of Čapek's imaginary researchers concludes that this ritual is the "very source and origin of the marvelous Newt collectivism" (159).

Čapek's and Martini's novels were written in 1936; their apocalyptic visions of an unstoppable collective force suggest an antifascist allegory. The connection between fascism and a nightmare vision of male dominance is made explicit in Katharine Burdekin's 1937 novel *Swastika Night*. Writing as "Murray Constantine," Burdekin posits a dystopian Nazi future set seven centuries after Hitler's hypothetical triumph over Europe and Africa. Here the Nazis establish a semifeudal society based on what Burdekin calls the "cult of masculinity": women are kept in cages throughout their lives, their entire world limited to their reproductive function. The men's sexual contact with women is limited to rape; otherwise, male homosexuality is the norm. For a discussion of the cult of masculinity and "brotherhood" in Nazi Germany, see Mosse and Theweleit.

42   René Girard's theory of mimetic desire also deserves a place on this list. Girard is discussed in more detail in chapters 1 and 5.

43   Indeed, Tiger's essential argument is that "male bonding *as a biological propensity* is not only a phenomenon unto itself, but ... in part it is the very cause of the formation of those various male groups observable around us" (Tiger xv, emphasis added). For detailed rebuttals to such "biological" psychology, see Ashley Montagu's anthology *Man and Aggression*, especially his introduction (3–18), and Erich Fromm's critique of "instinctivists" (13–32).

44   A lay sociological approach does characterize Nikolai Klimontovich's 1993 article on

such "male unions" (*muzhskie soiuzy*) as military hazing (*dedovshchina*), the mafia, and new "patriotic" groups in Russia. Klimontovich finds a "ritual" element to all such groups, whose members he characterizes as "infantile" or "primitive" (166).

45 The Russian word *tovarishch* (comrade) was appropriated by Russian Marxists at the turn of the century; the usage was inspired by the term's currency among European Social Democrats. "Comrade" was the exclusive form of address among party members and took on a more popular use among workers during the 1905 revolution. Though still considered less impersonal than "citizen," the term "comrade" enjoyed popular use in the 1920s, the word was used in a wide variety of situations, eventually becoming an official, nearly neutral term (Stites, *Revolutionary Dreams* 134).

46 See Gorky's 1906 fairy tale "Comrade!" ("Tovarishch") which includes perhaps the most "promiscuous" usage of this form of address in Russian literature. In Gorky's story, "comrade" is a "simple, light word" whose main function is to unite the downtrodden "with new ties, strong ties of mutual respect, of respect for human freedom. The word's scope expands with each page, lifting the spirits of workers, cabbies, and a prostitute; by the story's end, the word "comrade" has inspired "people's great faith in everyone's brotherhood." As the word "brotherhood" suggests, the family metaphor is repeated throughout ("the joy of the rejected in joining the great family of laborers"), and yet the trait that defines this family is one of class rather than blood; the word "comrade" eclipses all other social and moral distinctions (Gor'kii 7: 151–56).

47 Though the grammatically masculine noun *tovarishch* was applied to both men and women, anecdotal evidence does suggest that in the 1920s, it may have been easier for men to qualify as "comrades" than women. Among the difficulties encountered by female Komsomol members in the NEP era, Anne Gorsuch includes issues relating to language: "Women were commonly called 'baba' or 'moll' rather than 'comrade' " (Gorsuch 650).

48 For a discussion of comradeship among British soldiers in World War I, see chapter 3 of Joanna Bourke's *Dismembering the Male* (124–70).

49 My discussion of *pobratimstvo* relies on Eve Levin's *Sex and Society in the World of the Orthodox Slavs, 900–1700* (149–50).

50 In contemporary Russian, the word *pobratim* has survived largely as a metaphor in certain fixed expressions; since the word for "city" in Russian is masculine, the equivalent to the English phrase "sister cities" is *goroda-pobratimy*.

51 My discussion of the Cossack myth is indebted to Judith Deutsch Kornblatt's book-length study of the Cossack in Russian literature. In Kornblatt's view, the Cossacks of Gogol's "Taras Bulba" take on a "decidedly religious aura," and his "depiction of the Cossacks' 'multiplicity-in-unity' was no doubt influenced by the Orthodox ideal of sobornost', a term coined by Gogol's friend Aleksei Khomyakov" (49; 192n24).

52 The Cossack world is discussed at greater length in chapter 2.

53 The influence of Fyodorov's ideas on Russian literature is well documented, as is the high esteem in which Fyodorov was held by such contemporaries as Dostoevsky, Tolstoi, and Solovyov. The links between Fyodorov and the nineteenth-century literary

tradition have been explored by Lukashevich (20-24) and Semenova (*Nikolai Fedorov* 304-20). Masing-Delic's book-length study *Abolishing Death,* while not specifically a study of influences, traces the myth of physical immortality (elaborated in greatest detail by Fyodorov) through the works of Blok, Gorky, Sologub, and Zabolotsky (passim). Fyodorov's influence on twentieth-century writers is also treated by Lukashevich (24-34) and Semenova (*Nikolai Fedorov* 346-81). Fyodorov's role in early-twentieth-century thought is also explored by Todorov (59-61, 63-66).

However, it is Fyodorov's influence on Andrei Platonov that has received the most critical attention. In addition to Ayleen Teskey's book-length *Platonov and Fyodorov,* one can find discussions of the links between the two writers in Bethea (159-61), Geller (30-54), Kiselev (237-48), Langerak ("Andrei Platonov v Voronezhe"), Naiman ("Andrej Platonov" 324-326), Osipovich (29-37), Paramonov (344-46), Seifrid (20-24), Semenova (*Nikolai Fedorov* 363-74; "Mytarstva ideala" 498-502; "'Tainoe tainykh'" 83-86), and Tolstaia-Segal ("Ideologicheskie konteksty" 246-55). Fyodorov's role in Platonov's thought will be discussed in chapters 5 and 6.

54 Fyodorov's view of resurrection and reproduction as two mutually exclusive categories will still resonate in the early twentieth century, especially in the works of Platonov. Matich argues that Fedorov's ideas "must have contributed to the further demotion of procreative love in the Symbolist era" and notes that the "preference for resurrection or transformation over procreation continued into the Soviet period" in Gladkov's *Cement* and in Mayakovsky's poetry (Matich, "Merezhkovsys' Third Testament" 161). For more on Fyodorov's role in twentieth-century Russian thought, see Masing-Delic (102-4).

55 Fyodorov felt that socialism was an attempt to replace Christian brotherhood with class warfare and a promotion of vice. For a brief English-language summary of Fyodorov's argument against socialism, see Lukashevich (257-61).

56 Hence Fyodorov's influence on "Godbuilders" such as Gorky and Lunacharsky. Godbuilding (*bogostroitel' stvo*) was an attempt to reconcile "scientific" socialism and religion, a recognition of religion's role in facilitating a powerful human bond (Stites, *Revolutionary Dreams* 102). Stites sees the seemingly improbable importance of Fyodorov's thought in the early years of the revolution as evidence of "millenarianism and a utopianism fed by serious erudition of a special sort and by the unbounded Promethean belief in man's ability to transform nature and reverse its laws" (*Revolutionary Dreams* 170).

57 This scene is analyzed in more detail in chapter 6.

58 Platonov spent his literary apprenticeship as a member of the Smithy (*Kuznitsa*), an offshoot of the Proletcult. See chapter 5.

59 Robert C. Williams finds the roots of Bogdanov's collectivism in "a growing movement of Bolsheviks intrigued by European syndicalism after 1905" (389). Williams considers "collectivism" in pre-1917 Russia a Bolshevik "Aesopian code word that operated on three levels of meaning. It was, first, a philosophical and quasi-religious notion of collective immortality, whereby individuals die, but the collective group, class, or party is

said to endure eternally. Second, it represented a political strategy, close to syndicalism that viewed any ideology . . . as useful political myth, not true doctrine. . . . Third, it encompassed a utopian culture of the future in which the proletariat would create its own science, art, and literature with the guidance of intellectuals." Williams argues that these three levels of meaning correspond to the evolution of Bolshevik collectivism from Godbuilding through syndicalism to proletarian culture (388).

60   The influence of Fyodorov on Bogdanov is discussed by Langerak ("Andrei Platonov v Voronezhe" 453), Osipovich (28), Teskey (23–28), and Tolstaia-Segal ("Ideologicheskie konteksty" 243).

61   Fyodorov felt that in order for paradise to be realized on earth, the Russian tsar had to go beyond his traditional role of "gatherer of the Russian land" (*sobiratel' zemli russkoj*) to become the "gatherer of the earth" (*sobiratel' zemli*) (Lukashevich 269).

62   In addition to *Red Cavalry*, Maguire's examples include Khadzhi-Murat Mugaev's 1927 "The Death of Nikolai Bunchuk" ("Smert' Nikolaia Bunchuka") and Vsevolod Ivanov's "Duty" ("Dolg," 1923) (Maguire 345–46).

63   For Platonov in particular, World War II provided the opportunity to return to this theme that was so prominent in his earlier works; see his 1942 short story "Inspired People" ("Odukhotvorennyie liudi"). For a more detailed examination of comradeship in this period of Platonov's life, see my "Tekst kak mashina smerti."

64   Even the decidedly individualist Serapions, for whom Lev Lunts suggested the rallying cry "We are not comrades! We are brothers!" (*My ne tovarishchi! My—brat'ia!*) (Lunts 200) relied on a sense of fellowship whose "familial" character was purely metaphorical. Yes, they wanted to be individuals, but they wanted to be individuals together.

65   Mosse's analysis of the centrality of masculinity to the development of nationalism is too complex to be fully reproduced here, as it touches upon numerous movements, countries, and time periods. Mosse provides his most concise historical interview in the book's introduction (Mosse 1–22).

66   On the reaction against turn-of-the-century decadence, see Dijkstra's *Idols of Perversity*, especially pp. 210–71, and Elaine Showalter's *Sexual Anarchy*, especially chapters 1 and 9.

67   In his *History of Sexuality*, Michel Foucault discusses the significance of an 1870 article about homosexuality by Karl Westphal: "The sodomite had been a temporary aberration . . . The homosexual was now a species" (Foucault 43).

68   Though Mosse concentrates primarily on Germany, he also includes numerous examples of the cult of male friendship in England, particularly in the world of the English public school (Mosse 81–89). In England and America, nineteenth-century phrenologists claimed to have isolated the portion of the brain responsible for "adhesiveness," or the capacity for friendship; the "organ" for adhesiveness was considered to be more highly developed in men (Lynch 68–74). Michael Lynch argues that Walt Whitman deliberately "modified the effects of this organ to refer only to same-sex relationships" in order to praise "adhesive love" or "comradeship" among men (Lynch 69).

69 On masculinity in the literature inspired by World War I, see Adrian Caesar's *Taking It like a Man*, and also Mosse (114–32).

70 Eric Naiman makes a convincing case for the importance of War Communist nostalgia in the NEP era due to the greater ideological "purity" attributed to the ethos of the civil war years (*Sex in Public* 57–59; 79–82).

71 On the dwindling role of the family under Nazism, see Theweleit (1: 252–56).

72 Sedgwick finds "correspondences and similarities between the most sanctioned forms of male-homosocial bonding, and the most reprobated expressions of male homosexual sociality.... For a man to be a man's man is separated only by an invisible, carefully blurred, always-already-crossed line from being 'interested in men'" (89). Her view is prefigured by that of Otto Weininger, whose theory of "sex and character" is based on the different amounts of "masculinity" and "femininity" found in each individual: "There is no friendship between men that has not an element of sexuality in it, however little accentuated it may be in the nature of the friendship ... there would be no friendship unless there has been some attraction to draw men together" (49). Weininger's observation, however, may well be colored by his inability to come to terms with his own sexuality. For Weininger's reception in Russia, see Engelstein (301–2, 310–13) and Naiman ("Historectomies" 262–68).

Though homoeroticism plays an important part in all the works to be discussed here, care will be taken not to reduce these works to symptoms of "latent homosexuality"; no attempts are made to psychoanalyze the authors with the help of their texts. To focus only on the homoerotic elements of these works would be to ignore a broad range of other factors that will be discussed in the course of this book.

73 Joe Andrew's *Women in Russian Literature* departs from traditional "images of women" criticism by including sections on male/male relationships and images of the male. This addition enriches his analysis of Pushkin, Lermontov, and Gogol, but its scope does not extend to the Soviet period.

74 In numerous poems by Proletcult writers such as Kirillov and Gastev, and in Mayakovsky's communist epic *150,000,000*, the new world is symbolized by one enormous body, invariably a male one. For more on the "collective body," see Nesbet and Naiman (92) and Todorov (45–70).

1. THE LADYKILLERS

1 Ambivalence over attempts to "masculinize women" can even be found in the early fiction of Andrei Platonov, who spent the first years of the Soviet period extolling male comradeship and castigating women as the "embodiment of sex" (see chapter 5). In his "Descendants of the Sun" ("Potomki solntsa," 1922), Platonov imagines the future earth to be entirely deserted save for one "watchman and chronicler," who narrates the tale; the rest of humanity, having accomplished socialism and conquered nature, has abandoned its native world in favor of distant stars. The narrator did have a wife,

whom he describes as "more severe than a man, there is nothing of the so-called woman within her—a soft, formless creature." In the next paragraph, however, he admits that his wife's lips are thicker and her eyes moister than his; moreover, "within her there is impatience and alarm—the power of maternity, not transferred into thought, is still aroused within her" (Platonov, *Chevengur* 399–402).

2   Lévi-Strauss views exogamous marriage as the "widened social application" of the prohibition on incest (51), requiring that marriage serve to cement two preexisting families or clans. As such it is a "dramatic encounter between nature and culture": the "bond of alliance with another family ensures the dominance of the social over the biological, and of the cultural over the natural" (489, 479).

3   The exceptions to this rule are few, but still significant. Boris Lavryonov's 1924 "The Forty-First" tells of the remains of a Red Army division consisting of only twenty-five soldiers: the leader, Yevsukov, twenty-three men, and a young orphan named Maryutka. After twelve years gutting fish in a small town on the Volga, Maryutka volunteered to join the army as a sharpshooter. When the story begins, she has forty kills to her credit, and when the soldiers capture a White lieutenant, she assumes he will be the forty-first. The lieutenant tries to charm his captor, whom he repeatedly calls an "Amazon" (*amazonka*), but she remains unmoved. When the two of them end up shipwrecked together on a desert island, they of course begin to fall in love; she even begins to convince him of the righteousness of her cause. But when the ship that comes to rescue them turns out to belong to Whites rather than Reds, Maryutka kills her beloved rather than allow him to return to the enemy, thus rendering him her forty-first victim after all.

The end of "The Forty-First" resonates strongly with the end of Ehrenburg's *Kurbov*, cited above; in each case, the revolutionary chooses violence over love and marriage. But in Lavryonov's story, gender adds an interesting dimension to the plot: we sense that Maryutka's love for the lieutenant is inevitable, and that she is overcoming her "natural" femininity by choosing to shoot him. Moreover, even though Maryutka is accepted by her comrades when she joins the Red Army, the narrator admits that "the Red Army men made affectionate fun of her, but they protected her better than themselves in battle" (335). Despite her ostensible equality, the woman Maryutka is still to be protected by the men around her.

4   See chapter 5 for a more detailed discussion of this story.

5   Olga Matich's typology of the fallen woman posits four models for the relationship between the fallen woman and her male complement: female victim/male victimizer, female victim/male redeemer, female victim-redeemer/male victim, and female victimizer/male victim (Matich, "Typology" 327). The examples discussed here fit Matich's second and third models. For more on the attempts to "save" the literary prostitute, see Siegel (81–107) and Zholkovsky ("Topos" 317–68).

6   On the function of Mary Magdalene in these authors' works, see Matich ("Typology" 337–40; "What's to Be Done" 47–64) and Zholkovsky ("Topos" 365).

7   See, e.g., Zholkovsky: "The hero is usually a sensitive and lonely intellectual man" ("Topos" 319).
8   Such is the case in Chekhov's "A Nervous Breakdown," and also in Tolstoi's *Kreutzer Sonata*.
9   Matich, "Typology" 342; Siegel 107; Zholkovsky, "Topos" 318.
10 Grigory Vasiliev's companions also appeal to group solidarity in order to keep the hero of "A Nervous Breakdown" from leaving the brothel without them: "Gri-gri, be a comrade! We came here together, we'll leave together" (Chekhov 7: 209).
11 Of course, prostitution is far from eradicated; the survivors are turned into "wandering, solitary streetwalkers" (Kuprin 6: 311). Nonetheless, the soldiers, whose crusade was sparked by being cheated in one of the "ruble institutions," have avenged themselves on their deceivers.
12 In *Deceit, Desire, and the Novel*, Girard postulates that the well-known phenomenon of the love triangle does not describe a simple conflict between two men who love the same woman, but is rather a cover for a man's fascination with his rival. The woman, ostensibly the object of desire, is actually a displacement of the subject's desire to be like his rival; the subject pursues the woman because of, and not in spite of, his rival. Girard's theory is discussed in greater detail in chapter 5. For a Girardian analysis of the romantic entanglements of the historical and fictional Russian radicals of the nineteenth century, see Eidelman and Paperno (especially 112–17 and 136–50).
13 Elisabeth Bronfen has argued that, in certain literary texts, "the death of a beautiful woman emerges as the requirement for a preservation of existing cultural norms and values or their regenerative modification . . . a sacrifice of the dangerous woman reestablishes an order that was momentarily suspended due to her presence" (181). If for "cultural norms" we substitute "male comradeship," Bronfen's formulation can be applied to the early Soviet context.
14 Bronfen comes to a similar conclusion about the murder of Carmen by José in Mérimée's novel: "By killing the object of his desire, José is able in fact to kill his desire as this manifests itself as a force that overpowers him, that lies beyond his control" (186). Again, Bronfen's approach must be slightly modified. Though repression of sexuality is an important theme in Soviet revolutionary literature, the motivations for this repression are substantially different from those Bronfen offers in her work; in the Soviet context, one must sublimate one's sexual desire into socially constructive work and eliminate all forces that could separate one from the collective.
15 The Russian word *baba* means "peasant woman" or "old woman"; when it is applied to women of other classes, it is pejorative, roughly equivalent to "dame" or "broad." When a man is reproached for being weak, cowardly, or effeminate, he is called a *baba* (and never the more neutral *zhenshchina*).
16 One can also make the connection with the Russian folk song about the Cossack rebel Stenka Razin. After Razin spends the night with a woman, his comrades accuse him of turning into a *baba* himself, a charge Razin refutes by tossing his bride into the Volga

and leaving her to drown. I am grateful to Thomas Seifrid for bringing this connection to my attention. For more on the importance of female sacrifice to the Cossack myth, see Kornblatt.

17 In his analysis of the story, Hongor Oulanoff sees the combination of the "gang" plot and the "triangle" plot as a "certain weakness," since the end of the gang does not result from "a dramatic play between 'pro-gang' and 'anti-gang' interests" (132). Oulanoff fails to recognize that the very existence of the love triangles involving Ekaterina Ivanovna constitutes an "anti-gang" force, for it interferes with the orderly operations of the criminal group.

18 For a longer discussion of the sexual and sacrificial motifs in this story, see chapter 2.

19 Such scenes in Babel's work are not limited to *Red Cavalry*. In "Our Father Makhno's" ("U bat'ki nashego Makhno"), the story centers on the gang rape of Rukhlya, a young Jewish girl by six anarchist soldiers. As in "At Saint Valentine's," the narrator's political sympathies side with the soldiers (it is he who calls Makhno "ours"), and his account appears entirely dispassionate: "I decided to find out what a woman looks like after a rape that has been repeated six times" (1: 110). Like Sashka, Rukhlya "stinks like freshly chopped meat," and their encounters with their attackers are both described in terms of horseback riding: Vasya Kurdyukov mounts Sashka and shakes as though "in the saddle" (2: 87), while Rukhlya walks like a "cavalryman who has just set his swollen feet on the ground after a long crossing" (1: 111). In both stories, the men are accompanied by a young boy who travels with the soldiers and wants to "join the fun": Kurdyukov in "At Saint Valentine's" and Kikin in "Makhno." Kikin, who held Rukhlya down for his six comrades, refrained from raping her only because he knew that one of the soldiers had a venereal disease; as if to compensate himself for this inconvenience, he humiliates Rukhlya by describing the rape to her the next day as she tries to work.

20 There is no doubt that Babel was familiar with Gorky's story. In the 26 Aug. 1920 entry of his wartime diary, Babel describes a woman who has slept with every soldier in the brigade. Babel's laconic comment: "The sister—26 and 1" (1: 422). That Gorky's work might serve as a model for Babel's should be no surprise, as Babel's admiration for Gorky is well known. On more than one occasion, Babel credits Gorky with inspiring him to "go to the people" and become a war correspondent, making him, in a sense, the godfather of the *Red Cavalry* stories ("Nachalo" 2: 369; "Vystuplenie na zasedanii sekretariata fosp" (2: 373). In 1937, Babel wrote an article praising Gorky in a special issue of *SSSR na stroike* (2: 364–65). Gorky defended Babel in print against Budyonny's denunciation of *Red Cavalry* (*Pravda*, 27 Nov. 1926). Gorky's and Babel's correspondence can be found in volume 70 of *Literaturnoe nasledstvo*. For an analysis of the intertextual links between Babel and Gorky, see Zholkovsky ("Topos" 157–73).

21 The connection between women and counterrevolution appears again in "Betrayal" ("Izmena"), also narrated by Balmashev. Here Balmashev and two wounded comrades refuse to shed their uniforms for hospital gowns, despite the insistence of the nurses. The nurses nonetheless remove the men's army clothes as they are sleeping, causing the patients to go on a rampage. In "Salt," women and counterrevolution become practi-

cally one and the same thing. In the second story, women become so thoroughly identified with treachery that "betrayal" is personified as a woman in the last two paragraphs: "Betrayal . . . laughs at us from the window, betrayal walks barefoot in our house, betrayal has hung her boots over her shoulder, so that the floorboards won't creak in the house it's robbing" (2: 117). The identification of woman with counterrevolution in both stories is, of course, satirical; by presenting such a viewpoint in Balmashev's substandard language, Babel implicitly identifies this point of view with ignorance and poor education.

22 Babel's exploration of the fratricidal metaphor is discussed in the following chapter.
23 More precisely, this is the time span between the one-day revolt of 1917 and 10 Mar. 1921, the exact midpoint of the second uprising (Poulin 515).
24 Here it should be noted that none of the family relationships are made clear immediately; when the young woman arrives on the scene, the group says that the blood on the floor belongs to her "brother / or husband" (Khlebnikov 321). As a rule, the revolutionary marauders who encounter families in the literature of the civil war period display an almost willful disregard for the specifics of family ties; see, for example, the discussion in chapter 2 of Lyutov's confusion about the structure of the Jewish family he encounters in "Crossing the Zbrucz."
25 In Babel's story "There Were Nine of Them," one of the Cossacks takes a prisoner's shirt before shooting him. In *Chevengur*, Sasha Dvanov is shot by a band of anarchists, and the near-death experience he undergoes after this penetration causes him to ejaculate. When Nikita, the man who shot him, realizes Dvanov is still alive, he asks him to remove his clothes before Nikita finishes the job. Dvanov readily obliges, and Nikita even helps him with his pants. But Nikita is disappointed to discover that Dvanov has wet himself, and complains that most of his victims similarly spoil their clothes during execution. Only one local commissar left behind clean underwear: "He was a special man!" (Platonov, *Chevengur* 102). For more on this scene, see chapter 6. It should be noted that the stripping of victims is, like the frequency with which men sleep in groups in *Red Cavalry*, a "neutral" fact of life in the civil war that can nonetheless take on an erotic dimension when brought into the realm of literature.
26 This is not to say that a woman cannot become a Christlike martyr; rather, the woman who does so is obliged to cross gender lines.
27 Khlebnikov's use of the icon of Christ once again connects "Night Search" to "The Twelve." In the final lines of "The Twelve," Christ is shown to be at the head of the marauding band of revolutionary soldiers. Masing-Delic argues that "[I]n the androgynous Christ of the Twelve, the murdered Katka is resurrected together with her murderer Petrukha in ultimate perfect union. The fact that Katka forms part of [the] immortal Christ is shown by the pearl imagery of the poem, Katka having 'pearly' teeth and Christ being adorned by snow pearls . . . Thus her resurrection in Christ 'resolves' the ethical problems raised by her murder. Her death, as it turns out, is entirely positive, since it allows the Red Guard apostles to carry out a task of which she is the major beneficiary" (Masing-Delic 213–14). Whether or not one completely accepts Masing-

Delic's conclusion, her emphasis on both the ambivalence and the androgyny of the Christ image in Blok is also appropriate for the Christ icon in Khlebnikov.

28 This is, of course, from the point of view of the male group, rather than Khlebnikov (or, for that matter, Babel): certainly the women in "Night Search" are sympathetic characters.

29 I am grateful to Elisa Shorofskaia Frost for bringing the function of the *khoziaika* ("hostess" or "landlady") in Russian literature to my attention.

30 One recalls Dostoevsky's parody of "progressive" social thinking in *Crime and Punishment*; when Raskolnikov visits his friend Razumikhin not long after murdering Alyona Ivanovna and her sister, Razumikhin has just begun a translation of the German tract *Is Woman Human?* (*Chelovek li zhenshchina*). The German's answer is yes, but he comes to his conclusion only after long deliberations and proofs.

31 "Men were bonded together by their sexual contact with this single female; instances of female 'bonding' through sexual contact with the same man are rarer." Naiman's primary example is Vadim Okhremenko's "The Crime of Kirik Basenko" (1926), in which the title character attempts to convince his lover to sleep with other Komsomol members in order to induce an abortion (*Sex in Public* 280).

32 Here I have in mind the standard litany of such works that, despite their moralizing tone, were condemned for their "cynicism": Panteleimon Romanov's "Without Cherry Blossom," Lev Gumilevsky's *Dog Alley*, and Sergei Malashkin's *The Moon from the Right Side*, all published in 1926. For more on the reaction to these publications, see Naiman (*Sex in Public* 99–108) and Stites (*Women's Liberation Movement* 359–62).

33 For a more extensive discussion of necrophilia in *Chevengur*, see chapter 6.

34 Andrei Platonov, *Chevengur* (Moscow: Vysshaia shkola, 1991). All references to Platonov will use this edition.

35 Eric Naiman argues convincingly that Platonov's conception of utopia depends on a "negation, or nonrecognition, of sexual urges . . . If Platonov is repeatedly compelled to excise sexuality from his utopia, it is only because sexuality is implicitly, essentially present within it" (Naiman, "Andrej Platonov" 319).

36 See chapter 6 for a more extensive discussion of homoeroticism in *Chevengur*.

37 The Chevengurian love of comradeship and hostility to women have been noted throughout the critical literature on the novel. See Langerak ("Andrei Platonov v perelomnom periode" 318), Naiman ("Thematic Mythology," 207), Osipovich (72–102), Paramonov (332–87), Piskunova and Piskunov (20), Semenova ("'Tainoe tainykh'" 105–109), Teskey (52–76), and Tolstaia-Segal ("Ideologicheskie konteksty" 253–56).

38 Osipovich calls Klavdyusha the "Judas of Chevengur who betrays the principal values of proletarian ethics—comradeship and hatred of private property" (Osipovich 73). Günther, however, sees in Klavdyusha a different biblical parallel, as the Virgin Mary to Prokofy's John the Baptist and Chepurny's Christ. According to Günther, Klavdyusha represents a compromised incarnation of the communist future (Günther 264).

39 There are, of course, some notable exceptions. Vsevolod Vishnevsky's popular play *An Optimistic Tragedy* (1933) features a female commissar in charge of a boat full of revo-

lutionary sailors. The stage is set for a misogynist drama similar to the texts discussed above; after first meeting the commissar, the sailors even lightheartedly discuss chopping her up and throwing her overboard. But revolutionary consciousness wins out (this tragedy is, after all, an optimistic one), and when the commissar dies a martyr's death at the end of the play, she is mourned by all her comrades.

2. DEAD FATHERS AND SONS

I am grateful to Clare Cavanagh for bringing the epigraph quote to my attention.

1   See, for example, Kornblatt and Andrew.
2   The role of the horse, as well as its relationship to masculinity, has been particularly well covered in Babel criticism. For reasons of space, I have confined my observations about horses to those stories where the man-horse bond has a direct bearing on the cycle's central character, Lyutov.
3   With two exceptions, all of the *Red Cavalry* stories were first published between 1923 and 1926, appearing in book form in May 1926. "Argamak" was published in 1932 and was included by the author in the seventh and eighth editions of the book. "The Kiss" appeared in 1937, and though he apparently planned to include it somewhere in the *Red Cavalry* cycle, Babel's arrest in 1938 put a halt to subsequent editions of the author's work. All but one of the posthumous editions of *Red Cavalry* in both Russia and the West end with "Argamak"; the 1990 two-volume *Collected Works* edition ends with "The Kiss."

The history of *Red Cavalry*'s publication is unusually complex; for a detailed examination of the textological questions surrounding the book, see S. Povartsov's commentary to the 1990 edition of Babel's works, Livshits, Grongaard, and the *Voprosy literatury* round table "How I. Babel Was, Is, and Should Be Published," especially V. Kovskii's "Sud'ba tekstov v kontekste sud'by" (23–78). Kovskii and Sarnov disagree about the significance of the changes in *Red Cavalry* required by the censors; Sarnov provides a long list of intriguing examples of political and sexual material that was removed from Babel's stories (88–91).
4   This fact has been noted by Carol Avins (695).
5   Violence in Babel's work is not restricted to the context of the family. In "Guy de Maupassant," Babel writes that "[n]o iron can pierce the human heart as coldly as a well-placed period" (2: 219). This quote is usually interpreted purely on the level of Babel's aesthetics and stylistics, but it also establishes connections between the text, the body, and violence. Babel's prose yields both exquisite sentences and dead bodies with equal mastery. For examinations of the question of violence in Babel's work, see Andrew (passim), Edward Brown (passim), chapters 4 and 5 of Carden's *Art of Isaac Babel*, Ehre (82–84), Kornblatt (118–23), Luplow's *Isaac Babel's "Red Cavalry"* (16–20), O'Connor (passim), Sicher's *Style and Structure* (39–47, 90–94), and Stine (passim).
6   According to Ehre, the male-centered ethos of *Red Cavalry* is reflected in the cycle's style: "Babel's epic manner is aggressively masculine" (68).

7 Kornblatt observes that despite the misogyny of Cossack fictional characters, "Cossacks did marry and have children, who themselves became Cossacks by birth rather than choice. It is the choice itself, however, that makes a Cossack authentic" (66).
8 For a discussion of *Taras Bulba* as an example of the Cossack myth, see Kornblatt (49–60).
9 One could make a case for the presence of even more fathers in the first half of the cycle. The fifth and seventh stories, "Pan Apolek" and "Gedali," both feature men who, both for their age and for their spiritual searching, could conceivably be called father figures for Lyutov. Lyutov, however, is no Kavalerov, nor is he a Dvanov: though he seeks out the company of both Gedali and Apolek, he does not spend his life looking for new fathers.
10 Literally, "Sashka the Christ."
11 Even potential father figures, such as the brigade or division commanders, are far removed from the paternal realm by the cycle's end. As more and more soldiers die, the commanders get younger and younger. Baulin, the Squadron commander of "Argamak," is "just a boy in years" (2: 130).
12 Nakhimovsky (71) notes that the Jews in *Red Cavalry* "are never 'we' outright, though even early on they are sometimes 'my' Jews."
13 Isaak Babel', *Sochineniia*, vol. 2 (Moscow: Khudozhestvennaia literatura, 1990), 7. All references to the author's texts use this edition and will be cited by page and volume number only. All translations are my own.
14 Babel uses the word *monastyr'*, which can be either a monastery or a convent. Since the word for buckwheat is a feminine noun in Russian, and since it is described as virginal, "convent" seems more appropriate here.
15 The woman never uses the informal *papa* to describe her father; rather, she chooses the less emotional, but perhaps more dignified, *otets*.
16 Jan van der Eng interprets the question more broadly, finding that it "directs the reader to a universal problem . . . : the deficiency of human existence, the frustration of human desires and emotions, the irreplaceableness of what is dearest to man and taken by death" ("The Pointed Conclusion" 587). I hope to show, however, that it is no accident that this "universal problem" is embodied in the corpse of the father.
17 Despite Babel's repeated appeals to the epic tradition in general and the Homeric tradition in particular, the problem of fathers is presented in a particularly "Jewish" manner: it is not a "father quest," but a "father question." The Jewish woman's words recall the question-and-answer format of traditional Jewish religious instruction, which we will see once again in "The Rabbi."
18 Instead, the commander finds Lyutov when he hears Lyutov cry out after being startled.
19 Benya, Levka, and Dvoyre Krik flirt with parricide in both versions of Babel's "Sunset" ("Zakat"). Their father, Mendel, survives their combined attack, but he is reduced to a figurehead in the family he once ruled with an iron hand.
20 As Carden notes, all of the stories told by a narrator other than Lyutov are related to violence (119).

21 Brodal notes the "similarity between the nature of the General [Denikin] and that of the Father, both being representatives of the old order and of an authoritarian way of life" (31).
22 His name also serves as a connection with Nikitinsky in "The Life of Pavlichenko, Matvei Rodionovich," the story immediately following "Sashka Christ." When Nikitinsky tells Pavlichenko that he has "messed up all your mothers," he uses the verb *tarakanit'*, whose root also means "cockroach." Nikitinsky steals the hero's wife and insults his mother, while Tarakanych has long since displaced Sashka's absent father and now threatens to "defile" Sashka's mother. Tarakanych considers this his right and will not tolerate any interference from Sashka.
23 This point is often lost on critics of *Red Cavalry*, who tend to ascribe to Sashka purer motives than the evidence suggests. Brodal praises Sashka for maintaining his "spiritual integrity" in the face of the "stupidity and recklessness" of the older generation. He admits that "Sashka's choice involves treachery against his mother" but is convinced that Sashka is "only making the best of a bad situation, because his step-father would in the long run have forced his mother to have intercourse whatever action Sashka had taken" (31–32). There is, however, no evidence that any such consideration entered Sashka's mind. Sashka was making the best of a bad situation, but he took the path of self-interest over selflessness.

In the critical literature, Sashka Christ has a reputation for selflessness that must be reexamined. In his new life he does bring what Zsuzsa Hetényi calls "spiritual consolation," but with it he also spreads his disease ("Eskadronnaia dama" 168). In "The Song," Sashka offers comfort to the old woman Lyutov has been threatening, even going to bed with her. Upon reading that story, it is tempting to see Sashka's action as one of charity, but one must remember the events of "Sashka Christ." By the end of the story, Sashka has most likely given the woman syphilis.
24 Carden observes that the "hero figures" of Babel's stories are "without psychology" (107).
25 See Trilling and Andrew.
26 The words describing Lyutov's heart (*skripelo i teklo*) echo the fate of the goose's head, which "cracked and bled" (*tresnula i potekla*). Milton Ehre finds that the author's "choice of words points to an identification with the victim that is at the root of Lyutov's conflict" (82).
27 James Falen breaks with earlier criticism of the story when he finds that the "initiation" in *Red Cavalry* has limited effect: "As an initiatory ritual of blood sacrifice, the narrator's action has been facile, cheap, and even perverse. The young hero has faced no monstrous dragon, only a goose, and the killing is linked to a grim, repressed sexuality." Falen suggests that the killing of the bird represents "self-mutilation" rather than "the attainment of manhood" (144). Though he is absolutely correct to point out the ineffectiveness of the "initiation," I must disagree with him about Lyutov's "self-mutilation." One can agree with Andrew's statement that the goose symbolizes, among many other things, the passive side of Lyutov's own personality (Andrew, "Babel's 'My

First Goose'" 76), but such an identification does not entail self-mutilation. If there is any way in which Lyutov is punishing or hurting himself, it is in forcing himself to act completely antithetically to his own nature. If one must search for a dramatic metaphor, the action is more self-rape than self-mutilation. Peter Stine calls the killing of the goose "a violation of the soul" (241). Lyutov's crushing of the goose's neck calls to mind Vladimir Mayakovsky's later assertion in his uncompleted "At the Top of My Voice": "I have stepped on the throat of my own song." Such a connection is purely coincidental, but it does point to the nature of Lyutov's action: forcing himself to go against the grain.

28 As mentioned in the introduction, Tiger asserts that "the male bond selection . . . is functionally equivalent and analogous to mate selection in the reproductive sphere" (135). Tiger pays particular attention to initiation ceremonies, which "symbolize a concern men have with the qualities of courage, competence, and loyalty, of the young who will be their colleagues and successors." Such concern is "akin to the preference men have for women thought lovely by the community, or women who are talented, or powerful, wealthy, good mothers and wives" (142). Tiger then gives several examples of male-male "courtship" in initiations, from street gangs to fraternities. The initiations Tiger describes, however, are all successful, and thus Tiger does not discuss long, protracted "courtships" like that of Lyutov and the Cossacks.

29 Lyutov watches what may be an attempted rape of the female nurse Sashka, but he makes no comment and none of the participants give any sign that they are aware of his presence ("At Saint Valentine's") ("U sviatogo Valenta") (2: 87). The narrator of "First Love" ("Pervaia liubov'") first observes the romantic interplay between the dominant Galya and her submissive husband, then sees his father humiliated by a Cossack (2: 154). In "The Crack" ("V shchelochku"), the protagonist pays a landlady for the privilege of spying on a prostitute and her clients while hiding on a staircase (1: 71–72). For more on scopophilia in Babel's works, see Zholkovsky and Iampolskii (74–75; 285–316).

30 Carden suggests a similar connection, but between the horse and the reader rather than the horse and Lyutov: "the story is a psychological weapon directed at the reader to force him to attend to the claims of Dyakov's virtuosity" (41).

31 Later, in "The Story of A Horse," Savitsky's effeminate qualities will be exaggerated as he is found to be living in a very un-Cossack-like domestic setting. But at this point neither the reader nor Lyutov knows that Savitsky will be guilty of behavior unbecoming a Cossack; in "My First Goose," Savitsky is a rugged specimen of Cossack manhood, one before whom Lyutov feels envy and attraction.

32 In Babel's war diaries, when describing the love affair between a young Jewish woman and Prishchepa, a Cossack soldier, Babel writes, "who can understand her soul better than I?" (*komu ee dusha poniatnee, chem mne?*) (1: 387; Nakhimovsky 80).

33 The term *laska* ("tenderness," "caress") is difficult to translate in this context; Walter Morison's rendition of the line drains it of all sexual ambiguity: "you'll have the boys patting you on the back" (Babel, *Collected Stories* [1955] 74), while David McDuff's

version goes to the opposite extreme: "our fighting lads will give you a fond caress" (Babel, *Collected Stories* [1994] 120).

34 This has been noted by Efraim Sicher (*Style and Structure* 87–89).

35 According to Nakhimovsky, "My First Goose" would appear earlier in the collection if chronology were the organizing principle of *Red Cavalry*. Instead, the story comes between "Gedali" and "The Rebbe," two stories that are strongly linked in terms of time and content (94).

36 This approach is adopted by Jovanovic and Iribarne. Nakhimovsky asserts that the "fullness of life is associated with Cossacks, the whiff of death with Jews" (71). Not all evaluations of the Cossack-Jewish dichotomy are as favorable to the gentiles. In his infamous anti-Semitic tract *Russophobia* (*Rusofobia*), Igor Shafarevich asserts that "[c]ontempt and distaste for Russians, Ukrainians, and Poles as not-quite-human beings of a lower order are felt in every story of I. Babel's *Red Cavalry*" (467).

37 Otto Weininger's *Sex and Character* was translated into Russian in the first decade of the twentieth century, and the misogyny and anti-Semitism of his theory were discussed in reviews by Gippius, Bely, Platonov, and Rozanov. Rozanov found the book flawed but, writing in 1913 and 1915, approved of the identification of Jews with women: "the womanish nature of Jew is my *idée fixe*" (Rozanov, *Sochineniia* 98).

38 This characterization of the Sabbath puts Lyutov implicitly on the side of Ilya, since each is a Sabbath-breaker. Though Lyutov does nothing to offend his hosts in "The Rebbe," the first paragraph of "The Rebbe's Son" is the metaphorical equivalent of Ilya's chain-smoking. Ilya profanes the laws of the Sabbath by smoking, whereas Lyutov degrades the idea of the Sabbath by turning "her" into a merciless woman in red, high-heeled shoes.

39 Nakhimovsky connects "fecundity" with "gentile sexuality" in *Red Cavalry*, whereas Jews are associated with morbidity (89–90). This opposition does roughly correspond to the imagery surrounding Jews and gentiles in the cycle, but, as the examples listed above demonstrate, fertility in *Red Cavalry* is more often described in negative rather than positive terms.

40 Maurice Friedberg views Ilya's death as both the end of one line and the beginning of another: "if the death of Ilya Bratslavsky marks the end of an old Hasidic dynasty, it may also be interpreted as the death of the *founder* of a *new* dynasty of *Communist* Bratslavskys" (196, emphasis in the original). Friedberg's terminology ("dynasty") fails to differentiate between the filiative line of Hasidism and the affiliative bonds of communism, but so do Babel's own words ("brother"). To refer to Ilya's new "dynasty" as communist, however, oversimplifies the complex "middle path" shown by Ilya's example.

41 Babel's later work, with the exception of the childhood stories, continues this trend. "Sunset" leaves the patriarch of the Krik family thoroughly humiliated. By the end of "Maria," the Mukovin family has been evicted from its apartment, though the family that settles there is pointedly fertile and prosperous.

42 Thus here I must take issue with Nakhimovsky's assertion that Lyutov's identification of Ilya as "my brother" is a sign of the narrator's growing identification with Jewishness (71). Rather, Ilya is Lyutov's "brother" precisely because neither man belongs in a world that is exclusively Jewish or exclusively Cossack and revolutionary.
43 Maguire calls this approach "the way of qualified commitment" (328).
44 Here it should be noted that Ilya reconciles masculinity and femininity as well. Physically, he is androgynous, with the face of a nun (2: 35) and weak, bare knees like those of an old woman (2: 129).
45 For a more detailed interpretation of Ilya's Hebrew name, see Friedberg (196).
46 The role of Vasily had been largely ignored before Carol Avins's 1994 article on *Red Cavalry* and Babel's 1920 diary. Avins and I have independently drawn primarily the same conclusions about Vasily's role as a third "brother," although Avins also makes the intriguing case that Vasily, like Lyutov, is a Jew masquerading as a Russian. See Avins (707–8).
47 In his description of that night, he quotes "The Rebbe" word for word: "*Za oknom rzhali koni i vskrikivali kazaki. Pustynia voiny zevala za oknom*" (2: 37, 128).
48 "*Pomnish' li ty Zhitomir, Vasilii? Pomnish' li ty Tererev, Vasilii*"; "*Pomnish' li ty etu noch', Vasilii*"; "*I vot tret' ego dnia, Vasilii*"; "*Ia uznal ego totchas, Vazilii*" (2: 128–29).
49 Metaphorical brotherhood is also a hallmark of military comradeship. "Comrades," Gray tells us, "love one another like brothers" (89).
50 This resembles the "successful" resolution of the oedipal complex: rather than literally "taking the father's place" in his own family, the boy grows up and "takes the place of the father" in a new family unit that he himself will start.
51 Here *Red Cavalry* represents numerous forms of popular entertainment, including the television program "M.A.S.H." (which itself lasted several years longer than the American participation in the Korean War). For a fascinating discussion of the narrative devices that make such temporal "distortions" possible, see Morson's *Narrative and Freedom*.
52 I must, however, agree with Luplow and Nakhimovsky that "Argamak" does not have to be accepted as the capstone of the cycle. Nakhimovsky notes that the story is a "chronological anomaly" and "does not add anything new in a substantive way, since the theme of acceptance and assimilation is already present" (233n87). Luplow questions whether the story might have been "added for reasons of political pressure" rather than owing to Babel's desire to have the cycle end "more optimistically" (116n24).
53 A similar folkloric inconsistency can be found in Babel's "Benya Krik" cycle, in which the gangster Benya marries two different women in two different stories without any implications of divorce or bigamy.

3. THE FAMILY MEN OF YURI OLESHA

The source of the epigraph is Iurii Olesha, *Povesti i rasskazy* (Moscow: Khudozhestvennaia literatura, 1956), 282. The lack of a "collected works" edition of Olesha's writing presents a problem for scholars discussing his work. Whenever possible, any citations of Olesha's short stories or articles will refer to this edition, abbreviated within the text as "PR." All translations are my own.

1. William Harkins's 1966 article "The Theme of Sterility in Olesha's *Envy*" was the first to analyze the role of fathers in Olesha's work, though Robert A. Maguire arrived at similar conclusions independently in his 1968 study *Red Virgin Soil*. Elizabeth Klosty Beaujour's 1970 *The Invisible Land* continues Harkins's argument. Andrew Barrat examines the ideological implications of the father-son conflict in his 1981 monograph *Yurii Olesha's "Envy."* Their approaches to the problem will be discussed later in this chapter.

2. "Legend" first appeared in *Oktiabr'skaia gazeta* on 8 Nov. 1927, a month after its completion (Badikov 438). Although it has been reprinted several times since its original publication, it was left out of the 1956 *Povesti i rasskazy* edition of Olesha's work and is thus absent from the Ardis *Complete Short Stories*. Perhaps its omission from the more standard collections explains why this remarkable story, so rich in psychological implications and so Kafkaesque in theme and structure, has drawn little attention from either Western or Soviet critics. The most detailed analysis of "Legend" was made by Burdin ("Chelovek i mir"), whose work with drafts of the story is invaluable. In the present book, all references to the text use the 1988 *Izbrannoe* edition (99–101), abbreviated "I."

3. Olesha, unlike his narrators, had a sister, though she died when he was still young (Olesha, *Zavist', Tri tolstiaka, Ni dnia bez strochki* [Moscow: Khudozhestvennaia literatura, 1989], 330. All subsequent references to either *Envy* or *No Day without a Line* will use this edition.).

4. For a discussion of Olesha as autobiographer, see Beaujour's "Imagination of Failure." As Beaujour demonstrates, Olesha fictionalizes his autobiography. One can argue that his representation of his own childhood in *No Day without a Line* was influenced by his earlier semi-autobiographical stories such as "Human Material."

5. All the same, the names Olesha gives his protagonists are often significant; certainly, the root of "Babichev" has been noted repeatedly, as has "Kavalerov." Examination of drafts of his work shows that he often went through several different names before settling upon the one by which his characters would be called. Valya, for example, was originally to be named Lelya Tatarnikova (Shitareva 83). The fact that he gave essentially the same name to two characters in two different stories could be purely coincidental, but given Olesha's preoccupation with both the semantic and acoustic properties of his character's names, some kind of connection might well have been intended.

6. This emphasis on vision is one of the many features Olesha shares with Babel. Both authors create protagonists whose reliance on vision and observation underscores their passivity and emphasizes their distance from the objects of their gaze.

7. Volodya's letter is intercepted by Kavalerov, who thinks he has retrieved his own message to Babichev. Kavalerov's letter is thus left behind at Babichev's apartment, but

at no point in the narrative is there any indication that anyone has actually read it. Kavalerov's letter is not a means of communication, but a function of the novel's narrative and Kavalerov's own psychological needs. The letter advances the plot by explicitly laying out Kavalerov's challenge to authority, at the same time satisfying Kavalerov's own desire to verbally abuse Babichev on paper. The novel's narration creates the illusion of communication between Kavalerov and Babichev, but most of Kavalerov's "speeches" to Babichev are left unspoken. If the story were told from Andrei's point of view, the reader would hear no more than a few words from Kavalerov.

8   This issue is developed in more detail in Olesha's other stories of childhood. The very title "Human Material" refers in part to the son's relation to the paternal model. Dosya is expected to live according to his father's "plan," which consists of the father's own unachieved goals that must be fulfilled by the son. Fathers, grandfathers, and older brothers form a "gallery of examples" (*galereia-primerov*) that Dosya and his fellow schoolboys must imitate. If Dosya does not want to be like these "model men" (*liudi-obraztsy*), his opinion has no value, for "Papa knows exactly how I must live in order to be happy . . . This plan is considered the best, and I have no right to discuss it" (PR 242). It is the father's ambitions that Dosya must fulfill. Dosya must succeed where his father has failed, continuing the work of his father's plan.

The narrator of Olesha's autobiographical novel was equally constrained by his father's ambitions. *No Day without a Line* describes a time in Olesha's boyhood when his father brings him to the barber, saying "Give the heir a haircut!" (*Postrigite naslenika!*). This lighthearted phrase, which was apparently not even original with Olesha's father, leaves a lasting impression on the boy: "This was oppressive to hear. And, for some reason, shameful. And for some reason I still remember this burden. What kind of heir am I? Heir to what? I knew that Papa was poor. Heir to what? To Papa himself, a repetition of Papa?" (111).

9   For a discussion of the links between Fyodorov and Platonov, see Bethea, Seifrid, Semenova (*Nikolai Fedorov*), Teskey, and Tolstaia-Segal.

10 The furniture in Kavalerov's life is more hostile, actively tripping him rather than merely forcing him in a particular direction.

11 In his article "Yuri Olesha's Three Ages of Man: A Close Reading of 'Liompa,'" Andrew Barrat finds that the central theme of "Liompa" is "the problem of how man assigns meaning to the phenomena of the physical world" (599). Barrat's article is perhaps the most complete and original treatment of Olesha's short story. Further relevant discussion of the story can be found in Harkins ("The Philosophical Stories of Iurii Olesha," 1966) and Ingdahl ("The Life/Death Dichotomy in Jurij Olesha's Short Story 'Liompa,'" 1982).

12 Nils Ake Nilsson's 1965 "Through the Wrong End of Binoculars" was the first in-depth study of vision and perspective in Olesha's work. Nilsson remarks that Olesha's world is never straightforward, but instead always caught in "distorted glimpses . . . through glass windows and bars" or "enlarged or diminished through binoculars, telescopes, or microscopes" (40). Other critics since Nilsson, Beaujour included, have expanded

on his observations. The most provocative work is that of Neil Cornwell, who finds that distortion in *Envy* is a "formula" in which the exterior world or memories of the past become transformed by the artist, "colliding with reality and emerging invariably in a distorted, grotesque, or parodistic version of the original idea" ("Principle of Distortion" 29). The result for the artist is usually disillusionment.

13   Thus, when *Envy* begins to follow the perspective of Ivan Babichev, one of the novel's primary father figures, the narration moves from first person to third. This is consistent with the rest of Olesha's work: every one of his first-person stories is told from the point of view of either a child or a childlike adult. Kolya and Dosya, who narrate three stories between them, are both literally sons. The narrator of "The Chain" ("Tsep'") is a little boy. Kavalerov is the figurative son of both Babichev brothers. Fedya, the narrator of "The Cherry Pit" ("Vishnevaia kostochka"), is the young, defeated rival of the older Boris Mikhailovich. The fellow traveler Zand is a childless adult who is strongly attached to his mother. Olesha does have some older protagonists, even fathers (the professor in "Natasha," for example), but none of them serves as narrator.

14   All of the three statements concern death: "—*Kolia, bud' gordym. My umrem, kak dvoriane.*" "—*Pododi,—prodolzhal otets,—seichas ia vyidu. My umrem vmeste.*" (I 100). "—*Zastegnist' na vse pugovitsy,—prikazal on mne. . . .—Vstretim smert' dostoino*" (I 101).

15   Kavalerov's emotional backwardness has been treated by a wide range of scholars. Harkins finds that Kavalerov's love of beds and sleep is indicative of a desire to "return to childhood" ("Theme of Sterility" 451). Beaujour discusses childishness throughout her study, especially in reference to Fedya of "The Cherry Pit" (*Invisible Land* 18). The predominance of a child's-eye view is part of the focus of Victor Peppard's study of Olesha's "poetics of dialogue" (*Poetics* 98), while Richard Borden asserts that childhood and a child's perspective are at the heart of the greater part of Olesha's metaphors, often providing "a means of 'escape' to childhood from threatening adult situations" ("Magic and Politics" 168). Borden also finds that the conflict between Olesha's protagonists and a "threatening adult world" reflect "the awkward relationship of an entire generation of intellectuals with the new social order."

16   Olesha himself resented the suggestion that he looked like his father. In *No Day without a Line*, he writes: "When I was a child, everyone said I looked like my father. But when I had already, as it were, learned to look in a mirror—I, on the contrary, saw a resemblance to my mother, and not my father. When I told people about my discovery, they laughed at me . . . All the same, little by little others started to exclaim, 'He looks like his mother!'" (117). He claims that this resemblance grew more pronounced as he matured and came nearer to the age of first love. From then on, "I could only imagine myself looking like my mother" (118). Though physical resemblance to the father is usually threatening in Olesha's work, there is one exception to the rule. In "From the Notebooks of Fellow Traveler Zand," the title character laments that he looks so much like his mother: "How can one be a strong man and look like one's mother?" (I 170). Zand, unlike Kolya in "Legend," worries that he is effeminate. Zand is by no means the

only Olesha character to feel inadequate as a man, but he is the only one to assert that he looks like his mother. When Kolya and Kavalerov distance themselves from their fathers, neither one claims a resemblance to his mother.

17 Milton Ehre finds that this passage signifies not only a "biological pessimism" about aging and paternity, but also Kavalerov's desire to "become a man and enter the world of the parents, to partake of their power" ("Olesha's *Zavist'*" 604–5). Certainly Kavalerov's narration is marked by an ambivalent attitude toward adulthood and parents, but the passage about Kavalerov's father is unequivocally negative.

18 Again, Harkins's "Theme of Sterility" was the first article to explore this aspect of Anechka's character. Barrat (*Yurii Olesha's "Envy"*), Beaujour (*Invisible Land*), and Maguire all continue this approach in their respective studies.

19 This bed, according to William Harkins, "is at once the goal of Kavalerov's yearnings and the symbol of his fears of and disgust at sexuality," serving as a "vaginal symbol" due to its "implicit connection with its owner and its function in the sexual act" (451).

20 Though Anechka's widowhood might lead one to believe she is an old woman, she is only forty-five years old (21).

21 Kavalerov's frustration has its parallel in the great twentieth-century novel of paternity, Joyce's *Ulysses*. Whereas the cuckolded Bloom learns to accept his place as one in a long line of men in Molly's bed, neither the first nor the last, Kavalerov is inconsolable. Ivan's toast to indifference and his suggestion that they share Anechka has more in common with the spirit of Bloom's resignation with his lot, though Ivan's defeat is far more total than Bloom's. Both Bloom and Ivan have lost their children before the action of their respective novels, one to death, the other to ideological enemies. Bloom ends his day by bringing home his newfound "son" Stephen Daedalus and finds himself more at ease both as father and as husband. Ivan's surrogate son rejects him, but they still find themselves in the same apartment at the novel's close. Both have come to stay with Anechka, just as Stephen and Bloom come home to the moonlike gravitational pull of Molly.

22 According to Beaujour, "[i]t is really Andrei, not Ivan, who has invented himself," despite Ivan's assertion to the contrary (*"Ia sam sebia vydumal"*). This is why Volodya and Valya choose him as a father and "reduce their natural parents to the status of mere 'relatives'" (Beaujour, "On Choosing One's Ancestors" 26). I would add that the qualities that draw Volodya and Valya to Andrei hold an equal fascination for Kavalerov.

23 Andrei, by contrast, is connected with glass that blinds, rather than reflects. When Andrei turns toward Kavalerov in the airport, the latter is horrified to see that, instead of eyes, Babichev has only "the two dull, mercurially shining badges of his pince-nez" (32). Andrei's eyes are hidden from Ivan as well. When Ivan asks his brother how he can allow Volodya to insult him, Ivan only sees the sheen of Andrei's glasses (60). In each case, Andrei denies familial and pseudo-familial bonds, rejecting both his brother and the man he took in from the street.

24 This trait of Ivan's has its parallel in *The Three Fat Men* (*Tri tolstiaka*), in which the mythical kingdom's rulers completely control the life of their adopted heir Tutti. They

determine what Tutti may and may not see and forbid him to play with other children. In attempting to remake the boy in their own image, they go to the grotesque extreme of convincing him that his natural heart has been replaced by one made of iron. This in turn is reminiscent of Volodya's desire to stamp out "petty feelings" by becoming a human machine, and of Ivan's attribution of his imaginary machine with human emotions.

25 Olesha's characterization of the sausage as a "bride" is one of the novel's many elements that clearly allude to the works of Nikolai Gogol. Akaky Akakievich's overcoat is cherished and desired much like a bride, while the scene in which Kavalerov considers throwing away the sausage while carrying it across Moscow is reminiscent of Ivan Yakovlevich's attempt to dispose of the human nose that has mysteriously appeared in one of his wife's pies. I am grateful to Thomas Seifrid for pointing out this connection.

26 One might argue that the sausage is both phallic and excremental; Zholkovsky notes its anal and phallic imagery without seeing the two terms as mutually exclusive (Zholkovsky 197).

27 Of course, this formulation breaks down when Shapiro and Babichev cook the sausage on the grill and eat it, but so too (one hopes) does the excremental reading. Such a collapse of symbolism is inevitable to any psychoanalytic treatment of a literary text, since a good author's symbols doggedly refuse to be tied to just one interpretation. Whatever other associations the sausage might suggest, for the purpose of the novel's narration it still has to function as food. To paraphrase a statement often attributed to Freud, sometimes a sausage is just a sausage.

28 The elder Makarov merits only occasional brief mentions in *Envy*: Andrei mentions that Volodya is visiting his father in Murom (17), where the latter works in locomotive construction (73). Apparently Volodya's father knows and approves of his son's living arrangements, for Volodya writes in his letter to Andrei, "*Papasha klianiaetsia tebe*" (44). His words are a standard greeting, but more formal than necessary. Volodya's father is disposed of in one short sentence, using a phrase that connotes respect and literally means, "Dad bows down to you." This brief reference establishes that although Volodya's father is still among the living (Olesha does not share Platonov's predilection for orphans), Andrei Babichev is above him in the paternal hierarchy.

29 Because of the complexities of Olesha's narrative, it would be a mistake to accept Andrei's monologue as completely unmediated. Though the second half of the novel is related by a third-person narrator, the reader is nonetheless presented with a series of subjective viewpoints filtered through a supposedly objective narrator.

30 "*A znaiu: massa, a ne sem'ia, primet moi poslednii vdokh.*" Cf. Lyutov's consolation of Ilya, the rebbe's son, in Babel's *Red Cavalry*: "*ia prinial poslednii vzdokh moego brata*" ("I took the last breath of my brother") (2: 129). Andrei wants only the abstract masses at his deathbed, but Ilya and Lyutov cannot completely abandon a familial context.

31 Thompson, as quoted in Barrat (*Yurii Olesha's "Envy"* 44), notes that Andrei's scar shows that he has been cut off from the past. Barrat takes this idea further, noting that the scar resembles a lopped-off branch. Joining this simile to the branch imagery

surrounding Valya and the resemblance between Ivan's hand and a tree, Barrat sees Andrei's scar as a symbol of his rejection of the romanticism of the past that provides the impetus for Ivan's conspiracy of feelings.

32 See Matt F. Oja, "Iurii Olesha's *Zavist'*: Fantasy, Reality, and Split Personality" (1986). Though Oja's thesis is provocative, his assertion that Kavalerov actually goes mad in the course of the novel is not supported by the evidence of the text. The general predominance of subjective viewpoints in *Zavist'* has been explored by Beaujour (*Invisible Land*) and R. Jones (passim), but the best analysis of the novel's various narrative voices is found in Cornwell's 1980 essay on the subject. Cornwell notes that even when Kavalerov's perspective is supposedly absent, the narrative point of view is basically constant.

33 In this Andrei is like Olesha's Three Fat Men, who adopt a young heir rather than conceiving one with a woman.

4. THE OBJECT OF *ENVY*

1 The designations "eunuch" and "hermaphrodite" are from Harkins and are discussed below. Most Western critics, including Harkins ("Theme of Sterility" 450) and Peppard (*Poetics* 79), find Andrei to be a parody, whether of true creativity, the Bolshevik ideal, or other characters in the novel. R. Lauer sees the entire Babichev clan as a parody of the Ulyanov (Lenin) family. Viktor Pertsov (*My zhivem* 243) refers to Andrei as a "rock-hard financial manager" who over-enthusiastically follows Lenin's call to entrepreneurship under NEP. In the introduction to his translation of *Envy*, Clarence Brown wonders aloud about Andrei's relationship to Volodya: "Are they adopted father and son, or old pederast and young catamite?" (231). This question is addressed in chapter 3 of this book, albeit in different terms.

2 Androgynous characters also figure prominently in Olesha's play *A List of Assets*: the actress Lelya Goncharova appears in the role of Hamlet, despite the fact that "one can tell from her feet that she is a woman" (P 93). Her ironic explanation of her choice of roles connects androgyny to the new world: "Now women must think like men. The Revolution. Male scores are being settled" (P 145). Androgyny in a man, however, is associated with the decadent West: The "great" actor Ulyulyam, the "champion of sexuality," is "a man for men, a woman for women" (P 137).

3 The name "Valya," like many Russian names, is itself ambiguous, for it can refer to either a woman or a man. Olesha's friend and rival Valentin Kataev was also called Valya.

4 Cf. Clarence Brown's 1985 introduction to *Envy*: "[Volodya] strikes us not only as disgustingly fawning and devious, but also as more than a little sissified; the strange wrist-slapping tone of poor-little-me against big-strong-you induces considerable dubiety about their real relationship" (231). While one can take issue with both the value judgments implicit in Brown's choice of words, Brown has identified the aspects of Volodya's personality that are at odds with his traditionally masculine character.

5   Kavalerov, too, can be cast in this same role. Often Kavalerov is compared with Dostoevsky's underground man (Jackson; Shenshin 1980), but critics fail to note that his relationship with Andrei can be seen as a parodic inversion of the second half of *Notes from Underground*: Olesha's underground man, rather than dreaming of redeeming a prostitute, is himself the "fallen woman" whom Babichev is moved to rescue. The prostitute in Dostoevsky's novel leaves after the underground man is deliberately rude to her, while Kavalerov runs from Andrei in response to a slight that he himself has imagined.

6   Andrei's isolation from women was a relatively late development in the writing of *Envy*. In the original draft, Andrei is married to Lelya Tatarnikova, Valya's precursor. In the next version, Lelya is the wife of Kostya Belov, a character completely absent from subsequent drafts. Nonetheless, Lelya abandons Kostya to marry Andrei. Andrei's subordinates gloat over their superior's marriage, since they expect to discover that Andrei's married life is miserable, thus finally staining Babichev's impeccable reputation. On the contrary, the Babichevs' marriage is a happy one (Shitareva, "Tvorcheskaia istoriia" 83–87). Shitareva, whose research brought the earlier drafts to light, finds the pages devoted to Andrei's family life unremarkable, concluding that Babichev has no family in the final version precisely because his interactions with Lelya serve only to show that Andrei is happily wedded to a beautiful woman. But even during this happy marriage, Andrei exhibits no real connection to women. Shitareva writes that "even in relation to Volodya in the final version Babichev opens up more than he does with his wife Lelya" ("Tvorcheskaia istoriia" 87). Babichev is far more forthcoming in his relationships with men (Volodya) than he is with women (Valya). By the time the novel is published, the only references to a romance between Andrei and Valya come from Kavalerov, who accuses the sausage maker of trying to "corrupt" (*razvrashchat'*) his own niece. Kavalerov's charge, however, is completely unfounded.

7   In his analysis of puberty initiation rites, Bruno Bettelheim sets forth the generalization that "one sex feels envy in regard to the sexual organs and functions of the other" (19). In *Male and Female*, Margaret Mead concludes that it is essential in most civilizations for the male to "reach a solid sense of irreversible achievement, of which his childhood knowledge of the satisfactions of childbearing have given him a glimpse" (160). The ramifications of this "womb envy," along with the male attempts to compensate for it through achievement, are discussed by Chodorow in *Feminism and Psychoanalytic Theory*.

8   Andrei expands on the significance of these names in *The Conspiracy of Feelings*, Olesha's dramatic adaptation of *Envy*, asserting that there are poetic sciences. In the play, he vetoes not one but two female names for the candy bar: Rosa Luxemburg and Odalisque ("*Odaliska*," P 51). Andrei's out-of-hand rejection of the name "Rosa Luxemburg" is noteworthy in connection to *Chevengur*, since in Platonov's novel the dead German revolutionary becomes a symbol of the Eternal Feminine.

9   See, e.g., Kavalerov's reaction to Andrei's laughter: "'You are a philistine, Kavalerov. You don't understand anything.' He doesn't say it, but it's understood without words"

(18). Here he is like his younger namesake in "Legend," who is also sure he is privy to his father's thoughts: "You thought you were my ideal" (I 99). Dosya in "Human Material" is also convinced that he knows what his father is thinking.

10 Pushkin's Bronze Horseman crushes the pathetic, mad Yevgeny, only to reappear in a different form in Bely's *Petersburg*. Gogol's wild troika, the symbol of Russia at the end of *Dead Souls*, returns in a context contemporary to Olesha: in his 1908 essay "The People and the Revolution" ("Narod i revoliutsiia"), Blok asks if this troika is racing toward the intelligentsia (5: 329). Blok superimposes the coming upheaval onto the familiar troika, calling attention to the destructive potential of the revolution. For an overview of the horse as apocalyptic symbol, see David M. Bethea's introduction to his *The Shape of the Apocalypse in Modern Russian Fiction*.

11 Other triangles include Kavalerov-Valya-Volodya, Kavalerov-Valya-Ivan, Kavalerov-Valya-Andrei, Kavalerov-Anechka-Ivan, Kavalerov-Anechka-Anechka's husband, and Ivan-Valya-Andrei. This is by no means an exhaustive list.

12 Michael Naydan briefly discusses the pervasive triangles in "The Cherry Pit," connecting them to the various triangles of *Envy*. He also includes the triangle of Fedya, Avel, and the "flock of comrades from Kursk." More provocatively, he postulates that the triangle formed by the postrevolutionary world, the old world, and the invisible land of the imagination is "the most significant triad in the story" (383).

13 Here Olesha's representation of triangular desire differs from that of the Russian triangular "master plot" of Chernyshevsky's *What Is to Be Done?* In Chernyshevsky's novel, the third man is, according to Irina Paperno, "the husband's 'magical helper,' an intermediary between a man and a woman, and, as such, is the husband's mirror image" (152). Indeed, Vera Pavlovna, the novel's heroine, would not have consummated her first marriage to Lopukhov were it not for her awakening passion for Kirsanov (153). The Chernyshevskian triangle, when successful, is the antithesis of rivalry, resulting in a "triple union" that benefits all parties. For a discussion of the evolution of this triple union in the Silver Age and the early Soviet period, see Matich ("Dialectics of Cultural Return," "Merezhkovskys' Third Testament," and "Symbolist Meaning of Love"), Paperno, and the introduction to the present volume.

14 Gladkov reports that Olesha used the word "demon" (*demon*), but Kataev reproduces the statement with the word "devil" (*chert*). Kataev, however, belabors the point that *My Diamond Wreath* is not a book of memoirs in the traditional sense, and that no direct quotes should be taken as a faithful representation of events.

15 Victor Peppard speculates that Olesha is the narrator's alter ego in *My Diamond Wreath* (8). Certainly, Kataev acts as Olesha's active double in the events detailed in his memoirs.

16 Treating women as "prizes" to be "abducted" is also a recurring motif in *Envy*: Kavalerov writes in his letter that he will get Valya as "his prize" and thinks to himself while listening to Ivan that he will "tear Valya loose" from the grasp of Volodya and Andrei (39, 67).

17 Olesha's marriages to two of the Suok sisters, as well as his first wife's subsequent mar-

riages to Vladimir Narbut and to Olesha's friend Viktor Shklovsky, also fit this pattern. Sketchy references to Olesha's marriages are found in Beaujour ("Imagination of Failure" 133), Belinkov (73), and Sheldon (912). It is possible that the "little friend" and the rival of Kataev's memoirs are Serafima Suok and Vladimir Narbut, but nowhere does Kataev mention that Olesha and "little friend" were married. Given the vague distinction between registered and unregistered marriages in the 1920s, as well as the generally loose usage of the terms "husband" and "wife" that has continued in Russia to the present day, it is possible that Olesha's first marriage was common law.

18 For a detailed analysis of the sexual dynamics present in *A Strict Youth*, see Heil. Comradeship, homoeroticism, and love triangles are all central to Heil's treatment of the film. *A Strict Youth* is only briefly treated in this book not only because Heil has so deftly explored them, but also because this film represents a markedly different stage in Olesha's literary career.

19 Girard's blind spots (women and gay men) are extremely vulnerable to feminist critique. If Freud, by means of the oedipal triangle, is often accused of sexualizing everything to the extreme, Girard's triangle is guilty of the opposite: he removes eroticism from what is most clearly erotic. First the (female) object of desire is reduced in stature, which requires a corresponding decrease in her erotic status. Then the potentially erotic element between the two men is also defused. Even Proust's acknowledged homosexuality, a given in literary history, is reduced in Girard's hands to a mere outgrowth of mediated desire. Toril Moi argues convincingly that Girard makes no provisions to explain "feminine desire." She also asserts that Girard's theory of sexuality, while pointing to a "homosexual" structure of sexual rivalry (Girard, *Things Hidden* 337), is forced to posit heterosexuality as instinctual. For a reinterpretation of Girard in feminist terms, see Eve Kosofsky Sedgwick's *Between Men*.

20 The reverse also holds true: Olesha could have been a perfect case study for Girard's *Deceit, Desire, and the Novel*. Olesha even wrote a film version of one of the works Girard devotes the most attention to: Dostoevsky's *The Idiot*.

21 Indeed, this is precisely the arrangement that Valya has with Andrei and Volodya: one is a father figure, while the other is (eventually) to be her husband.

22 Olesha discusses his study of Latin in the Rishelevsky gymnasium in *No Day without a Line* (166–68).

23 Once again, the parallel between Valya and Ophelia is implicitly reinforced. In the previous chapter, Ivan uses almost the exact same words in reference to Ophelia: "I will show you my machine" (85).

24 This is not to suggest that the text gives us any reason to consider Valya a victim; as a character, she is little more than a cipher, and thus nothing can be said about her state of mind or personal views.

25 In her research on early Soviet political art, Victoria Bonnell finds that female allegorical figures (such as Freedom, Liberty, or History) had for the most part disappeared by 1921. The 1920s saw the proliferation of peasant women and women workers in government propaganda (Bonnell 269–77, passim). These women substantively differ from the

stern *rodina-mat'* ("motherland") who would return later. They were meant to inspire by their example rather than by their allegorical content or their appeal to solidarity. See also Waters (225–33).

26 Ehre writes that Volodya and Valya "have formed a society of adolescent peers, free from anxiety because free from authority" ("Olesha's *Zavist'*" 607). This is certainly true of the scene in which the two are exercising at the end of the novel, but Volodya's letter to Andrei shows that even the "new man" is not free from anxiety.

27 Volodya's self-characterization as a "man-machine" is only one of many contemporary references to the early Soviet ideal of what Toby Clark calls the "human-machine hybrid." Clark cites the avant-garde filmmaker Dzhiga Vertov's dreams of the "perfect electrical man" and Aleksei Gastev's vision of mechanized collectivism as two of the more prominent examples of this "recurring formula of the new man" (Clark 35–36).

28 The juxtaposition of woman and machine as the symbols of the previous and the present centuries is not unique to Olesha. In response to the Great Exposition of 1900, Henry Adams wrote an essay entitled "The Dynamo and the Virgin," in which he laments the decline of the feminine ideal in the age of science. Sex and reproduction have been eclipsed by science and production. In earlier ages, a goddess was worshiped "because of her force; she was the animated dynamo; she was reproduction—the greatest and most mysterious of all energies; all she needed was to be fecund" (384). More contemporary artists and writers could not see the goddess as power: "They felt a railway train as power" (388). The conflict between the old and new worlds in 1920s Soviet literature is so keenly felt because official ideology emphasized the replacement of the old by the new. The anxiety expressed by Soviet authors can be viewed as simply a more extreme version of a general "future shock" that was not exclusive to revolutionary Russia.

29 The substitution of a human female by a mechanical replacement is also a major part of *The Three Fat Men,* in which the acrobat Suok, a young girl, is repeatedly confused with a mechanical doll that looks exactly like her. The doll belongs to Tutti, the heir to the tyrants that rule Suok's land. When Suok is substituted for the doll, she awakens human feeling in Tutti. As noted above, Tutti himself was told that his human heart had been replaced by a mechanical one. The substitution of a mechanical doll by a human girl leads him to find that his "mechanical" heart is as human as hers.

30 Ophelia can also be seen as a combination of Anechka (the castrating, threatening woman) and Valya (the ethereal, untouchable beauty).

5. PURITANS AND PROLETARIANS

1 Andrei Platonov, *Chut'e pravdy* (Moskva: Sovetskaia Rossiia, 1990), 118. Whenever possible, all references to Platonov's essays will use this edition, which is the most complete collection of the author's nonfiction.

2 See Naiman's "Andrei Platonov and the Inadmissibility of Desire" (passim), Osipovich (62–102), and Paramonov (passim).

3   This is not to say that Platonov's work is entirely without heroines; his "Teacher of the Sands" ("Peschanaia uchitel' nitsa," 1927) whose central character is modeled on Platonov's future wife, is the exception that proves the rule. Women are the central characters in "Fro" (1936) and "The Girl Roza" ("Devushka Roza"); also noteworthy is the number of well-rounded female supporting characters in Platonov's later work, including Lyuba in "The Potudan River" (1937) and the wife in "The Homecoming" ("Vozvrashchenie," 1945). Nonetheless, Platonov would continue to give prominence to absent heroines in his later stories, such as the long-lost Aphrodite of the story of the same name (1944–45).

4   For the role of "Antisexus" as a turning point in Platonov's worldview, see Thomas Langerak ("Andrei Platonov v perelomnom periode," passim), Naiman ("Andrej Platonov" 322), and Semenova ("'Tainoe tainykh'" 92–99).

5   The division of Platonov's career into three stages is most clearly elucidated by Osipovich. Osipovich terms the period from 1918 to 1926 Platonov's "Proletcult" period, which is followed by the 1927–1934 period of "spiritual crisis" and "reevaluation." The final period (1934–1951) is centered on the family as the source of "the meaning of human existence" (i, iii). See also Semenova ("'Tainoe tainykh,'" passim).

For a discussion of the sexual politics of "The Potudan' River," see Geller (363–64), Naiman ("Andrej Platonov" 345–54; "'Iz iztiny'" 234–35), Osipovich (141–48), and Semenova ("'Tainoe tainykh'" 117–20).

6   Osipovich points to Platonov's 1922 courtship of his future wife as a possible reason for the tempering of his antifamily rhetoric by the end of that same year (24–25).

7   In addition to his novel, plays, and numerous short stories, Platonov left behind a large body of articles and essays, the bulk of which were published during the first few years of his career. His most productive period of political-philosophical writing was between 1919 and 1923, when his articles frequently appeared on the pages of journals whose very names leave little doubt as to their communist orientation: besides his work for the above-mentioned *Voronezh Commune*, Platonov was a regular contributor to *The Iron Path* (*Zheleznyi put'*) and *The Red Village* (*Krasnaia derevnia*). By the mid-1920s his nonfiction publishing comes to a near halt, to be resumed with any sort of regularity only with the appearance of his reactions to the desert reclamation campaign in Turkmenia, the literary-critical articles in the late 1930s, and the wartime journalism that was a common occupation of Soviet writers in World War II. The drop in Platonov's journalistic output can be explained by a number of objective circumstances: his move from Voronezh to Tambov, and subsequently to Moscow; the rise of NEP and, later, Stalinism, both of which clashed with the young Platonov's views; the growing strength of the censor; and, finally, Platonov's own growing predilection for longer and more complicated fictional projects.

8   As Savel'zon points out in his commentary to one of Platonov's recently rediscovered early short stories, one can find in Platonov's work not only attacks on sexuality and reproduction, but also admissions of the "mysterious and wonderful power" of physical love (317). Seifrid notes that Platonov was "hardly a consistent thinker" and that his in-

311

consistencies extend to his writings on sexual desire (38–39), hence Seifrid's argument that the "notion of an abrupt *volte-face*" on Platonov's part amounts to an "oversimplification" of the author's thought.

9   Chalmaev's term for Platonov's early journalism, "fossilized rhetorical psychosis," at times seems particularly apt ("Plennik svobody" 20).

10 Iablokov argues this point rather differently, since he believes that no typology of Platonov's women is appropriate: "In Platonov's prose we see basically a single feminine image that acts in one or another 'social role' depending on the plot: mother-sister-wife-love-beloved-beautiful lady [*Prekrasnaia dama*]"; in her relations with male characters, this "feminine image" takes on "that 'hypostasis' which is psychologically closer to him" ("O filosofskoi pozitsii" 246). Though the examples that Iablokov takes from *Chevengur* serve him well, I cannot agree that all Platonov's female characters are aspects of a single "image." Iablokov's assertion makes sense within a Jungian context; but since, from a Jungian point of view, all female characters in any literary work would be aspects of the "Great Mother," such an insight would not be limited only to Platonov.

11 Crones do, however, play a small but significant role in Platonov's early work. When Maria Nikiforovona, the young protagonist of "The Teacher of the Sands," sees that all the good works she has accomplished in a Russian desert settlement have been ruined by Asiatic nomads, she realizes that she will have to devote all her efforts to "civilizing" these barbarians. She asks herself if it is really possible for her to "bury [her] youth in this sandy desert" (*Na zare* 115). Where, she wonders, will she find a "husband and companion" in this wilderness? Briefly, she remembers her attraction to the nomads' chieftain, but the implication of a possible romance between the two is left undeveloped. Instead, when she agrees to educate the nomads, she tells her supervisor that she will "come back in fifty years as an old woman" and will travel on the new roads that she will have constructed (*Na zare* 116). For the sake of the future, she imagines herself a crone, skipping motherhood and middle age. Thus the only strong heroine in Platonov's early fiction can work for the common good only at the expense of her sexual, feminine self.

12 Platonov's early nonfiction begs to be analyzed in terms of genre. For the sake of brevity, Seifrid treats "the Voronezh journalism more or less as single text," as does Eidinova (Seifrid 201n2). Yet the form in which these works were published clearly had an effect on their content. Moreover, like all of Platonov's boundaries, that between his fiction and nonfiction is quite fluid: a large part of his 1922 short story "The Descendants of the Sun" reads very much like his most programmatic articles, while "A Story about Many Interesting Things" (1923) and "The Ether Tract" (1926–27) contain miniature scientific treatises whose style and content would be familiar to readers of Platonov's nonfiction. The connections between "The Ether Tract" and an earlier, unpublished article called "The Symphony of Consciousness" ("Simfoniia soznaniia") was brought to light by Kornienko ("V khudozhestvennoi masterskoi" (308–21); " 'Efirny trakt" passim); the results of Kornienko's painstaking works in Platonov's archives suggest

that the relationship between the author's fiction and nonfiction could be a rewarding avenue of inquiry.

13 My treatment of the spontaneity-consciousness dialectic is indebted to the work on this subject of Katerina Clark (15–24). Clark sets forth this dichotomy as the primary subtext of the "master plot" of socialist realism. While Platonov cannot be called a socialist realist, his communist reinterpretation of Fyodorov's opposition between the "learned" (*uchenye*) and "unlearned" (*neuchenyei*) can be seen as the mirror image of Lenin's ideas, as Platonov's "fools" (*duraki*) are portrayed far more sympathetically than his Bolshevik "brains" (*umniki*). For a discussion of Platonov's work in the context of socialist realism, see Seifrid (176–98).

14 For an analysis of various avant-garde and Stalinist theories on the "transformation" of the world, see chapters 1 and 2 of Groys.

15 Platonov's worship of science is not, however, without reservations. As early as 1921, Platonov wrote a story of scientific experimentation that leads to tragic results ("Markun"). Seifrid treats Platonov's growing unease with scientific utopianism in his discussion of the author's early science fiction (52–56).

16 Geller (45), Osipovich (19–20), and Tolstaia-Segal ("Ideologicheskie konteksty" 238–39, 248) see the influence of Gastev in Platonov's cult of the machine. Bethea (152–60) compares Platonov's views on the machine with those of Gastev, Fyodorov, and Bogdanov.

17 Cf. the foreman's unfavorable comparison of women and machines in *Chevengur*. This passage is discussed in the next chapter.

18 Boris Paramonov discusses the identification of women with nature and the bourgeoisie in *Chevengur* (338–39).

19 Though the opposition between the two is made explicit in several of Platonov's articles, Osipovich was the first critic to discuss Platonov's early work specifically in terms of "sex and consciousness," which is the title of her first chapter (10–58). Seifrid sees this binary opposition in terms of a larger dialectic of "consciousness and matter" (32–55).

20 Though Platonov's thought is on the other extreme of the political spectrum, the bulk of his early writings on woman and sexuality are reminiscent of Otto Weininger's *Sex and Character*. Weininger writes that "[w]oman . . . has an unconscious life, man a conscious life" (113) and that the "female, who is sexual, can appear to be asexual because she is sexuality itself, and so her sexuality does not stand out separately from the rest of her being, either in space or time, as in the case of the male" (200). Platonov, however, was harsh in his criticism of Weininger's work, though he never addressed the content of Weininger's argument (see note 36).

21 This conflation of the physiological with the sociological not only is reminiscent of some of the postrevolutionary pseudo-science (such as Bogdanov's faith in immortality through blood transfusions [O'Connor 25]), but also is consistent with Platonov's treatment of the categories of matter and spirit. Platonov renders the process of consciousness (thinking) in physical terms, deliberately erasing the boundaries be-

tween the two categories (Seifrid 76–78) — hence the near-synonymous use of the terms "brain" (*mozg*) and "soul" (*dusha*) in "The Battle of the Brains."

22 Osipovich sees a similarity between Platonov and Bogdanov in that both attach "a tremendous amount of importance to the biological factor in history" (17).

23 Cf. Todorov's *Red Square, Black Square*: "Platonov insists on virility as the major feature of the future disgendered being. Woman according to him creates the gender difference" (82).

24 It is in his treatment of women and sex in "The Culture of the Proletariat" that Platonov shows his debt to Fyodorov. To Fyodorov, sex is the enemy of ancestor worship, since it focuses on reproduction rather than resurrection, and is thus the biological expression of that most odious notion, progress. Woman as sexual object or mother has no place in Fyodorov's utopian schemes, for in these roles she can only distract men from the task at hand.

25 In his commentary on "On the Culture of Harnessed Light," Chalmaev asserts that this article is a sign of Platonov's growing "doubts" and "inner discord" on the subject of love and sex (*Chut'e* 451). Certainly, such signs are present in Platonov's later writings, and 1922, the year this essay was published, was a turning point in Platonov's life (see note 6). Yet there are no signs that Platonov has modified his attitude in this article. "On the Culture of Harnessed Light," printed in the second issue of the journal *Art and Theater*, belongs to the earlier part of 1922, probably before Platonov's courtship of his future wife.

26 Cf. Kollontai's "love-comradeship" (*liubov'-tovarishchestvo*). See note 14 of the introduction to the present book.

27 See, e.g., the beginning of "The Future October," from which this chapter's epigraph was taken: "Anyone who says that, in the future communist society, there will be *absolutely* no differences among people is an idle dreamer with a bovine, feminine heart rather than a thinker" (*Chut'e* 117, emphasis in the original). Not only is the subject presumed to be a man, but the contrast between the male body and female heart suggests that Platonov's affirmation of difference is particularly applicable to gender.

28 Cf. "Woman, the source of sexual provocation, becomes the enemy" (Naiman, "Andrej Platonov" 325).

29 The two essays appear within a day of each other: "But Man Has Only One Soul" was printed in *Voronezh Commune* on 17 July 1920, and "The World Soul" was published in the 18 July edition of *The Red Village*.

30 All citations in this essay refer to Platonov, *Vozvrashchenie*. The essay is printed in both *Gosudarstvennyi zhitel'* (547–48) and vol. 3 of *Sobranie sochineniia* (519–20), but a key paragraph is missing from these editions.

31 In *Deceit, Desire, and the Novel*, Girard selects *The Idiot* for detailed study according to his model of mediated desire. Note that both Platonov and Olesha pay particular attention to *The Idiot* in their work: Platonov writes a review of a stage production of the novel, whereas Olesha is the author of a film scenario based on the same novel. See chapter 4 for a discussion of triangular desire in Olesha.

32 Though the association of Rogozhin with femininity is counterintuitive, Platonov's unorthodox reading of *The Idiot*'s sexual politics is facilitated by the prevalence of androgyny in the novel. Matich argues that "the traditional masculine-feminine roles are reversed rather than re-evaluated: . . . In spite of her hysteria, [Nastasya Filippovna] represents the active male principle in the novel. Myshkin is the embodiment of passivity" (Matich, "Androgyny" 172). While Platonov and Matich differ in their interpretations of Myshkin, both associate Nastasya Filippovna with something other than traditional femininity.

33 According to Platonov, Christ's message is that "the kingdom of God must be taken with efforts." The love of Christ is not the "limp, powerless, shelterless love of the dying," but a powerful love that can burn down and rebuild the world. It is proletariats who can build Christ's kingdom on earth, for they know Christ's true teachings. People used to see Christ as God, but "we" know him as a friend (*Chut'e* 51). This essay appeared a month before Platonov's review of *The Idiot*.

34 Here Platonov appears to be indebted to his symbolist predecessors, though the connection may well be unconscious. The Platonic ideal of the transcendent androgyne gained new currency among the first generation of symbolists, especially Gippius, Merezhkovsky, and Vyacheslav Ivanov. Ivanov made a distinction between the masculine noun *dukh* (spirit) and the feminine *dusha* (soul), one that prefigures Jung's animus and anima (Matich, "Androgyny" 171). Considering Platonov's repeated identification of woman with the soul, Ivanov's ideas are a possible subtext. However, I have found no evidence that Platonov deliberately contrasted soul and spirit in terms of gender.

35 The otherwise exhaustive studies by Langerak, Naiman, and Tolstaia-Segal do not treat "The World Soul." Osipovich quotes from it briefly in her treatment of "The Ether Tract" (50). S. Liubushkina touches on the essay in her article "Ideia bessmertiia u rannego Platonova." She elides the apparent contradiction between "The World Soul" and Platonov's other articles by noting that "Platonov perceives woman not in the esthetic realm, but on the philosophical and ethical planes" (404). Semenova does, however, discuss this essay at some length (" 'Tainoe tainykh' " 80–81).

36 One possible explanation is that "The World Soul" is a book review in the sense that "But Man Has Only One Soul" is a response to the staging of a play. Toward the end of the article, Platonov changes his subject and begins a brief critique of Otto Weininger's *Sex and Character*. Platonov berates Weininger for his misogyny (indeed, *Sex and Character* is one of the most misogynistic approaches to sex ever to pass for science), proclaiming that "I could refute this book from beginning to end, but will do so elsewhere" (*Chut'e* 68). There is no record that he ever undertook such an extensive critique, but even his short criticism of the book is of interest. At first glance, Platonov's nonfiction is no less misogynist than Weininger's (see note 20). But there is a substantial difference between the two. Platonov criticizes femininity as an abstraction but rarely attacks women. Weininger makes both femininity and women the target of a several-hundred-page study, writing that "[n]o man who really thinks deeply about women retains a high opinion of them; men either despise women, or they have never thought seriously

about them" (236). It is possible that Platonov was moved to write "The World Soul" after reading Weininger. For a brief discussion of Weininger and Babel, see chapter 2, note 37.

37 As Chalmaev observes, when Platonov has anything at all positive to say about women, it is only about mothers (*Chut'e* 439).

38 It has been argued that the cause of Nastya's death is precisely that superhuman significance accorded to her: "The symbol of the future descends to earth and settles in the body of the orphan Nastya. But it nonetheless remains a symbol. They have forgotten about the fragility of childhood" (Urban 190). Nastya's dead mother is replaced by a typically Platonovian collection of idealistic "fathers," none of whom can come up with an adequate replacement for maternal warmth. The failure of men to be a self-sufficient "family" will be discussed in the next chapter.

39 Platonov's mother-worship has been treated in the critical literature, though usually not in connection to the articles. Naiman sees Platonov's emphasis on the importance of the mother as the author's major departure from Fyodorov ("Andrej Platonov" 325-26). Chalmaev finds that Platonov is willing to praise only woman as mother (*Chut'e* 439). "In the poetics of Platonov, a mother symbolizes the soul and all that is humane," according to Osipovich (50).

40 Though Platonov's article is reminiscent of the Silver Age worship of the Eternal Feminine, Platonov's use of the term "World Soul" does not correspond with the Symbolist or ancient understanding of the term (Shimak-Reifer 270). However, in the 1930s, Platonov would work on a novel called *Happy Moscow* (*Schastlivaia Moskva*), whose female protagonist resembles, as Natasha Drubek-Maier writes, a "Soviet Sophia" (Drubek-Maier 253).

41 In *The People of the Moonlight* (*Liudi lunnogo sveta*), Rozanov devotes several pages to a discussion of conception, childbirth, and the care of the fetus (2: 56-58). He also states that the "souls" of each sex are analogous to their sexual organs (2: 33).

42 Echoes and refutations of Rozanov can be found throughout his fiction and essays. Platonov singles out Rozanov for criticism in his 1920 essay "The Culture of the Proletariat" (*Chut'e* 98-109). For more on the connection between Platonov and Rozanov, see Chalmaev ("Primechaniia" 435-36, 443-44), E. A. Iablokov ("Kommentarii" 634), Paramonov (353), and Tolstaia-Segal ("Ideologicheskie konteksty" 256-63).

43 Platonov would again connect maternity and female consciousness in his notebooks from the years 1941 to 1950: "The consciousness of a woman is the mother herself" (*Soznanie zhenshiny—sama mat'*) (*Gosudarstvennyi zhitel'* 602).

44 Cf. Naiman ("Andrej Platonov" 320-21, "Thematic Mythology" 190, 210) and Anninsky (98).

45 Boris Paramonov accuses Berdyaev of being antilife (349-50), but his conclusion is based on a reading of Berdyaev through the prism of Fyodorov and Platonov. For a discussion and critique of Paramonov's article, see the next chapter.

46 Here Platonov's portrayal of the mother as Moses can be linked to the heroine's fate

in "The Teacher of the Sands": Maria Nikiforovna must sacrifice the rest of her life in order to bring happiness to others.

47   Platonov clearly connects mothers to the earth elsewhere. In "Repairing the Earth," he writes: "The earth is where we've come from and where we will go. . . . That's what the people think. And that is correct" (*Chut'e* 49).

48   Osipovich notes that, for Platonov, the term "bride" is "a synonym for the impossible, a synonym for the ideal" (44).

49   "Let not woman . . . but though be the bride of man" ("But Man Has Only One Soul," *Chut'e* 72); "Every man [*chelovek*] in this world has a bride, and only because of this is he able to live. For one her name is Maria, for another it is a mysterious image seen in a dream, and for a third it might be a stove door or the lamenting wind of spring" ("Notes," *Chut'e* 175); "The impossible is the bride of humanity, and our souls fly to the impossible" ("Zhivia glavnoi zhizni' [1921], *Gosudarstvennyi zhitel'* 568).

50   Early on Ivan gets advice from a regional doctor who "loved books" and "lived without a wife," existing only for his studies (*Starik* 55). The Sturdy Man has an elderly female housekeeper but otherwise lives without female company. The man who reads Johann Pupkov's essay aloud has a daughter, but no wife is in evidence, while the engineer-space traveler is quite clear about the need to be unencumbered by women. Only Ivan's mentor Kondrat has a wife, and it is her labor that is portrayed in such grotesque terms.

51   The theme of love for the distant recurs throughout Platonov's work. See Shepard (passim).

6. BURIED IN THE FAMILY PLOT

The epigraph is from Andrei Platonov, *Chevengur* (Moscow: Vysshaia shkola), 177. Because of the vast explanatory notes included by E. Ia. Iablokov, this is the preferred edition of the many different publications of *Chevengur* that have appeared in the former Soviet Union since 1988, at least until a new collected works edition appears. All references to the novel and notes use this edition and will be cited by page number only.

1   When comparing *Chevengur* to other works of "Soviet Russian revolutionary romanticism," Jurij Striedter finds that the novel is "genuinely ironic" (195). For Striedter, however, this term does not imply abject cynicism and disillusionment; instead, irony is an integral component of the romantic aesthetic, one that is lacking in other Soviet revolutionary romantic works (194–95). Thomas Seifrid concludes that it would be a mistake to consider the novel either a parody or a sincere expression of revolutionary romanticism. Rather, the ambiguity of *Chevengur* is itself the novel's theme (102–3). Eric Naiman also sees the novel as a balance between irony and sympathy: both *Chevengur* and *The Foundation Pit* ridicule Platonov's early "fanaticism" without completely rejecting it (Naiman, " 'Iz istiny' " 234).

2   Both Bethea (161) and Paramonov (368) reject the notion that *Chevengur* is satire. Borrowing Sinyavaksy's term, Paramonov calls the novel "fantastic realism." Todorov goes

even further, asserting that "[t]here is no critique" in Platonov's works. Nor is Platonov an anti-utopian: "There works an ecstatic vision for the universal orgy of revolution that periodically is overcome with melancholy and grief but soon bursts out again vehemently" (Todorov 72).

3. This story is not to be confused with another story by that name, also written by Platonov in the same year: originally entitled "The Satan of Thought" ("Satana mysli"), it has also been published as "Descendants of the Sun."

4. Geller, 180–81. The definition of menippean satire is from Mikhail Bakhtin, *Problemy poetiki Dostoevskogo* (Moscow, 1975), 197–98, as quoted in Geller.

5. Simon Serbinov tells Dvanov that "people in Chevengur are ideas for each other" (384).

6. Even Sasha Dvanov is, in the words of Serbinov, a "semi-intellectual" (*poluintelligent*, 370), while his half brother Prokofy uses his relative eloquence to create glib ideological "formulations" that allow him to retain personal property and privileges.

7. In a complete reversal of Fyodorov's priorities, the rare female character in *Chevengur* either is removed from the family context (Sonya) or serves as a mother or sister. Women in *Chevengur* give birth but are not themselves born; the issue of any sexual union is always male. Daughters begin to play a major role in Platonov's work only in *The Foundation Pit*.

8. The scene is also noteworthy for its intricate play with gender, based on the masculine noun *kon'* ("steed") and the female *loshad'* ("horse"). Before the kiss, Proletarian Strength urges Kopyonkin into action and is consistently referred to as *kon'*. Immediately afterward, the steed turns into a *loshad'* and is now sly, knowing, and shameless. For similar wordplay, see the discussion of Babel's "The Remount Officer" in chapter 2.

9. The ambiguity of this phrase is noted by Seifrid (230n44).

10. Were it not for the novel's preponderant emphasis on male relationships and masculinity, one could argue that this interest in naked men is part of what Seifrid calls the characters' recognition of "the problem of possessing a body, and the acuteness with which they experience that possession as a burden" (107). This is not to dispute Seifrid's thesis that so much of Platonov's work is an exploration of the struggle between matter and spirit, but rather to say that Platonov's exploration of corporeality in *Chevengur* is thoroughly gendered: it is male bodies that are the object of the comrades' curious gaze.

11. Osipovich calls Kopyonkin "the only character in the novel whom Platonov actually associates with homosexuality" (Osipovich 78). Osipovich overstates her case, as demonstrated by the above discussion of homoeroticism involving other men besides Kopyonkin. Kopyonkin, however, makes more of an effort to court other men than any other character in the novel, with the possible exception of Chepurny.

12. For Paramonov, the homosexual (and, in his view, death-worshiping) impulse is paramount: "[N]atural [*sic*] relations are abolished here not because the Chevengurians are the victim of utopian consciousness, but, on the contrary: utopia has taken hold of them because they hated these natural relations from the very beginning. The revolution is only a motivation for this preexisting hatred of life" (Paramonov 342).

13 "Without a doubt," writes Paramonov," the undercurrent that makes Berdyaev's philosophy so capricious and unstable in its judgments is that of homosexuality." Paramonov claims that "this is simply a statement of fact, which is clear to anyone who knows psychoanalysis" (348).

14 As Osipovich argues, Paramonov's analysis is dependent on an absolute definition of "normalcy" and the behavior of the "normal man" (Osipovich 77–78). The homoeroticism of Platonov's work is also discussed by Geller (89) and Seifrid (119, 230n44).

15 The example of Whitman is instructive in that it shows how easily sociological theorizing can be adapted to individual predilections. According to Michael Lynch, Walt Whitman was able to adapt popular notions from phrenology in order to create a social theory that provided an ideological justification for his own erotic attachments to men. Nineteenth-century phrenologists posited the existence of a special "organ" in the brain that results in "adhesiveness," or the tendency to develop strong friendships. Though adhesiveness was considered possible among men and women, the phrenologists' examples were almost exclusively same-sex friendships. Eventually "excess adhesiveness" would be diagnosed as a "disease." Though adhesiveness was not identified as homosexual, it was often contrasted with "amativeness," or the sexual instinct: "For the phrenologists, Amativeness was opposite-sex but could be abused into same-sex activity; Adhesiveness was possible between the sexes, but was most often described in same-sex examples" (Lynch 91). Whitman was able to redefine adhesiveness and amativeness in a manner that resembles homosexuality and heterosexuality while still couching them in sociological rather than erotic terms: "Whitman was more eager to set Adhesiveness — the manly love of comrades — over against Amativeness — marriage and the family — as a basis of social organization" (Lynch 92). This view formed the basis of his 1871 *Democratic Vistas,* which argued that same-sex comradeship was inherently more democratic than heterosexual marriage. In Whitman's appropriation of adhesiveness, we can see homosexuality as both cause and effect; clearly, Whitman was searching for a model that rendered his own desires intelligible, and one can charge that Whitman added an overt homoerotic component where there was none. Yet Lynch's examination of the history of adhesiveness demonstrates that this phrenological concept was at the very least homosocial, and certainly suggestive of what would now be recognized as homosexual passion. If one takes the model of adhesiveness seriously, then Whitman's own well-known homosexuality becomes merely an extreme consequence of a strong faculty for friendship combined with democratic inclinations. But if one looks at homosexuality as the primary cause for Whitman's theorizing, the content of *Democratic Vistas* can be reduced to torturous self-justification. Clearly, neither approach is entirely acceptable.

16 The gypsy's proposition to "share bodies" is a direct challenge to the form taken by male comradeship in Chevengur: with the arrival of women, the Chevengurians no longer "share their bodies with each other by means of labor" in order to create gifts for each other (390).

17 Naiman argues that a basic component of Platonov's textual strategy is "the acknowl-

edgement and limitation of his debt to Freud," whose oedipal theories pose "an obvious threat" to Platonov's aim to "return to the womb while denying the presence of sexual desire within this goal" (Naiman, "Andrej Platonov" 329). Platonov accepts only part of Freud's theory: the father serves as a model for the son, showing him how to desire and directing him toward his proper place in the social order. With the exception of Prokofy, Platonov's men show no sign of rivalry with their fathers.

18 The importance of orphans in Platonov's works is widely recognized, but critics have failed to make a distinction between those who knew their parents and those who did not. Kornienko correctly recognizes that for Platonov, the heroes' orphanhood "is not an individual trait," but I cannot entirely agree with her conclusion that orphans are a "sign-symbol of the destruction of the wholeness of national life and the removal of God from the world" (Kornienko, "V khudozhestvennoi masterskoi" 330). In *Chevengur*, at least, the absence or presence of God is not a primary concern.

19 " 'Fatherhood' for a man is a second, and he can understand it as 'pleasure'; for a woman her 'motherhood' is a process, and one of such complication and labor that it is impossible to combine with 'pleasure.' " (Rozanov 1: 242). "The meaning of 'fatherhood' remains tangential, elusive. To 'father' a child suggests above all to beget, to provide the sperm which fertilizes the ovum. To 'mother' a child implies a continuing presence, lasting at least nine months, more often for years" (Rich xiv).

20 In *The People of the Moonlight* (1912), Rozanov recommends that married couples have sex once a week, to insure that "the children will be very healthy and very talented." Because he sees semen as the source of the life force ("we are attached to everything in this world through our seed"), he asserts that a fetus can only develop naturally if its mother is regularly caressed by its father. The efficacy of semen is born out in nursing as well: a lactating woman who has sex with her husband will produce healthier milk (2: 55–57).

21 Writing at the peak of the Stalinist terror, Platonov would subsequently transfer this developmental function from the individual father to the people in general. In his 1937 essay on Ostrovsky's *How the Steel Was Tempered* ("Pavel Korchagin"), Platonov writes: "The main and highest purpose of the Soviet people in fact consists of giving birth to Korchagins; any woman who has pledged herself to a man can give birth to a child, but it depends on the people whether or not this child will subsequently be a pitiful creature or a wonderful man [*chelovekom*]" (*Vozvrashchenie* 182).

22 Mead and Nancy Chodorow agree that the fundamental lessons boys and girls learn as they develop are vastly different: the girl thinks, "I am," while the boy says to himself, "I do" (Mead 148; Chodorow 33). According to Mead, "[t]he boy learns that he must make an effort to enter the world of men, that his first act of differentiating himself from his mother . . . must be continued into long years of effort," whereas the girl's life "starts and ends with sureness, . . . with the simple identification with the mother" (Mead 157, 158). Chodorow diverges from Mead in asserting that individuation is complex for girls as well, but she accepts the basic premises of Mead's analysis. For a more recent elaboration of these ideas, see Badinter's *XY*.

23 A similar distribution of roles between mother and father can be found in the beginning of "A Story about Many Interesting Things"; by the third chapter, Ivan Kopchikov's mother is nowhere to be seen. His father, the werewolf Yakim, apparently never takes part in Ivan's upbringing, yet early in Ivan's childhood he is befriended by a nameless wolf, who remains with Ivan until adulthood.

24 The term *bezotsovshchina* ("fatherlessness") is, of course, essential to Nikolai Fyodorov's *Philosophy of the Common Cause*. For more on Fyodorov and fatherlessness, see the introduction.

25 The quote is from the E. V. Rieu translation of *The Odyssey*, as quoted in Davis. Davis notes that this traditional English rendering of the original Greek is "an aphorism as old as it is familiar," though not completely accurate. The Greek reads, "Who has known his own engendering?" Davis's interpretation of the answer to both formulations of the question is the same: "the father's absence creates a predicament wherein a son must discover wisdom within the limitations of his own efforts" (Davis 5). In the context of *Chevengur*, the miscellaneous have far fewer resources for this endeavor than Sasha Dvanov.

26 The exhausted masses who are driven by basic needs rather than human desires become the half-starved nomads of Platonov's 1934 "Dzhan." Naiman sees in "Dzhan" and *Chevengur* the common thread of "the utopia as a community built upon the negation, or non-recognition, of sexual urges" (Naiman, "Andrej Platonov" 319).

27 Juliet Mitchell explains the difference between need and desire in terms of the nature of the object: "Desire is . . . always a question of a significant interrelationship, desire is always the desire of the other. Need can be satisfied by an actual object; demand is *for* something whereas desire is the desire to have one's desire recognized—it is a yearning for recognition. Desire can thus be recognized but never satisfied, for, as the desire for what the other desires, it necessitates the wish to *be* the other one, or not to be different from the other one" (396; emphasis in the original).

28 See Todorov's similar characterization of Fyodorov's "collective man" as "vegetal," controlled by an "external brain center" (52, 61).

29 With the exception of the woman who brings her dying child to Chevengur, the miscellaneous are only men. There is, of course, nothing in the term "miscellaneous" that excludes women. The lack of women among the miscellaneous is a result of Prokofy's selection of new Chevengurians: before he is given the instruction to bring women to Chevengur, he rounds up only men. The potential "brides" who later arrive in Chevengur clearly have suffered the abandonment and privation endured by the male miscellaneous, but by the time these women appear on the scene, the term "miscellaneous" is reserved for the homeless men who preceded them in Chevengur.

30 As Bethea notes, Platonov's work is fundamentally different from other "apocalyptic" Russian novels. Platonov, he writes, is a "*failed utopian*, not a confirmed apocalypticist" (Bethea 163; emphasis in the original).

31 The most serious study of necrophilia in Platonov's work is that of Paramonov, whose analysis of Fyodorov's opposition of father and grave to wife and life has some bear-

ing on Platonov's novel (Paramonov 345–46). Paramonov's conclusions, however, are too extreme, associating homosexuality with necrophilia to a greater extent than the text justifies. Paramonov's overall approach is informed by Shafarevich's *Socialism as a Phenomenon in World History* (*Sotsializm kak iavlenie mirovoi istorii*, 1977), which concludes that socialism's ultimate goal is the "death of humanity" (358). Though *Chevengur* can be understood as the rejection of theory over nature, and perhaps even a renunciation of communism, to say that Platonov's view of communism came to resemble Shafarevich's would be to project on Platonov an outlook that the evidence does not support.

Necrophilia in Platonov is also discussed by Podoroga (194–95) and Bethea (177), both of whom pay special attention to Dvanov's near-death orgasm. Like Paramonov, Bethea sees the influence of Fyodorov in the novel's "almost morbid" preoccupation with death (161), noting as well the macabre "Dulcinea," who sparks the passion of the quixotic Kopyonkin (178). Naiman sees both the necrophilous implications of Serbinov's encounter with Sonya on his mother's grave and the novel's homoeroticism as the "perversion of the utopian ideal" (357).

Seifrid treats Platonov's predilection for describing even living bodies in a state of decay as a sign of the alienation of consciousness from matter (108–9). While recognizing that the "frequent desire of Platonov's characters to be near, if not in physical contact with, a corpse" bears a "certain resemblance to necrophilia," Seifrid sees this as an "ironic surrogate for resurrection" (127). Seifrid's focus on resurrection is based on the importance of Fyodorov's philosophy to the development of Platonov's thought, yet some scholars (Paramonov 344–46) argue that Fyodorov's entire philosophical system is based on necrophilia rather than resurrection (see note 39).

32 Fromm quotes this last phrase from H. von Hentig, *Der Nekrotope Mensch* (Stuttgart: F. Engke Verlag, 1964).

33 According to Fromm, "the engineer who is passionately interested in the construction of machines of all kinds" is not necessarily an example of the necrophilic character, for it is possible to be fascinated by machines and still have a "great love of life," people, and nature (343). This is certainly the case with Sasha Dvanov, who, unlike the foreman, is "interested in machines as much as he is in other active and living objects" (*Chevengur* 65).

34 Podoroga (195) also notes the conflation of sexual reproduction and graveyards in the novel: "Sexual energy is used not for the birth of life, but for its rebirth. This is why Platonov's necrophilia is to be understood as an attempt to work out a new conception of human time: it is due only to a feeling of love for the dead that we become closer to dead, forgotten time . . . and revive it, draw it into the present and change ourselves, helping the dead become closer to the living."

35 Fromm cites "malignant incestuousness" as "one of the earliest roots, if not *the* root, of necrophilia" (364; emphasis in the original).

36 Zakhar Pavlovich's desire for a living mother resembles Simon Serbinov's rationale for later regretting the death of his own mother: "Wherever little Zakhar Pavlovich went,

he knew that he had a mother, who was waiting for him forever, and he feared nothing" (57–58). Serbinov's reasoning is stated more baldly: "Simon lived because he felt his mother's pity for him." Simon could "fail to love her, he forgot her address, but he lived because his mother had at some point fenced him off for a long time from many other people with her need for him" (360). In both Zakhar Pavlovich's and Serbinov's cases, the Fyodorovian emphasis on memory and filial duty is reversed: it is the parents whose memory serves to anchor their children in the world, and not the other way around.

37 The same dream reinforces the connection between sons and their dead fathers: Zakhar Pavlovich's father tells his wife to bury him in his old pants, so that his new ones can go to his son.

38 In his later work, Platonov was able to shake off the grip of the dead father, but only at great cost. Naiman argues that in his 1939 play "The Father's Voice" ("Golos ottsa") Platonov "once and for all renounces Fyodorov's philosophy in favor of Stalinist ideology" (" 'Iz istiny' " 248). There is no longer any need to resurrect the biological father; in the figure of Stalin, the hero has the only father he will ever need.

39 Thanks to the coincidence of Fyodorov's recent revival with the publication of Fromm in Russian, *Nezavisimaia gazeta* featured a polemic on whether or not Fyodorov could be termed a necrophile. In her review of the philosophical journal *Put'*, Elena Ivanitskaia asserts that Fyodorov's fixation on graves, dead bodies, and cemeteries makes him a classic case of necrophilia (*Nezavisimaia gazeta*, 31 Mar. 1993). On 15 May of the same year, Pavel Gurevich printed a rebuttal, claiming that Ivanitskaia confuses Fyodorov's philosophy with his personality. Their difference of opinion essentially amounts to a value judgment: Ivanitskaia, who is critical of Fyodorov, finds that his insistence on resurrection is merely a cover for his obsession with death, while Gurevich, who finds Fyodorov more appealing, concentrates on the positive side of Fyodorov's message rather than on his morbid preoccupations.

40 In his elaboration of Platonov's "archdiscourse about the world," Zholkovsky asserts that family life in Platonov's work, while usually unhappy, is often improved "by establishing 'additional links,' outside or inside the family: extrafamilially, by adopting a child, parent, or spouse . . . ; intrafamilially, by upgrading existing relationships (by a reconciliation of the spouses after an affair or even an alternative marriage; by a mutual adoption of children and parents; by a child's assumption of mediational, sometimes androgynous functions; by a resurrection of the parents, restoration of their graves, or through rejoining them in death" (Zholkovsky, *Text Counter Text* 292, 293). Zholkovsky's typology is an excellent explanatory tool, summarizing in a few short lines all the possible outcomes of family crises in Platonov's fiction. But the very breadth of possible solutions shows that some choices preclude others; in attempting to compensate for the loss of his father, Dvanov formed "extrafamilial" ties with Kopyonkin and the Chevengurians, but he chooses to return to his dead father rather than "upgrade" his existing relationship with Zakhar Pavlovich.

CONCLUSION

1. Naiman contrasts the discursive terrors of NEP with the actual Terror of the 1930s: "Liberated from the ideological terrors of coexistence and of indefinite political anticipation, Bolshevism was free to enjoy to the hilt the exercise of its own naked power and all of the material benefits that power could bring" (*Sex in Public* 289). Much of his argument is persuasive; the stark disparity between state-sanctioned mass murder and the eerie, unrelenting happiness of official propaganda makes the Stalin era all the more horrifying. Nonetheless, his suggestion that true understanding of the Stalinist Terror requires probing "the depths of the discursive terror that preceded it" is fraught with complex ramifications: are we to understand that the "Gothic" mentality of the 1920s paved the way for the physical extermination of millions?
2. The novel was finished in August 1929 and published in 1930.
3. Both the story and the novel were written in 1929; the publication of "Mahogany" abroad did serious damage to Pilnyak's career. Browning argues that one should not look at *Volga* as a retreat from "Mahogany," since Pilnyak had apparently been planning to write a novel all along. The publication of a smaller part of the novel first was consistent with Pilnyak's prior publishing history; Browning points to Pilnyak's inclusion of previously published stories and sketches in *The Naked Year* to justify his claim. While most of the novella is, indeed, included in *Volga*, the most politically troubling passages were not; the Trotskyite Akim is nowhere to be found in the novel. In addition, Pilnyak's already unflattering portrayal of Yakov Karpovich and the Bezdetov brothers takes on entirely new significance in the novel; when Ozhogov tells Yakov Karpovich that he has interrupted the Bezdetovs' visit in order to "take a look at the forms of counterrevolution," he is correct only insofar as these men do embody the idea of counterrevolution within the text. When he makes the same statement in the novel, he is referring to the conspiracy of Yakov Karpovich, the Bezdetovs, and Poltorak to blow up the dam (Pil'niak, *Povesti* 656; *Romany* 445). The abstract, metaphysical enemies of "Mahogany" have now become consummately evil saboteurs, perhaps suggesting that neither kind of counterrevolution should be tolerated.
4. The phrasing is almost identical in both versions of the text, although the novel adds the word "themselves" (*sami*): "zheny sami ushli ot nikh" (Pil'niak, *Povesti* 659; *Romany* 490).
5. Solidarity among prostitutes also connects *The Pit* to "The Twelve": as part of his satire on the new language of the revolutionary times, Blok briefly describes a set of prostitutes who discuss their fees as though they were at a party meeting (348).
6. For a discussion of the negative associations evoked by the term *babii bunt*, see Viola (23).
7. Pilnyak's novel is dated "February–August 1929" (606). Goldman discusses the *bab'i bunty* as a phenomenon of the spring of 1929, while Viola discusses a number of such riots during the same year (Goldman, "Industrial Politics" 60; Viola 34–37). The *bab'i bunty* continued into 1930.

8   Here it is important to recall the not-insignificant role Pilnyak himself played in the motif's development. Gruesome rapes are described in his 1923 short story "Old Cheese" ("Staryi syr"), and the heroine of his 1924 "Moist Mother Earth" ("Mat' Syra-zemlia") endures a long and agonizing death after being impaled on a stake. At one point in his novel *The Naked Year* (*Golyi god*, 1920–22), the revolution itself is identified with the desire to rape every woman in one's path. For a discussion of sexual violence in Pilnyak's early work, see Naiman (*Sex in Public* 59–63).

9   The manner in which the women advance toward Laslo, slowly and wordlessly, is reminiscent of the last section of Gogol's "Viy," in which the dead witch rises at night and attempts to kill Khoma Brut.

10 Bonnell argues that Mukhina's statue is the "definitive statement" about the feminization of the countryside in Soviet propaganda, "using gender differences to convey the relationship between the worker (male) and peasant (female) and, by implication, between urban and rural spheres of Soviet society" (122).

WORKS CITED

Adams, Henry. "The Dynamo and the Virgin." *The Education of Henry Adams.* New York: Modern Library, 1946. 379-90.

Andrew, Joe. "Babel's 'My First Goose.'" *The Structural Analysis of Russian Narrative Fiction.* Ed. Joe Andrew and Christopher Pike. Keele: Keele University Press, 1984. 64-81.

———. *Women in Russian Literature, 1700-1863.* Basingstoke: Macmillan, 1988.

Anninskii, Lev. "East and West in the Work of Andrei Platonov." *Soviet Studies in Literature* 4.4 (1968): 79-105.

Attwood, Lynne. *The New Soviet Man and Woman: Sex Role Socialization in the USSR.* Bloomington: Indiana University Press, 1990.

Avins, Carol. "Kinship and Concealment in *Red Cavalry* and Babel's 1920 Diary." *Slavic Review* 53.3 (1994): 694-710.

Babel, Isaac. *Collected Stories.* Ed. and trans. Walter Morison. New York: New American Library, 1955.

———. *Collected Stories / Isaac Babel.* Trans. David McDuff. London: Penguin, 1994.

Babel', Isaak. *Sochineniia.* 2 vols. Moscow: Khudozhestvennaia literatura, 1990.

Badikov, V. V. "Primechaniia." *Izbrannoe.* By Iurii Olesha. Sverdlovsk: Uralskogo universiteta, 1988. 435-47.

Badinter, Elisabeth. *XY: On Masculine Identity.* Trans. Lydia Davis. New York: Columbia University Press, 1995.

Bakhtin, Mikhail. *The Dialogic Imagination.* Ed. Michael Holquist. Trans. Caryl Emerson and Michael Holquist. Austin: University of Texas Press, 1981.

Barrat, Andrew. *Yurii Olesha's "Envy."* Birmingham Slavonic Monographs 12. Birmingham, 1981.

———. "Yury Olesha's Three Ages of Man: A Close Reading of 'Liompa.'" *Modern Language Review* 75.3 (1980): 597-614.

Beaujour, Elizabeth Klosty. "The Imagination of Failure: Fiction and Autobiography in the Work of Yury Olesha." *Autobiographical Statements in Twentieth-Century Russian Literature.* Ed. Jane Gary Harris. Princeton: Princeton University Press, 1990. 123-32.

———. *The Invisible Land: A Study of the Artistic Imagination of Iurii Olesha.* New York: Columbia University Press, 1970.

———. "On Choosing One's Ancestors: Some Afterthoughts on *Envy.*" *Ulbandus Review: A Journal of Slavic Languages and Literatures* 2 (1979). 24-36.

Beauvoir, Simone de. *The Second Sex.* Trans. and ed. H. M. Parshely. New York: Vintage Books, 1974.

Belinkov, Arkadii V. *Sdacha i gibel' sovetskogo intelligenta: Iurii Olesha.* Prepared for publication by N. Belinkova. Madrid, 1976.

Belyi, Andrei. "Veininger o pole i kharaktere." *Russkii Eros, ili Filosofiia liubvi v Rossii.* Comp. and ed. V. P. Shestakov. Moscow: Progress, 1991. 100-105.

Bernstein, Frances L. "'What Everyone Should Know about Sex': Gender, Sexual Enlightenment, and the Politics of Health in Revolutionary Russia, 1918-1931." Diss. Columbia U, 1997.

Bethea, David M. *The Shape of Apocalypse in Modern Russian Fiction.* Princeton: Princeton University Press, 1991.

Bettelheim, Bruno. *Symbolic Wounds:*

Puberty Rites and the Envious Male. New rev. ed. New York: Collier Books, 1971.

Biale, David. *Eros and the Jews: From Biblical Israel to Contemporary America*. New York: Basic Books, 1992.

Blok, A. A. *Sobranie sochinenii v vos'mi tomakh*. Moscow-Leningrad: Khudozhestvennaia literatura, 1960–63.

Bogdanov, A. A. *Voprosy sotsializma*. Moscow: Politizdat, 1990.

Bonnell, Victoria E. *Iconography of Power: Soviet Political Posters under Lenin and Stalin*. Berkeley: University of California Press, 1997.

Borden, Richard C. "The Magic and Politics of Childhood: The Childhood Theme in the Works of Iurii Olesha, Valentin Kataev, and Vladimir Nabokov." Diss. Columbia U, 1987.

Borenstein, Eliot. "Slavophilia: The Incitement to Russian Sexual Discourse." *Slavic and East European Journal* 40.1 (1996): 142–47.

———. "Tekst kak mashina smerti: voennye rasskazy A. Platonova." *Voina i literatura, 1941–1945*. Ekaterinburg: Ural State Pedagogical University Press, 2000. 109–17.

Bourke, Joanna. *Dismembering the Male: Men's Bodies, Britain, and the Great War*. Chicago: University of Chicago Press, 1996.

Brodal, Jan. "Fathers and Sons: Isaac Babel and the Generation Conflict." *Scando-Slavica* 17 (1971): 27–43.

Brod, Harry, and Michael Kaufman, eds. *Theorizing Masculinities*. London: Sage Publications, 1994.

Bronfen, Elisabeth. *Over Her Dead Body: Death, Femininity, and the Aesthetic*. New York: Routledge, 1992.

Brown, Clarence. "Yuri Olesha." *The Portable Twentieth-Century Russian Reader*. Ed. Clarence Brown. New York: Viking Press, 1985. 230–34.

Brown, Edward J. "Isaac Babel: Horror in a Minor Key." *Russian Literature since the Revolution*. Cambridge: Harvard University Press, 1982.

Browning, Gary. *Boris Pilniak: Scythian at a Typewriter*. Ann Arbor: Ardis, 1985.

Bulgakov, M. A. *Sobranie sochinenii v piati tomakh*. Moscow: Khudozhestvennaia literatura, 1989.

Burdekin, Katharine (Murray Constantine). *Swastika Night*. New York: Feminist Press of the City University of New York, 1985.

Caesar, Adrian. *Taking It like a Man: Suffering, Sexuality, and the War Poets: Brooke, Sassoon, Owen, Graves*. Manchester: Manchester University Press, 1993.

Čapek, Karel. *War with the Newts*. Trans. M. and R. Weatherall. Evanston, Ill.: Northwestern University Press, 1985.

Carden, Patricia. *The Art of Isaac Babel*. Ithaca: Cornell University Press, 1972.

Chalmaev, V. "Plennik svobody ('Nechaiannye' i vechnye katastrofy v prekrasnom i iarostnom mire Andreia Platonova)." Kornienko, *"Strana filosofov"* 3–50.

———. Primechaniia. *Chut'e Pravdy*. By Andrei Platonov. Moscow: Sovetskaia Rossiia, 1990. 429–58.

Chekhov, A. P. *Polnoe sobranie sochinenii i pisem v tridstati tomakh*. Moscow, 1985.

Chernyshevskii, Nikolai. *Chto delat'?* Gor'kii: Gor'kovskoe knizhnoe izdatel'stvo, 1953.

Chodorow, Nancy J. *Feminism and Psychoanalytic Theory*. New Haven: Yale University Press, 1989.

Cioran, Samuel D. *Vladimir Solov'ev and*

the Knighthood of the Divine Sophia. Waterloo: Wilfrid Laurier University Press, 1977.

Clark, Katerina. *The Soviet Novel: History as Ritual*. Chicago: University of Chicago Press, 1985.

Clark, Toby. "The 'New Man's' Body: A Motif in Early Soviet Culture." *Art of the Soviets: Painting, Sculpture, and Architecture in a One-Party State, 1917–1992*. Manchester: Manchester University Press, 1993. 33–50.

Clements, Barbara Evans. *Bolshevik Feminist: The Life of Aleksandra Kollontai*. Bloomington: Indiana University Press, 1979.

Cornwell, Neil. "The Principle of Distortion in Olesha's *Envy*." *Essays in Poetics* 5.1 (1980): 15–35.

Costlow, Jane T., Stephanie Sandler, and Judith Vowles. Introduction. *Sexuality and the Body in Russian Culture*. Ed. Jane T. Costlow, Stephanie Sandler, and Judith Vowles. Stanford: Stanford University Press, 1993. 1–38.

Davis, Robert Con. "Critical Introduction: The Discourse of the Father." *The Fictional Father: Lacanian Readings of the Text*. Ed. Robert Con Davis. Amherst: University of Massachusetts Press, 1981. 1–26.

Dawson, Graham. *Soldier Heroes: British Adventure, Empire, and the Imagining of Masculinities*. London: Routledge, 1994.

Dellamora, Richard. *Masculine Desire: The Sexual Politics of Victorian Aestheticism*. Chapel Hill: University of North Carolina Press, 1990.

Dijkstra, Bram. *Idols of Perversity: Fantasies of Feminine Evil in Fin-de-Siècle Culture*. Oxford: Oxford University Press, 1986.

Disch, Thomas M. *The Man Who Had No Idea*. London: Victor Gollancz, Ltd., 1982.

Dostoevskii, F. M. *Sobranie sochinenii v piatnadtsati tomakh*. Leningrad: Nauka, 1989.

Drubek-Maier, Natasha. "Rossia—'pustota v kishkakh' mira." *Novoe literaturnoe obozrenie* 9 (1994): 251–68.

Dunham, Vera S. *In Stalin's Time: Middle-class Values in Soviet Fiction*. Enlarged and updated edition. Durham: Duke University Press, 1990.

———. "The Strong-Woman Motif." *The Transformation of Russian Society: Aspects of Social Change since 1861*. Ed. Cyril E. Black. Cambridge: Harvard University Press, 1960. 459–83.

Durfee, Thea Margaret. "*Cement* and *How the Steel Was Tempered*: Variations on the New Soviet Woman." *A Plot of Her Own: The Female Protagonist in Russian Literature*. Ed. Sona Stephan Hoisington. Evanston: Northwestern University Press, 1995. 89–101.

Eco, Umberto. "The Myth of Superman." *Contemporary Literary Criticism: Modernism through Poststructuralism*. Ed. Robert Con Davis. New York: Longman, 1986. 330–44.

Ehre, Milton. "Olesha's *Zavist'*: Utopia and Dystopia." *Slavic Review* 50.3 (1991): 601–11.

Eidelman, Dawn D. *George Sand and the Nineteenth-Century Russian Love-Triangle Novels*. London and Toronto: Associated University Presses.

Eidinova, V. "K tvorcheskoi biografii A. Platonova." *Voprosy literatury* 3 (1976): 213–26.

Eng, Jan van der. "The Pointed Conclusion as Story Finale and Cyclic Element in *Red Cavalry*: In Honor of Ladislav

Matejko." *Language and Literary Theory.* Ed. Benjamin Stolz, I. R. Titunik, and Lubomir Dolazel. Ann Arbor: University of Michigan Press, 1984. 585–94.

Engelstein, Laura. *The Keys to Happiness: Sex and the Search for Modernity in Fin-de-Siècle Russia.* Ithaca: Cornell University Press, 1992.

Erenburg, Il'ia. *Neobychainye pokhozhdeniia Khulio Khurenito: Zhizn'i gibel' Nikolaia Kurbova.* Moscow: Moskovskii rabochii, 1991.

Falen, James. *Isaac Babel, Russian Master of the Short Story.* Knoxville: University of Tennessee Press, 1974.

Farnsworth, Beatrice. *Aleksandra Kollontai: Socialism, Feminism, and the Bolshevik Revolution.* Stanford: Stanford University Press, 1980.

Fedorov, Nikolai Fedorovich. *Sochineniia.* Ed. S[vetlana] G[eorgievna] Semenova. Filosofskoe Nasledie 85. Moscow: Mysl', 1982.

Fitzpatrick, Sheila. *The Cultural Front: Power and Culture in Revolutionary Russia.* Ithaca: Cornell University Press, 1992.

———. "New Perspectives on the Civil War." *Party, State, and Society in the Russian Civil War: Explorations in Social History.* Ed. Diane P. Koenker, William G. Rosenberg, and Ronald Grigor Suny. Bloomington: Indiana University Press, 1989. 3–23.

———. *The Russian Revolution, 1917–1932.* Oxford and New York: Oxford University Press, 1984.

Flieger, Jerry Aline. *The Purloined Punchline: Freud, Comic Theory, and the Postmodern Text.* Baltimore: Johns Hopkins University Press, 1991.

Foucault, Michel. *The History of Sexuality.* Vol. 1: *An Introduction.* Trans. Robert Hurley. New York: Vintage Books, 1990.

Freud, Sigmund. *Jokes and Their Relation to the Unconscious.* Trans. and ed. James Strachey. New York: Norton, 1989.

———. *Totem and Taboo.* Trans. and ed. James Strachey. New York: Norton, 1950.

Friedberg, Maurice. "Yiddish Folklore Motifs in Isaak Babel's *Konarmiia*." *American Contributions to the Eighth International Congress of Slavists.* Vol. 2. Ed. Victor Terras. Columbus, Ohio: Slavica, 1978.

Fromm, Erich. *The Anatomy of Human Destructiveness.* New York: Holt, Rinehart and Winston, 1973.

Gallop, Jane. *Reading Lacan.* Ithaca: Cornell University Press, 1985.

———. *Thinking through the Body.* Gender and Culture Series. New York: Columbia University Press, 1988.

Gasiorowska, Xenia. *Women in Soviet Fiction, 1917–1964.* Madison: University of Wisconsin Press, 1968.

Geller, Mikhail. *Andrei Platonov v poiskax schast'ja.* Paris: YMCA, 1982.

———. See also Heller, Mixail.

Gessen, Masha. "Sex in the Media and the Birth of the Sex Media in Russia." *Postcommunism and the Body Politic.* Ed. Ellen E. Berry. Genders 22. New York: New York University Press, 1995. 197–228.

Girard, René. *Deceit, Desire, and the Novel: Self and Other in Literary Structure.* Trans. Yvonne Freccero. 4th ed. Baltimore: Johns Hopkins University Press, 1988.

———. *Things Hidden since the Foundation of the World.* Research undertaken in collaboration with Jean-Michel Oughourian and Guy Lefort. Trans.

Stephen Bann (books 2 and 3) and Michael Metteer (book 1). Stanford: Stanford University Press, 1987.

Gogol, Nikolai. *The Complete Tales of Nikolai Gogol.* 2 vols. Trans. Constance Garnett. Ed. Leonard J. Kent. Chicago: University of Chicago Press, 1985.

Goldman, Wendy Z. "Industrial Politics, Peasant Rebellion, and the Death of the Proletarian Women's Movement in the USSR." *Slavic Review* 55.1 (Spring 1996): 46–77.

———. *Women, the State, and Revolution: Soviet Family Policy and Social Life, 1917–1936.* New York: Cambridge University Press, 1993.

Gor'kii, Maksim. *Sobranie sochinenii.* Moscow: Khudozhestvennaia literatura, 1950.

Gorsuch, Anne E. "'A Woman Is Not a Man': The Culture of Gender and Generation in Soviet Russia, 1921–1928." *Slavic Review* 55.3 (Fall 1996): 636–60.

Goscilo, Helena. *Dehexing Sex: Russian Womanhood during and after Glasnost.* Ann Arbor: University of Michigan Press, 1996.

Gray, J. Glenn. *The Warriors: Reflections on Men in Battle.* New York: Harper and Rowe, 1959.

Greiner, Donald J. *Women Enter the Wilderness: Male Bonding and the American Novel of the 1980s.* Columbia: University of South Carolina Press, 1991.

Grongaard, Ragna. *An Investigation of the Composition and Theme in Isaak Babel's Literary Cycle "Konarmiia."* Aarhus: Arkona, 1979.

Groys, Boris. *The Total Art of Stalinism: Avant-Garde, Aesthetic Dictatorship, and Beyond.* Trans. Charles Rougle. Princeton: Princeton University Press, 1992.

Günther, Hans. "Zhanrovye problemy utopii i 'Chevengur' A. Platonova." *Utopiia i utopicheskoe myshlenie: Antalogiia zarubezhnoi literatury.* Ed. V. A. Chalikovskii. Moscow: Progress, 1991. 252–76.

Halfin, Igal. "The Rape of the Intelligentsia: A Proletarian Foundational Myth." *Russian Review* 56 (Jan. 1997): 90–109.

Harkins, William E. "The Philosophical Stories of Iurii Olesha." *Orbis Scriptus Dmitrii Tschizewski, zum 70. Geburtstag.* Ed. Dietrich Gerhardt et al. Munich: Wilhelm Fink Verlag, 1966. 349–54.

———. "The Theme of Sterility in Olesha's *Envy.*" *Major Soviet Writers: Essays in Criticism.* Ed. Edward Brown. New York: Oxford University Press, 1973. 281–94.

Heil, Jerry T. *No List of Political Assets: The Collaboration of Iurii Olesha and Abram Room on "Strogii iunosha" [A Strict Youth (1936)].* Munich: Otto Sagner, 1989.

Heldt, Barbara. *Terrible Perfection: Women and Russian Literature.* Bloomington: Indiana University Press, 1987.

Heller, Mikhail. *Cogs in the Wheel: The Formation of Soviet Man.* New York: A. A. Knopf, 1988.

———. See also Geller, Mikhail.

Hetényi, Zsuzsa. "Eskadronnaia dama, vozdvedennaia v Madonnu. Ambivalentnost' v *Konarmii* Isaaka Babelia." *Studia Slavica Hungaricae* 31 (1985): 161–69.

Hoberman, John M. "Otto Weininger and the Critique of Jewish Masculinity." *Jews and Gender: Responses to Otto Weininger.* Ed. Nancy A. Harrowitz and Barbara Hyams. Philadelphia: Temple University Press, 1995.

Hodgson, Katharine. "Myth-Making in Russian War Poetry." *The Violent Muse: Violence and the Artistic Imagination in Europe, 1910–1939.* Ed. Jana Howlett and Rod Mengham. Manchester: Manchester University Press, 1994. 65–76.

———. *Written with the Bayonet: Soviet Russian Poetry of World War II.* Liverpool: Liverpool University Press, 1996.

Hoeveler, Diane Long. *Romantic Androgyny: The Women Within.* University Park: Pennsylvania State University Press, 1991.

Horney, Karen. *Feminine Psychology.* Ed. Harold Kelman. New York: Norton, 1967.

Iablokov, E. A. "Komentarii." *Chevengur.* Moscow: Vysshaia skola, 1991. 518–650.

———. "O filosofskoi pozitsii A. Platonova (Proza serediny 20-kh–nachala 30-kh godov)." *Russian Literature* 32 (1992): 227–52.

Ingdahl, Kazimiera. "The Life/Death Dichotomy in Iurii Olesha's Short Story 'Liompa.'" *Studies in Twentieth-Century Russian Prose.* Ed. Nils Ake Nilsson. Stockholm: Almqvist and Wiksell, 1982. 156–85.

Irigaray, Luce. *This Sex Which Is Not One.* Trans. Catherine Porter with Carolyne Burke. Ithaca: Cornell University Press, 1985.

Ivantskaia, Elena. "Fedorov—Nekrofil?" *Nezavisimaia gazeta,* 1 March 1993, 7.

Jackson, Robert L. *Dostoevsky's Underground Man in Russian Literature.* The Hague: Mouton, 1958.

Jones, R. "The Primacy of the Subjective in the Work of Jurij Olesha." *Melbourne Slavonic Studies* 3 (1969): 3–11.

Kataev, Valentin. *Almaznyi moi venets.* Moscow: DEM, 1990.

———. *Sobranie sochinenii.* Moscow: Khudozhestvennaia literatura, 1983.

Kastsis, L. "Tvorchestvo I. E. Babelia: problemy interpretatsii." *Literaturnoe obozrenie* 1 (95): 73–76.

Kaverin, V. A. *Sobranie sochinenii v vos'mi tomakh.* Moscow: Khudozhestvennaia literatura, 1980.

Khlebnikov, Velimir. *Tvoreniia.* Moscow: Sovetskii pisatel', 1987.

Kiselev, A. "Odukhotvorenie mira: N. Fedorov i A. Platonov." Kornienko 237–48.

Klimontovich, Nikolai. "Zakliuchenie muzhskogo soiuza." *Muleta Z: EoroAsiia.* Paris: Edition "Vivirisme," 1993. 161–168.

Kon, Igor'. *The Sexual Revolution in Russia: From the Age of the Czars to Today.* Trans. James Riordan. New York: Free Press, 1995.

Kornblatt, Judith Deutsch. *The Cossack Hero in Russian Literature: A Study in Cultural Mythology.* Madison: University of Wisconsin Press, 1992.

Kornienko, N. V. "'Efirnyi trakt' (K istorii teksta povesti)." *Russian Literature* 32 (1992): 253–70.

———, ed. *"Strana filosofov" Andreia Platonova: problemy tvorchestva.* Moscow: Nasledie, 1993.

———. "V khudozhestvennoi masterskoi Platonova." Kornienko 306–41.

Kovskii, V. "Sud'ba tekstov v kontekste sud'by." *Voprosy literatury* 1 (1995): 23–78.

Kruchenykh, A. *Pobeda nad solntsem.* St. Petersburg: 1914.

Kuprin, A. I. *Sobranie sochinenii v deviati tomakh.* 9 vols. Moscow: Pravda, 1964.

Lacan, Jacques. *Écrits: A Selection.* Trans. Alan Sheridan. New York: Norton, 1977.

Langerak, Thomas. "Andrei Platonov v perelomnom periode tvorchestva:

Zametki ob 'Antiseksuse.'" *Russian Literature* 9 (1981): 303–22.

———. "Andrei Platonov v Voronezhe." *Russian Literature* 22 (1988): 437–68.

Lapidus, Gail. *Women in Soviet Society.* Berkeley: University of California Press, 1979.

Lauer, R. "Zur Gestalt Ivan Babichevs in Oleshas *Zavist'.*" *Die Welt der Slaven* 7 (1962): 46–54.

Lavrenov, Boris. *Sobranie sochinenii.* Vol. 1. Moscow: Khudozhestvennaia literatura, 1963.

LeBlanc, Ronald D. "The Soccer Match in *Envy.*" *Slavic and East European Journal* 32.1 (1988): 55–71.

Levin, Eve. *Sex and Society in the World of the Orthodox Slavs, 900–1700.* Ithaca: Cornell University Press, 1989.

Lévi-Strauss, Claude. *The Elementary Structures of Kinship.* Boston: Beacon Press, 1969.

Liubushkina, S. "Ideia bessmertiia u rannego Platonova." *Russian Literature* 23.4 (1988).

Livshits, L. "Materialy k tvorcheskoi biografii I. Babelia." *Voprosy literatury* 4 (1964): 110–35.

Lukashevich, Stephan. *N. F. Fedorov (1828–1903): A Study in Russian Eupsychian and Utopian Thought.* Newark: University of Delaware Press, 1977.

Lunts, Lev. *Vne Zakona; P'esy; Rasskazy; Stat'i.* St. Petersburg: Kompozitor, 1994.

Luplow, Carol. *Isaac Babel's "Red Cavalry."* Ann Arbor: Ardis, 1982.

Lynch, Michael. "'Here Is Adhesiveness': From Friendship to Homosexuality." *Victorian Studies* 29.1 (1985): 67–96.

Maegd-Soëp, Carolina de. *The Emancipation of Women in Russian Literature and Society: A Contribution to the Knowledge of the Russian Society during the 1860s.* Ghent: Ghent State University, 1978.

Maguire, Robert A. *Red Virgin Soil: Soviet Literature in the 1920s.* Princeton: Princeton University Press, 1968.

Maiakovskii, Vladimir. *Polnoe sobranie sochinenii v trinadtsati tomakh.* 13 vols. Moscow: Khudozhestvennaia literatura, 1955–61.

Mandel'stam, O. E. *Sobranie sochinenii v chetyrekh tomakh.* Moscow: Terra, 1991.

Mann, James A., ed. *The Rediscovery of Man: The Complete Short Science Fiction of Cordwainer Smith.* Framingham: NESFA Press, 1993.

Martini, Virgilio. *The World without Women.* Trans. Emile Capouya. New York: Dial Press, 1971.

Masing-Delic, Irene. *Abolishing Death: A Salvation Myth of Russian Twentieth-Century Literature.* Stanford: Stanford University Press, 1992.

Matich, Olga. "Androgyny and the Russian Religious Renaissance." *Western Philosophical Systems in Russian Literature.* Ed. Anthony M. Mlikotin. Los Angeles: University of California Press, 1979. 165–75.

———. "Dialectics of Cultural Return: Zinaida Gippius's Personal Myth." *Cultural Mythologies of Russian Modernism: From the Golden Age to the Silver Age.* Ed. Boris Gasparov, Robert P. Hughes, and Irina Paperno. Berkeley: University of California Press, 1992. 19–51.

———. "The Merezhkovskys' Third Testament and the Russian Utopian Tradition." Ed. Robert P. Hughes and Irina Paperno. *Christianity and the Eastern Slavs.* Vol. 2: *Russian Culture and Modern Times.* Berkeley: University of California Press, 1994. 158–71.

———. "The Symbolist Meaning of Love: Theory and Practice." *Creating Life: The Aesthetic Utopia of Russian Modernism*. Ed. Irina Paperno and Joan Delaney Grossman. Stanford: Stanford University Press, 1994. 24–50.

———. "A Typology of Fallen Women in Nineteenth Century Russian Literature." *American Contributions to the Ninth International Congress of Slavists*. Vol. 2: *Literature, Politics, History*. Columbus, Ohio: Slavica, 1983. 325–43.

———. "What's to Be Done about Poor Nastja: Nastasja Filipovna's Literary Prototypes." *Wiener Slawistischer Almanach* 19 (1987): 47–64.

———. "Zinaida Gippius: Theory and Praxis of Love." *Readings in Russian Modernism To Honor Vladimir Fedorovich Markov*. Ed. Ronald Vroon and John E. Malmstad. Moscow: Nauka and Oriental Literatures, 1993. 237–50.

Mead, Margaret. *Male and Female: A Study of Sexes in a Changing World*. New York: William Morrow, 1953.

Mitchell, Juliet. *Psychoanalysis and Feminism: Freud, Reich, Laing, and Women*. New York: Vintage, 1975.

Mitscherlich, Alexander. *Society without the Father: A Contribution to Social Psychology*. Trans. Eric Mosbacher. New York: Harper-Collins, 1993.

Moi, Toril. "The Missing Mother: The Oedipal Rivalries of René Girard." *Diacritics* 12.2 (1982): 21–31.

Moller, Peter Ulf. *Postlude to the Kreutzer Sonata: Tolstoi and the Debate on Sexual Morality in Russian Literature in the 1890s*. Trans. John Kendal. Leiden: E. J. Brill, 1988.

Montagu, Ashley. "The New Litany of 'Innate Depravity,' or Original Sin Revisited." *Man and Aggression*. Ed. Ashley Montagu. 2nd ed. London: Oxford University Press, 1973. 3–18.

More, Thomas. *Utopia*. Ed. George M. Logan and Robert M. Adams. Cambridge: Cambridge University Press, 1989.

Morris, Marcia A. *Saints and Revolutionaries: The Ascetic Hero in Russian Literature*. New York: State University of New York Press, 1993.

Morson, Gary Saul. *Narrative and Freedom: The Shadows of Time*. New Haven: Yale University Press, 1994.

Mosse, George L. *Nationalism and Sexuality: Middle-Class Morality and Sexual Norms in Modern Europe*. Madison: University of Wisconsin Press, 1985.

Murphy, Peter F., ed. *Fictions of Masculinity: Crossing Cultures, Crossing Sexualities*. New York: New York University Press, 1994.

Nabokov, Vladimir. *Sobranie sochinenii*. 4 vols. Moscow: Pravda, 1990.

Nakhimovsky, Alice Stone. *Russian-Jewish Literature and Identity: Jabotinsky, Babel, Grossman, Galich, Rozner, Markish*. Baltimore: Johns Hopkins University Press, 1992.

Naiman, Eric. "Andrej Platonov and the Inadmissibility of Desire." *Russian Literature* 23 (1988): 319–67.

———. "The Case of Chubarov Alley: Collective Rape, Utopian Desire, and the Mentality of NEP." *Russian History/Histoire Russe* 17.1 (Spring 1990): 27.

———. "Historectomies: On the Metaphysics of Reproduction in a Utopian Age." *Sexuality and the Body in Russian Culture*. Ed. Jane T. Costlow, Stephanie Sandler, and Judith Vowles. Stanford: Stanford University Press, 1993. 255–76.

———. " 'Iz istiny ne sushchestvuet vykhoda': Andrei Platonov mezhdu dvukh utopii." *Novoe literaturnoe obozrenie* 9 (1994): 233–50.

———. *Sex in Public: The Incarnation of Early Soviet Ideology.* Princeton: Princeton University Press, 1997.

———. "The Thematic Mythology of Andrej Platonov." *Russian Literature* 21 (1987): 189–216.

Naydan, Michael M. "Intimations of Biblical Myth and the Creative Process in Iurii Olesha's 'Vishnevaia kostochka.'" *Slavic and East European Journal* 33.3 (1989): 273–85.

Nesbet, Anne, and Eric Naiman. "Формы времени в 'Формах времени...'" *Новое литературное обозрение* 2 (1993): 90–109.

Nilsson, Nils Ake. "Through the Wrong End of Binoculars: An Introduction to Iurii Olesha." *Major Soviet Writers: Essays in Criticism.* Ed. Edward Brown. New York: Oxford University Press, 1973. 254–279.

Nivat, George. "Les Aquarelles de Iouri Olecha." Preface to *L'Envie.* 1978. Rpt. in *Vers la fin du mythe russe: Essais sur la culture russe de Gogol à nos jours.* Lausanne: L'Age d'Homme, 1982. 237–45.

Noble, David F. *A World without Women: The Christian Clerical Culture of Western Science.* New York: Knopf, 1992.

Nyman, Jopi. *Men Alone: Masculinity, Individualism, and Hard-Boiled Fiction.* Costerus New Series 111. Amsterdam: Rodopi, 1997.

O'Connor, Timothy E. "Bolshevism and the Ideology of Resurrection." *European Studies Journal* 11.1 (1992): 19–37.

Oja, Matt F. "Iurii Olesha's *Zavist'*: Fantasy, Reality, and Split Personality." *Canadian Slavonic Papers: An Inter-Disciplinary Quarterly Devoted to the Soviet Union and Eastern Europe* 28.1 (1986): 52–63.

Olesha, Iurii. *Izbrannoe.* Sverdlovsk: Izdatel'stvo Ural'skogo universiteta, 1988.

———. *P'esy: Stat'i o teatre i dramaturgii.* Ed. G. Mokrushcheva. Moscow: Iskusstvo, 1968.

———. *Povesti i rasskazy.* Moscow: Khudozhestvennaia literatura, 1965.

———. "Strogii iunosha: P'esa dlia kinematografa." *Novyi mir* (8) 1934: 66–89.

———. *Zavist'; Tri tolstiaka; Ni dnia bez strochki.* Moscow: Khudozhestvennaia literatura, 1989.

Osipovich, Tatiana. "Sex, Love, and Family in the Works of Andrei Platonov." Diss. U. of Pittsburgh, 1988.

Ostrovskii, Nikolai. *Kak zakalialas' stal'.* Moscow: Russkii iazyk, 1985.

Oulanoff, Hongor. *The Serapion Brothers: Theory and Practice.* The Hague: Mouton, 1966.

Paglia, Camille. *Sexual Personae: Art and Decadence from Nefertiti to Emily Dickinson.* New York: Vintage Books, 1991.

Paperno, Irina. *Chernyshevsky and the Age of Realism: A Study in the Semiotics of Behavior.* Stanford: Stanford University Press, 1988.

Papernyi, Z. S. *Proletarskie poety pervykh let sovetskoi epokhi.* 2nd ed. Leningrad: Sovetskii pisatel', 1959.

Paramonov, Boris. "Chevengur i okrestnosti." *Kontinent* 54 (1987): 333–75.

Peppard, Victor. *The Poetics of Yury Olesha.* University of Florida Humanities Monograph 63. Gainesville: University of Florida Press, 1989.

Pertsov, Viktor Osipovich. *"My zhivem vpervye": O tvorchestve Iuriia Oleshi.* in *Sovremenniki: Izbrannye literaturno-kriticheskie stat'i v dvux tomax.* Vol. 2. 169-325.

Pil'niak, Boris. *Povesti i rasskazy.* Moscow: Sovremennik, 1991.

———. *Romany.* Moscow: Sovremennik, 1991.

Pirozhkova, A. N., and N. N. Iurgeneva, comps. *Vospominaniia o Babele.* 2nd expanded ed. Moscow: Knizhnaia palata, 1989.

Piskunova, S., and V. Piskunov. "Sokrovennyi Platonov: K vyxodu v svet romana 'Chevengur,' povesti 'Kotlovan' i 'Iuvenil'noe more.'" *Literaturnoe obozrenie* 1 (1989): 17-29.

Platonov, Andrei. *Chevengur.* Ed. E. A. Iablokov. Moscow: Vysshaia skola, 1991.

———. *Chut'e pravdy.* Ed. V. A. Chalmaev. Moscow: Sovetskaia Rossiia, 1990.

———. *Gosudarstvennyi zhitel'; Proza; Rannie sochineniia; Pis'ma.* Minsk: Mastackaia literatura, 1990.

———. *Na zare tumannoi iunosti: Povesti i rasskazy.* Ed. M. B. Dolotseva. Moscow: Sovetskaia Rossiia, 1990.

———. *Starik i starukha: Poteriannaia proza.* Ed. Fol'ker Levin. München: Verlag Otto Sagner, 1984.

———. *Vozvrashchenie.* Ed. M. Platonova. Moscow: Molodaia gvardiia, 1989.

Podoroga, Valery. "The Eunuch of the Soul: Positions of Reading and the World of Platonov." *Late Soviet Culture: From Perestroika to Novostroika.* Ed. Thomas Lahusen with Gene Kuperman. Durham: Duke University Press, 1993. 187-231.

Popovskii, Mark. *Tretii lishnii: on, ona i sovestskii rezhim.* London: Overseas Publications, 1980.

Porter, Cathy. *Alexandra Kollontai: A Biography.* London: Virago, 1980.

Poulin, Francis. "Velimir Xlebnikov's *Nočnoj obysk^*, $3^6 + 3^6$, and the Krondstadt Revolts." *Slavic and Eastern European Journal* 34.4 (1990): 511-19.

Povartsov, S. "'Mir, vidimyi cherez cheloveka': K tvorcheskoi biografii I. Babelia." Pirozhkova and Iurgeneva 320-334.

Remy, John. "Patriarchy and Fratriarchy as Forms of Androcracy." *Men, Masculinities, and Social Theory.* Ed. Jeff Hearn and David Morgan. London: Unwin Hyman, 1990. 43-54.

Rich, Adrienne. *Of Woman Born: Motherhood as Experience and Institution.* New York: Bantam, 1977.

Rosen, David. *The Changing Fictions of Masculinity.* Urbana: University of Illinois Press, 1993.

Rosenshield, Gary. "Afterword: The Problems of Gender Criticism; or, What Is to Be Done about Dostoevsky?" *A Plot of Her Own: The Female Protagonist in Russian Literature.* Ed. Sona Stephan Hoisington. Evanston: Northwestern University Press, 1995. 114-27.

Rozanov, Vasilii Vasilievich. *Sochineniia.* 2 vols. Moscow: Pravda, 1990.

Rubin, Gayle. "The Traffic in Women: Notes toward a Political Economy of Sex." *Toward an Anthropology of Women.* Ed. Rayne Reiter. New York: Monthly Review Press, 1975. 157-210.

Said, Edward. *The World, the Text, and the Critic.* Cambridge: Harvard University Press, 1983.

Sarnov, B. "Kak opredelit' avtorskuiu voliu." *Voprosy literatury* 1 (1995): 87-92.

Savel'zon, I. "Kommentarii k 'Volod'kinu muzhu.'" *Russian Literature* 32 (1992): 307-28.

Scheglov, Yuri K. "Some Themes and Archetypes in Babel's *Red Cavalry*." *Slavic Review* 53.3 (Fall 1994): 653–70.

Schlesinger, Rudolf, ed. *The Family in the USSR: Documents and Readings.* London, 1949.

Schwenger, Peter. *Phallic Critiques: Masculinity and Twentieth-Century Literature.* London and Boston: Routledge and Kegan Paul, 1984.

Sedgwick, Eve Kosofsky. *Between Men: English Literature and Male Homosocial Desire.* Gender and Culture Series. New York: Columbia University Press, 1985.

Seifrid, Thomas. *Andrei Platonov: Uncertainties of Spirit.* Cambridge Studies in Russian Literature. New York: Cambridge University Press, 1992.

Semenova, Svetlana. "Mytarstva ideala: K vykhodu v svet 'Chevengura,' Andreia Platonova." *Chevengur.* By Andrei Platonov. Moscow: Vysshaia shkola, 1991. 489–517.

———. *Nikolai Fedorov: Tvorchestvo zhizni.* Moscow: Sovetskii pisatel', 1990. 363–73.

———. "'Tainoe tainykh' Andreia Platonova (Eros i pol)." Kornienko 73–131.

Shafarevich, Igor'. *Est' li u Rossii budushchee?* Moscow: Sovetskii pisatel', 1991.

Sheldon, Richard. Review of *The Invisible Land: A Study of the Artistic Imagination of Iurii Olesha.* By Elizabeth Klosty Beaujour. *Slavic Review* 4 (1971): 911–12.

Shenshin, V. K. *Traditsii F. M. Dostoevskogo i sovetskii roman 1920-kh godov. (K. Fedin, Iu. Olesha, L. Leonov).* Krasnoyarsk: Izd. Krasnoiarskogo universiteta, 1980.

Shepard, Joe. "Liubov' k dal'nemu i liubov' k blizhnemu v tvorchestve A. Platonova." Kornienko 249–54.

Shimak-Reifer, Jadviga. "V poiskakh istochnikov platonovskoi prozy. Zametki perevodchika." *Novoe literaturnoe obozrenie* 9 (1994): 269–75.

Shitareva, O. G. "Tvorcheskaia istoriia sozdaniia romana *Zavist'* Ju. Oleshi." *Filologicheskie nauki* 4 (1969): 82–92.

Showalter, Elaine. *Sexual Anarchy: Gender and Culture at the Fin de Siècle.* New York: Viking, 1990.

Sicher, Efraim. *Style and Structure in the Prose of Isaak Babel'.* Columbus: Slavica Publishers, 1986.

Siegel, George. "The Fallen Woman in Nineteenth Century Literature." *Harvard Slavic Studies* 5 (1970): 81–107.

Sobolev, Vl. "Izgnanie metafory." *Literaturnaia gazeta* 17 May 1933.

Spackman, Barbara. *Fascist Virilities: Rhetoric, Ideology, and Social Fantasy in Italy.* Minneapolis: University of Minnesota Press, 1996.

Stern, Mikhail, with August Stern. *Sex in the USSR.* Ed. and trans. Mark Howson and Cary Ryan. New York: Times Books, 1980.

Stine, Peter. "Isaac Babel and Violence." *Modern Fiction Studies* 30.2 (1984): 237–55.

Stites, Richard. *Revolutionary Dreams: Utopian Vision and Experimental Life in the Russian Revolution.* New York: Oxford University Press, 1989.

———. *The Women's Liberation Movement in Russia: Feminism, Nihilism, and Bolshevism (1860–1930).* Princeton: Princeton University Press, 1988.

Striedter, Jurij. "Three Postrevolutionary Utopian Novels." *The Russian Novel from Pushkin to Pasternak.* Ed. John Garrard.

New Haven: Yale University Press, 1983. 177–201.

Suok-Olesha, O., and E. Pel'son, comps. *Vospominaniia o Iurii Oleshi.* Moscow: Sovetskii pisatel', 1975.

Tertz, Abram (Andrei Siniavsky). "On Socialist Realism." Trans. George Dennis. *"The Trial Begins" and "On Socialist Realism."* New York: Vintage Books, 1960.

Teskey, Ayleen. *Platonov and Fyodorov: The Influence of Christian Philosophy on a Soviet Writer.* Trowbridge-Wiltshire: Avebury, 1982.

Theweleit, Klaus. *Male Fantasies.* Vol. 1: *Women, Floods, Bodies, History.* Trans. Stephen Conway in collaboration with Erica Carter and Chris Turner. Theory and History of Literature Series. Minneapolis: University of Minnesota Press, 1987.

———. *Male Fantasies.* Vol. 2: *Psychoanalyzing the White Terror.* Trans. Erica Carter and Chris Turner in collaboration with Stephen Conway. Theory and History of Literature Series. Minneapolis: University of Minnesota Press, 1989.

Tiger, Lionel. *Men in Groups.* New York: Marion Boyars, 1984.

Todorov, Vladislav. *Red Square, Black Square: Organon for Revolutionary Imagination.* Albany: SUNY Press, 1995.

Tolstaia-Segal, Elena. "Ideologicheskie konteksty Platonova." *Russian Literature* 9.3 (1981): 231–80.

———. "'Stikhiinye sily': Platonov i Pil'niak (1928–1929)." *Slavica Hierosolymitana* 3 (1978): 89–109.

Tolstoi, A. N. *Sobranie sochinenii v desiati tomakh.* 10 vols. Moscow: Khudozhestvennaia literatura, 1958.

Tolstoi, L. N. *Sobranie sochinenii v dvenadtsati tomakh.* Moscow: Pravda, 1987.

Trilling, Lionel. Introduction. *The Collected Stories.* By Isaac Babel. New York: New American Library, 1955. 9–37.

Urban, A. "Sokrovennyi Platonov." *Zvezda* 7 (1989): 180–93.

Vail', Petr, and Aleksandr Genis. *Rodnaia rech': Uroki iziashchnoi slovesnosti.* Moscow: Nezavisimaia gazeta, 1991.

Viola, Lynne. "Бабьи Бунты and Peasant Women's Protest during Collectivization." *Russian Review* 45 (1986): 23–42.

Waters, Elizabeth. "The Female Form in Soviet Political Iconography, 1917–32." *Russia's Women: Accommodation, Resistance, Transformation.* Ed. Barbara Evans Clements, Barbara Alpern Engel, and Christine D. Worobec. Berkeley: University of California Press, 1991. 225–42.

Weininger, Otto. *Sex and Character.* New York: G. P. Putnam's Sons, 1975.

Williams, Robert C. "Collective Immortality: The Syndicalist Origins of Proletarian Culture, 1905–1910." *Slavic Review* 39.2 (1980): 389–402.

Zholkovskii, A. K., and M. B. Iampol'skii. *Babel'/Babel.* Moscow: Carte Blanche, 1994. 317–68.

Zholkovsky, Alexander. *Text Counter Text: Rereadings in Russian Literary History.* Stanford: Stanford University Press, 1994.

———. "Topos prostitutsii." *Babel'/Babel.* By A. K. Zholkovskii and M. B. Iampol'skii. Moscow: Carte Blanche, 1994. 317–68.

Ziolkowski, Margaret. *Hagiography and*

Modern Russian Literature. Princeton: Princeton University Press, 1988.

Zolotonosov, Mikhail. "Masturbanizatsiia: 'Erogennye zony' sovetskoi kul'tury 1920–1930-kh godov." *Erotika v russkoi literature: Ot Barkova do nashikh dnei, teksty i kommentarii, literaturnoe obozrenie, spetsial'nyi vypusk.* Ed. I. D. Prokhorova, S. Iu. Mazur, and G. B. Zykova. Moscow, 1992. 93–99.

INDEX

Abstinence, 8–10
Adams, Henry, 309n. 28
Affiliation vs. filiation, 14–18, 36–37, 40–41, 75, 125–127, 241, 245, 248–249
Akhmatova, Anna, 206
Andrew, Joe, 37, 92–93, 96, 98, 277n. 4, 297n. 27
Androgyny, 65, 151–154, 163–170, 187, 210, 300n. 44, 306nn. 1–4
Apollinaire, Guillaume, 73
Armand, Inessa, 12
Attwood, Lynne, 283n. 35
Avins, Carol 300n. 46

Baba, 55, 69, 291nn. 15–16
Babel, Isaak, 3, 5–6, 39–40, 133, 162, 191, 217, 226, 229, 231, 232, 248, 277n. 3, 292n. 20, 301n. 6; "The Crack," 298n. 29; "First Love," 298n. 29; "Guy de Maupassant," 295n. 5; *Maria*, 299n. 41; "Our Father Makhno," 292n. 19; *Red Cavalry*, 3, 23, 31, 39, 40, 43, 58–61, 64, 65, 66, 73–123, 149, 217, 226, 229, 234, 272, 276, 284n. 40, 288n. 61, 292nn. 19 and 22, 293n. 25, 295n. 5, 296n. 12, 297nn. 23 and 27, 299nn. 36 and 39, 300nn. 46 and 51, 305n. 23, 318n. 8; *Sunset*, 299n. 41
Babii bunt, 218–219, 324n. 7
Badinter, Elisabeth, 123
Bakhtin, Mikhail, 114, 122, 124, 318n. 4
Barrat, Andrew, 154, 301n. 1, 302n. 11, 305n. 31
Bataille, Georges, 53–54, 58
Beaujour, Elizabeth, 125, 301n. 1, 302nn. 4 and 15, 304n. 22
"Beautiful lady," 3, 52, 203, 205, 311n. 10
Bed and Sofa (film), 54
Bely, Andrei, 161, 213, 299n. 37
Berdyaev, Nikolai, 214, 316n. 45

Bernstein, Frances, 278n. 8, 283n. 33, 319n. 13
Bethea, David, 308n. 10, 313n. 16, 317n. 2, 321n. 30, 322n. 31
Bettelheim, Bruno, 123, 307n. 7
Biale, David, 105
Blok, Alexander, 3, 51–53, 64, 213, 287n. 52, 308n. 10; "The Twelve," 52–53, 55–56, 61, 62, 63, 71, 272, 293n. 27, 324n. 5
Bogdanov, Alexander, 28–30, 67, 196, 197, 211, 288n. 60, 313nn. 16 and 21
Bonnell, Victoria, 274–275, 309n. 4, 325n. 10
Borden, Richard, 303n. 15
Brodal, Jan, 297nn. 21 and 23
Bronfen, Elisabeth, 291n. 13–14
Brooke, Rupert, 33
Brotherhood: blood brotherhood (see *Pobratimstvo*); as metaphor, 24–25, 27–30, 48, 61–63, 113, 300nn. 46 and 49; as social structure, 20
Brown, Clarence, 301nn. 1 and 4
Browning, Gary, 324n. 3
Bulgakov, Mikhail: *Heart of a Dog*, 45
Burdekin, Katharine, 285n. 41

Campbell, Joseph, 115
Čapek, Karel: *The War with the Newts*, 285n. 41
Carden, Patricia, 119, 296n. 20, 297n. 24, 298n. 30
Chalmaev, V., 311n. 9, 315n. 25, 316nn. 37 and 38
Chekhov, Anton, 1; "A Nervous Breakdown," 50, 391nn. 8–10
Chodorow, Nancy, 123, 307n. 7, 320n. 22
Chernyshevskii, Nikolai: *What Is to Be Done?*, 8–10, 281nn. 22–26, 282nn. 27–28, 308n. 13

Christ, 61, 63–66, 230, 293nn. 26–27, 315n. 33
Chubarov Alley, 68, 71, 267–269, 279n. 7
Cioran, Samuel, 52
Civil War, Russian, 61, 71, 73–123, 276
Clark, Katerina, 197, 281n. 25, 313n. 13
Clark, Toby, 309n. 27
Clements, Barbara Evans, 282n. 31
Communist Youth League. *See* Komsomol
Comradeship, 5, 23, 26, 126–127, 284nn. 45–47; compared to friendship, 23–24, 30, 103–104, 115, 150; definitions of, 23
Cossacks, 18, 25–26, 39, 58–61, 73–123, 162, 231, 272, 286nn. 51–52, 291n. 16, 296nn. 1 and 7, 298nn. 28, 31, and 32, 299n. 36
Cycles (story cycles), 75, 90–91, 113–124

Davis, Robert Con, 81, 130–131
Delacourte, Marie, 165
Disch, Thomas M., 285n. 41
Domostroi, 274
Dostoevsky, Fyodor, 195, 205–210, 216, 277n. 4, 288n. 53; *Crime and Punishment*, 49, 294n. 30; *The Eternal Husband*, 53; *The Idiot*, 195, 205–210, 217, 309n. 20, 315n. 31, 316n. 32; *Notes from Underground* 49–50, 307n. 5
Drubek-Maier, Natasha, 316n. 40
Dunham, Vera, 277n. 3, 278n. 18

Eco, Umberto, 120–122
Ehre, Milton, 167, 295n. 6, 297n. 26, 304n. 17, 309n. 26
Ehrenburg, Ilya, 46–47
Eidinova, Violetta, 312n. 12
Engels, Friedrich, 10, 136
Eternal Feminine, 3, 52, 161, 185, 187, 194, 210, 214, 307n. 8, 316n. 40

Family: alternative structures, 8, 10–11, 13, 15, 19, 26; in Chernyshevsky, 8, 10; in Fyodorov, 27–28; juxtaposition with revolutionaries and soldiers, 3, 5; as "revolutionary cell," 14; struggle against, 11–14, 16, 17, 39, 76, 82–83, 125–128, 140, 192–193, 227–230
Family law and policy, Soviet, 6–7, 12
Fantomas, 122
Fascism, 31–36, 283n. 36, 285n. 41, 287n. 71
Fathers and sons, 17, 18, 19–21, 75–91, 124–151, 154–161, 177–180, 225–227, 242–263, 296nn. 9, 11, and 15–19, 297nn. 21–22, 300n. 1, 302n. 8, 303nn. 13 and 16, 304nn. 17, 18, and 21
Fellow travelers, 5, 136
Femininity, 16–18, 162–190, 191–196, 198–224, 229–231, 237–242, 264–276; as enemy, 17, 34–35, 47, 59–61, 66–67, 69–71, 126, 130, 191–192
Feminism, 10, 35, 43
Fertility and infertility, 82, 109–110, 134, 161, 164
Filiation. *See* Affiliation and filiation
First Five-Year Plan, 6, 264, 271, 276
Fitzpatrick, Sheila, 4, 278n. 6, 279n. 13, 280n. 15
Flex, Walter, 33
Flieger, Jerry Aline, 53–54
Foucault, Michel, 288n. 67
Fratriarchy, 21–23, 36, 61, 76. *See also* Brotherhood
Fratricide, 61, 64, 83–84
Free love, 7–8
Freud, Sigmund, 36–37, 129, 151, 175, 207, 236, 260, 305n. 27, 325n. 17: *Jokes and Their Relation to the Unconscious*, 53–55, 58, 60, 67; *Totem and Taboo*, 19–21, 83
Friedberg, Maurice, 299n. 40
Friendship, 11, 32. *See also* comradeship
Fromm, Erich, 253–255, 322n. 32–33, 322n. 35, 323n. 39
Fyodorov, Nikolai, 26–28, 29, 133, 196, 211, 215, 220, 225, 243, 279n. 9, 286n. 53,

287nn. 54–56, 288nn. 60–61, 313nn. 13, 16, and 24, 316nn. 39 and 45, 318n. 7, 321nn. 24 and 28, 322n. 39
Furies, 168, 270–271

Gastev, Alexei, 279n. 11, 289n. 74, 309n. 27, 313n. 16
Geller, Mikhail, 226, 261
Genis, Alexander, 282n. 27
Girard, René, 37, 53, 163, 175–176, 206, 285n. 42, 291n. 12, 309nn. 19–20, 315n. 31
Gilman, Charlotte Perkins, 18
Gippius, Zinaida, 282n. 28, 299n. 37, 315n. 36
Gladkov, Alexander, 173
Gladkov, Fyodor: *Cement*, 2, 18, 44, 278n. 45, 283n. 38, 287n. 54
Gogol, Nikolai, 305n. 45, 308n. 10, 325n. 9; "Taras Bulba," 25–26, 77, 84, 286n. 52, 296n. 8, 305n. 25
Gorky, Maxim, 39, 265, 286n. 46, 287nn. 53 and 56, 292n. 20; "Twenty-Six Men and a Girl," 57–59, 64, 68
Gorsuch, Anne, 278n. 8, 286n. 47
Gray, J. Glenn, 24, 31, 33, 36, 48, 103–104, 116, 150, 300n. 49
Groys, Boris, 283n. 34
Gunther, Hans, 284n. 38

Hagiography, 8
Halfin, Igal, 4–5, 279n. 11
Harkins, William, 164–165, 167, 301n. 1, 302n. 15, 304n. 19, 305n. 27, 306n. 1
Hasidim, 105–107, 114–115, 122. *See also* Jews
Heil, Jerry, 36
Heldt, Barbara, 1, 277n. 4
Heller, Mikhail. *See* Geller, Mikhail
Hemingway, Ernest, 1, 277n. 1
Herzog, Rudolf, 33
Hetenyi, Zsuzsa, 297n. 23
Homoeroticism, 26, 64–66, 69, 93, 96–101, 104, 154–155, 229–237, 289n. 72, 301n. 1, 306n. 4, 318nn. 11–12, 319nn. 13–15
Homosexuality, 164–165. *See also* Homoeroticism
Homosociality. *See* Comradeship
Horses and masculinity, 74, 83–84, 88, 101–103, 295n. 2, 298nn. 30–31, 318n. 8

Iablokov, E. A., 311n. 10
Incest, 19
Initiation, 91–99, 101–103, 115, 123–124, 297n. 27, 307n. 7
Irigaray, Luce, 19, 175
Isaev, Andrei, 11, 37
Ivanov, Vyacheslav, 315n. 34

Jews, 73–74, 75–80, 104–113, 296nn. 12 and 17, 299nn. 37–38, 300n. 42
Joyce, James, 304n. 21

Kataev, Valentin, 172–174, 306n. 3, 308nn. 14–15, 309n. 17
Kaverin, Valentin: "The End of the Gang," 56, 292n. 17
Khlebnikov, Velimir: "Night Search," 61–67, 293nn. 24 and 27, 294n. 28
Kirillov, Vladimir, 28, 67, 289n. 74
Kitchen, fight against, 11–12, 16, 162–170
Kollontai, Alexandra, 1, 7, 11–12
Komsomol (Communist Youth League), 7, 30, 35, 68, 106, 165, 175, 286n. 41
Kon, Igor, 281n. 19
Kornblatt, Judith Deutsch, 25–26, 107–108, 110, 111, 286n. 51, 296n. 8
Kornienko, N. V., 312n. 12, 320n. 18
Kronstadt revolts, 62, 64, 292n. 23
Kuprin, Alexander: *The Pit*, 49–51, 266, 291n. 11, 324n. 5

Lacan, Jacques, 137, 207, 245
Lenin, Vladimir, 10, 28, 77, 111, 112, 196–197, 199, 282n. 31, 306n. 1, 313n. 13

Lévi-Strauss, Claude, 19, 36–37, 46, 175, 290n. 2
Love triangles, 52–57, 163, 170–184, 206, 308nn. 11–14, 308nn. 13 and 17, 309nn. 11 and 19. *See also* Girard, René
Lunts, Lev, 288n. 64
Luplow, Carol, 300n. 52
Lynch, Michael, 288n. 18, 319n. 15

Machine, 227, 254–257, 309n. 27: as feminine ideal, 2, 163, 166, 186–188, 210; as metaphor for earth, 16, 198–199
Maegd-Soëp, Carolina de, 278n. 4
Maguire, Robert, 288n. 61, 300n. 43, 301n. 1
Male bonding. *See* Comradeship; Fratriarchy
Male collective, 45–63, 68, 72. *See also* Comradeship; Fratriarchy
Mandelstam, Nadezhda, 174
Mandel'stam, Osip, 1
Männerbund, 34
Marriage plot, 44–47, 69–71
Martini, Virgilio, 284n. 41
Marxism, 10, 136, 199, 247
Masculinity: cult of, in Europe, 31–33; and genre, 74–75, 113–124; and labor, 16–18. *See also* Comradeship; Fratriarchy
Masing-Delic, Irene, 55, 287n. 53, 293n. 27
Matich, Olga, 26, 290n. 5, 315n. 32
Mayakovsky, Vladimir, 33, 39, 287n. 54, 288n. 74, 298n. 27
Mead, Margaret, 123, 245, 307n. 7, 320n. 22
Mediated desire. *See* Love triangles
Merezhkovsky, Dmitri, 315n. 34
Mitscherlich, Alexander, 246–247
Mitchell, Juliet, 137, 321n. 27
Moi, Toril, 309n. 19
Monasticism, 25, 284n. 40
More, Thomas, 283n. 39
Morozov, Pavlik, 13, 275
Morris, Marcia, 115, 281n. 20, 287n. 27
Morson, Gary Saul, 305n. 51

Mosse, George, 31–34, 288nn. 65 and 68
Motherhood, 59–60, 76, 105–113, 130, 195, 210–217, 233, 242–247
Mukhina, Vera, 273, 325n. 10

Nabokov, Vladimir, 381n. 22
Naiman, Eric, 68, 236–237, 260, 271, 279nn. 9 and 11, 280n. 19, 281n. 21, 283n. 37, 289n. 70, 294nn. 31 and 35, 299n. 8, 316n. 39, 317n. 1, 319n. 17, 321n. 26, 322n. 31, 323n. 37, 324n. 1, 325n. 8
Nakhimovsky, Alice Stone, 296n. 12, 299n. 39, 300nn. 42 and 52
Naydan, Michael, 308n. 12
Nazism. *See* Fascism
Necrophilia, 68, 225, 253–263, 321n. 31, 322nn. 33–36, 323nn. 37–39, 324n. 1
NEP (New Economic Policy), 6, 34, 193, 241, 264, 271; and sexual mores, 6, 68
Noble, David, 284n. 40

The Odyssey, 81, 247, 321n. 25
Oedipus, 20–21, 58–59, 131, 134, 188–189, 300n. 50
Oja, Matt F., 301n. 32
Olesha, Yuri, 3, 5–6, 39–40, 54, 76, 125–190, 191, 199, 225, 231, 232, 236, 248, 251, 256, 277n. 3, 300nn. 4–5, 302nn. 8 and 12, 303n. 16, 308n. 17, 309n. 22, 315n. 31; "Aldebaran," 170; "The Black Man," 171; "The Chain," 171, 303n. 13; "The Cherry Pit," 170, 175, 303n. 13; *The Conspiracy of Feelings*, 152, 171, 307n. 8; "The Death of Zand," 171; *Envy*, 2, 31, 39, 46, 73, 93, 94, 106, 126–130, 132–135, 140–190, 199, 202, 204, 232, 236, 306n. 4, 307nn. 5, 6, and 8, 308nn. 12 and 16; "From the Notebooks of Fellow-Traveler Zand," 128, 154, 157, 303nn. 13 and 16; "Human Material," 128, 132, 143, 153, 154, 157, 301n. 4, 302n. 8, 308n. 9; "I Look into the Past," 125,

128, 132, 154; "Legend," 127-141, 145, 146, 153, 156, 166, 301n. 2, 303n. 16, 308n. 9; "Liompa," 136, 307n. 11; *A List of Assets*, 1, 171, 306n. 2; "Natasha," 171, 303n. 13; *No Day without a Line*, 301nn. 3-4, 302n. 8, 303n. 13, 309n. 122; *A Strict Youth*, 35-36, 170, 174-175, 309n. 18; "Summer," 171-172; *Three Fat Men*, 304n. 5, 309n. 29; "Three Stories," 171

The Oresteia, 270-271

Orphans, 4, 14, 70, 235, 242, 243, 245-263, 320n. 18

Osipovich, Tatiana, 277n. 1, 294n. 38, 313n. 22, 317n. 48, 318n. 11, 319n. 14

Ostrovsky, Nikolai, 2, 38, 278n. 5, 311nn. 5-6, 313n. 19, 320n. 21

Oulanoff, Hongor, 292n. 17

Paglia, Camille, 161

Paperno, Irina, 308n. 13

Paramonov, Boris, 236, 249, 277n. 1, 313n. 18, 316n. 45, 317n. 2, 318n. 12, 319nn. 13-14, 321n. 31

Peppard, Victor, 147, 308n. 15

Pertsov, Viktor, 190, 306n. 11

Piercy, Marge, 18

Pilnyak, Boris, 264-273; "Che-Che-O," 265; "Mahogany," 30, 265-266, 324n. 3; "Moist Mother Earth," 325n. 8; *The Naked Year*, 324n. 3, 325n. 8; "Old Cheese," 325n. 8; *The Volga Flows into the Caspian Sea*, 264-273, 324nn. 3 and 7

Platonov, Andrei, 3, 5-6, 9, 13, 39, 76, 162, 191-265, 279n. 9, 287nn. 53-54, 285n. 58, 288n. 63, 289n. 1, 299n. 37, 305n. 28, 311nn. 3-8, 312nn. 9-12, 313nn. 13, 15, and 19-21, 314n. 31, 315nn. 33 and 36, 316nn. 37, 39, 40, and 42-43, 317nn. 48 and 51, 321n. 31, 323n. 40; "About Science," 197; "Antisexsus," 192, 311n. 4; "The Battle of the Brains," 197, 199, 200, 201, 262, 311n. 21; "But Man Has Only One Soul," 200, 205-211, 216, 314n. 29, 315n. 36, 317n. 49; "Che-Che-O," 265; *Chevengur*, 2, 28, 39-41, 44, 48, 54, 56, 68-71, 106, 133, 191-193, 203, 212, 216, 222, 223, 224-263, 284n. 40, 293n. 25, 307n. 8, 313nn. 17-18, 317nn. 1-2, 318nn. 5, 7, and 10-12, 319n. 16, 321nn. 25 and 29; "The Culture of the Proletariat," 196, 199, 200, 201, 202, 204, 213, 262, 313n. 24, 314n. 25; "Descendants of the Sun," 226, 289n. 1, 312n. 12; "Dzhan," 214; "The Ether Tract," 212, 312n. 12; *The Father's Voice*, 323n. 38; *The Foundation Pit*, 212, 214, 258, 316n. 38, 317n. 7; "Fro," 311n. 3; "The Future October," 191, 204, 315n. 27; "The Girl Roza," 311n. 3; *Happy Moscow*, 316n. 40; "Inspired People," 288n. 63; "Ivanov's Family," 192, 311n. 3; "Markun," 313n. 15; "May Your Name Be Blessed," 199; "Notes," 223; "On the Culture of Harnessed Light," 199-200, 202-203, 205, 316n. 42; "Pavel Korchagin," 320n. 31; "The Potudan River," 192, 311nn. 3 and 5; "Proletarian Poetry," 199; "Repairing the Earth," 16, 198, 199, 211, 317n. 47; "The Return" (see "Ivanov's Family"); "The Satan of Thought," 318n. 3; "A Story about Many Interesting Things," 43, 47-48, 191, 195-196, 217-224, 312n. 12, 317n. 50; 321n. 23; "Symphony of Consciousness," 312n. 12; "The Teacher of the Sands," 2, 311n. 3, 312n. 11, 317n. 46; "The World Soul," 195, 205, 210-217, 221, 229, 313n. 29, 315nn. 35-36

Pobratimstvo, 24-25, 29, 286nn. 49-50

Podoroga, Valery, 322n. 34

Production vs. reproduction, 3, 16-17

Proletcult (proletarian culture), 28, 287n. 58, 289n. 74, 311n. 5

Prostitutes, 48-51, 290n. 5, 298n. 29

Poulin, Francis, 62

Pushkin, Alexander, 1, 308n. 16

Rape, 43, 58–60, 64, 85–86, 324n. 8; gang rape, 48, 68, 71, 290n. 29; of intelligentsia, 5. *See also* Chubarov Alley
Remy, John, 21–23, 36, 76
Revolution, 1–2, 6; and fiction, 1–2
Revolutionary asceticism, 7–13
Revolutionary sublimation, 13
Rich, Adrienne, 243
Rites of passage. *See* Initiation
Romanov, Panteleimon, 7, 294n. 32
Room, Abram, 35, 54
Rosenshield, Gary, 278n. 4
Rozanov, Vasily, 213, 214, 243, 299n. 37, 316nn. 41–42, 320nn. 20–21
Rubin, Gayle, 19

Sacrifice, female, 53–61, 64, 87, 92–99; male as "female" victim, 64–66
Said, Edward, 14–18, 36, 245, 281n. 23
Sand, Georges, 8
Scopophilia. *See* Voyeurism
Sedgwick, Eve Kosofsky, 36–37, 69, 289n. 72
Seifrid, Thomas, 211–216, 292n. 16, 311n. 8, 312n. 12, 317n. 1, 318nn. 9–10, 322n. 31
Semenova, Svetlana, 194–195
Sexual revolution, 6–14
Shafarevich, Igor, 299n. 36, 322n. 31
Shkolvsky, Viktor, 54, 244
Smith, Cordwainer (Paul Linebarger), 284n. 41
Socialist realism, 39
Solovyov, Vladimir, 213, 214, 286n. 53, 287n. 13
Spackman, Barbara, 34, 283n. 36
Stalin, Joseph, 7, 43, 264, 273–276
Stalinism, 7–8, 280n. 17, 283n. 34, 313n. 14, 320n. 21
Stites, Richard, 7, 287n. 56
Striedter, Jurij, 317n. 1
Superfluous man, 1, 38
Superman, 120–121
Symbolic Order, 137–139, 242, 246

Theweleit, Klaus, 34–35
Tiger, Lionel, 22–23, 36, 285n. 43, 298n. 28
Tkachev, Pyotr, 11
Todorov, Vladislav, 30, 313n. 23, 317n. 2, 321n. 28
Tolstoi, Alexei, 44–45
Tolstoi, Lev, 286n. 53; *The Kreutzer Sonata*, 282n. 32, 291n. 28; *Resurrection*, 49
Trilling, Lionel, 93
Turgenev, Ivan, 17, 161, 277n. 4

Utopianism and dystopianism, 3–4, 6, 18, 36–37, 69–72, 284n. 41

Van der Eng, Jan, 291n. 16
Viola, Lynne, 268
Vishnevsky, Vsevolod, 294n. 39
Voyeurism, 94, 298n. 74

War Communism, 6, 30, 34, 61, 68, 116, 264, 265, 268, 270, 271, 275
Waters, Elizabeth, 274
Weininger, Otto, 289n. 72, 299n. 37, 313n. 20, 315n. 36
Whitman, Walt, 288n. 68, 319n. 15
Williams, Robert C., 287n. 58
Woman question, 10
Women: absence of, 2–3; abstraction of, 3; emancipation of, 6, 9–10, 12, 16; masculinization of, 16, 44–45, 70; as witnesses to violence, 78–79, 88. *See also* Femininity; Sacrifice, female; Woman question
World War I, 33–34

Zalkind, Aron, 12–13, 280n. 14, 282n. 32, 283n. 33
Zhenotdel, 11, 71, 268, 272, 275
Zholkovsky, Alexander, 291n. 7, 305n. 26, 323n. 40
Zolotonosov, Mikhail, 280n. 9

Eliot Borenstein is Assistant Professor of Russian and Slavic Studies, New York University.

Library of Congress Cataloging-in-Publication Data
Borenstein, Eliot, 1966–
Men without women : masculinity and revolution in Russian fiction, 1917–1929 / Eliot Borenstein.
p. cm. Includes bibliographical references and index.
ISBN 0-8223-2578-0 (cloth : alk. paper)
ISBN 0-8223-2592-6 (pbk. : alk. paper)
1. Russian fiction—20th century—History and criticism.
2. Men in literature. 3. Masculinity in literature. 4. Man-woman relationships in literature. I. Title.
PG3096.M45 B67 2001
891.73′4209352041—dc21 00-030309

www.ingramcontent.com/pod-product-compliance
Lightning Source LLC
Chambersburg PA
CBHW061343300426
44116CB00011B/1972